Praise for *A Madm...*

"Mystery drives *A Madman's Will*, Gregory May's enlightening, suspenseful book. . . . [A] compelling case history of the complexities of enslavement and emancipation in the young American nation."

—David S. Reynolds, *Wall Street Journal*

"Eye-opening and vigorously researched. . . . May cogently reveals how white supremacy was not restricted to the South but permeated the nation, depicting a culture of fear and resentment around free Black settlement. . . . Ultimately, May shows how such deprivations have lasting, generational consequences, illuminating inequities that persist to this day."   —Ilyon Woo, *New York Times Book Review*

"An engrossing story of good intentions, selfishness, racism, and Black initiative during and after the era of slavery. Gregory May weaves a century of legal struggles and human strivings into a seamless fabric, vividly reminding us of how white supremacy shaped American life in both the South and North."

—Melvin Patrick Ely, Bancroft Prize–winning author of
*Israel on the Appomattox: A Southern Experiment in Black Freedom
from the 1790s Through the Civil War*

"*A Madman's Will* is a reminder that even promised freedom rarely came easily—or without an exacting price. Gregory May takes readers through the tangled family squabbles and legal machinations surrounding the life and death of one of the strangest and most tempestuous figures of the early republic, all while the fates of hundreds of enslaved people hung in the balance."

—Joshua D. Rothman, author of *The Ledger and the Chain:
How Domestic Slave Traders Shaped America*

"Lawyer-turned-historian May offers a fascinating account of Virginia senator John Randolph's posthumous efforts to free nearly 400 enslaved people and provide for their resettlement. . . . May lucidly untangles the legal proceedings and draws vivid character sketches of Randolph and others, while building an irrefutable case that freedom is only the first step to equality. This is history at its finest."

—*Publishers Weekly*, starred review

"A twisty story that illuminates the elaborate legal system built to defend slavery and silence its discontents." —*Kirkus Reviews*

"Exhaustively researched but written for a general audience, this book urges readers to consider the consequences of enslavement, racism, and the reality that manumission was less about people and more about money and power." —*Library Journal*

"In 1833, the Virginia congressman John Randolph freed his nearly four hundred slaves while on his deathbed. This detailed history untangles the much-publicized legal dispute that ensued. . . . May cautions against ascribing honorable motives to Randolph, and stresses that those he freed continued to face prejudice and violence in the North." —*The New Yorker*

A MADMAN'S WILL

Juba with Vixen, attributed to Joseph Wood, c. 1820

A MADMAN'S WILL

·······

John Randolph,
400 Slaves, and the
Mirage of Freedom

GREGORY MAY

LIVERIGHT PUBLISHING CORPORATION

A Division of W. W. Norton & Company

INDEPENDENT PUBLISHERS SINCE 1923

Epigraph: David W. Blight, *Race and Reunion: The Civil War in
American Memory* (Cambridge, MA: Belknap Press of Harvard
University Press, 2001), 110, by kind permission of the President and
Fellows of Harvard College

For information about permission to reproduce selections from this book,
write to Permissions, Liveright Publishing Corporation, a division of
W. W. Norton & Company, Inc., 500 Fifth Avenue, New York, NY 10110

For information about special discounts for bulk purchases,
please contact W. W. Norton Special Sales at
specialsales@wwnorton.com or 800-233-4830

Manufacturing by Lakeside Book Company
Book design by Lovedog Studio
Production manager: Julia Druskin

Library of Congress Control Number: 2023006557

ISBN 978-1-324-09562-0 pbk.

Liveright Publishing Corporation, 500 Fifth Avenue, New York, N.Y. 10110
www.wwnorton.com

W. W. Norton & Company Ltd., 15 Carlisle Street, London W1D 3BS

10 9 8 7 6 5 4 3 2 1

For Peter S. Onuf

Evil almost always has a historical logic, and therefore an explanation.

—David W. Blight, *Race and Reunion*

CONTENTS

Part Three
FREEDOM AND LOSS, 1845–46

LIST OF ILLUSTRATIONS

To those whom it may concern; I John Randolph of Roanoke in the county of Charlotte & commonwealth of Virginia do constitute this writing written with mine own hand, my last will & testament, hereby revoking all others.

1. I give & bequeathe unto my deservedly esteemed friends Major Joseph Scott of Amelia & Ryland Randolph of Powhatan all the property of every specie & description of which I die possessed in the fullest confidence that they will take upon them the troublesome office of complying with the requests stated below.

I desire that my just debts which are few & of little consequence (except those inherited from my late father) be paid.

I request that the management of my estate continue under my friend Major Scott who will direct every thing relative to it as if it were his own, & that the profits, after my debts are paid be accumulated & vested in some eligible fund for the support of the helpless slaves & when that purpose is effected it is my desire that every individual negro of whom I May die possessed be restored to that freedom which is his just & natural right & of which he has been so long & basely deprived

I desire that my friend Major Scott receive four hundred dollars out of the annual profits of my estate for his trouble in managing the same; not that I conceive such a sum to be a recompense for his services; they are above my ability to reward.

I desire that my landed estate be divided into three portions as nearly equal as possible & that my brothers Henry & Beverly & my sister

First will of John Randolph, November 17, 1800

RANDOLPH-TUCKER FAMILY TREE

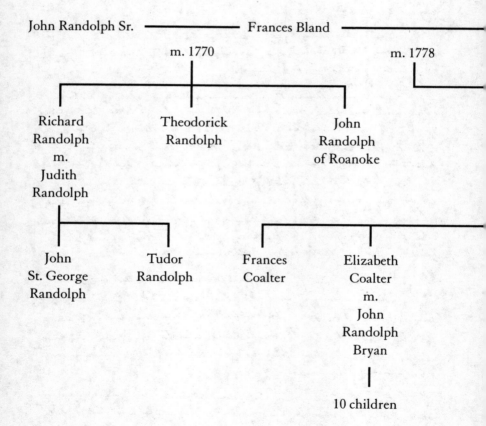

John Randolph Sr. ———————— Frances Bland ————————

m. 1770   m. 1778

Richard Randolph m. Judith Randolph

Theodorick Randolph

John Randolph of Roanoke

John St. George Randolph

Tudor Randolph

Frances Coalter

Elizabeth Coalter m. John Randolph Bryan

10 children

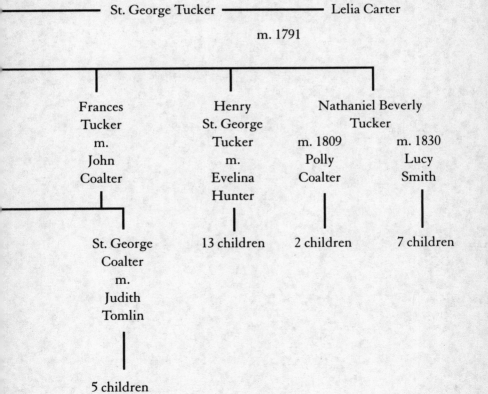

St. George Tucker ——————— Lelia Carter

m. 1791

Frances
Tucker
m.
John
Coalter

Henry
St. George
Tucker
m.
Evelina
Hunter

Nathaniel Beverly
Tucker

m. 1809
Polly
Coalter

m. 1830
Lucy
Smith

St. George
Coalter
m.
Judith
Tomlin

13 children

2 children

7 children

5 children

PREFACE

From where John White stood on the first morning of July 1846, the climb ahead looked steep. Beyond the rough pavement of the Cincinnati steamboat landing was an unbroken row of four-story brick warehouses, pierced toward the eastern end by an opening onto what everyone told him was Main Street. Behind the warehouses, the bank of the Ohio River rose so sharply that he could see only the tops of the buildings on the bluff above him and the shimmer of the morning sun on the rooftops.

Once he and the others who were with him walked past the warehouses onto Main Street, the fronts of tall Italianate brick buildings with big glass windows came into view. The glittering glass fronts ranked along both sides of the street as far up the hill as the walkers could see, broken at regular intervals by glimpses of cross streets lined with more buildings that looked just the same.

They had seen these blocks of buildings spreading toward the green hills on the horizon as their steamboat approached Cincinnati that morning. But only John White and a few of the others could imagine what it would be like to walk through them. White was a short, middle-aged man with an air of self-assurance. He had been to Philadelphia and New York, even London and Saint Petersburg. A few of his companions knew some large Virginia towns, such as Lynchburg and Petersburg, or perhaps the capital city of Richmond.

The rest had never before left the vicinity of the place where they were born, a large plantation on the Staunton and Little Roanoke Rivers in the rolling hills of the tobacco country 50 miles above Virginia's southern border.

Main Street remained steep as White and the others walked up into the city, and the rising heat of the morning began to take its toll. The line of walkers soon stretched more than half a block down the street. The young men and women, some with children in arms, stayed in front. John White followed among the older people along with his wife Betsy, who wore a stack of hats on her head to protect them from damage. At the rear came a clutch of women held back by half-grown children and a few men hobbling on canes.

Pale faces began peering through the tall windows on both sides of the street, and some men stepped out of doors to gawk as the procession passed. Free African Americans were a familiar enough sight in Cincinnati, but this group was unusual. Most of them wore the rough sort of clothing given to the enslaved, and except for the size of the group, they could easily have been mistaken at a distance for a slave coffle like the ones these bystanders were used to seeing across the river in Kentucky. Yet this crowd was full of small children, the men wore no chains, and they walked with a purpose all their own. There were 383 of them—the largest group of Blacks that anyone in this booming free city had ever seen.[1]

The women, men, and children walking up Main Street had been enslaved: property of the estate of John Randolph of Roanoke. Everyone in the United States knew who he was. From the time he entered Congress a year before Thomas Jefferson's election until the day he died during Andrew Jackson's second term as president, Randolph had courted fame. His extravagant speeches, savage wit, and eccentric manners made him one of the most famous public men in America. Newspapers throughout the country reported his antics under the headline "Randolphiana." Even on the other side of the Atlantic, a leading London magazine told readers that "no speaker in congress could draw an audience like him; his sayings were in every man's mouth, his reputation filled every corner of the Union."[2]

John Randolph had made a name for himself as one of the most strident early defenders of the states' rights to enslave Black workers. So when he died thirteen years before the warm July morning when the people he once owned appeared in Cincinnati, the public was surprised to read in the newspapers that John Randolph's will had freed his slaves.

John Randolph's will became a national sensation. The liberation of his slaves was one of the largest and most widely discussed manumissions in American history. The freedmen's journey to Ohio was the largest single migration of African Americans to a free state before the Civil War. When angry white farmers drove the freedmen away from the land that the freedmen had purchased in western Ohio, the outrage grabbed attention in Congress and headlines in newspapers throughout the country. The many pages of newsprint blotted to tell their story testify to the complexity of antebellum America's dilemma over slavery and racial prejudice.[3]

The story of John Randolph's will resonates today because we still struggle with the consequences of slavery and racial prejudice. Our struggle has prompted us to ask hard questions about the origins of American freedom and the men who proclaimed it. In one of his widely read commentaries for *The Atlantic*, Ta-Nehisi Coates used John Randolph's example to ask why we should forgive Thomas Jefferson for failing to free his slaves. Randolph, who scorned Jefferson's political platitudes and ridiculed him as "St. Thomas of Cantingbury," would have liked that. Yet Randolph, who kept his own workforce enslaved throughout his life and became a patron saint for states' rights ideologues, is hardly a hero for our times. The story of his slaves' manumission should grip us not because they gained freedom, but because they lost the land that would have helped them to exercise it.[4]

To understand the tragedy of John Randolph's will, we must confront an ugliness that most modern treatments of American slavery tend to obscure. The history of slavery is usually told in terms of Black self-assertion and white guilt. While that formulation is revealing, it has diverted attention from a more troubling historical truth that continues to have devastating consequences. That truth is white incomprehension and indifference. Antebellum abolitionists knew it was their greatest challenge. When William Lloyd Garrison launched *The Liberator* with the defiant proclamation that he would be heard despite all obstacles, his very next sentence gave the imperative reason. "The apathy of the people is enough to make every statue leap from its pedestal and to hasten the resurrection of the dead."[5]

If we approach John Randolph's will with Garrison's words in mind, we gain a new perspective on America's long encounter with race and slavery. Inertia is not as uplifting a theme as Black agency, but it has been a more powerful historical force. Randolph's will failed to give his slaves their rightful place in freedom because neither he nor they could escape the underlying pull of prevailing white assumptions about race and social order.

Randolph and other men who freed their slaves (and they generally were men) were not really so different from the white men who kept their slaves in bondage. They came to a different conclusion about what to do with their human property, but almost none of them set out to change their world. Their decision to free their slaves was an exercise of their will more than a rejection of their entitlement. For almost all of them, that was the main point. Manumission was a matter of self-expression rather than an expression of fellow feeling. The men who freed their slaves were thinking about what their God or their world would make of them, not what those they freed could make of themselves. That is why these men made so little difference.[6]

Enslaved people whose manumission forced them to migrate to the free states found scant welcome there. Most white men and women believed their own liberty and well-being were more pressing concerns than the plight of slaves or the reparation of the freedmen's condition. They pointedly excluded Blacks from the protection that the poor laws gave to the white population. They denied them the vote and the right to testify in court against whites who wronged them. Many free states tried to exclude Blacks altogether. Except for its rowdy celebrations of liberty, the freedmen's new Canaan was sometimes not so different from the ancient land that refused refuge to a people fleeing from their slavery in Egypt.[7]

A Madman's Will is a book about the lives of many individual people—famous and unknown, free and enslaved, self-righteous and much wronged—who experienced the difficult contradictions in antebellum American life in ways quite different than we usually imagine. At the center of the book is a sharply contested will that freed more slaves than almost any other will in American history. The story told here, however, is about much more than the battle over a legal document. It is about the will that made slaveholding white men act as they did. It is about the limits that other white Americans put on freedom when they rejected a remedy for past wrongs. It is not a parable about justice, but an enormously powerful encounter with the enduring pain and provocative ambiguity of our past. What it means for us today depends, as James Baldwin put it, on "what we make of the questions with which the story leaves us."[8]

John Randolph of Roanoke, engraving by
John Sartain after George Catlin, 1831–32

Part One

INTIMATIONS OF FREEDOM, 1833

Chapter 1

A DEATH IN PHILADELPHIA

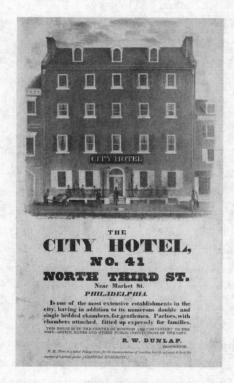

The City Hotel, Philadelphia, lithograph by
M. E. D. Brown, c. 1832

F OR ALL ITS SIZE AND SPLENDOR, THE OLD SENATE
chamber in the United States Capitol was an intimate space on
a winter day. The half-domed ceiling rose high above the visitors' galleries in the mezzanine, elegant marble columns screened the front of

the room, and crimson curtains spilled from a towering valence above
the presiding officer's desk. But on the floor, the forty-eight senators'
desks sat close together, and members had to brush by each other to
get to their chairs. A few hard sofas for invited guests sat crammed
against the back wall. As the day passed, the air grew heavy with heat
from the floor vents, coal vapor from the fireplaces around the walls,
and whiffs of wool, leather, and tobacco.[1]

John Randolph had been out of Congress for four years when he
came to the Senate floor late one afternoon at the end of February
1833, but he was no stranger there. He had served in Congress almost
continuously for thirty years. He personally knew most of the men in
the chamber, and he himself was still among the best-known political figures in the country. There had not been a session of Congress
during his long career, said one consummate politician, "in which his
sayings and doings did not contribute the principal staple of the political gossip of Washington."[2]

Randolph had first come to Congress as a member of the Jeffersonian Republican opposition when John Adams was president. He
was an exceptionally slender, russet-haired youth of twenty-six with
a beautiful, small-featured face and beardless cheeks. There was a
haughty feistiness about him, and he quickly called attention to himself through his outspoken opposition to a larger standing army.
Randolph disdainfully dismissed the federal troops as "a handful of
ragamuffins," and when some of the officers he had offended with
those words jostled him at the theater, he lodged a complaint with
the president himself. The newspapers picked up the story, and the
fresh-faced young congressman got more than his share of notice. It
was a telling beginning.

Few men in Congress were as articulate as John Randolph, and
even fewer as bright. When the Republicans took power, Thomas Jefferson saw him as a natural leader for the party on the floor of the
House of Representatives. Randolph took the chair of the powerful
Ways and Means Committee, and Jefferson entrusted him with the
administration's most important measures, such as the reduction of

federal spending, the repayment of public debt, and the purchase of Louisiana. The role seemed to suit Randolph at first. He relished the deference of others, and he had no doubt that his talents far exceeded those of most men.

But Randolph overplayed his hand. He wounded many of his colleagues with the sharp sarcasm he used to enforce party discipline, and they began to look for ways to escape his scourge. He also refused to follow the administration's lead when it seemed to him that James Madison, the secretary of state, was luring Jefferson away from true Republican principles. Randolph particularly opposed the trade restrictions that Madison wanted to impose on British shipping in the years leading up to the War of 1812, so Jefferson turned to other congressmen to take the lead on trade matters. When one of those men tried to strip a bill from Randolph's committee, Randolph simply exploded.[3]

No one ever forgot the sensational speeches in which Randolph turned on the Jefferson administration. They drew crowds from both chambers of Congress. Randolph was a brilliant speaker, and the very recklessness of what he was doing made the speeches spectacular performances. He denounced Jefferson for exercising "back-stairs influence" on Congress, he hurled Madison's pamphlet on trade policy to the floor, and he described the measures introduced by the administration's minions as the "handbills and nostrums" of "political quacks." "It was the most bitter, severe and eloquent philippic I ever heard," wrote a senator after one of the speeches. No stenographer could possibly capture "its spirit and highly finished eloquence, elegance, and well turned periods."[4]

But Randolph had crossed the Rubicon, and those speeches marked the end of his role as a party leader. He emerged on the other side of the river as the defiant leader of a small band of Southern congressmen who called themselves Old Republicans, a badge meant to emphasize that they were the true adherents to the party's original principles of free trade, low taxes, and weak central government. "Perhaps you may have heard," he wrote to a friend in Virginia, "that

I have made overtures to the reigning powers . . . to forgive & forget" the party breach. "Nothing can be farther from the truth."[5]

Randolph's opposition to the war against Britain in 1812 led to his only defeat in an election for Congress, and he found the rejection and the loss of public attention extremely painful. Even after his constituents—chastened by the cost and economic disruption of the war—reelected him two years later, he felt forgotten, unappreciated, and morose in Washington. Signs of the madness that would plague him throughout his life grew more evident to his friends during and after those years.[6]

It was the debate over admission of Missouri to the Union as a slave state in 1819–20 that revived Randolph's career and offered him the role he would play for the rest of his life. Randolph became Cassandra, the Trojan seer cursed to deliver prophecies of doom that no one else would believe. Randolph had always contended that intrusive central government was antithetical to the Constitution and inconsistent with the interests of slaveholding Southern planters. He had claimed that any central government attempt to limit slavery would threaten the Union. So for him the assault on Missouri's right to enslave Black workers was a clear augury of worse things to come, and like the great Trojan seer, Randolph never ceased warning his countrymen of the grief and destruction that lay ahead.[7]

His role as prophet of doom and relentless defender of states' rights made Randolph a political phenomenon. Unconstrained by party discipline or the need to compromise, he gave full vent to his extravagant rhetoric and his instinct for self-display. "No government extending from the Atlantic to the Pacific can be fit to govern me or those whom I represent," he declared in a debate over representation in Congress. "There is death in the pot, compound it how you will." He would no longer deign to quibble over the constitutionality of measures that threatened Southern agricultural interests, he cried on another occasion, because mere parchment barriers were clearly not enough to protect planters from central government interference. "A fig for the Constitution! When the scorpion's sting is probing us to the quick, shall we stop to chop logic?" "I am content to act the part of Cassandra," he proclaimed as his reputation mounted, "to lift up my voice, whether it be heeded, or heard only to be disregarded, until too late." The nation knew who Randolph was because what he said was so memorable and what he did was so singular.[8]

"I have heard John Randolph speak," reported one visitor to the House as he launched into a breathless description of the fifty-five-year-old man. "A slim, hollow-backed, round-shouldered figure, with his lemon skin, and little retreating nose, and sharp scooping chin" and "his smooth light brown hair kemped back from his forehead" by a string loose down his back, with "his shrill feminine voice, which can swell to a wonderful compass, and his unabashable self-possession, and searching twinkling eye, and his long slender denoting finger." Yet the man's flaws were evident. "He is fitter to pull down than to build up," wrote the visitor, "a clog to both parties," who regard him as "a kind of amusing, yet dreaded" satirist.[9]

Many of the men in the Senate chamber on the late winter afternoon when Randolph visited in 1833 vividly remembered the two years he had spent there as a Virginia senator during John Quincy Adams's administration. Randolph had opposed Adams's nationalistic policies with a vehemence so astonishing that it prompted even the states' righters in Virginia's legislature to replace him with a more moderate man. In the meantime, Randolph had fought a duel with Adams's secretary of state, Henry Clay, and earned the gratitude of Andrew Jackson, who despised Clay for arranging his defeat when the presidential election went to the House of Representatives in 1824.[10]

The rough-hewn Jackson and the delicate-featured Randolph could hardly have looked more different, yet they shared an unruliness of spirit and an antipathy for the power of national government. Jackson must have sensed, however, that the two of them could easily come to blows over Jackson's view of himself as an independent tribune of the people unaccountable to members of Congress. And after Jackson crushed Adams in the 1828 presidential election, he deftly removed Randolph from the Washington scene by appointing him the American minister to Russia.[11]

Randolph's health had collapsed soon after he reached his post in Saint Petersburg, and he spent a year in London trying to recover it. His critics claimed he had accepted the diplomatic mission in order to get the large up-front payment that came with it and then taken an extended holiday on the government's money. The accusation dishonored him, and Randolph returned to Virginia embarrassed, embittered, and too late to stand for election to his old seat in the House.[12]

Randolph was gravely ill when he came to the Senate in 1833. John White, his enslaved manservant, had to help him into the Senate chamber, and Thomas Hart Benton, the Missouri senator who had invited him, needed assistance to get him settled on one of the sofas in the rear. Randolph had always been strikingly thin. Now he was a husk. His flesh had wasted to almost nothing, and his thin skin had withered into countless lines. Although most of his hair was still russet brown, the part that framed his face had turned stark white. His long, dark coat had a distinctive high collar to protect his neck from drafts, and the folds draping closely around him showed that it was too large for what remained of him.[13]

John C. Calhoun and Henry Clay were speaking that afternoon, one to insist on states' rights and the other to finesse the issue. States' rights claims were now at the center of a great national stalemate remembered as the Nullification Crisis. Southern politicians like Randolph had long objected to increases in federal import duties because high duties protected Northern manufacturers at the expense of staple-exporting Southern planters—who had to pay higher prices for the goods they bought and worry about retaliatory foreign duties on the commodities they exported. But those objections had grown sharper after Northern resistance to the admission of Missouri as a slave state reemphasized the potential for federal interference with slave-based agriculture. Just a few months earlier, Calhoun and a South Carolina state convention had taken the objections to a new level by formally declaring that their state had a constitutional right to nullify the federal tariff law and to block the collection of duties within its borders. The declaration was the first major constitutional challenge to the integrity of the Union.

President Jackson had denounced nullification and asked Congress for authority to send federal troops into South Carolina to enforce tax collections. Jackson's call for force alienated many of his Southern supporters in Congress, and Calhoun played on sectional feelings in an effort to block Jackson's maneuver. Clay proposed a compromise that would gradually reduce the offensive duties, and both houses of Congress were about to adopt it. Calhoun supported the compromise, but he wanted the Senate to sustain his constitutional point by passing a resolution that the federal union was a compact made by sovereign states.[14]

Randolph believed in state sovereignty, and Jackson's call for military action against a sovereign state raised his hackles. Shortly before he came to Washington, Randolph had rallied his old constituents in Southside Virginia to adopt strident resolutions on both points. But Randolph's conception of states' rights grew from his long-standing commitment to weak central government and liberal free trade, not the shrill proslavery sectionalism that Calhoun was coming to personify. Calhoun had remained an outspoken nationalist long after Randolph began warning that federal power could jeopardize slavery and Southern agriculture, and when Calhoun pivoted to nullification in order to protect his political position in South Carolina, Randolph lost all respect for the man. By now, Randolph told Jackson, Calhoun must realize that he is a "thrice double ass." Clay on the other hand, Randolph had told his constituents, possessed the patriotism and the firmness to save the Union. The resolutions passed by Randolph and his constituents had explicitly defended states' rights, denounced nullification, and backed compromise.[15]

While Calhoun and Clay were speaking, many of the other senators left their seats and worked their way to the rear of the room to greet Randolph. This was why he had come, and he warmed to their attention. But until Henry Clay approached, he remained seated.

Clay was just four years younger than Randolph but he had begun life with fewer advantages, and by the time Clay entered the House in 1811, Randolph had been there for a dozen years. They clashed immediately. Randolph stoutly opposed the preparations for war with Britain that Clay and other new members supported. Finding himself in a dwindling minority, Randolph had turned the formidable forensic powers he once used to discipline the Republican majority into weapons of derision. He brought his hunting dogs to the House floor, he ridiculed other members in debates, and he stalked out when he wanted to show his disrespect for certain speakers. Clay had deployed charm as adeptly as Randolph used scorn. The Republican majority elected him Speaker of the House within a week of his arrival, and among his early acts was an order removing dogs from the floor. Clay remained Speaker for most of the next fifteen years, served four years as secretary of state, and became leader of the progressive Republicans who opposed Andrew Jackson. Clay and Randolph never reconciled their wide political differences, although after they shot at each other on the dueling field, they buried their personal hostility.

When the Senate adjourned, Clay walked back through the chamber to speak to Randolph. "Mr. Randolph," he said, "I hope you are better, sir." Randolph struggled to his feet with the help of those around him and grasped Clay's hand. "No, sir," he replied, "I am a dying man, and I came here expressly to have this interview with you." Randolph had been saying things like that for years, but this time Clay believed him. He looked, Clay reported to a friend in Virginia, "as if he were not long for this world."[16]

Thomas Hart Benton could see that Randolph was dying. The two of them had been close friends ever since they roomed at the same boarding house in Washington years earlier. Both men were insomniacs, and Randolph had taken to knocking on Benton's door when he saw light beneath it and then talking late into the night. Benton named one of his sons for Randolph, and his memories of his friend's last visit to Washington would remain with him for years. He remembered they were sitting together quietly one evening when Randolph began to recite Samuel Johnson's memorable verses about dementia:

> *And in life's last scene what prodigies surprise,*
> *Fears of the brave, and follies of the wise?*
> *From Marlb'rough's eyes the streams of dotage flow,*
> *And Swift expires a driv'ler and a show.*

Benton had witnessed Randolph's spells of mental excitement over the years, and he believed that Randolph sometimes had been mad. But that evening, Benton tried to reassure him. Surely, he said quietly, you do not believe you will unravel like Jonathan Swift. Yes, Randolph replied, "I have lived in dread of insanity."[17]

. . . .

THREE MONTHS LATER, Randolph set out for England in a desperate attempt to escape the damage a hot Virginia summer would do to his failing lungs. He wanted to catch one of the packet ships that made regular Atlantic crossings from Philadelphia and spend the summer in a cooler climate. Randolph was too weak to make arrangements for himself, so everything depended on his enslaved manservant John White. White packed Randolph's baggage and loaded him into his carriage, and they set off in late May through the splendid green foliage of Southside Virginia. At Richmond's river port on the James, they boarded a boat for Baltimore, where they caught one of the steamboats that ran to Philadelphia through a connecting canal.

Their boat reached Philadelphia in a spring downpour, and the storm had soaked Randolph by the time White could get him into a hackney. The carriage's broken windows leaked rain. They had to try several hotels before they could find room, and Randolph's rising agitation weakened him. As soon as Edmund Badger, a co-owner of the City Hotel, took them in, he called a doctor.[18]

Randolph insisted on an eminent physician, and he got one. Joseph

Parrish was a fifty-four-year-old Quaker who had practiced and taught medicine in the city for nearly thirty years. He was a plain-spoken man, and he got straight to business. How long, Parrish asked his new patient, had he been sick? "Don't ask me that question," snapped Randolph, "I have been sick all my life." Parrish could hear the old man's lungs wheeze when he spoke, so he started over by asking when the congestion began. He learned it had started before the patient sailed for Russia three years earlier and then grown worse in Saint Petersburg. A stay in England on the way home had relieved the condition, and the patient was bound there in the hope that he could survive the coming summer. Parrish reached for the sick man's wrist. "You can form no judgment by my pulse," the man said, "it is peculiar."

Parrish knew how to manage difficult patients. You have been "so long an invalid," he suggested to this one, that you must know a great deal about how to treat your own condition. And so Randolph did. Standard remedies such a camphor only made him worse, Randolph explained to his new audience, and ether "would blow me up." Not so opium and its derivatives, Parrish learned, for Randolph declared that "he either did or could (I am not clear as to the words *did* or *could*) take opium like a Turk." Doctor and patient then fell into a "curiously diversified" conversation that ran from Randolph's miserable arrival in Philadelphia that day to his admiration for the goodness of Quakers ("in every thing except politics," he said) before ending with Randolph's recitation of a passage from the Book of Common Prayer.

Parrish knew Randolph was a famous man whose death would attract public attention. The testimony that he later gave in the litigation over Randolph's will shows he paid careful attention to what happened during the next four days. Although Parrish's testimony had a purpose, accounts by other witnesses verified almost all of it.

After considerable experience with the sick and dying, Parrish testified, "I never met with a character so perfectly original and unique." Sometimes the man seemed to be a "spoiled and factious child," yet further conversation convinced Parrish that "in the midst of his extreme constitutional irritability, petulance, impatience, and sarcasm, there were some noble traits of character." Among them were a keen sense of propriety and a willingness, at least when challenged, to acknowledge his indiscretions.[19]

Randolph had some interesting visitors as he lay dying. Several friends from Virginia who happened to be in Philadelphia came to see him, including a medical student who noticed he was taking morphine and a Southside planter named William Barksdale who was among Randolph's good friends. Nicholas Biddle, president of the Bank of the United States, and his cousin Colonel Clement Biddle called to help Parrish put the $2,000 in banknotes that Randolph was carrying into the bank for safekeeping. Condy Raguet, a banker, diplomat, and financial journalist, asked the Biddles for an introduction to Randolph, and the two of them fell into conversation easily because Raguet admired Randolph's politics and Randolph approved of the free trade, states' rights slant in Raguet's papers.[20]

After three days of suffering, Randolph grew too weak to cough up the phlegm that was choking him. His breathing became labored and his anxiety increased. He asked Parrish to find a substitute attendant to relieve his poor man John so that John could go to bed. Yet even in the shadow of death, his petulance scarcely diminished. The substitute attendant was unable to find the little things Randolph kept demanding from the mass of baggage brought for the voyage to England. The newspapers, Randolph fretted, were publishing slanders and lies about him. The Atlantic packet ship would sail without him. "I believe," said Parrish, "the patient never fully relinquished his hold on life until the day he died. It is true, he had often said he was dying, he must die—or words to that effect," yet those had been just "the ebullitions of a morbidly irritable mind."

Randolph's darkening eyes never left Parrish when he returned to Randolph's room the next morning. After the hotel servants had gone, Parrish testified, Randolph declared quite distinctly that he wanted to "confirm every disposition in my will, especially that respecting my slaves, whom I have manumitted, and for whom I have made provision." Although the good Quaker—who had been president of the Pennsylvania Abolition Society—expressed approbation, the declaration took him by surprise. He was even more surprised when Randolph refused to let him leave the room. The laws of Virginia, Randolph insisted, were quite particular on the subject of slavery. They would not enforce a man's dying provision for his slaves unless a white witness who had heard it remained with the man until he was dead.

Parrish needed to see other patients that morning, so he persuaded Randolph to accept as his witnesses the innkeeper Edmund Badger and two young doctors, Parrish's son Isaac and his former student Francis West. While he and Randolph waited for the other three to arrive, Randolph steeled himself to die. He asked John White to retrieve from their baggage a large, gold shirt stud that had belonged to Randolph's father and to button it into the breast of Randolph's shirt. The shirt had buttons sewn on, so after White had passed the stud through one of the front buttonholes, there was no hole on the other side of the shirt through which he could fasten it. Randolph had him cut one with a pen knife and hang a clean white napkin over the rebuttoned shirt front. He then closed his eyes.

For a while, Randolph seemed to sleep. But he awoke with loud cries of "Remorse! remorse! Let me see the word!" He asked Parrish to write it on the back of one of Randolph's calling cards, which were lying on a nearby table. Randolph then took the card and stared at the word intently. "You have no idea what [remorse] is," Randolph told Parrish; "you can form no idea whatever." He directed White to draw a line under the word. Parrish asked him what they should do with the card. "Put it in your pocket—take care of it—when I am dead, look at it."[21]

When young Parrish and West arrived, their first sight of Randolph was unforgettable. He was propped up in bed with a blanket draped over his head like a hood and a well-worn tall hat pulled down toward his ears to hold the blanket in place. Joseph Parrish formed the two young men, Badger, and himself into a semicircle around Randolph's bed. John White stood by the head, and Randolph repeated the solemn testamentary declaration he had made earlier.

The words that the other three witnesses recorded were not as precise as those Parrish remembered, but they left little doubt about Randolph's intention. "I wish the provisions of my will, particularly in regard to my slaves to be enforced, & especially in providing for *this man*"—and here Randolph brought his hand down on White's shoulder with what force he still could muster. He paused, looked at them, and raised his long forefinger. "Remember that you four," he pointed at each man in turn, must bear witness.[22]

A little later, Randolph asked for pencil, paper, and his spectacles. He put the paper on a tray propped against his knees and began writing earnestly. He filled three-quarters of a page with widely spaced, irregular lines, handed the paper to Badger, and asked him to send it "over the way" to Mr. Coalter. White recognized the name of Randolph's brother-in-law John Coalter, who lived at a place called Chatham just outside Fredericksburg, Virginia. When Badger had left with the paper, Randolph began writing again—this time to Coalter's daughter Elizabeth and her husband, Randolph's godchild John Randolph Bryan. The lines wavered, broke, and drifted down across the page: "Dying   Home &   Adieu   Randolph & Betty my children adieu! Get me to Bed at Chatham or elsewhere . . . To Bed I conjure you all."[23]

John Randolph died quietly within the hour, just before noon on Friday, the 24th of May, 1833. The Philadelphia evening newspaper carried the notice of his death, which quickly appeared in papers throughout the country.[24]

. . . .

RANDOLPH DIED A very wealthy man, and newspapers everywhere eagerly speculated about the value of his estate. Some said it amounted to nearly $1 million—a staggering sum at the time—in "tobacco plantations on the Roanoke, negroes, race horses, dogs, bank stock, &c. &c." Others disputed that extravagant estimate. The tendency to exaggerate the wealth of Virginia planters, sniffed the editor of a New York business paper, amused Southern men who knew better. "*Millionaires* are as scarce in Virginia as they are elsewhere." Tobacco planting was difficult business, and Randolph had spent most of his lifetime redeeming the property he inherited from the heavy debts that came with it. "That Mr. Randolph was rich, there is no doubt; and that he had become so, under many disadvantages, is highly honourable to him." But a more reasonable estimate of the value of his estate was about $175,000—consisting of 4,000 acres of bottomland at $20 per acre, $80,000; 200 slaves at $300 each, $60,000; horses, carriages, and furniture, $15,000; books and wine, $10,000; and ready cash, $10,000. The leading business paper in Baltimore raised the slave count to 318 and noted that 120 of Randolph's 160 horses were valuable blood stock. A newspaper in Lynchburg, the commercial town nearest Randolph's plantations, reported the estimates from other papers and then pegged the value at "$250,000 to $300,000!"— still astonishing enough to warrant an exclamation point.[25]

Randolph's slaves represented a substantial portion of the estate. The population figures in census returns and the head counts in property tax records do not reconcile because they were kept on different bases, but they show that Randolph was enslaving about 240 men, women, and children when he died. Their average value on the market in Virginia was $300 to $360, and slave prices were moving sharply higher as cotton production on fresh land in the Deep South exploded. That put the aggregate value of the slaves at no less than $75,000 to $90,000, or roughly a third of the estate.[26]

Early newspaper reports on Randolph's death mentioned the possibility that he had freed his slaves. The story no doubt came from talk in Philadelphia about his deathbed declaration, although some reporters may have sought corroboration from some of Randolph's friends who had inklings of his intentions. The reports appeared in the same newspaper columns that described the British Parliament's debates on a bill to abolish slavery in the West Indies, a bill that would become law just a few months later. But by the middle of June—when no one had offered Randolph's will for probate at the Charlotte County Courthouse as everyone expected—it was becoming clear that something must be awry.[27]

The problem was that Randolph's final *written* will did not free his slaves, and a deathbed declaration was not enough to alter a written will. Either Randolph had been confused or mistaken about the law and the facts—or he had left another will that his executors could not find. The last will they had found was written in January 1832, about seventeen months before Randolph died. It left substantially all of his estate to the first child of his niece Elizabeth Bryan, a two-year-old boy whom Randolph had never seen. If the boy died without fathering children, the property would go to a son of Randolph's half-brother Henry St. George Tucker. The will appointed Henry Tucker and Randolph's close friend William Leigh as executors and directed them to sell all but a hundred of Randolph's slaves. The slaves to be sold would join many thousands of other Virginians who were being shipped south to meet the harsh labor demands of cotton production. The will contained no other provision for any of Randolph's slaves, not even his faithful manservant John White.[28]

Chapter 2

BURIAL AT ROANOKE

Roanoke, the Seat of John Randolph, woodcut in
Historical Collections of Virginia, 1845

B Y THE TIME JOHN WHITE BROUGHT RANDOLPH'S BODY
back to his Roanoke plantation, the men and women enslaved
there already knew that the man was dead. It was the end of May.
The brood mares were out on pasture. The days had grown long, and
for the past month, every hand capable of the work had been setting
out tobacco seedlings from sunrise until nightfall. The news of Randolph's death did not surprise them. They had watched him decline
during the winter and fail to revive with the spring. The accompanying rumor that he might have set them free was another matter altogether. It seemed too much for them to believe.

Fear inevitably pierced enslaved men and women when the man who owned them died. They were often his most valuable and readily salable assets. Even if one of the heirs was going to maintain his plantation, some of the slaves on it were likely to be divided among other members of the dead man's family or sold to settle his debts. The division inevitably separated friends and relatives, and it could split couples and scatter their children. Where a man such as Randolph had no obvious successor, fear could turn to dread. All of his slaves were quite likely to be sold, and because the most able-bodied ones were worth far more money to cotton planters farther south than they were to anyone in Virginia, their futures were especially grim. They could expect to march away in chains to clear the damp forests and die in the hot fields of Georgia, Florida, Alabama, Mississippi, or Louisiana.[1]

John White had heard Randolph's deathbed declaration, yet he had his own reasons to doubt whether he and his family would ever go free. White and his parents, Essex and Hetty, had been Randolph household servants all their lives. After Randolph entered Congress, White spent much of each year in Washington, where he and another of Randolph's personal servants named Juba became such familiar figures that their names sometimes appeared in the newspapers. But living directly under Randolph's thumb was not easy, and White had begun to drink. Randolph punished him by sending him to work in the fields, where White quarreled with the overseer and ran away. He was arrested in the river port of Dumfries about 30 miles south of Washington, and Randolph left him in jail there for three months before bringing him home and returning him to the fields for three years.

Imprisonment and rustication were standard procedures for humbling an enslaved manservant, and White knew that. He had chosen to bear up under the treatment, and his good work out in the fields eventually restored him to Randolph's favor. But he found that Randolph's favor had a down side. When Randolph's brother Richard died leaving a will that emancipated his half of the family's slaves,

Randolph took pains to see that John White and his parents were not assigned to Richard's share.[2]

White was now fifty years old, and his parents were decrepit. But their age and long years of service had not spared them from Randolph's tantrums during the past two years. Randolph accused Essex and Hetty of stealing from him while he was in Russia. He claimed that White had connived with Juba to pilfer his baggage on the trip home, and he said that White's five- and six- year-old sons were becoming liars and thieves. At one point, he threw all of them out of the house and brought in field hands to serve him. Just three months before John took him to Philadelphia, Randolph had John whipped for gambling with stolen money. These memories were too raw to be forgotten as White brought John Randolph's body home.[3]

• • • •

THE JOURNEY FROM Philadelphia took five days. Although Randolph had wasted away to nothing, the plain wooden box containing his coffin was heavy. The coffin was made of lead, and the big box had been packed with enough salt and ice to keep the coffin completely covered. White put the box onto a steamboat back to Baltimore, where another boat brought it down the Chesapeake Bay to Norfolk, and there a third boat took it up the blossom-lined James River to Richmond. There was an Episcopalian service for the dead man in Richmond, and after pallbearers loaded the heavy box on a black funeral wagon, a cortege followed it through the city as it began its 100-mile southwestern journey back to Roanoke.[4]

Toward the southern end of Charlotte County, the black wagon left the public road and passed through dense forest for nearly a mile before the driver caught sight of two cottages about 30 yards further on. The one on the left seemed to be an ordinary Virginia planter's house, a small story-and-a-half building with an exterior chimney at each end and a low-slung shed porch. But the porch columns were unhewn, and the whole structure was made of logs. It was the sort of thing that might have been built for an overseer or the occasional visits of an absentee owner. The frame building to its the right was not much larger, only better designed and finished. An enclosed vestibule extended from the front, and a matching porch on the rear had glass-paneled doors around all three sides to admit light and air. Beyond the cottages were a simple kitchen, a blacksmith's shop, and two houses for household slaves. The compound was meticulously clean, but the trees and bushes surrounded the buildings and the grounds were just part of the forest floor.[5]

Word of the wagon's arrival raced through the county, and by the next morning, a hundred men and perhaps a few women had gathered to see Randolph buried. His long-suffering slaves dug his grave at the place Randolph had described to White, beneath a tall pine tree just beyond the frame house. There were no rites. Afterward, the visitors looked around this place to which many of them had never been invited.[6]

The door of Randolph's log house opened into the main room, which served multiple purposes. There were two drop-leaf tables, a mahogany sideboard, a pine cupboard filled with elegant plate and glassware, a pine writing desk, and various chairs. On the walls and in the corners were some exquisite English pistols and fowling pieces. The small adjacent room contained Randolph's bed, a small table, mirror, and rocking chair. Both rooms were crammed with books, and bookshelves completely surrounded the walls in the sleeping parlor, except for a space above the mantelpiece where Randolph had hung an elegant portrait of himself by Gilbert Stuart.

Stuart painted the picture when Randolph was thirty-two, although some visitors who were seeing it for the first time thought he must have been an adolescent at the time. "In the fresh rosy complexion . . . of this beautiful little boy," wrote one, "it would be difficult to trace any resemblance to the thin, cadaverous lineaments" of the sixty-year-old man they had just buried. In the main room hung another arresting portrait. It pictured Juba dressed as a sportsman with his neck wrapped in a fine dark cravat, a double-barreled shotgun over his shoulder, and a terrier on his lap. Visitors did not know quite what to make of it. Although slaves occasionally appeared in portraits as part of the white subject's self-display, this stylized picture of an enslaved man by himself was transgressive enough to shock.[7]

The frame house was higher off the ground. It had a sitting parlor and a dining room on the ground floor and bedrooms for company upstairs. Here the mantelpieces were marble, the furniture much finer, and the upholstery done in a fashionable rose color. The bulk of Randolph's large library lined the walls. The vestibule held serial reports of debates in the British Parliament and the United States Congress, and beside them sat bound volumes of leading newspapers. In the main rooms were shelves of Latin texts, speeches, and books on politics, history, and philosophy. There were multiple editions of the New Testament in Greek and a few books of sermons. English and European literature heavily predominated. "'What! You cry out,'" Randolph had once imagined a friend exclaiming about his choice of books, are you reading "'nothing but poetry & novels?'" Well why not, Randolph answered. "I read to amuse [myself] & wherefore should I incur a headache with Scotch metaphysics, or a heartache with history, or a nausea with politics?"[8]

The two plain buildings for household servants were the only slave houses in sight. The other slaves on the plantation occupied small houses near the fields where they worked. A few of the visitors who hunted on Randolph's land had seen them clustered on the edges of the forests. Some had been in those places ever since John Randolph's grandfather established slave labor camps to clear the land a hundred years earlier.[9]

Richard Randolph of Curles, as the grandfather was known, never lived at Roanoke. He was probably the richest member of one of the wealthiest families in colonial Virginia. He made his home in a large frame house on a fine plantation beside the James River south of Richmond. Roanoke was just part of roughly 70,000 acres he acquired throughout the southern Piedmont during the 1730s–40s when he and other great tobacco planters began pushing west in search of fresh land and speculative property investments. Richard Randolph had bought newly enslaved African captives to clear and plant the most promising parts of the land, and he sent some of them to work this 2,800-acre tract along the Staunton and Little Roanoke Rivers.[10]

Richard Randolph put a white man named Joseph Morton in charge. Morton was an early settler in what would become Charlotte County, a small planter and land speculator in his own right who also served as steward for others. The slaves at Roanoke did their daily work under the direction of enslaved overseers sent up from Randolph's Tidewater plantations, and the kind of houses they built for themselves revealed that they were more autonomous than most enslaved communities in Virginia. Their houses were not the regular, symmetrically organized buildings familiar to Anglo-Virginians. They had peaked roofs and lopsided fenestration, and they stood in loose knots rather than tidy straight lines.[11]

Richard Randolph left the upcountry plantation at Roanoke to the youngest of his seven children, John. For a few years after John married, he and his wife, Frances Bland, lived about 40 miles away on an Appomattox River plantation called Bizarre, but the year after Frances gave birth to a son they named John in 1773, the family moved back downriver to a plantation just above Petersburg. They called the new place Matoax to celebrate John Sr.'s descent from the woman of that name better remembered as Pocahontas.[12]

Within a year after moving downriver, John Randolph Sr. died at the age of thirty-three. He left Matoax and Bizarre to his eldest son Richard and different parts of Roanoke to his younger sons Theodorick and John Jr. Four years later, young Frances Randolph married a handsome Bermudan lawyer named St. George Tucker, who became the trustee of his three stepsons' inheritance.[13]

Frances and St. George Tucker stayed at Matoax, leaving the upcountry plantations in the care of white stewards and resident Black overseers. The small planters who lived in their own clearings near the Randolph plantations disapproved of that. They did not trust enslaved overseers to maintain good order, and they feared that loosely managed slaves would steal from them and undermine the discipline of their own enslaved labor force. Men of their class usually felt obliged to defer to the big planters—the rich Randolphs in particular—but that did not stop them from grumbling. As the enslaved population on the Randolph places grew with descendants of the captives first sent there, these men worried. The irregular slave houses at Roanoke became a symbol for their concern, and they muttered that the oddly clustered buildings "had more the appearance of an old Indian town than any thing else."[14]

But the autonomy of the slaves at Roanoke and Bizarre appeared to make them more content. They had not joined the thousands of enslaved Virginians who ran away during the Revolution. When British troops invaded southern Virginia in the spring of 1781, St. George Tucker took his young family to Bizarre to get them away from the fighting before he went off to join his rebel militia regiment. There, the family heard that slaves around Petersburg were fleeing to the British. Among them were Thompson, Phil, and Jack, who absconded from Matoax on three of the best horses. Many more slaves left a nearby plantation belonging to Frances Tucker's brother, and some of their names appear on the list of Black refugees who managed to sail with the British when they evacuated New York at the end of the war.[15]

Although Thompson and Phil returned to Matoax, Jack and some other slaves from the place apparently got away. Among the refugees who embarked with the British was a woman from the area named Nancy Johnston, who told the clerk recording her departure that she had belonged to a man whose name sounded to him like "John Randall." The slaves on the upcountry places who had been left to themselves, however, stayed put. Frances Tucker praised the "faithful Servants" at Bizarre, and slaves at Roanoke apparently did not join the Black refugees who asked a French commander for asylum when his troops camped in Charlotte County the following year.[16]

What appeared to be a rich inheritance for John Randolph and his brothers actually came burdened with heavy debts. A Virginia tobacco planter typically borrowed against his next crop, which sometimes failed to bring enough to cover his personal and production expenses. Young planters were often particularly indebted because they were setting up new households and buying the land and slaves needed to expand their operations. An early death therefore could leave a man's widow and children with challenging obligations. That appears to be what happened to John Randolph's father.[17]

The senior John Randolph's debts were very large, perhaps almost equal to the value of the estate passed to his children. He died owing more than £12,000 sterling to British merchants and another £1,000 Virginia currency to his brother Ryland for the remaining purchase price of Bizarre. A substantial part of the debt traced to a £4,000 settlement that John and his brothers made with a firm called Hanburys a few years earlier. It was secured by a mortgage on Roanoke and all of John's slaves other than his manservant Syphax Brown, who wore his exclusion as a badge of honor. The debts were still unpaid when John's three sons came of age in the early 1790s. By 1796, the two older sons were dead, Matoax had been sold to pay the accumulated interest, and the full burden of those debts fell on John Randolph Jr., who had just turned twenty-three.[18]

The debt burden was especially pressing because young John Randolph's brother Richard had directed the executors of his will to free his share of the family's slaves. John could not free them as long as his father's creditors had claims on them, and he feared they could ruin his father's unsettled estate if they successfully brought suit for their freedom. The pressure almost broke him.[19]

John Randolph had been an exceptionally clever, sometimes studious, but rather careless youth. Although he took a passing interest in the management of Roanoke after he came of age, he had lived with Richard at Bizarre in a household full of relatively irresponsible young people. They included Richard's lively wife and cousin Judith, their two infant sons, Judith's attractive younger sister Nancy Randolph, Richard's tubercular brother Theodorick, and sometimes a first cousin named Anna Dudley who needed a home for her children after the death of a wastrel husband. John spent most of his time riding around the country to hunt, shoot, and socialize. When Richard died unexpectedly, John experienced a psychological crisis. He became moody, fretful, and insomniac. He paced the floors at night, sometimes saddling his horse to ride alone through the darkness. "I have not been even in a doze since the night before last," he wrote to his stepfather in the early morning hours of one sleepless night; "nor am I at all sleepy."[20]

John Randolph battled his father's debts for the next ten years. He dug through piles of old warehouse receipts to prove that the Hanburys had failed to credit his father for all of the tobacco he had shipped. He insisted that his first cousins should share the debt because his father had entered into the £4,000 settlement with Hanburys as an accommodation to their father. He sold some of his father's slaves, with no recorded regret, in order to pay part of the balance. The Hanburys' Richmond agent, John Wickham, gave Randolph an accommodation for repaying the rest. Randolph's cousins were another matter. They refused any responsibility for the debt, and although John Randolph sued them twice, he lost.[21]

As the years passed, Judith Randolph grew anxious to execute her dead husband's will. It was not that she shared his commitment to emancipation; she planned to buy new household slaves to replace the ones he had freed. She simply believed it her duty to see her husband's wishes fulfilled, and more to the point, the slaves who worked at Bizarre were insisting on their rights. Judith reported to Richard's stepfather, St. George Tucker, that it took her "continual mediation . . . to keep even tolerable peace between the Negroes & their Overseer," and she thought their continued "subordination was entirely out of the question."[22]

John Randolph thought he and Judith should keep the family's whole workforce together until he could lift the mortgage on them, and he resented Judith's insistence on dividing his father's estate. In his diary, he described their discussions on the subject as her "tantrums," yet the following day, it was he who rose an hour after midnight and complained when he could not find John White until three o'clock in the morning.[23]

Judith's letters to St. George Tucker reveal her to have been a knowledgeable and intelligent person corseted by society's expectation that she would defer to the senior male member of her husband's family on business matters. She thought she should sell her husband's land once she no longer had the slaves needed to work it. John urged her just to lease it instead so that her sons eventually could inherit the kind of property on which gentry status in Virginia traditionally depended. But Judith knew that poor agricultural practices made Virginia land a wasting asset, and she pointed out that she could not rent it for "anything like the interest of the money it would sell for." Judith nevertheless yielded to John's judgment and rented the plantations to him. You know, she explained to Tucker, "that he cannot bear the least opposition."[24]

Judith and John began to divide John Randolph Sr.'s property in 1810, and each of them received 155 slaves appraised at £10,622. There were more slaves at Roanoke than at Bizarre, so the chancery commissioners making the division allocated thirty-one of the Roanoke slaves to Judith. Judith's slaves had to be released from the Hanburys' mortgage so that she could free them, and since the slaves remaining at Roanoke were worth less than the unpaid principal and accumulated interest, John had to sell some slaves to pay down the debt. A few of them sold to local planters; the rest went to the slave market in Lynchburg. Richard Randolph's will directed Judith to give the group he emancipated 400 acres of his land, and she had already settled Syphax Brown, his family, and several others on a hilly tract along the Appomattox River in Prince Edward County. The freedmen called the place Israel Hill.[25]

John Randolph sold no slaves after he settled his father's estate, and despite hard work, rough living conditions, parasitic worms, and annual bouts of malaria, the community descended from the slaves he inherited grew considerably. By the time he died, there were about 240 of them. Slightly more than half were male, and 150 were older than sixteen, the age at which Virginia taxed slaves as full adult workers.[26]

The increase in slave numbers had been a problem for Virginia tobacco planters until they found a profitable solution in the interstate slave trade. Tepid prices and soil exhaustion discouraged planters from putting out more tobacco, and alternative cash crops such as wheat required less enslaved labor. But the agricultural boom in the new Cotton Belt changed everything.[27]

The explosion of cotton production in the Deep South was the most dramatic economic development in the United States during the early nineteenth century. European industrialization created a strong demand for cotton fiber, and following the War of 1812, Americans scrambled to satisfy it. The rich, dark-soiled lands running from western Georgia into eastern Louisiana were perfect for cotton production, and the surplus of enslaved workers in the old slave states offered a supply of labor. After white governments began expelling the thousands of Native American inhabitants who stood in the way, speculators, planters, farmers, merchants, bankers, and slave traders from all parts of the United States swooped in.[28]

Cotton soon became the country's leading export, and a sharp spike during the early 1830s drove up cotton prices by 80 percent. By the time overspeculation triggered an economic panic in 1837 and slowed the boom, planters and speculators had snapped up more than 30 million acres of previously uncultivated land in the Cotton Belt. The free population there had nearly tripled, and the number of slaves had more than quadrupled. The slaves cleared vast moss-laden forests, tilled the dank soil, and picked billowing seas of cotton one prickly boll at a time.[29]

A popular jingle of the time expressed the white masculine energy behind the cotton boom. "All I want in this creation," it ran, "Is a pretty little wife and a big plantation / Away up yonder in the Cherokee nation." Native expulsion, Black exploitation, and the scramble for new wealth shaped the cotton states, and they became the heartland for the white male Democracy that dominated national politics after Andrew Jackson became president in 1828. Celebrations of Jacksonian democracy as the rise of the common man overlook a darker reality. Nothing better predicted political affiliation with the Jacksonian Democrats than support for Native removal, territorial expansion, and slavery.[30]

The rising demand for labor in the aggressive new cotton states had a profound effect on men and women enslaved in Virginia. Slave prices in the Deep South spiked even more sharply than cotton prices, and Virginia slaveholders sent tens of thousands of slaves to the market. Between 1820 and 1860, they dropped more than a fifth of the slaves who lived in Virginia into the maw of the interstate slave trade. More than half of the slaves were driven away without their families. Many of them soon died from overwork and subtropical diseases.[31]

Even though John Randolph himself did not sell slaves after he and Judith divided his father's property, he was keenly aware of the economic importance of interstate slave trading. During his early years in Congress, he stridently opposed a federal ban on the use of small ships in the coastal slave trade. And in a friendly letter of advice to a cousin who had decided to sell out and move north, Randolph argued that planting in fact was not such a bad business because the "increase of Slaves alone will yield 5 per Cent: on Capital [in]vested in them."[32]

The unusually good conditions for tobacco planting in Charlotte and the other Piedmont counties south of the James River allowed John Randolph to keep his growing slave population employed. The soils in Southside Virginia continued to produce good quantities of bright tobacco—the light-colored varieties that brought the best prices because their clean taste and lower nicotine content made them easier to smoke and chew. Indeed, planters found that the thinner leaves of plants grown in depleted soils tasted sweeter and got the fanciest prices. The best bright leaf could sell for several times the price of other tobacco. A successful Southside planter therefore could keep additional slaves profitably employed by buying more land and expanding production.[33]

John Randolph had taken good advantage of this opportunity.

He bought neighboring plantations in Charlotte County, including a large one called Bushy Forest, and some smaller tracts across the river in Halifax County that his slaves could work together with the nearby property of his close friend William Leigh. The slaves not needed at Roanoke were sent to make crops on the new places.[34]

Wherever Randolph's enslaved laborers worked, their daily lives were much the same. They rose early in the bleak cold light of winter mornings to feed the livestock and carve fresh tobacco fields from the bare forests. Those who cared for the blood horses Randolph raised as his other main source of income watched over the foaling, cleaned out the barns, and carried countless cartloads of manure to the tobacco fields. When spring came, everyone stooped for months on end to plant tiny tobacco seeds in mucky seedbeds. Each adult field worker was then expected to transplant ten to fifteen thousand of the tender seedlings into the fields. They also planted some wheat for the market as well as corn and oats to feed themselves, the cattle, and the horses. In the blinding hot light of long summer afternoons, they hoed weeds away from the tobacco and made hay in the meadows and waste fields where they could find enough grass to justify the effort.[35]

With late summer and autumn came the heavy work of harvest. The grain and corn could be stacked for processing during the winter, but the endless thousands of tobacco plants demanded immediate care. Slaves walked through the tobacco fields daily to cut down the stalks with the ripest leaves. They carried the stalks to drying sheds, strung them on long poles, and hoisted them in ranks to cure. In curing barns set aside for the best tobacco, they carefully tended fires that smoldered to achieve the finest cure. Overseers expected these efforts to produce 1,500 to 2,000 pounds of tobacco from each adult worker.[36]

All that the men, women, and children enslaved at Roanoke got in return for their hard labor was coarse food and rough clothes. The cornmeal and meat that Randolph and his overseers allowed them were not enough to keep them healthy, so they were expected to raise their own vegetables and forage in the forests for berries, nuts, and small game. One suit of clothes for each season was all that a field hand could expect. Summer cloth was woven from the hard tow remaining after the good fibers were beaten from flax, and winter cloth was the brittle hard wool taken from old sheep. Wearing such a shirt for the first time, Booker T. Washington remembered many years after his freedom, was like wearing "a dozen or more chestnut burrs or a hundred small pin-points." This harsh regime was typical of the treatment meted out to the people enslaved on other large Piedmont plantations.[37]

Few details of slave management escaped John Randolph's notice when he was a young planter still shocked by the encounter with his father's debts. He counted out slave clothing and reckoned slave rations with the same care he had applied to his father's warehouse receipts. Although he did not sell slaves, he never hesitated to use slave labor to rebuild his family's lost fortune. And after many years of perseverance, he had succeeded.[38]

By the time Randolph died, he was the largest planter in Charlotte County and one of the largest slaveholders in the country. His 240 slaves and their overseers worked almost 8,400 acres—more than twice what he had inherited and considerably more than the newspaper reports on his estate estimated. Perhaps only half a dozen other Virginians and fewer than three hundred planters anywhere in the United States owned as many slaves. The large workforce on Randolph's sprawling plantations fit comfortably in the rolling forests and tobacco fields of Charlotte County, where 62 percent of the population was enslaved.[39]

Chapter 3

RUMORS

John Randolph, by Gilbert Stuart, 1804–05

A FAMOUS MAN AS COLORFUL AS JOHN RANDOLPH attracted many rumors. Most of them scattered with the winds that blew in other good stories. But among the rumors that swirled around Randolph was one that persisted throughout his life—and every one of the men and women enslaved at Roanoke must have heard it. People said that John Randolph was going to free his slaves. Whether or not they believed it, everyone who repeated the rumor seemed to agree on one thing. It had some intriguing foundations.

To begin with, there was Richard Randolph's decision to free his share of the Randolph family slaves. Although Richard had been dead for nearly forty years when John Randolph died, the free Black community living on the land he had given them at Israel Hill in Prince Edward County was a constant reminder of what he had done. The liberation of his 155 slaves was unusual enough; scarcely any Virginians had ever freed so many. The settlement of the freedmen in a single community was even more extraordinary. Yet what had made the manumission so notorious was Richard Randolph himself.

Richard died in the shadow of a scandal that had erupted three years earlier when a slave saw a bloody white fetus in a pile of shingles behind the house of Richard's cousin Randolph Harrison. Richard, his wife Judith, his brother John, and Judith's sister Nancy were visiting there at the time, and the whole household knew that eighteen-year-old Nancy Randolph had suffered pain and bleeding during the night. Richard had left the house in the darkness soon afterward. The Harrisons were discreet enough not to ask questions, but the slave's report quickly spread through the Southside.

Rumor was a powerful tool for enslaved people in Virginia. Because few of them could read or write, they depended on oral communication to share knowledge, pass warnings, and examine the weaknesses of the white men and women who oppressed them. Through careful observation, slaves could gather the intelligence needed to avoid danger and exploit opportunities. And undernourished enslaved women were credible witnesses to the painful signs of fetal mortality. The slave's report of the bloody fetus passed to slaves on other plantations and trickled out to white people just as surely as the words printed in a newspaper.

Many of Richard's neighbors and Nancy's family concluded that Richard had seduced Nancy while she was living in his household and then concealed a stillborn or murdered fetus. Perhaps they were too ready to believe those things because, despite his charm and intelligence, twenty-two-year-old Richard seemed immature and irresponsible. He had studied law with George Wythe, his stepfather's teacher, an opponent of slavery, and one of Virginia's finest lawyers, yet Richard never put his education to any public or private use. He had married his attractive young cousin Judith Randolph over her mother's objection, paid scant attention to running his plantations, and gone around styling himself and his friends "Citizen" this and "Citizen" that in imitation of the French revolutionaries. He had declared that he meant to free all of his slaves. He was not the only young Virginian to do such things, yet something about Richard made others more willing to accuse him.[1]

The dishonor of failing to protect the virtue of a woman under his roof was a serious problem for Richard no matter what had happened. And Nancy's potential exposure was graver still because the mere concealment of a dead fetus might be evidence enough to convict her of infanticide. Richard decided to address both problems by challenging his accusers to present charges against him in the county court. Although men of his class were rarely prosecuted in the county courts, Richard took no chances. He consulted with his stepfather, St. George Tucker, who had succeeded Wythe as law professor at the College of William and Mary. He hired John Marshall of Richmond, acknowledged to be one of Virginia's best lawyers. And to leave nothing undone, he persuaded the aging Patrick Henry—a masterful trial lawyer and a powerful political figure in the Southside—to join Marshall on the case.[2]

The county court brought no charges against Richard on the evidence they heard, but that did not satisfy public opinion. A newspaper broadside from St. George Tucker in support of Richard also failed to end the gossip, leaving Richard, Nancy, and to some extent their whole household dishonored. John Randolph's chagrin over the scandal revealed itself in an impulsive decision, quashed by St. George Tucker, to join the French Revolutionary Army. What Richard perceived as the vulgar public's self-righteousness made him very angry, and when he sat down before the glazed doors of his tall secretary to write his will nine months later, he attacked his slaveholding neighbors at their weak point.[3]

The testamentary language by which Richard Randolph freed his slaves crackled with indignation. "To make retribution, as far as I am able," he began, "to an unfortunate race of bondmen, over whom my ancestors have usurped and exercised the most lawless and monstrous tyranny, and in whom my countrymen (by their iniquitous Laws, in contradiction of their own declaration of rights, and in violation of every sacred Law of nature; of the inherent, unalienable & imprescriptible rights of man; and of every principle of moral & political honesty;) have vested me with absolute property. . . ." He went on like that for pages. He blamed his father for having mortgaged the slaves—"to gratify [the] pride & pamper [the] sensuality" of a dissolute brother—as well as the "british Harpies" whose mortgage prevented outright emancipation. And he ended with a blast at all "tyrants of the Earth—from the throned Despot of a whole nation, to the [more] despicable, but not less infamous petty tormentor of single wretched Slaves, whose torture constitutes his wealth and enjoyment."[4]

Richard was not the only member of John Randolph's family who had taken up his pen against slavery. In the year Richard died, his stepfather St. George Tucker denounced slavery as a danger to the new American nation and offered the Virginia legislature a plan for gradual emancipation.

St. George Tucker was a practical man, and his *Dissertation on Slavery* had none of the sharpness of Richard's will. Although he declared slavery to be incompatible with the natural rights principles of the American Revolution, that was not his main point. Tucker's concern was with the security and stability of the white population's new republican government. The bloody slave uprising in Saint-Domingue during the 1790s was a warning, he said, that the principles of the Revolution could destroy a slave society unless it took steps to protect itself. The first step was to recognize that slavery must end. The next steps, however, had to be cautious. Men and women brutalized by slavery were not ready for freedom. Immediate emancipation would lead to mass starvation, social disorder, or perhaps even a destructive race war like the one in the French West Indies. The safest way forward was through gradual emancipation along the lines of plans adopted in some of the Northern states.

Tucker proposed that female children born in slavery should go free after serving as apprentices for twenty-eight years and that all children in the following generation should go free after serving until age twenty-one. Those long apprenticeships would compensate slaveholders for the cost of raising the young. The apprenticeships also would train the young for occupations that could support them in freedom. Free Blacks would have no right to own real property, testify against whites, or vote, and those disabilities would encourage them to move from Virginia to some unsettled part of the vast American continent. Thus, within a hundred years, Virginia could become a truly free and largely white society.[5]

Tucker's plan was the first systematic emancipation proposal ever presented to the Virginia General Assembly, and he knew it would be controversial. He had included the proposal to deny free Blacks basic civil rights, he told the legislature, because he understood emancipation would be impossible without that concession to white prejudice.[6]

The reaction to Tucker's plan surprised him. His concessions to white prejudice and slaveholder self-interest were not enough to get even a hearing. The General Assembly tabled the plan with no comment other than a perfunctory personal letter to Tucker from the member who had undertaken to introduce it. Sensible and well informed though he was, Tucker had failed to comprehend the depth of white Virginians' commitment to slavery. Tucker never again proposed emancipation, although he published his plan in the edition of *Blackstone's Commentaries* that he used to teach his law students.[7]

Those had been reasons enough for voters to question whether John Randolph was sound on slavery when he first ran for Congress in the spring of 1799. Some said he advocated universal emancipation. Others claimed he was selling his father's slaves and pocketing the proceeds in order to defraud his creditors. And many thought the loose management of slaves on the Randolph plantations was a poor reflection on his character. According to one clerk of court in the district, Randolph had asserted that as he meant to serve no man, he thought it was wrong to make anyone serve him. The phrase sounds like Randolph, and more than one witness heard him use it. Years later when they had become bitter enemies, Nancy Randolph taunted John with her recollection that he had gone around boasting about his intention to free his slaves until he saw that it could keep him out of public office.[8]

When Randolph realized that rumors about his unreliability on slavery could wreck his political prospects, he published a refutation in a leading Richmond newspaper. He pointed out that he still owned "a considerable portion" of his father's slaves. And he declared that even if he advocated emancipation—*"which is not the case"*—he would adamantly oppose any congressional interference with slavery. No sensible man, he wrote, could dare to claim that the Constitution gave the central government any jurisdiction whatsoever over the subject.[9]

Randolph held to that position for the rest of his life. Slaveholding was his lot because he had been born to it. He considered it no more shameful to be a slaveholder "than to be born in a particular country," he told congressmen from the Northern states that were gradually abolishing human bondage. Slavery in the South was simply a fact of life, he said. It could not be denied, the risks associated with it were grave, and the Constitution had left the management of those risks to the state governments. Any attempt by the central government to restrict property rights in slaves would "blow up the Constitution." If the country ever faced disunion, he warned, "the line of severance would be between the slaveholding and the non-slaveholding States."[10]

But Randolph privately believed that slavery was wrong, and he wished to free his own slaves. He vividly remembered the impression that British abolitionist Thomas Clarkson's first essay against slavery made on him as a young man. He could almost imagine himself walking with captives on the road to the great West African slave markets in Calibar or Bonny. Although he confessed that he had allowed "pleasure or business"—he might have added political ambition—to shift his attention away from that youthful impression, he did not forget it. And testimony given by the Black men prosecuted in Richmond for their part in Gabriel Prosser's failed slave uprising during the summer of 1800 deepened Randolph's concern about slavery. The rebels' "sense of their rights," their "contempt of danger," and their "thirst for revenge," he told a friend, were dangerous portents.[11]

Randolph wrote his first will in November 1800, a few months after Prosser's uprising. It left his entire estate to two friends who were to operate his plantation until they had paid his father's debts and accumulated a fund for the support of his slaves. When they had done that, he wrote, "it is my desire that every individual negroe of whom I may die possessed be restored to that freedom which is his just & natural right & of which he has been so long & basely deprived."[12]

Augustus John Foster was intrigued by "gentleman Jacobins" like Randolph who held slaves and yet talked of natural rights. Foster was a British diplomat who spent four years in Washington during the run-up to the War of 1812, and he came to know Randolph fairly well because Randolph was one of the few Republicans friendly to Britain at the time. Foster had the arrogant superficiality of a young man of his class, and to some extent Randolph's good looks and patrician pretensions took him in. Randolph dressed like an English squire, spoke of his landed patrimony, and kept Juba and John White about him as part of his self-display.[13]

Yet Foster's very superficiality helped him understand the honor culture that had shaped Randolph. When Randolph told him that "possession of slaves was necessary to the formation of a perfect gentleman," Foster instinctively knew why. Honor depended on appearances. Slaves gave a man not just leisure, but the ability to display power and mastery. Such a man could afford to condescend; he could even play the demagogue, as Foster thought Randolph had done when he first entered politics. Randolph and other elite Virginians could "profess unbounded love of liberty and of democracy" with impunity, wrote Foster, because they had enslaved "the mass of the people who in other countries might become mobs." Indeed, they had done even better than that. The federal Constitution effectively let white Virginians cast votes for three-fifths of the slaves even though the slaves had "no check upon their masters' political conduct."[14]

The link unmentioned in Foster's analysis, of course, was deference. What gave the Virginia gentry their political influence was the deference they received from poorer whites when voters went to the polls. A large landowner like Randolph who successfully presented himself as alert to the people's interests could expect to win elections over and over again. In fact, Randolph lost only one popular election during thirty years in public life, and Virginia congressmen generally retained their seats at a higher rate than the congressmen from other states. A man like Foster simply took deference for granted, so he did not entirely understand the connection between it and the gentry's embrace of republicanism after the Revolution.[15]

Virginia was a scattered rural society in the first decades of the nineteenth century, and the self-perpetuating county courts composed of leading local gentlemen still held most of the political power they always had exercised. They collected taxes, authorized roads, and organized marketplaces. They commanded the militia and gave subsistence to the poor. Their sheriffs decided who could vote and counted the votes given. If gentry candidates wanted to get those votes, however, they had to keep the confidence of their poorer neighbors. To do that, candidates had to extol the people's liberty and protect their property. That meant keeping their taxes low, their crops moving, and their slaves secure.[16]

The formula gave John Randolph and other elite Virginians outsized influence in the central government. Nearly one-sixth of all congressmen were Virginians, and a Virginian had been president for all except four years since the national government began. But the Virginia gentry could never dominate the central government as thoroughly as they dominated Virginia politics, and they knew it. Their power base was in the Virginia county courthouses and the rural byways where some poor whites still tipped their hats to passing carriages, and the best way for them to maintain their position was to keep as much power as they could at the state level. Their defense of states' rights and their insistence on keeping the central government small and frugal were part of their essential localism. So were their views on slavery.[17]

A Virginia gentleman could lament slavery in the abstract; Thomas Jefferson, James Madison, and many other good republicans did. Slavery was inconsistent with the laws of nature, the commands of Christ, and the political principles of the Revolution. According to Adam Smith and other modern political economists, slavery was also so inefficient that it would eventually wither away. The economists said that free men worked harder than those compelled to work, so wage labor would replace slave labor as free populations grew. In the meantime, however, white Virginians understood that slavery was a hard fact of life. It was an evil they had inherited from the colonial past, a wrong for which they did not hold themselves entirely responsible.[18]

In fact, Virginia had been a slave society long before the living were born, and more men than Randolph had inherited slaves encumbered with mortgages. Until those debts could be cleared and the Blacks colonized elsewhere, white Virginians believed they had to bear with the system. General emancipation was out of the question. They thought it would wreck the economy, loose a horde of freedmen unfit for self-government, and perhaps lay the ground for a race war. So republican gentlemen could deplore slavery all they wanted, but if they cared for the people and their own fortunes, they would leave it undisturbed until the day when a merciful Providence paved the way to a solution.[19]

Even manumissions were unpopular. After the Revolution, Virginia Quakers who wanted to rid themselves of slavery persuaded the General Assembly to let individual slaveholders free their slaves. Private manumissions had been illegal for almost sixty years because of the fear that free Blacks would disrupt social order, but the Quakers argued that the ban unjustly interfered with a slaveholder's property rights. In the new dawn of freedom, they said, the state should no longer prevent a man who had qualms about slavery from doing what he wanted to do with his own property.[20]

The Virginia legislators agreed, and in 1782 they passed a statute that allowed a slaveholder to free his or her slaves by a "last will and testament, or by any other instrument in writing." The statute was about the property rights of slaveholders, not the welfare of slaves, and the legislators were careful to protect the public interest. The statute made an emancipator liable to support freedmen too young or too old to support themselves, so that they would not become charges on the county governments. Any freedman who failed to pay his or her taxes could be hired out to raise the amount due, and the emancipator's creditors could seize and sell freedmen to satisfy the emancipator's antecedent debts.[21]

The manumission statute still drew formal protests from voters in eight counties, most of them in the tobacco country south of the James River. The protesters declared they had fought the Revolution to protect their property rights, and they maintained that manumissions endangered those rights because free Blacks would steal from them and encourage their slaves to run away. The legislature left the law unchanged, and the complaints about freed slaves continued. The problem was that one person's exercise of property rights could interfere with the property rights of others. "It appears to me (witnessing the consequences)," wrote a neighbor of one planter who was emancipating his large workforce, "that a man has almost as good a right to set fire to his own building though his neighbors is to be destroyed by it, as to free his slaves."[22]

The General Assembly finally bent to those concerns in 1806. It required all slaves freed thereafter to leave the state within one year on penalty of reenslavement. In practice, this removal statute was widely ignored. Manumissions typically involved only a few slaves, whites living nearby knew them, and almost no one really believed they were a threat. Whites often supported local freedmen who made formal petitions for permission to stay in Virginia. The 1806 statute nevertheless discouraged manumissions significantly because it created uncertainty. Slaves did not want to be forced to leave their friends and relatives, and slaveholders did not want to banish them.[23]

Richard Randolph had been dead for ten years when the removal statute passed, so no one tried to force those freed by his will to leave Virginia even though they got their freedom after the statute went into force. The unusual free Black community at Israel Hill nevertheless had to live with legal disabilities and white suspicions. When the freedmen failed to pay their taxes, the county court ordered their children bound out as apprentices to raise the money. The order appears to have gone unenforced, yet the threat was real enough because the law allowed it. And the widespread concern that free Blacks would steal from whites and corrupt their slaves was inescapable. John Randolph had particular reason to worry because his slaves had many friends and relatives at Israel Hill. He gave "express and peremptory" orders that slaves running errands to the nearby town of Farmville were not to go there. "I am resolved," he wrote two days after Christmas in 1814, "on breaking up all communication between my estate and that neighborhood."[24]

. . . .

JOHN RANDOLPH'S ANXIETIES about the freedmen at Israel Hill did not stop him from writing wills that freed his own slaves. The will he wrote in 1800 did not come to light until long after his slaves were free, but two others did. Randolph had written the first one in 1819, the second in 1821, and over the course of the next ten years, he amended the second will with four codicils. Both wills freed all of Randolph's slaves and provided funds to resettle them outside Virginia.[25]

On the face of things, Randolph was typical of the men who freed all of their slaves for other than religious reasons during the early decades of the nineteenth century: he was a childless son of the Revolution. He grew up surrounded by Revolutionary notions about natural liberty, and he did not have the family responsibilities that made other men hesitate to abandon valuable slave property. Randolph had once felt paternal concern for his brother Richard's sons, St. George and Tudor, but the curse that seemed to haunt his family soon relieved him of the need to provide for them. St. George, who was congenitally deaf and mute, lost whatever prospects he might have had in Virginia society when he became mad in 1814, and Judith Randolph's estate was nearly sufficient to pay for the care he needed for the rest of his life. Poor Tudor died of tuberculosis the following year.[26]

Had Tudor lived, Randolph might never have freed his slaves. It was after Tudor died that Randolph began to put cash remaining after payments on his debts into a fund for the emancipation and resettlement of his slaves. When the Richmond firm that held the money went broke in the panic of 1819, Randolph claimed to worry less about the financial loss than the setback it gave to his plans for a release from "the *daily nightmare* that has so long oppressed me."[27]

Randolph also appeared to be a relatively decent, although exacting and frequently willful, master to his slaves during the years when he was planning to free them. He wrote cordially about his household servants Essex and Hetty, their daughter Nancy, and the cook Queen. Essex accompanied St. George Randolph when he went to England for special education, and John Randolph professed to be as grateful to Essex as he was to James Monroe, the American minister to Britain who took St. George under his wing.[28]

During years when Randolph felt isolated at Roanoke, he described his household servants as "my best friends." "They are a loyal & for their opportunity good people," he wrote to a friend in New York. While they were "not very scrupulous perhaps in distinguishing between meum & tuum," he said, "this ought not to surprise us." They were liberal in sharing with each other and reliable in their conduct toward him. "I sleep with windows open to the floor, my doors are never fastened, seldom shut." Randolph's closest neighbor believed he was "a kind and indulgent master" as long as his slaves obeyed him, but he "punished severely" when they did not. Although Randolph did not have slaves whipped very frequently, said his friend William Leigh, "a quarrel from him . . . was equal to a whipping from most masters."[29]

Randolph spent most of his time with John White and Juba, and although the question was not as unavoidable then as it is now, some of Randolph's contemporaries may have wondered whether his relationship with them was sexual. Few descriptions of Randolph at the time failed to mention or hint at his sexual ambiguity. A genetic abnormality or perhaps an adolescent illness had impaired his sexual development. He remained slight-bodied and boyish, and his voice did not change. Randolph recognized in himself a "delicacy or effeminacy of complexion, that, but for a spice of the devil in my temper, would have consigned me to the distaff or the needle," and some members of Congress openly ridiculed his impotence. These things inescapably concerned him because virility was entwined in prevailing cultural notions about strength, courage, and honor. An allusion to a sexual relationship with a male slave therefore would have been a dangerous step for Randolph's political enemies to take—especially against a man whose devil had armed him with lacerating invective and fine dueling pistols—and none of them ever went that far.[30]

Randolph's relationship with the slaves who worked in his fields was more distant, but at least in his early years as a planter, Randolph knew something about them. A list for distributing winter blankets in 1810 is in Randolph's handwriting, as are several other lists of the family groups working at each of the plantation's quarters. Planters usually despised the white overseers they employed to direct the slaves' field work, and Randolph was no exception. He thought they were crude, lowborn fellows inclined to overwork and abuse his slaves in order to make bigger crops. What annoyed Randolph was not so much any resulting injuries to his slaves as the disrespect that such abuse showed toward him as their master. The birth of mixed-race children to two enslaved women at Roanoke drove him into a frenzy. He gathered the women, their children, and some of his neighbors to confront the overseer he held responsible. He fired the man and then sued him. The children, of course, remained Randolph's property.[31]

Randolph was less attentive to other types of abuse. In his autobiographical narrative, a Maryland man named Charles Ball remembered passing by the property of "Mr. Randolph, a member of Congress" on his forced march to the slave markets in Georgia. The slaves Ball saw working there appeared ill clothed and underfed, and the overseer he saw with them "carried in his hand a kind of whip which I had never before seen; though I afterward became familiar with this terrible weapon." It was probably a long plaited lash tipped with a foot of soft buckskin—a type of whip that could be used unsparingly because it made a terrifying crack and delivered penetrating pain without breaking the victim's skin.[32]

But Randolph's greatest fault was his failure to prepare his slaves for freedom. They had useful skills. Some of them were blacksmiths, coopers, or carpenters. The rest were experienced farmworkers. Bouts of spiritual enthusiasm did sometimes prompt Randolph to give them religious instruction, but nothing else seems to have occurred to him. "True humanity to the slave," he told a good friend, "was to make him do a fair day's work, and to treat him with all the kindness compatible with his subordination." In that way, the master could afford to clothe and feed him, to care for him in sickness and old age, and to keep him from falling into the clutches of a slave trader on the master's death.[33]

Randolph simply assumed that his slaves would support themselves in freedom by working the land he intended to give them, and he left it at that. Toward the end of his life, he expressly drew a connection between the ignorance of slaves and their tractability. Yet lack of education was one of the reasons white Virginians commonly gave for refusing to free their slaves, and even men like Thomas Jefferson who had ceased thinking about emancipation knew that freedmen would require training of some sort. While it was illegal to teach reading or writing to an assembly of slaves, private instruction remained lawful until 1831, and some Virginians who planned to free their slaves did educate them.[34]

The Roanoke slaves' freshest memories of John Randolph were not of his neglect, but his violence. In the two years between his return from Russia and his death, Randolph's relationship with them had changed radically.

Randolph's behavior became noticeably more erratic during his Russian mission. On the voyage out aboard a government ship, he had claimed command, demanded that a pilot be thrown overboard, and eaten his breakfast from the head of a barrel rather than sit down with the captain. At the Russian court, it was said, he had knelt to the emperor and screamed at the young friend he had taken along as his secretary that he never wanted to see him again in this world. Randolph denied everything except the screaming (for which he offered his young friend a brittle apology), but there was no mistaking his loss of self-control.[35]

What Randolph found when he got home sent him spiraling. A major slave revolt led by Nat Turner had just killed well over a hundred men, women, and children. The rebels indiscriminately exterminated every white person they encountered, and the whites who responded killed just as many Black persons. Turner's revolt caused many white Virginians to reexamine their views on slavery. Virginia had the largest slave population in the United States at the time, and Turner's action made it impossible to ignore the inherent danger, especially in the Southside counties where the enslaved outnumbered the free. Some whites pushed for amelioration and gradual emancipation; others advocated stronger measures to control the slave population.[36]

The whole affair was more than an ailing old man frightened by his loss of vitality could take. "He said many wild things," recalled Randolph's closest neighbor: "that the people of Virginia were cowards—that if he had been tied on the back of his horse Radical with a broad sword in his hand, he would have ridden over 5,000 of the insurgents." When the Virginia legislature did debate emancipation the following spring for the first time in its history, Randolph savagely dismissed the whole discussion as a waste of time.[37]

His physical suffering, his anxiety about death, his embarrassment over the stories about his diplomatic mission, his fears of servile insurrection—Randolph took out all of them on his slaves. He convinced himself that they and their overseers had let his property run to ruin in his absence. "I have lost two crops at my three best plantations," he complained to Andrew Jackson. "Every overseer . . . proved to be a scoundrel who bribed the negroes with the plunder of my property to wink at their own depredations." He said that his close friend and agent William Leigh had spoiled the slaves with kind indulgence. And he bought a whopping 250 barrels of cornmeal for the ensuing winter, thought Leigh, simply to uphold his bitter complaint that his slaves could not even feed themselves and the horses.[38]

The very sight of his household servants enraged Randolph, and he accused them of everything he could imagine. He was sure all of them had stolen from him, except perhaps Queen who was too lazy. He thought that John White and Juba were drinking again. He said that Queen was too busy coupling with white men to get her work done, and his fantasies about her grew obscene enough to embarrass his male visitors. When Queen dropped a lamb chop in the dining room, he attacked her with a fork and knife. By the end of the year, Randolph had put vindictive notices in the newspaper advertising upward of one hundred slaves for sale. He meant them to suffer the biting fear of banishment from the community in which they and their ancestors had lived ever since anyone could remember.[39]

Essex, a dignified old man of perhaps eighty, was the special focus of his rage. Randolph had always favored him, but now he convinced himself that Essex was the root of all evils. "My good servants are the greatest rascals in Virginia," he wrote to his godchild John Randolph Bryan. "I have determined to eradicate the whole of them that ever have had the benefit of that old scoundrel Essex's lessons" and replace them with "honest (for negroes) corn field hands." He relented only after Moses, the best field hand, proved to be too awkward around the house.[40]

Randolph's fears and resentments came to a climax on New Year's Day, 1832. The previous day, he had sent word summoning William Leigh to help him write a contract for the purchase of land from his neighbor Elisha Hundley. Randolph also asked Leigh to bring along his last will and codicils. Leigh thought the contract negotiation with Hundley went well enough, although Randolph had stormed every time one of his slaves came into the room. But Leigh believed what happened next was insane.[41]

After Hundley left, Randolph unsealed his will, read through it, and started to pitch it into the fire. Leigh stopped him. Randolph had not been himself since he came home, and Leigh thought the man had no business destroying his will without explanation. Randolph then unfolded the document and read out the passages that freed his slaves. He reached for a Bible and read out the verses from Genesis in which Moses lays a curse on the descendants of Ham, the son who has seen him drunk and naked. His slaves had behaved so badly in his absence, he told Leigh, that his feelings toward them had changed. Whether manumission was a gift or a reward, they were no longer worthy to receive it.[42]

Leigh persuaded Randolph not to burn the will, but simply to cancel it by cutting out the signatures. The two of them ate dinner, and Leigh must have remonstrated with Randolph about the possibility of dying intestate. That night Randolph walked over to the frame house where Leigh was sleeping and gave him a new will. "My dear Leigh," read the accompanying note, "to guard against the *impossibility* of dying intestate I have Scribbled a hurried Will on the envelope of the Cancelled one, the chief alteration . . . regards the poor devils of Slaves. . . . If it please God to spare me," the noted ended, "I will draw a better one tomorrow."

Randolph put his old will on the mantelpiece where his household slaves would see it, walked back through the darkness to his log house, and went to bed.[43]

Chapter 4

HEIRS AT LAW

Henry St. George Tucker, attributed to
William James Hubard, c. 1833–37

WILLIAM LEIGH DID NOT OFFER JOHN RANDOLPH'S
last will for probate in the month following Randolph's death
because he believed there was another will—or at least that Randolph
had revived the part of his canceled will that freed his slaves. "We
have sent for trunks" left in Philadelphia, the good lawyer explained

to a friend in late June 1833, "and in a few days we shall know fully how he has disposed of his estate."[1]

Leigh and his older brother Benjamin Watkins Leigh had been Randolph's close friends for decades. Their father was the Anglican priest who married St. George Tucker to John Randolph's mother. Although the good clergyman's early death had left the Leigh brothers in pinched circumstances, both managed to become successful lawyers. Benjamin Watkins Leigh's achievements were more conspicuous. He was a leader among the elite lawyers in Richmond, an influential member of the General Assembly, and in the year after Randolph's death, a United States senator. William had chosen the life of a country lawyer, riding from court to court within the circuit that included Halifax, Charlotte, and adjacent counties.[2]

William Leigh was a quiet, introverted man who lacked his elder brother's flair and imagination. His brother's portrait depicts a handsome, outgoing fellow in fine clothes; William's shows an unremarkable, bespectacled man in a plain black suit. But William Leigh had an orderly mind, sensible manners, and steady habits. A friend said he never made an unnecessary stroke of the pen because he believed that flourishes were ostentatious and interfered with reading. He kept a plantation with the help of his wife and the forced labor of about fifty slaves, and he became known as the leading lawyer in his circuit. Just two years before John Randolph died, the General Assembly had elected Leigh to the General Court and designated him the judge for that circuit.[3]

William Leigh and John Randolph grew especially close after Randolph moved from Bizarre to Roanoke in 1810. Leigh's route to the courthouses in Charlotte and Prince Edward Counties passed by Roanoke, and he frequently stopped to visit or spend the night. On the face of things, the two had little in common. Leigh was an earnest young man pursuing the sort of law practice that Randolph once scorned, and Randolph—ten years older—was the impetuous heir to a sprawling old tobacco plantation. But Leigh admired Randolph, who was well read and hugely articulate, and Randolph valued Leigh, who was capable and unassailably honest. Leigh began keeping an eye on Roanoke when Randolph attended Congress. As the years passed, Randolph came to rely on Leigh, and Leigh looked to Randolph as one of his few close friends. When Randolph made his will in 1821, he named Leigh both his executor and his principal beneficiary. It seemed natural. He is "the soundest & best of men," Randolph told a mutual friend.[4]

Randolph's death was a personal blow to Judge Leigh. "We had been so long such close friends," he wrote three months after Randolph's burial, that "I could not part with him without the deepest grief." Yet as Leigh reflected on his friend's physical and mental decline during his last years, he could see that Randolph's death had been "a release from suffering—perhaps too an escape from loss of fame, which was the breath of [his] nostrils."[5]

When Leigh looked beyond Randolph's death, he saw trouble. He thought Randolph had "left his affairs in the best possible condition to give rise to litigation." Randolph's estate was large. He had written his last will under disturbing circumstances. And neither his last will nor his earlier one was likely to satisfy those who stood to inherit his property if the wills could be set aside. The earlier will emancipated Randolph's slaves and gave them much of his estate. The last will favored Elizabeth and Randolph Bryan's two-year-old child to the exclusion of everyone else in Randolph's family.[6]

Virginia's intestacy statute would divide the estate among Randolph's siblings and their heirs. A double share would go to Richard Randolph's disabled son St. George, the only surviving descendant of John Randolph's full brothers. He would get two-fifths. John Randolph's two Tucker half-brothers would get one-fifth each, and the remaining fifth would go to the surviving children of Randolph's half-sister Fanny, Elizabeth Bryan and her brother St. George Coalter. Randolph had long complained to Judge Leigh that his half-brothers Henry and Beverley Tucker cared less about him than they did about his property, and although Randolph had loved Elizabeth Bryan, he deeply distrusted her brother. Leigh expected the whole lot of them would object to the manumission of Randolph's slaves and contend for their statutory shares. In slaveholding Virginia, a will that freed a man's slaves was always more about his white heirs than the Black slaves.[7]

. . . .

LONG-STANDING TENSIONS about property within John Randolph's family had shaped his will, and Judge Leigh understood that those same tensions would drive the family to contest Randolph's will with particular tenacity. The tensions arose not only from clashing personalities within the family, but also from the economic and social upheaval that followed the American Revolution. From John Randolph's perspective—and even in ways that Randolph never consciously acknowledged—his stepfather St. George Tucker was at the root of them all. That was not entirely Tucker's fault. He was an upright man and, in many ways, a wise one. Yet like most men, he was what his circumstances had made him.[8]

St. George Tucker was an outsider whose values differed from those of the Virginia gentry. Tucker was born into a well-established family of merchants in Bermuda, a small island where opportunities were limited and even the established families encouraged their children to find places for themselves in other parts of the British Empire. This outward-looking, self-making attitude came naturally to merchants caught up in the economic changes that were transforming the Atlantic world during the late eighteenth century. It bespoke bourgeois values rather different from the more conservative pretensions of the agrarian gentry that Tucker encountered when he came to Virginia to study law at the College of William and Mary shortly before the Revolution.[9]

Although relatively few of the Virginians who possessed large lands and big houses were themselves more than a generation or two removed from great striving, that only stiffened their commitment to the styles and values they borrowed from English country gentlemen. Their well-being and self-worth depended on land

and, in this colonial setting, slaves. They imported fine furnishings, rich clothing, and expensive carriages to demonstrate their status, and their education—which the wealthiest young men acquired in Britain—was an ornament more than an occupational credential. They aimed to do the work required to maintain their position with as little apparent effort as possible.[10]

Tucker won access to Virginia gentry society with his good looks and happy wit, and he gained entry through his fortunate marriage to Frances Randolph. She was a charming young widow with a fine house and a large plantation on the Appomattox River. The Blands, from whom she sprang, and the Randolphs, with whom she had married, were both leading families. She held her share of her husband's property free from the sizable debts that encumbered her children's shares. When she and Tucker married in 1778 and he took charge of her property, he found himself one of the wealthiest men in Virginia. He moved in with her at Matoax and began buying some smaller plantations for himself. Tucker did his duty for Virginia during the Revolutionary War. He smuggled supplies from Bermuda, suffered a wound in battle, and served in the victorious army at Yorktown. The economic depression that followed the war, however, prompted him to reassess his plans. The family's plantations made little money, and the downturn lingered for years.[11]

Tucker's bad experience with the plantations convinced him that the striving, bourgeois values of his birthplace made more sense than the aristocratic pretensions of the Virginia gentry. He began to practice law. His great ability quickly vaulted him to the top of the profession, where a gentleman could work without too much embarrassment. When Frances Tucker died in 1788 leaving Tucker with three older sons from her first marriage and five small children, he gathered up the eight of them and moved to a house in Williamsburg. He became a law professor and, six years later, a judge. He married Lelia Carter, another attractive young widow who had large plantations and two children of her own. Tucker took a demanding, patriarchal approach to rearing the big combined family. From the

Randolph boys who were away at school, he expected sober effort and good academic progress. For the children at home, he posted "Garrison Articles" to enforce discipline at what he playfully called "Fort St. George." He insisted that his sons and stepsons prepare to support themselves in the law or some other respectable occupation.[12]

The Randolph boys' landed inheritance and their assumption about their place in Virginia society set them at odds with Tucker's expectations. At college in Princeton and New York, they studied to please him more than to achieve anything. When Tucker tried to inspire them with the examples of men like Benjamin Franklin who had attained greatness, his exhortation fell flat. The sort of recognition they expected was not achieved, but ascribed. Young men with their background were respected on account of who they were and what they owned. Although their own accomplishments could enhance their reputations, achievements were not the main thing. Had their own father lived longer, the Randolph boys might have thought differently. John Randolph Sr.'s will directed their mother Frances to educate her sons "in the best manner without regard to expence . . . even to the last shilling," and it stipulated that none of them should be "brought up without learning either Trade or profession." Frances had been of a similar mind, but she was dead, and the boys' stepfather alone could not bridle them.[13]

Tucker tried to get the boys' attention by exploiting the fear of their father's debts. "You will have heard," he wrote to John and his brother Theodorick on one particularly significant occasion, "that the Constitution has been adopted in this State." The federal courts to be established under the new central government, Tucker warned them, almost certainly would enforce the claims of British merchants that the Virginia courts had rejected. The Randolph boys therefore should expect to lose their entire patrimony of land and slaves to their father's creditors. "The consequence, my dear boys, must be obvious to you—your sole dependence must be on your own personal Abilities & Exertions." It was a resolutely manipulative message, and Tucker repeated it for years. It created anxieties about property that festered for the rest of John Randolph's life.[14]

Tucker nevertheless failed to change John Randolph's gentry mindset. John Marshall and other good lawyers kept the family's British creditors at bay for many years. And when Tucker sent Randolph to Philadelphia to read law with Edmund Randolph, President Washington's attorney general, the boy did not take to it at all. If he ever had to practice law, he told a friend, he would give it up as soon as he had earned enough to live without working. Tucker unwittingly increased Randolph's aversion to the profession by emphasizing to him how much energy it would take to develop a practice, and as soon as Randolph came of age, he dropped his studies and went to live with his brother Richard at Bizarre. Even as his father's creditors closed in a few years later, Randolph ruled out the idea of practicing law.[15]

Randolph's anxieties about property spiked as he struggled to settle his father's estate and free his brother's slaves. He was determined to keep the land and slaves on which his status depended, and he took the steps he thought necessary to achieve that goal. He moved to Roanoke so that he could exercise better control over operation of the plantation. He lived in the simple log house already standing there so that he could save money. He bought no furniture, and he put no rugs on the floors. The move signaled his retreat into a frugal austerity through which he intended to free himself from debt and the uneasiness it caused him.[16]

Planting tobacco is a trying business, and Randolph saw his share of agricultural disasters. The Staunton River, which sweeps down from mountain highlands in western Virginia, was prone to floods that wiped out the corn in his bottom fields. In other seasons, dry weather destroyed the crops and burned up the pastures. Some years, his fields suffered both inundation and drought. The weather changes wrought by plantation agriculture were avenging the wrongs done to "my red ancestors," he told a friend, just as surely as the gullies in old tobacco fields and the rivers full of dead fish were avenging the wrongs of the African slave trade. "God is just. Crime ensures punishment." Yet despite the difficulties, Randolph's enslaved workforce managed over the years to produce enough good tobacco leaf and rear enough fine horses to return him a profit.[17]

Randolph gradually reduced his debt. He saw his way clear to build the frame house for company, to add hundreds of books to his library, and to buy some fine English shotguns. He went to England for the first time in 1822—where he reveled in landscapes he had read about all his life and basked in the culture he regarded as his own—and two years later he visited the Continent. "Here then am I," he wrote to a friend from a well-fitted hotel in Paris, "where I ought to have been thirty years ago . . . had I not [entered] life overwhelmed with a load of DEBT." When Randolph finally paid off the Hanburys' mortgage in 1829, he bought a $350 carriage to replace the $50 one-horse gig he had driven for years. The year before he died he bought a $600 carriage, the sort of fine vehicle that British travelers more often sighted in the slaveholding South than in the free North.[18]

"It is strange, passing strange," Randolph mused as he began to reap the rewards of austerity, that most people with heavy debts still keep fine carriages and give fancy dinners. A wise man had once told him that a decayed family could never recover its rank in the world until it stopped dwelling on its past riches. He thought that was true. He had seen it borne out among his Randolph relatives, including Judith Randolph's siblings and the cousins who had refused responsibility for their share of his father's debts. They "will never thrive," Randolph said, "until they can become 'poor folks.'" Nothing was more respectable "than the independence that grows out of self-denial."[19]

Although what he said sounded sensible enough, the truth was that Randolph's long-standing anxiety about debt had left him emotionally scarred. I must "turn miser or take to the bottle," Randolph had predicted as he took up the struggle against his inherited debts. "He did both," his brother Beverley Tucker caustically observed years later. The anxious, frugal young man grew into an avaricious old miser. A Virginia newspaper could criticize Randolph for taking the Russian mission simply to get the government's money because the editor knew readers would believe it. Randolph's friends noticed that he developed the habit of coming to stay with them for months on end, and he even arranged things so that they would have to pay for his postage. When friends bought Randolph's horses while he was away from home, he would sometimes make a show of magnanimously returning their money so that he could get back the horses even though they had paid the full price he set before he went away. He once asked his cousin Anna Dudley to return—"dead or alive"—a young man named Isaac whom he had given to her.[20]

Those things were foibles compared with John Randolph's abiding anger toward his aging stepfather, St. George Tucker. That anger emerged a few years after Randolph moved to Roanoke. There were two reasons for it according to Randolph. Tucker had mismanaged the Randolph estate during his stepsons' minority, and he had appropriated slaves that Frances Tucker's father, Theodorick Bland, had given to their father. Mismanagement was difficult to show. The Randolph plantations were far from the only properties that failed to turn a profit during the long depression after the Revolutionary War. The Bland slaves were another matter.[21]

Randolph claimed that his grandfather Bland had given twenty slaves to his father as Frances's dowry. The slaves therefore belonged to his father's estate rather than to his mother. Tucker had connived to get them by pointing out that an undocumented gift of slaves was invalid and then asking Theodorick Bland to sign a deed that conveyed the slaves in trust to Frances as her separate property, which she could leave to Tucker on her death.[22]

How much of this might have been true was never established. Theodorick Bland did sign such a deed, Tucker had written it, and Tucker kept some of the Bland slaves after Frances's death. Whether Theodorick always meant the slaves to be Frances's separate property is simply unknown, although it appears that he did. Whatever his original intention, the deed confirming the slaves to Frances personally could have protected them from the claims of her first husband's creditors. That probably was what Tucker had in mind. After John Randolph came of age, Tucker conveyed a woman named Doll and at least five other Bland slaves to him in what appears to have been a settlement of accounts for his parents' estates. Tucker sold some of the others.[23]

Once Randolph decided that Tucker had wronged him, he was unrelenting. His letters to Tucker, which previously had been respectful and sometimes affectionate, ceased altogether. When the two of them met unexpectedly, Randolph refused to take Tucker's hand. Tucker asked his son-in-law and former law student John Coalter to try patching things up. Randolph would have none of it. He sent Tucker a long and rancorous declaration of grievances, and he even hired a lawyer to sue Tucker before thinking better of it. Three years later, moved by religious enthusiasm, serious illness, and another chance encounter, Randolph wrote Tucker one last letter purporting to forgive him. In it, Randolph maintained that his brother Richard's will would have freed his half of the Bland slaves, and he exhorted Tucker "to liberate as many as you have unjustly sold into bondage to the thousandth generation & for whose sufferings you are answerable to Heaven."[24]

Anger is a telling emotion, and Randolph's abiding hostility toward Tucker revealed more than his angst about property. It exposed a visceral dimension in the clash between Randolph's conservative agrarian insistence on the centrality of landed property and Tucker's practical bourgeois belief in the need for personal striving. Tucker's progress down the path Randolph refused to follow had given Tucker the things Randolph conspicuously lacked. Tucker had a comfortable house, an affectionate wife, and a family of clever children. He made friends easily, and he earned wide respect for his wisdom and integrity. The lectures on American law that he had published in his edition of *Blackstone's Commentaries* were attracting national interest.

Randolph's lot on his family plantation deep in the Piedmont seemed grim by comparison. Randolph lived alone in a shabby log building, and in the year before he refused to take Tucker's hand, fire had destroyed the house at Bizarre that still contained most of his library, a flood had ruined his crops at harvest time, war with Britain had wrecked the tobacco trade, and he had lost his seat in Congress. "I am as poor as a *rat*!" Randolph complained to a friend in New York. "The Government has ruined me & every planter in the Southern States, who had not some other resource except his land & slaves."[25]

Smoldering beneath all of this were unconscious emotions. Tucker was not only the father whose advice Randolph had rejected; he was the man who had displaced Randolph in his widowed mother's affections when Randolph was a sensitive young boy. Randolph was two years old when his father died, so his mother was the only birth parent he ever knew. In the three years before she remarried, he later remembered, he had shared her "widowed bed" and nestled at "her bosom." She had taught him to pray, to cherish his land, and to protect his slaves. Looking back on those early childhood years at the time he broke with Tucker, it seemed to Randolph that his mother had once loved him as no one else ever could.[26]

Then came St. George Tucker. "The first blow I ever received," Randolph claimed, was from that man. Tucker was a skeptic and free thinker who led the family away from its Anglican faith. He was a poor planter—and a parvenu, in Randolph's eyes—who failed to sustain the agrarian way of life on which their social standing depended. Worst of all, perhaps, was the passionate relationship St. George had enjoyed with Frances Tucker. She was a bright and spirited person who plainly adored her new husband. She died when she was thirty-five, leaving the image of her as a vibrant young woman forever fixed in Randolph's imagination.[27]

. . . .

JOHN RANDOLPH'S QUARREL with his stepfather troubled Randolph's half-brother Henry St. George Tucker, and two years after John Coalter had failed to appease Randolph, Henry tried to resolve it. Henry was serving his first term in Congress at the time, Randolph had just been reelected, and the two of them were seeing each other more frequently than they had since they were children. Henry asked his father about Randolph's grievances, and St. George explained the misunderstanding over the Bland slaves as he understood it. He even offered to forgive a $2,500 loan that he had made to Randolph many years earlier if that would settle things. But nothing came of Henry Tucker's efforts.[28]

Henry Tucker was St. George Tucker's oldest son, and it was he more than any of the other Randolph-Tucker children who had fulfilled his father's expectations. Henry was just a few months old when a British army led by Benedict Arnold raided southern Virginia in 1781 and drove the Tucker family to flee upcountry to Bizarre. John Randolph remembered that Frances Tucker had carried the infant boy swaddled in her arms. Henry grew up in Williamsburg, where he attended college and then stayed on to study law with his father. He was a serious, diligent boy, and St. George Tucker saw to it that he never got the opportunities for mischief that the Randolph boys had exploited when they went away to college. St. George told him that he would have the best chance of breaking into the legal profession if he started his practice in one of the western Virginia court towns where there was less competition, and Henry took that advice. St. George gave him a house, a slave named Johnny, and the promise of a grub stake for three years, and Henry Tucker rode off to the bustling country town of Winchester to face adulthood.[29]

Building a new law practice required the sort of perseverance that John Randolph had disdained, and Henry Tucker gave the task his full attention. When he had no paying work, which at first was often, he studied or volunteered to represent enslaved criminal defendants. Henry was not easily outgoing, so he sometimes felt lonely and homesick. He complained about Johnny and asked St. George Tucker whether he could sell him and move into a boarding house. St. George thought Henry should stay put, and he replaced Johnny with a young boy named Bob.[30]

Henry awoke one night to the sound of Bob's crying, and Bob's explanation taught Henry an important lesson. Bob missed home as much as Henry did. It had never occurred to Henry that a Black child could have the same feelings as a white person, and in a letter to his father, he marveled at the revelation. How wonderful, he wrote, were "the bonds of natural affection" that linked all mankind—the "civilized and the savage," the "American and the African." Perhaps as St. George read those words, he paused to consider why Henry had not learned such scant decency at home.[31]

Henry Tucker managed to thrive in Winchester, just as his father had hoped. He gradually found clients. He married a woman from a prosperous local family. Six years after coming to town, he won the district's seat in the General Assembly. Henry served several terms in the Assembly and then in Congress, and in 1824, the Assembly named him chancellor of the equity court in Winchester. The judicial salary was modest, so Henry opened a law school to replace some of his lost income. He rose at four o'clock in the morning, his son remembered, to prepare for classes before starting work at the court. He taught after court adjourned in the afternoon, and he spent the evenings working on his caseload. Henry became a popular teacher, and he eventually turned his lectures into a treatise on Virginia law far more practical and systematic than the rather philosophical notes his father had added to *Blackstone*. Two years before John Randolph died, the General Assembly had elected Henry president of the Court of Appeals, the highest civil court in Virginia.[32]

Despite what Bob had taught him about fellow feeling, Henry Tucker never questioned slavery. His treatise called it "a stern necessity" for the control of an alien race introduced to the American colonies by an "unwise and cruel policy." But Henry's opinions for the Court of Appeals generally showed respect for enslaved litigants. One of his early opinions freed a Virginian whose owner had taken her to Massachusetts (not because she had lived in a free state, but because the enslaver violated Virginia law by bringing her home). Another held that the creditors of a man who emancipated his slaves could not reenslave them once the executor of his estate had set them free.

Henry regularly gave liberal interpretations to faulty manumission provisions in wills and deeds so that the court could enforce them. Despite legal mistakes in the documents, he wrote, "the benevolent design to emancipate a slave" should prevail.[33]

The Revolutionary leaders who enacted Virginia's manumission statute had meant it to be generous, wrote Judge Tucker. They had looked upon slavery "not as a blessing but as a national misfortune" and considered a slave "not as property only, but as a man." Henry Tucker was not alone in these views. Virginia's five-member appeals court had bent toward freedom in manumission cases even before he joined it, and under Henry's leadership, the court continued to lean in that direction even as the appellate courts in the other Southern states hardened their positions on slavery. The Virginia judges' stance did not reflect antislavery feeling, but the belief that it was their duty to apply the law as those who wrote it must have intended.[34]

When John Randolph had warned Judge Leigh that both of his Tucker brothers were greedy, he was actually being unfair to Henry Tucker. Randolph's conclusion likely had more to do with his disdain for St. George Tucker and the lifestyle he associated with the legal profession than it did with Henry's own personality. Henry Tucker had chosen life on the bench even though he could have made more money as a practicing lawyer. He already had nine children to bring up, yet his affairs were in reasonably good order. He had begun building a country house on his wife's land west of Winchester. When Randolph complained to Henry that he could not afford to go to Europe for his health in 1829, Henry was concerned enough to send Randolph—with proper apologies—a check for travel expenses. Randolph could have taken Henry's gesture as a self-serving attempt to ingratiate himself with Randolph; he apparently did not.[35]

Although Leigh did not want to acknowledge it, Randolph seemed to have changed his mind about Henry Tucker before he died. In the will he wrote on New Year's Day, 1832, Randolph made Henry co-executor of his estate, and in a codicil to the canceled will that would come to light two years later, Randolph left Henry the sub-

Nathaniel Beverley Tucker,
daguerreotype, c. 1840–45

stantial plantation called Bushy Forest. When Henry had to decide
whether to accept Randolph's will or divide the estate under the intestacy laws, however, he was not sentimental. The question for him
was not what Randolph had wanted, but what would best serve his
family's interests.[36]

. . . .

BEVERLEY TUCKER WAS Henry's younger brother, and he grew
up admiring John Randolph. Randolph was eleven years older than
Beverley, and the life he led looked more attractive than the arduous
path St. George Tucker had set for his own sons. Randolph responded
to Beverley's admiration by treating him with particular affection.
Henry Tucker therefore was surprised when he heard that the two of
them had quarreled.[37]

Beverley was only four years old when his mother died and
St. George Tucker moved the family to Williamsburg. Those were
overwhelming changes for a small child, and to Beverley they
seemed like the fall from Eden. It was happy summer holidays
with John Randolph on the plantation at Bizarre that restored him

to the agrarian way of life he saw as his birthright. Randolph was the very image of the man Beverley thought he himself was meant to be—a landed gentleman with the leisure to read, shoot, socialize, and bask in the world's good opinion. Those holidays also spared Beverley the disciplined regimen of the Tucker household in Williamsburg, which he found increasingly oppressive.

Beverley never learned the steady habits his father expected from him, and St. George frowned on what he called the boy's "freaks & eccentricities." Beverley adopted a Romantic sensibility to hide his resulting sense of insecurity. His professors at William and Mary mistook that pose for smug self-satisfaction. They gave Beverley low marks in order to get his attention, but that only encouraged Beverley to think of himself as one of those exceptional souls whom the world cannot appreciate.

Beverley's legal studies with his father went about as poorly as both of them should have expected, so St. George sent Beverley across the mountains to read law with John Coalter. That was a good decision. Beverley liked Coalter, who had married Beverley's sister Fanny, and he managed to master enough law to qualify himself for the bar. He also fell in love with John's younger sister, Polly Coalter.[38]

Beverley and John Randolph decided that Beverley should settle in Charlotte County, work the county courts in that circuit, and help Randolph run his plantations. St. George Tucker objected on the sensible ground that there already were too many lawyers in Southside Virginia, but Beverley simply defied him. Although Beverley did get some business from William Leigh, who had one of the best practices in the area, winning clients in the Southside proved just as difficult as St. George had predicted. Beverley fretted about his slow progress because he was eager to marry Polly Coalter, and St. George let him stew.[39]

John Randolph offered to give Beverley enough land and slaves to support himself and a wife while his law practice developed. St. George Tucker angrily demanded that Beverley reject Randolph's offer. Not only had Beverley chosen a poor situation to begin with,

wrote St. George, he was now presuming to lead Polly into marriage without ever having shown that he was capable of supporting
her. Randolph, St. George admonished Beverley, already had obligations enough to his dead brother Richard's family and to his father's
creditors.[40]

Beverley waited a year before taking his half-brother's offer. Then
in the fall of 1808, he announced to his father that he had accepted
300 acres and fifteen slaves. They included some of the Bland slaves
and a few others not subject to the Hanburys' mortgage. Randolph's
gift, he wrote, would secure him and Polly "all the necessaries of life."
St. George conceded defeat by giving Beverley 500 acres that he still
owned in an adjacent county, two slaves, and $500. He did not attend
the wedding.[41]

It was inevitable that two men as high-strung as Beverley Tucker
and John Randolph would clash. Their first disagreement came just
two years later when Beverley got involved in discussions between
Judith and John Randolph over the settlement of the Randolph
estates. Beverley's views about gender roles were markedly traditional
even for the time, and perhaps he thought Judith needed a protector.
Or perhaps he simply presumed too much on his relationship with
John. Whatever Beverley thought he was doing, he managed to upset
both of them, and their reactions offended Beverley. Although he and
John tried to put the incident behind them, it helped convince Beverley to join the stream of white Virginians disappointed with their
economic circumstances who headed west after the War of 1812.[42]

The territory that would soon become the state of Missouri was
a favorite destination for small slaveholders from Virginia and other
states in the Upper South. Rich bottomland along the Missouri River
was still relatively cheap, and the Missouri and Mississippi Rivers
made it easy to ship crops to market through New Orleans. Just as
important was the temperate climate, which discouraged large planters from arrogating the land for extensive cotton production. To Beverley and other young men like him, Missouri offered a fresh start.
Beverley settled his affairs with John Randolph, packed his household

goods in two big, canvas-covered wagons, and arranged to move the slaves Randolph had given him in several groups. Then he, Polly, and their two young children set off through a gap in Virginia's western mountains. Behind their wagons walked the first group of slaves.[43]

The Missouri frontier was a good place for eccentrics, and it brought Beverley Tucker into his own. He opened a law office in the hollow trunk of an enormous sycamore tree, flaunted his old Virginia pedigree, and swaggered when he spoke on public occasions. His law practice flourished, and a few years later, the Virginia native acting as territorial governor made him a circuit judge. Beverley and a group of Southerners bought 6,000 acres near St. Charles on which to found a settlement of slaveholding planters. For Beverley, that place was the Promised Land. "I came here like the patriarch of old, leaning on my staff," he wrote to his father, "& behold I am become a great nation."[44]

The controversy in Congress over Missouri's admission as a slave state erupted a few years after Beverley settled at St. Charles. New York congressman James Tallmadge proposed an amendment to the statehood bill that would have stopped additional slaves from entering Missouri and emancipated enslaved children when they reached twenty-one. The amendment threatened the economic future of Missouri's small slaveholders, and Beverley gloried in the opportunity to defend the state's sovereignty and protect the slaveholders' property rights. He wrote a series of essays for the newspapers and saw to it that they were reprinted in Virginia. Slaveholders in Congress managed to defeat the Tallmadge amendment, the slaveholding party in Missouri got control of the new state government, and the first governor reappointed Beverley to be a judge on the state circuit court.[45]

Although Beverley took satisfaction in his achievements in Missouri, he also experienced his share of sorrows. His children died from malaria soon after the family arrived. He himself suffered an illness so debilitating that for months he could not speak or eat solid food. Polly Tucker died, and other settlers in the community at St. Charles began to move away. Beverley found solace in evangelical Presbyterianism, and after his second wife died, he picked up stakes and moved farther up the Missouri River to Saline County. There he met a young woman named Lucy Smith. Her radiant appearance quickly attracted Beverley's attention, and he also came to admire her father—a Virginia native and retired army general who had settled on a 6,000-acre tract that he called his Experiment.[46]

Although Lucy Smith had many admirers, it was the forty-five-year-old Beverley who married her in the spring after she turned seventeen. Such age differences in marriage were not so uncommon at the time, and the couple's devotion to each other was remarkable even by the Romantic standards they both accepted. When he was away, Beverley sent Lucy long, detailed, and unguarded descriptions of how he felt, what he hoped, and how much he loved her. Her articulate letters to him were steeped with love, admiration, and dependence—the emotional responses Beverley craved. In a novel called *George Balcombe* that he wrote half a dozen years later, the vibrant descriptions of the grizzled main character's attractive young wife pulse (in a nineteenth-century way) with his affection for Lucy.[47]

Missouri and Virginia were not far enough apart to keep Beverley and John Randolph from quarreling again, and when they did, it was about slaves. Randolph claimed that Beverley had left a deed reconveying to Randolph the slaves Beverley took to Missouri, perhaps as security for a promise to pay for them or to exchange them for other slaves once Randolph had lifted the Hanburys' mortgage. Sometime in the spring of 1820, Randolph demanded the slaves back and Beverley refused to send them. One or both of them complained to Henry Tucker. Henry thought Randolph just wanted the money, but Randolph's quarrels were never that simple. He actually may have wanted to reunite Beverley's slaves with the enslaved community at Roanoke. That spring, he had asked William Leigh to draft a will that would keep the plantation and slaves there together by putting them in trust for the support of a school. Although Randolph soon dropped that idea and his demand for return of the slaves, he could not let go of his real complaint—his belief that Beverley and the rest of the Tucker family were ungrateful.[48]

Elizabeth Tucker
Bryan, by William
James Hubard, 1839

It was very painful, Randolph told Beverley, to remember the affection he and the Tucker children had once shared. He recalled the trouble he had taken to organize their summer holidays at Bizarre, the money he had borrowed to pay for them, and the great warmth with which they had more than repaid him. "How little then did any of us dream of the estrangement which (with one dear exception) was to ensue!"[49]

• • • •

THE "ONE DEAR EXCEPTION" was their sister Fanny Coalter. John Randolph embraced her in a parenthesis because by the time he wrote his complaint to Beverley in 1820, Fanny had been dead for seven years. She died late one summer after a long struggle with tuberculosis, two weeks short of her thirty-fourth birthday. She left two young daughters and a four-year-old son.[50]

Fanny Coalter was Frances and St. George Tucker's eldest child and their only surviving daughter. After the Randolph-Tucker children grew up and scattered, Fanny worked hard to keep all of her brothers on good terms with each other. She wrote to them and their wives regularly, and she arranged for the family to meet at her house in the summers when they crossed the Blue Ridge for the cooler air of resorts around mountain springs. Fanny was frank and emotionally aware, and her siblings took her into their confidence. They also loved her husband John. He had lived in their household when he was their tutor and stayed there while he studied law at William and Mary. St. George Tucker respected him, and the family readily counted him as one of them when he married Fanny. They took pride in his appointments to the General Court in 1809 and to the Court of Appeals two years later.[51]

Fanny's daughter Elizabeth Tucker Coalter grew up to be much like her mother. Elizabeth looked a good deal like Fanny, and her uncles also were struck by her resemblance to their own mother. She had the same slender face, tawny complexion, and dark hair. She also had Fanny's winning personality. Her nanny had called her "Betty Obliging," and her mother thought she was the most "perfectly good tempered being I ever knew." Yet even as a child, she had baffled her uncles with a mock seriousness that left them wondering at her precocious self-confidence.[52]

Elizabeth Coalter's likeness to his mother particularly endeared her to John Randolph, and young Elizabeth saw in him a lonely old relative who needed a friend. In the year when her older sister died, she and her Uncle Randolph struck up a correspondence that became the liveliest in the family. Randolph's letters followed her everywhere. The friends she visited came to expect them and forwarded them to her when they arrived after she had gone home. Her letters followed Randolph too, and they came more frequently when she knew they would find him alone at Roanoke. The two of them wrote about their family and friends, education and reading, and inevitably a bit about politics, and their letters offer historians vivid glimpses into their times, their daily lives, and their private feelings.[53]

"When I first began to write to you, I loved you for my Mother's sake," Elizabeth confided to Randolph many years into their correspondence, "but now I know you & love you for your own dear sake—

In this I hope we are alike." "I have no friend now," he told her, "but William Leigh and yourself." Although Uncle Randolph was too discreet to ask about her courtships, he approved when she took an interest in his godchild John Randolph Bryan, the son of an old friend from Georgia whom Randolph had helped to educate after the boy's father died.[54]

Randolph had just returned from the 1829–30 Virginia constitutional convention when Elizabeth and Randolph Bryan visited Roanoke on their wedding trip, and the young couple's presence must have reified deep anxieties about the future of his class that Randolph brought home from the convention. The farmers of western Virginia came to the convention seeking equal representation in the state legislature, which would have ended the political dominance of the eastern planters. Randolph was among the eastern conservatives who stoutly resisted. He "would not live under King Numbers," Randolph told the convention. Once those without property got power, those who had property—especially property in enslaved men and women—would never be secure. Let all white men have an equal voice, he warned, and in less than twenty years, the General Assembly would take up a bill "for the emancipation of every slave in Virginia."[55]

The Virginia convention preserved the dominance of the eastern Virginia voters. But Randolph had already seen enough change in the state to know that he and slaveholders like him would remain exposed to the risks of democratic reform. His apprehension mingled with old sorrows about his family and new hopes for this marriage between his favorite niece and a well-educated young man he had treated as a son. There was a great storm on the last night that the young couple spent at Roanoke. Randolph's diary speaks of lightning, hail, high winds, toppled trees, and dead slaves on a nearby plantation. If he sensed an unpropitious omen in the upheaval, Randolph did not say so.[56]

Elizabeth and Randolph Bryan decided not to settle at Bizarre as Randolph had encouraged them to do. Perhaps cautioned by Beverley Tucker's unhappy experience as John Randolph's neighbor, they bought an old plantation in Gloucester County at the eastern tip of

Virginia's Middle Peninsula. Eagle's Point, as the place was called, was also closer to Elizabeth's father, who had moved to his new wife's house outside Fredericksburg a few years after he remarried. Randolph Bryan wrote to John Randolph in Russia to tell him about their decision, and Uncle Randolph responded with a warm letter full of advice about how they could live within their means.[57]

When the couple's first child arrived the following spring, they named him John Coalter Bryan in honor of his grandfather. The boy had a cleft lip, and his parents' efforts to deal with their anxieties about him drew them closer. John Randolph was less supportive. When he returned from Russia, he begged Randolph Bryan to visit Roanoke without bringing his wife or the child. "I have no accommodation for Ladies *now* & above all for children," Randolph wrote. "I do most heartily detest the nasty little wretches & never wish to see one in my house."[58]

Randolph's grossly insensitive letter says more about the mental decay that had overtaken him on the Russian mission than his feelings about the Bryan child. Only a month earlier, he had written the will in which he left the boy almost his entire estate. News of that bequest to her son came as a shock to Elizabeth Bryan when Randolph died a year later because the letter had convinced her that he found the child repulsive.[59]

. . . .

BEVERLEY TUCKER HAD his own reasons for surprise when he first heard of John Randolph's will. Beverley had spent the first months of 1833 by Randolph's side at Roanoke, and he thought the two of them had renewed the relationship they enjoyed as young men. Randolph had urged Beverley to move back to Virginia, and when Beverley got news of Randolph's death, he and his wife and their young child were on a boat in the Kanawha River working their way east through the verdant mountains of western Virginia.[60]

Randolph had called Beverley to Roanoke the previous autumn in a disjointed letter that ended with the pitiful plea "Come to me."

The plea found Beverley struggling with raw feelings of his own. His bid for a seat in Congress had just failed, dealing a nasty blow to his self-image. He had strutted forth not only to defend the states' rights that South Carolina was asserting in opposition to federal tariffs, but also to impress his young wife. Democratic Party leaders sidelined him, however, in favor of another candidate. It was an embarrassing way to fail. Reunion with his brother could repair their broken relationship, Beverley hoped, and perhaps even provide a bridge for him to return to Virginia and take up his brother's political mantle.[61]

By the time Beverley reached Randolph's side, President Jackson had called for troops to put down South Carolina's resistance to federal tariffs, and bitter congressional debates over the use of force brought the nullification question to a full crisis. The crisis pitted slaveholding planters against rising manufacturing interests in other parts of the country, and men like Beverley and Randolph felt that Jackson—who was himself a slaveholder—had betrayed them. As their spirits joined in the defense of states' rights, they seemed to rediscover the emotional connection they had lost more than a decade earlier. They spent the days reading the newspapers and plotting political strategies. They talked late into the nights. Beverley helped Randolph draft the states' rights resolutions that Randolph presented to his old congressional constituents, and the two of them launched the crusade to Washington that had brought Randolph to the Senate chamber on that late February afternoon just three months before he died.[62]

During those heady days and nights with Randolph, Beverley had thrilled at the prospect of gaining a role on the national stage. He also came to believe that Randolph meant to give him something more tangible than a political legacy, so he was taken aback when he learned of Randolph's last will. It left him nothing at all, not even a token remembrance like the small bequests Randolph made to other family members and friends.

Surely, Beverley thought, Randolph must have left another will. "I know," he insisted to Elizabeth Bryan, "that he meant to have distributed his property among us. Strange as it may seem, death *surprised him*." But Beverley did not tell her about the letter he had just received from Randolph's close friend John Brockenbrough, the president of the Bank of Virginia. Brockenbrough wrote to say that Randolph had removed all of his deposits from the bank as he departed for Europe, leaving nothing there to pay the drafts Beverley had written in reliance on Randolph's promise to cover them.[63]

Chapter 5

SEARCH FOR
THE WILL

Court House Planned By Thomas Jefferson, 1823, Charlotte C. H., Va.

Charlotte County Courthouse, early-twentieth-century postcard

JOHN RANDOLPH'S TRUNKS CAME BACK FROM PHILADEL-
phia in early July, and his brother Beverley Tucker rode up to
Charlotte Courthouse, where he and Judge Leigh planned to open
them in the presence of the clerk of court. The county's new brick
courthouse stood in an open green, and a rider coming up the road
from Roanoke could see it across the fields from some distance away.
Just beyond the whitewashed columns of the courthouse was a two-
story brick tavern that belonged to Wyatt Cardwell, an endeavoring
small planter and horse breeder who had bought the place a few years
earlier. Cardwell had ingratiated himself with John Randolph after
Randolph's return from Russia, and Randolph had asked Cardwell to
help manage his plantations. It was Cardwell who had gone to Phil-

adelphia for the trunks, and it was at his tavern that Beverley was to meet Leigh and the clerk.[1]

Judge Leigh and Beverley Tucker were looking for different wills in Randolph's trunks. What they found proved a sharp disappointment to both of them. Instead of a new will that freed Randolph's slaves or gave Beverley a legacy, there were only some disjointed papers crumpled among Randolph's clothes. They reflected both the deterioration of Randolph's mind and his renewed determination to free his slaves. None of the papers had been signed.[2]

"I leave my negroes their freedom as far as our unjust and illiberal laws will allow them to be free," began one fragment, "and I leave a sum of ten thousand dollars . . . to send them to the Country where god planted the sons of *Canaan*, such of them as he condemned to be black." Another passage left the same sum "to protect as many red men as it will provide for," an idea no doubt prompted by Randolph's pride in his descent from Pocahontas. The papers also included a miser's compulsive instructions for sorting his silver, Sheffield plate, and linens by quality and origin. They said nothing, however, about the disposition of any of those things or the rest of Randolph's property.[3]

Randolph believed that he had written his last will "under the influence of vindictive feelings" toward his slaves, his lawyer John Marshall explained later, "and that he could not face his God unless he changed it." Marshall practiced law in Charlotte Courthouse, and he and Randolph had been good friends for many years. After William Leigh took the bench, Randolph turned to Marshall for legal advice. But Marshall had hesitated when Randolph asked him for help with a new will in April 1832, and his concern about Randolph's disturbing state of mind must have been apparent as Randolph began writing the papers now crumpled in his trunk. "You will say I am deranged," Randolph had told him. "I know you will. I see it in you. But I am under the influence of the spirit of God."[4]

Leigh and Tucker did find something more useful when they looked in Randolph's portable writing case, which contained his 1821 will and the first codicil to it. Leigh believed that those were the documents Randolph had canceled and left on the mantelpiece in the dramatic events of New Year's Day, 1832. No one in the Tucker family had ever seen them until Beverley Tucker began unwrapping the thick trifold pages.[5]

The opening lines probably did not surprise him. "I give and bequeath all my slaves their freedom," the will began, "heartily regretting that I have ever been the owner of one." What followed were provisions for their removal from Virginia as state law required. The will set aside $8,000 to settle the freedmen in another state or territory and to purchase at least 10 acres for each one older than forty. There were special provisions for the household servants whom Randolph hoped would be allowed to stay in Virginia. Essex and Hetty were to receive an annual allowance of 3½ barrels of cornmeal, 200 pounds of pork, 20 pounds of brown sugar, 10 pounds of coffee, a pair of strong shoes, a suit of clothes, and a blanket. The same allowances went to Hetty's daughter Nancy, Juba, Queen, and John White. Essex was also to get a new hat.[6]

But as Beverley read on, his pulse quickened. The will appointed William Leigh as sole executor. It gave him the Middle Quarter of the Roanoke plantation, including Randolph's houses, his library, and his household goods. It authorized Leigh to sell the rest of Randolph's land and entrusted the sale proceeds to Randolph's friends Francis Scott Key and William Meade, who were to use the money for the benefit of the manumitted slaves. Frank Key, as his friends called him, was a prominent lawyer in Georgetown, an evangelical Episcopalian, and one of Randolph's closest friends. Meade was an evangelical Episcopalian priest who had recently become the assistant bishop of Virginia.

The rest of the will contained various specific bequests. It gave Randolph's godson John Randolph Bryan a gold watch. It gave Anna Dudley's son Theodore, a cousin through the Bland family, some land that Randolph expected to inherit from the Blands, although the first codicil made a few days later had revoked that bequest and given the expectancy to Leigh. Another short provision simply confirmed to Beverley Tucker the slaves Randolph had given him and for which Randolph claimed to have a reconveyance. Apart from that, the will gave the Tucker family nothing.

Worse than that, it explained why. Randolph had excluded the Tuckers from the will, the document declared, because their father St. George had taken not only the whole profits of the Randolph plantations while John Randolph and his brothers were minors, but also the twenty slaves their grandfather had given to their father as their mother's dowry. Then came the same moral indignation about the fate of those slaves that Randolph had heaped on St. George Tucker in life. "One half of them now scattered from Maryland to Mississippi were entitled to freedom at my brother Richard's death, as the other would have been at mine."[7]

An earnest search through Randolph's papers back at Roanoke turned up two uncanceled codicils. They did not alter the basic arrangements in the canceled will. One dated January 1826 gave John White's wife Betsy and Juba's wife Celia the same annual allowances that the will had provided for their husbands. It asked the General Assembly to permit Randolph's household servants and any other "old and faithful slaves" who desired it to remain in Virginia. It also left 600 acres and a pair of fine English dueling pistols to Senator Thomas Hart Benton. This codicil and another one written in 1828 gave Leigh all of the land Randolph had bought since making the original will, including some tracts in Leigh's home county of Halifax. The later codicil disinherited anyone who contested the will, "as lawyers and courts of law are extremely addicted to making wills for dead men, which they never made when living."[8]

For a man who had just brought his family all the way across the United States as it then existed so that he could live near Randolph, these papers were completely stunning. They left Beverley Tucker nothing except the slaves he already owned.

. . . .

THE BITTER ACCUSATION against St. George Tucker in Randolph's 1821 will was an obvious focus for Beverley Tucker's disappointment. He and the rest of the Tucker family had known for years that Randolph believed St. George Tucker had cheated him. They never doubted the claim was false—the product of Randolph's sometimes disordered imagination—and they regarded the breach within the family as an unfortunate and private matter. They probably never anticipated that it would lead Randolph to disinherit them. With Randolph's wills now available at the clerk's office, everything suddenly changed. Randolph's aspersion on St. George Tucker became public. Newspapers in New York and Baltimore published an autobiographical letter from Randolph to his nephew Tudor that made the same charge. The extraordinary last will leaving Randolph's estate to Elizabeth Bryan's infant son further complicated the situation because it pointedly excluded everyone else in the family.[9]

With the public now looking on, the family's handling of Randolph's will became a matter of honor in a society where honor was central to social identity. Honorable children would defend their dead father's good name. Honorable siblings would not quarrel over their dead brother's property. Unbefitting family differences needed to be veiled, and self-interested disappointment would have to dress itself in finer intentions.[10]

Beverley Tucker thought he saw an honorable solution on the face of the problem. Randolph's fixation on his grievances against St. George Tucker was irrational, he said, and the grievances were so inconsistent with facts known to Randolph that they proved he was mad. Showing the world that Randolph's accusation arose from an insane delusion would vindicate St. George Tucker's honor. It also would spare Randolph's honor because the world could not blame him for allegations made when he was not himself. And once Randolph's insanity had been established, the family could overturn his wills and divide his estate under the intestacy statute.[11]

It was true that the law gave men considerable freedom to leave their property to whomever they wished. That was especially true in the case of a man without wife or children, who could have claimed a share of his estate for their support whether he left it to them or not. But in practice the common law had always been suspicious of wills that left the bulk of a man's property to someone outside his family. Men were expected to love their families and close relatives, and even when natural bonds of affection had torn, men were supposed to recognize that the law protected their property so that they could use it to fulfill their social obligations. When a man's will left his property to "strangers," it was natural to ask whether he had been in his right mind.[12]

Although the common law had long recognized that an insane person lacked the capacity to make a valid will, courts typically invalidated wills only when the derangement was patent. In the decades before Randolph died, however, the law began to change. Courts responded to new medical theories about what doctors called mental alienation. Those theories postulated that otherwise sensible persons could become alienated, or unable to think in the usual way, about particular subjects. That confusion could lead them to do things they would not otherwise have done. Probate courts therefore sympathized with the claim that persons who had developed irrational antipathies toward the natural objects of their bounty were incapable of deciding how to dispose of their property. That, it seemed to Beverley Tucker, was John Randolph's case precisely.[13]

Within the context of the honor culture in antebellum Virginia, Beverley's solution to the problem presented by Randolph's wills was not as blatantly self-interested as it seems. Even St. George Tucker's widow Lelia, who had no interest in John Randolph's estate, thought the Tucker brothers owed it to their father's memory to challenge the will that accused him of dishonesty. She had heard it said, she told Henry Tucker, that "the World looked on with wonder" at the brothers' friendly relationship with a man who vilified their father. While she was willing to believe they had not realized Randolph was saying such things outside the family while he lived, she expected them to prove it by challenging the will now that Randolph's accusations were public.[14]

Although her own child had the most to lose, Randolph's niece Elizabeth Bryan thought the last will should be set aside. She took comfort from the note Randolph had written to her as he lay dying, but the will leaving everything to her infant son frightened her. A dispute over it could tear the family apart, and the possession of so much property at a young age could corrupt her son. She thought that Randolph's real objective had been to keep his land together, and he had simply pitched upon the bequest to her child as a way to do that. "My own belief," she wrote, "is that Uncle R. did wish his slaves emancipated, & Mr. Leigh handsomely rewarded for his tried friendship." She therefore hoped the law would free the slaves, make a generous provision for Leigh, and divide the rest of the property among the "natural heirs."[15]

Without divine intervention or another will, none of that seemed likely. Randolph's last will did not free his slaves, and his earlier will left nothing to his natural heirs. If both of the wills were invalid, only the heirs could benefit. William Leigh would get nothing, and Randolph's slaves would remain in bondage.

Behind all of Beverley Tucker's talk about honor, that was exactly what he had in mind. If Beverley ever had qualms about slavery, he had lost them during the fight over Missouri statehood. He regarded his community of Southern slaveholders at St. Charles as a proper model for agrarian society, and he had boasted that they would drive antislavery Northern settlers out of the state. By the time he returned to Virginia, Beverley had joined the vanguard of Southern conservatives who were weaving a strong connection between states' rights and the defense of slavery. And although Beverley wrote sentimental descriptions of the affectionate and enduring relationship between masters and slaves, he ultimately sold the forty slaves he had left in Missouri to a Texas cotton planter.[16]

Beverley's older brother Henry was also an enslaver, and notwithstanding the respect he showed for manumissions in his judicial opinions, he had no particular interest in freeing John Randolph's slaves. They were worth a lot of money. His country house west of Winchester was going to cost quite a bit, and he had not yet paid for the house he bought in Richmond when he was appointed to the Court of Appeals. "With nine children," he told his brother, "I find life an uphill business." Henry Tucker sensed the anger behind Randolph's direction to sell all but a hundred of his slaves, yet even that "denunciation of banishment"—as Henry called it—gave him little pause. If the heirs overturned Randolph's wills, they would need most of the slaves to keep his plantations running until they decided what to do with them. Should the last will hold up, at least the proceeds from the slave sales would go to Elizabeth Bryan's son.[17]

Few white people in Virginia would have objected to the way the Tucker brothers thought about John Randolph's slaves. In its debates after Nat Turner's revolt, the Virginia legislature had firmly rejected the possibility of gradual emancipation. It chose instead to increase the restrictions on slaves, free Blacks, and any whites who sympathized with them. Men and women of African descent who gathered to pray without white supervision, for example, could get thirty-nine lashes. And free people who distributed abolitionist literature or helped a slave escape bondage faced a prison term of up to five years.[18]

Having made those decisions, white Virginians began to accept a new orthodoxy about slavery. What the Revolutionary generation had considered an inherited evil their children now defended as a positive good—or at least better than the alternatives. Virginians had long ago embraced Thomas Jefferson's claim that white prejudice and Black resentment would forever prevent the two races from living together peacefully in freedom. And to that racial rationalization for slavery, they now bolted a class-based analysis borrowed from economists who were trying to explain labor unrest in industrializing Europe. Not only did slavery avoid race war, claimed the new pro-slavery thinkers, it also prevented the conflict between capital and free labor that was disturbing European societies. They said that American slaves were actually treated at least as well as workers in free labor systems. Slavery assured them employment, and it gave them as large a share of the profits as European workers received.

The proslavery argument effaced slavery's violence and degradation with a gloss of blindness and falsehood. Fatal violence was said to be rare because sensible men would not destroy their own slave property. Assaults and rapes were said to be unusual because they would produce anger and disorder. Physical punishments were scarcely harsher, ran the argument, than the ones administered in families and other hierarchical social relationships. Justifications for the racial basis of American slavery were a similar compound of empirical error and rank prejudice. Persons of African descent were better able to bear hard labor in hot climates, said white apologists, and they actually benefited from slave discipline because they were too ignorant and indolent to prosper on their own.[19]

Those beliefs made manumissions anomalous. Three decades earlier, planters had persuaded the General Assembly to force newly manumitted slaves out of the state so they could not steal from white planters and incite slave insubordination. Now, if the proslavery arguments were to hold together, it became important to believe that persons of African descent should not go free at all because they were better off in slavery. Indeed, the western states that were once the most attractive destination for manumitted Virginians had adopted laws to exclude them. "If the state of Ohio could not endure the admission of a few thousand Africans," asked a white Virginia educator, "what would have become of Virginia, if she must have half a million within her boundaries?"[20]

Richard Randolph's freedmen at Israel Hill in Prince Edward County became a signal example. The sort of white men who wrote letters to newspapers insisted that this free Black community had failed. As long as "the habits of industry" they acquired in slavery persisted, one told the proslavery *Farmers' Register*, the community grew and lived in some degree of comfort. Once "a new race, raised in idleness and vice, sprang up," however, the settlement became "wretched in the extreme." Not only were the residents pests and burdens on their white neighbors, the writer concluded, they were also "infinitely" worse off than they would have been in slavery. Newspaper writers repeated and magnified that tale for the next twenty years. While the number of Blacks in slavery had twice doubled since the founding of Israel Hill, one of them claimed, the free Blacks there had grown by less than 40 percent. A Randolph cousin predicted that in a generation or two, the freedmen of Israel Hill would become "entirely extinct."[21]

Antislavery reformers who worked with freedmen on Southern plantations during the Civil War would reach exactly the opposite conclusions. They found that the older adults who had grown up in bondage were less capable of improvement than the young people. "The first generation," one wrote, "might be unfitted for the . . . responsibilities of citizenship," but with the benefit of education, the next generation would be able to shoulder the duties of free men and women. Their industry was already putting to rest the claim that only enslaved labor could produce Southern staples. Prospects for their prosperity seemed bright. These contradictory assessments of free African American communities said more about the different preconceptions of the white observers than they did about the painful complexities that confronted the freedmen themselves.[22]

. . . .

JOHN RANDOLPH'S OWN public position on slavery migrated during the last ten years of his life, so his brothers could find reasons to convince themselves that he had given up on manumission by the time he died. It was true that during his first twenty years in Congress, Randolph had not defended slavery as an institution. He had simply insisted that the central government should leave the problem of slavery to the states because it had no constitutional power to meddle with slaveholders' private property. When the expansion of slave-based agriculture into Missouri and other territories increased opposition to slavery, however, Randolph joined in the defensive reaction. He swallowed his private reservations and stepped forward as a leader of the Southern politicians who made slavery a reason for resisting federal power.[23]

During his early years in Congress, Randolph had supported restrictions on slavery in federal territories. When white settlers in the Indiana Territory sought relief from the federal ban on slavery in the region north of the Ohio River in 1803, a House committee under Randolph's control bluntly rejected the proposal as "highly dangerous and inexpedient." Slave labor was "demonstrably" more expensive than free labor, said the committee's report, and it could not pay for itself in a climate unsuited to high-value staples such as tobacco. The burgeoning population of Ohio proved that agriculture in the Northwest could prosper without it. Randolph had also supported a ban on the importation of foreign slaves into the Louisiana Territory, where sugar and other staples were profitable. He thought the risk that rebellious slaves from the West Indies could incite uprisings justified this restriction on the Louisiana planters' rights.[24]

Prompted by his evangelical friend Frank Key, Randolph had launched a congressional investigation into slave trading in the District of Columbia, another place where the Constitution gave the central government local jurisdiction. The horrors of that trade sprang to Randolph's attention in the winter of 1815 when a woman named Anna, who was about to be trafficked away from her family, jumped from the attic window of a Washington tavern. She somehow survived the fall, and her desperate act unmasked a network of illegal slave traders. Key and others who opposed the slave trade leaped into action, and that spring, Randolph took the problem to Congress.[25]

Nowhere on earth, Randolph told the House, could a slave market be more infamous than at the seat of a nation that prided itself on freedom. The buying and selling of human beings in the very shadow of the Capitol was "a crying sin before God and man." While he would never support restrictions on slavery in the sovereign states, he believed that Congress should outlaw the slave trade in the federal district. His brother Henry Tucker, who chaired the House committee on the District of Columbia at the time, sidestepped responsibility for making an investigation, so the task went to a select committee chaired by Randolph. The report he delivered recounted abuses that ranged from the outright kidnapping of free Blacks to the illegal sale of Northern slaves before they reached the age at which they would go free under their home states' gradual emancipation laws.[26]

When Frank Key and other prominent men from both political parties founded the American Colonization Society in December 1816, John Randolph attended the organizational meeting. The purpose of the society was to promote the voluntary removal of free African Americans to a colony in West Africa. That objective appealed both to slaveholders who thought free Blacks threatened social order and to opponents of slavery who thought an outlet for freedmen would encourage manumissions and eventual emancipation. In his remarks at the organizational meeting, Randolph explicitly emphasized the connection. Colonization, he said, would "tend to secure" slave property by ridding the country of free Blacks, and removing that risk to slavery would open the way for hundreds of new manumissions.[27]

Colonizationists credited African Americans with the ability to build new lives in freedom, but they were more concerned with their own desire for a single-race society than the future of the Black emigrants. Given the white population's "unconquerable prejudice" against them, Kentuckian Henry Clay told the society's organizers, Blacks "never could amalgamate with the free whites of this country." He therefore thought it was best "to drain them off." The Colonization Society ultimately foundered when supporters intent on removal found themselves at cross-purposes with those more interested in emancipation. In the early years, however, their common interest in raising the enormous amount of money needed to resettle the first tens of thousands united them in the pursuit of government support. Three weeks after the organizational meeting, Randolph stifled his concerns about central government involvement with slavery and gingerly presented the new society's first memorial to the House.[28]

Religious feelings stoked Randolph's interest in manumission during these years. His friend Key was again an important influence. Randolph admired Key's benevolent concern for others, and that admiration drew him to Key's evangelical Episcopalian faith. Key encouraged Randolph to attend sermons by William Meade, then an attractive young minister in Alexandria, and when Randolph was in Washington, he often rode across the Potomac River on Sunday to hear Meade preach. This evangelical Episcopalianism suited Randolph. He saw it as a revival of the respectable Anglican faith his beloved mother had taught him. He could experience religious renewal while still holding himself aloof from the popular enthusiasm he disdained in the religious awakening of the time. "The great error" in the awakening was the belief in "miraculous conversions," he told a friend. When it came, however, Randolph experienced his own change of heart in much the same way other evangelicals were describing theirs.[29]

"O night of bliss," Randolph exclaimed in his diary at the end of August 1818; "Almighty God" had seen fit to "shew me the mighty scheme of his Salvation." In a letter to Meade, Randolph emphasized the emotional quality of the event. And after assuring his friend John Brockenbrough that the experience was the result of long striving rather than an overheated imagination, Randolph characterized it as "the consummation of my *conversion*." Frank Key understood Randolph's experience in the same way, yet he knew the man well enough to worry. He rejoiced at Randolph's conversion "with some trembling," Key confided to Meade. If Randolph was indeed a Christian, he would be "no ordinary one" for a man of his talents could do wonders. Still, Key thought it would be best for them to say nothing about it to anyone else until they saw what Randolph did next.[30]

Unlike most Virginia Episcopalians, Randolph recognized the tension between his new profession of faith and his ownership of other human beings. Days after his conversion experience, he preached to his slaves, and he began to reflect more intently on the wickedness of slavery and slave trading. Ambition found its reward in pride, pomp, and military glory, he wrote to a friend, "but where are the trophies of avarice?—the handcuff, the manacle, and the blood-stained cow-hide?" Yet arranging for the liberation of his own slaves would not be easy, and he now understood Saint Paul's admonition that the sinfulness of human nature defeats men's good intentions.[31]

Randolph struggled with this existential dilemma. Unless a Virginia planter stinted on his slaves' food, clothes, and housing, he explained to a friend, he could never earn anything from his plantation except an increase in the number of his slaves. And the growing slave population would just keep eating away at his resources until he failed, died, or gave up and sold the slaves to cotton country. Randolph began putting aside money to spare his own slaves from that fate, and the following spring he deposited with John Brockenbrough the earliest of the emancipatory wills that would come to light in the probate litigation after his death.[32]

But the controversy over Missouri statehood that erupted early in 1819 began to harden Randolph's views on slavery just as it hardened the views of other white Virginians. Congressman Tallmadge's proposal to make Missouri renounce slavery as a condition of statehood galvanized sectional differences. The Union already had as many free states as slave states, so the refusal to admit a state simply because it practiced slavery would create an unacceptable precedent. It would condemn the slave states to a minority and ultimately doom the labor system on which they depended. Pragmatic evasion of questions about the future of American slavery became impossible. The Northern majority in the House passed Tallmadge's amendment over the opposition of Southern members. The Senate rejected the amendment, and the Missouri question was still unresolved when Randolph returned to the House in December after sitting out a term for bad health.[33]

Thousands of slaveholders had legally settled prime lands along the Missouri River—including Beverley Tucker and others who brought their slaves from Virginia—and the direct assault on their property rights drove Randolph to fury. "God has given us the Missouri," he cried, "and the devil shall not take it from us."

His long, emotional, disordered speeches to the House were nearly impossible to report, and when he criticized the reporters' efforts, they simply stopped trying.[34]

Reported or not, Randolph's speeches drew large crowds. Secretary of State John Quincy Adams left his office at the other end of Pennsylvania Avenue to listen to one of them for nearly four hours. Adams had been a professor of oratory at Harvard College, and what he heard did not impress him. He thought Randolph's speech "had neither beginning, middle, nor end. Egotism, Virginia Aristocracy, slave-scourging liberty, religion, literature, science, wit, fancy, generous feelings, and malignant passions constitute a chaos in his mind, from which nothing orderly can flow." Even a friend from Virginia who heard one of the speeches called Randolph's behavior "perfectly childish." His wild looks and frantic gestures—mixed with occasional flashes of sheer eloquence—"still haunt my imagination and oppress my heart!"[35]

Randolph's position on Missouri was consistent with his past resistance to central government interference with slavery in the states, but his fury sprang from new feelings of vulnerability and shame. The House vote on Tallmadge's amendment had shown what the growth in Northern population and antislavery sentiment could do. The debate highlighted the threat to slaveholders' control over their own institutions and revealed the moral bankruptcy of their proslavery arguments.[36]

Randolph had always been defensive about slavery. That accounted for his characterization of slavery as an unavoidable fact, his interest in colonization, and his concern about abuses in the slave trade. But the abrupt frontal attack on slave property in Missouri, coming in the wake of his recent religious experience, drove his feelings to new heights. Gone was the brassy assurance with which he once told the House it was no more shame to be a slaveholder than to be born in a particular country. Now he confessed that "all the misfortunes of his life" seemed light in comparison to "the single misfortune of having been born the master of slaves." When the great compromiser Henry

Clay supported the exclusion of slavery from all other territory north of Missouri's southern border in order to get Missouri admitted as a slave state, Randolph voted against the plan. Randolph also insisted that Missouri had the constitutional right to exclude free Blacks, and in a final showdown on that question, he was the only Southerner to vote against a conciliatory face-saving resolution.[37]

Fear and shame are the fuel that stokes political reaction. "These Yankees have almost reconciled me to negro slavery," Randolph told John Brockenbrough during the Missouri debates. He claimed that the supporters of Tallmadge's amendment were just ambitious politicians who aimed to exploit antislavery feeling for their own selfish purposes. What they were doing, he said, would set back the possibility of true emancipation for at least a generation. He fingered Henry Clay and other slaveholders with presidential ambitions as the worst culprits. He said they had betrayed the slaveholding interest to curry favor with voters in the rest of the country.[38]

By the time Congress adjourned, Randolph was telling a cousin who had moved to Rhode Island that "necessity alone can *drive* me north of Mason's & Dixon's line." The Yankees there would not want his money anyway, he sneered, because it was "the earnings of Slave Labour & Philanthropists surely would not touch the wages of Sin."[39]

The following year, 1821, Randolph wrote the last of the wills in which he freed his slaves. In public, however, he no longer spoke about the evils of slavery. He began making naked appeals to Southern fears about slavery in order to defeat measures that would strengthen the central government. Randolph and the other Old Republicans who broke with Jefferson and Madison had long resisted centralizing policies. They reviled the standing army, the national bank, protective tariffs, and federal support for the construction of roads and canals. As the new nation began to flex its muscles after the War of 1812, the Republican majority in Congress had come to support all of those things, leaving Randolph and his band in lonely opposition. Federal threats to the extension of slavery now put Randolph's adherence to

old Republican principles in a new light, and what he had been saying about central government power during his years in the political
wilderness began to sound prophetic.[40]

Randolph's speeches to the House flaunted his appeals to slaveholders' self-interest. As more members of Congress began to take
him seriously, the long-suffering congressional reporters Gales and
Seaton took the trouble to get his outpourings on paper. Newspapers
throughout the country reprinted them, and Gales and Seaton found
it worth their while to publish some of them in a special pamphlet.
The speeches made slavery a wedge issue.[41]

In one of the most often quoted speeches, Randolph bluntly warned
that the same authority used to build federal roads and canals could
be used to "emancipate every slave in the United States." "Should this
bill pass," he said, those south of Mason and Dixon's line would eventually be forced either "to perish like so many mice in a receiver of
mephitic gas under the experiments of a set of new political chem-
ists" or "to maintain that independence which the valor of our fathers
acquired." Another speech declared that protective tariffs, by raising the price of goods needed for slave subsistence to ruinous levels,
would force masters to run away from their slaves. In other words,
said Randolph, the tariff laws gave the central government power to
do just what the anti-Federalist Patrick Henry had warned it could
do: "liberate every one of your slaves." As Randolph used fears about
slavery to uphold the states' rights principles he had always supported,
he began to corrupt those principles into a doctrinal foundation for
the defense of slavery.[42]

Randolph's rhetoric reached a fever pitch after John Quincy Adams
defeated Andrew Jackson in the bitterly contested presidential election of 1824. Adams was a strong nationalist from a New England
state where manufacturing had prospered, and he chose as his secretary of state one of the western nationalists whom Randolph despised.
Henry Clay and Randolph had opposed each other in Congress for
years, and Randolph was among those who claimed that Clay had
bought his appointment to the State Department by shifting votes to

Adams when the presidential election went to the House of Representatives. It was because of Randolph's strong opposition to Adams that the Virginia legislature elected him to the Senate, and there he became the Adams administration's most scathing critic.[43]

Randolph responded with particular venom when Adams nominated American representatives to a congress of newly liberated South American republics in Panama. The proposed meeting with men from those multiracial nations was an affront to the honor of Southern slaveholders, Randolph told the Senate, because the American representatives would have to discuss slavery with men of color. When another Southern senator suggested that slavery was not really at issue in this particular case, Randolph disagreed. The Senate could no longer overlook slavery just because the Constitution had "vainly attempted to blink" it, he said. "You might as well try to hide a volcano in full operation" or "a cancer in your face." When the Senate confirmed the nominations, Randolph responded badly. He accused the State Department of having altered the invitation to the Panama congress, and he complained that his opposition to the nominations had been defeated by the previously unheard of combination of "the puritan and the black-leg." The puritan was Adams, the cheating gamester was the cardplayer Clay.[44]

Clay did not let the insult pass. He challenged Randolph to a duel, and after they missed each other on the first shot, Clay insisted on a second. Clay's second bullet passed through Randolph's loose coat, and Randolph then discharged his pistol into the air as a gesture of reconciliation. The two men shook hands. "You owe me a coat, Mr. Clay," Randolph quipped. "I am glad the debt is no greater," replied Clay. Senator Benton later described the encounter as "the last high-toned duel" he ever witnessed. It was not, however, the end of the matter.[45]

Randolph had made many flamboyant speeches in his congressional career, but friends thought the raving extravagance of his speech against the Panama mission showed he was mad. When Randolph launched into other venomous tirades against the Adams administration, its supporters defanged him by walking out of the Senate chamber one by one until no quorum remained. Randolph's speeches grew so long, meandering, and irrelevant that Gales and Seaton stopped reporting them. The following year, the Virginia legislature quietly replaced him with the more moderate future president John Tyler, and in personal letters, Randolph himself seemed to recognize he had gone too far. The nationally read *Niles' Weekly Register* mockingly wondered how such an uproar over meeting with men of color could have come from "one who glories" in his own mixed-race heritage.[46]

Randolph's position on colonization also shifted. Although the American Colonization Society had established a West African colony named Liberia, Randolph called the organization a failure. Mortality in Liberia was high, funding was inadequate, and the number of immigrants remained extremely low. Public opinion in Virginia opposed federal funding. It was evident, said Randolph, that the society could never voluntarily remove all free African Americans from the slave states. When his old friends Frank Key and Chief Justice John Marshall asked him to present a new petition from the society to the Senate, he declined. The society, Randolph told them, was nothing more than an outlet for morbid sensibility, religious fanaticism, and self-righteous display.[47]

"Whether I have left the Society, or the Society has left me, I cannot tell, and do not care," Randolph told the Senate a few weeks later. His own object was to get rid of the free Blacks in order to ensure the happiness of the slaves and their masters. The society seemed more interested in emancipation, and Randolph was no longer prepared to speak for that. He could still remember how his feelings had revolted at slavery when he read essays by the great British abolitionist Thomas Clarkson as a child. But having read his way into such madness, he assured the Senate, he had also read his way out.[48]

Like others in Virginia, Randolph began claiming that his slaves were better off than menial workers in Europe and even New England. He described the miserable living conditions of laboring people he had seen in Ireland to anyone who would listen. His good man John had found them so shocking, he said, that it made him proud to be "a *Virginia slave.*" Randolph said he was for "the good old plan of making the negroes *work*" so that their masters could feed and clothe them and support them in sickness and old age. He had no doubt that American slaves got "a greater portion of the produce of their labor" than any other workers on earth.[49]

Although many European visitors to the United States did not quarrel with Randolph's assessment of the relative living conditions of slaves and some free laborers, they did not see how that justified slavery. The indominable British social commentator Harriet Martineau thought the very argument revealed the "grossness" of the enslavers' morals. While she would never attempt to excuse conditions in Ireland, she was surprised that slaveholders failed to see the difference between bad government and human bondage. In her famous account of life on her American husband's Georgia plantation, the celebrated English actress Frances Kemble vigorously dismissed the whole comparison. Although slaves might have food, clothes, and housing while shivering Irish peasants starved in roofless huts, she wrote, "the bare name of freeman" was a blessing "beyond food, raiment, or shelter." A British farmer who toured Virginia tobacco plantations put it more tersely. In England, he said, laborers are not driven by personal fear; in Virginia, fear was "the prevailing stimulus."[50]

It took years for Randolph's last will and testament to catch up with his new rhetoric. Despite his blustering defense of slavery, Randolph understood the value that a human being sets on freedom. He also knew that few emancipated slaves wanted to leave their home country. Just weeks after he declined to present the Colonization Society's petition, Randolph wrote a second codicil to the will that freed his slaves. It was the one that asked the Virginia legislature to let the slaves he liberated stay in Virginia. The codicil specifically committed the freedmen to the care of William Leigh, "who I know is too wise, just and humane, to send them to Liberia, or any other place in Africa or the West Indies."[51]

Not until five years later did Randolph write the last will in which he left a patriarchal legacy to a single heir and condemned most of his slaves to the market. The last will profoundly disappointed Beverley Tucker, but his brother Henry thought it had two important merits. It showed the world that Randolph had repented his false allegations against St. George Tucker and decided to keep his property in the family. And when read against the background of Randolph's political rhetoric, the last will could be seen as a defiant proclamation that Randolph had changed his mind about slavery.[52]

· · · ·

WILLIAM LEIGH READ John Randolph's last will from a different perspective. Leigh was with Randolph the night when he wrote it, and Leigh had persuaded Randolph not to burn his earlier will that night because he doubted Randolph was competent to make a new one. Leigh also believed that Randolph, when he was himself, had meant to free his slaves. Leigh therefore thought it was his duty as Randolph's executor to oppose the last will and present the canceled will for probate. He had performed a similar duty as executor for his brother-in-law Benjamin Watkins eight years earlier, when the wealthy bachelor died leaving freedom and property to an enslaved woman named Rachel and the children they had together.[53]

Judge Leigh knew how opposing Randolph's last will would look. He was the principal beneficiary under the canceled will. The world could say he was challenging his friend's last wishes in order to gain a large estate. Indeed, some would believe he had cultivated his friendship with Randolph with an eye toward getting the estate. Unless he renounced his interest under the canceled will, the courts would not even allow him to testify against the last will because his testimony would be self-interested. The rules of evidence, in other words, would presume that his testimony was unreliable because it could help to revive the will that favored him.[54]

Leigh would have welcomed a large inheritance. He was not a

wealthy man, and he had acted as Randolph's agent for many years without any compensation other than the occasional use of some of Randolph's slaves. He believed that Randolph had left him property partly as compensation for his efforts over the years. But Leigh's sense of duty toward his friend was stronger than his sense of entitlement. After he and Beverley Tucker opened Randolph's trunks at Charlotte Courthouse, Leigh had decided to renounce his interest under Randolph's will so that he could testify for the manumission of Randolph's slaves. "Unless I am greatly deceived," he told a friend, "I shall be able to secure to the negroes the advantages which their master intended [for] them."[55]

Few Virginians ever faced the choice Leigh had to make because few men emancipated all of their slaves and left their estates to someone outside the family. Perhaps it was best for his reputation and his own conscience, Leigh told his friend, that Randolph's cancellation of the earlier will had withdrawn the temptation he otherwise might have felt to accept the whole estate. Although others had advised him that he was giving up too much, he did not think so. He could "part with the prospect of affluence with very little concern." The loss of Randolph's library and papers as a token of their friendship bothered him more than anything else. He did hope, however, that he could insist on receiving the small tracts of land in Halifax County that Randolph had left him in the unrevoked 1828 codicil. They would work so well, as Virginia planters put it, with the Halifax plantation he already owned.[56]

About the Tucker brothers Leigh had nothing good to say. He agreed with Randolph's assessment of their characters. They had smiled to Randolph while he lived, despite what he was saying about their father, because they wanted his property. Now they made those allegations about their father a point of honor with which to attack Randolph's true wishes. Beverley Tucker openly declared that Randolph had been incompetent to make a will ever since 1806. He derisively dismissed Randolph's conversion experience—"the season of the vision," he called it—as evidence of Randolph's madness. Henry Tucker offended Leigh by describing the "extraordinary wishes" in Randolph's canceled will as "grossly unnatural." He then offered to free Randolph's slaves based on his deathbed declaration if Leigh would give up his claim to the Halifax County land and concede full intestacy.[57]

Had he known more about what the Tuckers were doing, Leigh would have been outraged. Beverley knew he could not challenge the last will himself because an overt assault on the interests of his niece's family would be unfriendly and dishonorable. Yet he could not reconcile himself to getting nothing at all from Randolph's estate. So he was hoping to use Leigh's testimony against the last will as a way out of this predicament. Once Leigh's testimony discredited the last will, the family could vindicate their father's honor by casting doubt on Randolph's capacity to make the earlier will. If none of the wills or codicils was valid, Beverley explained to his father-in-law, he would get $50,000 from the estate (he wrote the number in oversized bold script) instead of the mere $5,000 he could expect as his share of the property Leigh had renounced. The value of Randolph's slaves represented a significant part of that difference.[58]

Elizabeth Bryan's brother St. George Coalter, the only other member of the family who got nothing under any of Randolph's wills, sent his uncle Beverley a busy letter of encouragement. Young Coalter was a good-natured but immature fellow, boisterous about honor, rightly worried about the disease in his lungs, and only moderately improved by marriage to a sensible woman. He tried to camouflage his interest in Randolph's money behind his blustery concern for the honor of his namesake grandfather, and the utter obviousness of the self-interest that had prompted him to write to his uncle for the first time in his life seemed to escape him. Beverley's response was equally calculating. He began cultivating a friendship with St. George Coalter so that he would not be the only one in the family directly opposed to all of Randolph's wills.[59]

Henry Tucker took the practical position that a last will is presumed valid until proven otherwise. Since Randolph's last will did keep his property in the family, Henry thought they should defend it when Leigh tried to probate the earlier will. If Beverley wanted to contest all of the wills, Henry told him, he could do that later by invoking the Virginia statute that lets heirs bring suit in the chancery courts to challenge a probate court's decision.[60]

Conflict over an inheritance can set a family at odds, but at least in their letters to each other, the members of the Tucker family tried to remain cordial despite their differences. Elizabeth Bryan set the tone. She had assumed her mother's role as the person who held the family together, and when Randolph's exclusive bequest to her son put her on the spot, she rose to the occasion with strength and candor. "If you had heard of [that bequest] before you wrote," she scolded her uncle Beverley soon after Randolph died, "why did not you mention it?" She said that only openness could prevent suspicion and misunderstanding. She insisted to everyone that Randolph's property was far less important than their affection for each other. By the spring after Randolph's death, even the sometimes flighty Beverley Tucker seemed to think that the family would be able to handle the controversy "with perfect amity and good feeling."[61]

The three lawyers in the family—the Tucker brothers and Elizabeth's father, John Coalter—agreed on one thing. There must be another will. The codicil of 1828 referred to several provisions in an earlier will that simply did not appear in any of the wills they had found. The note that Randolph had written when he gave Leigh the last will said that the will made no significant changes except to keep the slaves in bondage. And the paper Randolph used for that note, which he had described as the wrapper around the canceled will, was much larger than the only canceled will they had discovered. Henry urged Beverley to use his time at Roanoke to gather more evidence and search for another will.[62]

A lost will drives the plot of Beverley Tucker's novel *George Balcombe*, which he probably conceived about this time although he did not finish it until 1836. The novel tells a rather stilted story about a young Virginian named Napier, who finds that the inheritance his family needs to maintain their standing in the world has gone to a distant relative because a ward of Napier's grandfather named Montague concealed the grandfather's will. Montague is an evangelical hypocrite, and his ungrateful self-seeking jeopardizes a fine old family, upsets its faithful slaves, and pretermits fated marriages for Napier and his sister. Napier follows the villain to the Missouri frontier, where Napier meets a noble Virginian settler named George Balcombe. Balcombe turns out to have been another of the grandfather's protégés and just the man to find the missing will. Balcombe's wisdom and courage help Napier face down mortal dangers, recover the will, and carry it triumphantly into a Virginia chancery court.[63]

The novel's characterization of George Balcombe obviously celebrates the author himself, and at least to a modern reader, young Napier resembles St. George Coalter. Other characters have parallels in the Randolph-Tucker family (including a young woman seduced by Montague). The author leaves readers to ponder who the hypocritical Montague might be.[64]

While Beverley Tucker was turning fact into fiction, Henry Tucker plotted a strategy for probating Randolph's last will. It went like this. Henry would ask Judge Leigh to bring all of Randolph's testamentary papers to Richmond when he came for the December 1833 sitting of the General Court. Then without having told Leigh what they meant to do, Henry's lawyers would present Randolph's last will to the General Court for probate. Leigh would have to recuse himself from the case and—here was the main thing—formally renounce his own interest under the earlier will so that he could testify against the last will and protect the interests of the slaves. Once the renunciation gave the family the property Randolph had left to Leigh, the slaves' claim for freedom would be the only issue. The family could then take control of the slaves by convincing the court that Randolph was mad when he wrote the earlier will.[65]

"I have spoken to Stanard & Johnson," Henry wrote to Beverley. Robert Stanard and Chapman Johnson were his choice of the elite lawyers who regularly practiced before the courts in Richmond. He had offered them $1,000 each if they could establish a total intestacy. He would pay them less if the last will survived, even less if the canceled will survived, and least of all if the codicils also survived. The Tucker heirs could split the legal fee in proportion to the shares they would receive in intestacy.[66]

"I beg you to remember," Henry cautioned Beverley after explaining all of this, that under no circumstances was Beverley to show Henry's letters to anyone other than John Coalter because "malice & ill will might possibly misinterpret what they contain." It was one thing to plot against a dead brother's will, quite another thing for the world to hear about it. Honorable men did not proceed by indirection and contrivance. The justice that was their due must appear to come unaided.[67]

The General Court formed when the circuit judges assembled in Richmond was not the usual forum for probate litigation. The county courts and the circuit superior courts had probate jurisdiction, and wills almost never came to the General Court unless the decedent had widely scattered landholdings. Because William Leigh was the circuit judge for Randolph's home district, however, he would have to transfer the case elsewhere if it began in his court or came there on appeal from the Charlotte County court. That made it simpler to bring the probate case in Richmond, and Henry Tucker probably saw an important additional advantage.[68]

County courts were traditional bodies composed of local worthies whose common sense exceeded their knowledge of the law. Their outlook was narrow and conservative, and they aimed to interfere in men's affairs as little as possible. If an old man with no wife or children had left all of his property to a favorite niece's young son, why should they question it? The will kept an ancestral property together, and although the boy was not among those who would have received a share in intestacy, he belonged to the next generation of the same family. Compared with the man's earlier will in which he had freed his slaves and left most of his property out of the family, the last will looked sensible enough. In a county where men had forgiven John Randolph his eccentricities and accepted his political leadership for decades, the court was unlikely to refuse probate.[69]

In Richmond, the judges were distinguished lawyers with liberal education and significant professional experience. Although they were acculturated in the same traditional norms as other white Virginians, their understanding of the law gave them a wider view. They gave credence to the views of doctors who postulated theories about mental alienation, and they read the decisions of English judges who were using those theories to reconceive legal ideas about testamentary capacity. The county courts' vernacular way of thinking about personality and acceptable behavior was giving way to professional conceptions of the mind and personal accountability. Peculiarities that lay judges probably would overlook when a man's will was patriarchal—leaving his whole estate to a single heir or giving his slaves their freedom—could invalidate the will in a court where professionals were open to understanding such peculiarities as symptoms of mental disorder.[70]

Judge Leigh did not bring Randolph's wills to Richmond when he came for the General Court. By that time, he probably had guessed what Henry Tucker had in mind. In fact, Leigh and the trustees for Randolph's slaves, Bishop Meade and Frank Key, were already making preparations to challenge the last will. They had engaged lawyers of their own, reported the correspondent for a New York newspaper, "and it is generally believed, that after a long course of litigation, the will . . . emancipating the slaves will be established."[71]

...those whom it may concern ... I John Rando...
Roanoke in the county of Charlotte & comm...
Virginia do constitute this writing, written...
...own hand, my last will & testament, her...
...oking all others.—

1. I give & bequeath unto my deservedly...
...ends Major Joseph Scott of Amelia & Ryla...
...udolph of Po...land all the property of...
...ries & descriptions of ... the p...p...
...fullest confidence that they will take up...
...the troublesome office of complying with...
...rusts ...ted below...

I desire that my good debts which are of...
...little consequence (except those inherited...
...(late father) be paid...

I request that the management of my est...
...come under my friend Major ... who ...
...being relative to ... as of it were his own...
...the profits, after my debts are paid be...
...lected & ...ed ... inton eligible fund for the ...
...the helpless slaves ... whom little purpose is...

Richmond from the Hill above the Waterworks, aquatint by
William James Bennett after George Cooke, 1834

Part Two

. . . .

FREEDOM CONTESTED, 1834–45

Chapter 6

THE
SLAVES' DEFENDERS

William Meade, engraving, c. 1840

THE GENERAL COURT FIRST HEARD MOTIONS ON JOHN Randolph's will at its July term in 1834, more than a year after Randolph's death. The court met in July and December, when half of its twenty judges came to Richmond from the districts where they sat as circuit judges during the rest of the year. They gathered in a lofty, capacious room on the main floor of the state capitol, an elegant white building modeled on a Roman temple that sat dramatically on the crest of a hill. From tall windows facing south, the judges, law-yers, litigants, and spectators had a sweeping view through the front columns, across the city, and down to the warehouses along the James River. On that particularly hot Monday morning, the windows stood open to the air and the flies.[1]

The judges had heard that the trustees for Randolph's slaves were planning to argue for their freedom, so they expected the case to become time consuming and sensational. Both of the trustees were formidable men prominent in the American Colonization Society. William Meade had been a leading fundraiser for the society before he became a bishop, and Frank Key was one of the Washington law-yers who regularly protected the society's interests at the Capitol. Each of them had freed some of his own slaves.

Chapman Johnson easily commanded the courtroom's attention when he rose to offer Randolph's last will for probate. He was a strap-ping, handsome man in his mid-fifties, a poor boy who had become a leader of the Richmond bar, and one of the few men who emerged from Virginia's recent constitutional convention with a reputation greater than the one he took into it. Johnson had known the Tucker family since he studied law at William and Mary thirty years earlier, and when he was trying to start his law practice in the western Vir-ginia town of Staunton, it was John Coalter—already well established there—who had encouraged him. He now rose to present the Ran-dolph will for Coalter on behalf of his three-year-old grandson John Coalter Bryan.[2]

Another prominent Richmond lawyer stood to respond on behalf of Randolph's slaves. John Robertson was the recently retired attor-ney general of Virginia, and he was appearing as local counsel for his friend Walter Jones. General Jones, as everyone called him because of his rank in the militia, was one of the finest lawyers in the country. He had grown up in Virginia, settled in Washington, and launched a notable legal career that would stretch to the eve of the Civil War. He was among the most active members of the American Colonization

Society, and he knew Key well from their work on some of the same cases before the Supreme Court.[3]

John Robertson made a completely unprecedented motion that must have caught the judges off guard. He asked the General Court to let John White, Juba, and Essex appear in the case as representatives for the slaves seeking freedom under Randolph's earlier will. Although each of those men was well known in Richmond, Robertson could not have expected the motion to be granted. Virginia courts did allow slaves to present a slaveholder's will in suits for their own freedom, but as far as Robertson knew, courts had never permitted slaves to stop a slaveholder's heirs from probating some other will. Robertson nevertheless offered the motion for two important reasons.[4]

First, Robertson wanted to remind everyone involved in the case that they could not resolve the controversy over Randolph's will without considering the claims of his slaves. If the General Court upheld the last will without making the slaves parties to the case, the court's judgment would not bind them. They therefore could—and would—bring a separate suit to claim their freedom under Randolph's earlier will.[5]

The second reason for Robertson's motion had nothing to do with the law, but it was extremely important to the slaves' trustees. Bishop Meade and Frank Key wanted to show the world why they were getting into the case. They were highly visible men who needed to stay on good terms with people of varied opinions. Meade was the assistant bishop in the Episcopal diocese of Virginia, and Key had recently become United States attorney for the District of Columbia. While both of them were sympathetic to manumission, many other people were not. So they needed to show that they were contesting Randolph's last will because their duty required it. If the court would not permit Randolph's slaves to join the probate case, then they as the slaves' trustees had to do what Randolph had trusted them to do. At least one of them would have to intervene.[6]

The scene in the General Court played out as Robertson must have expected. The judges overruled his motion to admit John White, Juba, and Essex on the ground that slaves had no right to appear in court except in suits for their own freedom. The judges then granted Robertson's alternative motion to admit Bishop Meade as a defendant against the Bryan child's claim for probate.[7]

Despite Robertson's efforts, the public perception of Meade's appearance in the case turned out to be just what the trustees had feared. Intervention made Meade look like the aggressor. Although he was technically a defendant, the newspaper reporters and even some of the lawyers took to calling the case *Meade v. Bryan*.[8]

. . . .

WILLIAM MEADE WAS a boy of seven in the summer of 1796 when young John Randolph tied a bundle of clothes to a stick, slung it over his shoulder, and trekked across the Blue Ridge Mountains to visit Meade's father. Uncle Kidder, as Randolph called him, had been married to one of John Randolph's aunts, and although she was long dead, Randolph honored the family connection. Richard Kidder Meade had served as George Washington's aide-de-camp in the Revolution, remarried, and then joined a wave of gentry migrants to the fertile land at the northern end of Virginia's Shenandoah Valley, where all of his children were born. Young William Meade grew up to value family connections just as much as John Randolph, so when the two of them met fifteen years later outside the church in Alexandria where Meade was preaching, Meade would have recognized Randolph as one of his family relations.[9]

Although William Meade's father seems to have been more of a churchgoer than many Virginia men of the Revolutionary generation, it was Meade's mother and his sisters who brought young William to his religious vocation. Mary Meade and her four daughters shared an almost mystical belief in the "continual presence of God," a presence they experienced so powerfully that it shaped their daily activities. They were among the relatively small number of Virginia Episcopalians enlivened by the Second Great Awakening who remained faithful to the devotional style of the church rather than joining in the enthusiasm of the Methodist movement. Although William Meade's faith was never as mystical as theirs, it was infused with the same conviction that God had a purpose for everything. The dissolute lifestyle of many of their friends and family, the post-Revolutionary decline of the Episcopal Church, the great curse of slavery—all of those evils contained within themselves the potential for some good. Their religious duty was to strive to find God's purpose and to advance it day by day.[10]

William Meade became a muscular Christian bent on reforming the Episcopal Church and Virginia's slave society. Soon after he was ordained to the priesthood in 1814, he and a few others bullied the more conventional clergy into accepting an evangelical named Richard Channing Moore as the new bishop of Virginia, and when Moore discouraged Meade from his enthusiastic itinerant preaching, Meade simply ignored him. Meade took no salary in order to combat the image of Virginia's old Anglican priests as overfed placemen. He got a dispensation from the ban on clergy doing manual labor so that he could work on his farm, and his house was so sparsely furnished that visitors said they could not find a comfortable chair. He drove an old gig that George Washington had given to his father, by then so dilapidated that wags said it ran on God's grace.[11]

Slavery was an intensely personal problem for William Meade. He and the rest of his family used enslaved labor to run their farms, but they wanted to free their slaves to cleanse themselves from sin. They accepted a frugal lifestyle in order to do that. Manual labor and self-denial were not enough, however, because the law required emancipated slaves to leave the state and the Meades believed they could not send them away illiterate and unredeemed. The family's efforts to educate their slaves and relocate them took decades. Meade still owned almost a dozen slaves when Randolph died, and he did not free the last of them until at least ten years later.[12]

The colonization movement appealed to the Meades because it seemed to offer a solution to their problem. They believed that religious instruction would prepare slaves for freedom. Yet without a suitable earthly destination, they feared, emancipated slaves could find true freedom only in heaven. An organized West African colony seemed to promise a more tangible redemption because it could give freedmen the support they needed to lead righteous and self-sufficient lives. The men and women who went there could escape white prejudice, combat the slave trade on the African coast, and spread Christ's message among African unbelievers.[13]

Most of the men who met to organize the American Colonization Society were Meade's personal friends, and his early passion for the cause appears in a sermon he preached to the Virginia diocesan convocation a few months later. Meade gave that sermon in the shadow of evil. Just days before and a few miles away, some angry slaves had ambushed the man who owned them, bludgeoned him to death, and burned his body in a big kitchen fireplace. Although Meade did not mention the crime, his sermon responded to it. "Even here in this dark vale of sorrow," he said, Virginia Episcopalians should find cause for rejoicing because African colonization offered their bondsmen homes in "another Canaan flowing with peace and plenty."[14]

The following year, Meade spent nine months traveling around the United States to raise money for the Colonization Society. He was a darkly handsome young man with a winning personality, and he brought in more money than the society ever again raised in such a short time. Meade's family and some of their wealthy cousins remained among the society's largest donors for years, and the local chapter in Meade's home county contributed more money than any other auxiliary in the country. Although Meade's return to parish ministry slowed the society's momentum, he continued to support the cause. When the United States observed its national jubilee in 1826, Meade saw to it that the Fourth of July sermon given to every Episcopal parish in Virginia celebrated freedom, emancipation, and colonization.[15]

Meade understood the power of his appearance, his austere lifestyle, and his gentry connections. He was a companionable fellow from a good family who conspicuously lacked the usual shortcomings of such men. He could talk about horses over Sunday dinner with an ease that scandalized a devout young tutor from New England, but he did not drink, dance, or gamble. When Washington's old gig finally broke down, Meade used its weatherworn seat as a visitor's bench in his study to remind people of who he was and how he had chosen to live.[16]

Meade's expression of his views on slavery and colonization had changed as white Virginians' attitudes toward racial slavery hardened. While he continued to believe that slavery was wrong, Meade as a bishop no longer spoke as freely about emancipation and colonization. He did not indict the slaveholders in his flock as sinners. He focused instead on their duty to ameliorate their slaves' condition, and he preached that religious instruction would help slaves accept their bondage. That message reflected his essential belief that Christians must seek the potential for good in the evils around them, and it fit comfortably within a broader movement for religious ministry to slaves that was appearing at other places in the South.[17]

In his ministry as bishop, Meade welcomed slaves to the altar to confirm their baptismal vows, and his confirmation sermons emphasized the spiritual equivalence of all human souls. That posed risks for Meade at a time when white Virginians were embracing the ugly conclusions that flowed from corrupt premises about race and slavery. It was one thing to preach to slaves on plantations or to invite them into the segregated galleries of a church; it was another to bring them to the same altar where white Episcopalians knelt. When the leading Richmond newspaper printed a violent objection to Meade's confirmation message some years later, Meade's alert response shows that he had long anticipated it.[18]

Although Meade remained sympathetic to manumission, his duty as trustee for Randolph's slaves made him uncomfortable for a number of reasons. In the first place, the responsibility was entirely unexpected. Meade had heard very little from Randolph since his conversion experience in 1818, and Randolph had never intimated that he planned to leave Meade such a responsibility. Then there was the problem of Randolph's competence. Because they had been out of touch, Meade had no way of knowing Randolph's state of mind in his later years. That left Meade with moral questions about what, if anything, he should do. Next came concerns about whether Randolph's slaves were ready to be self-reliant. Meade did not doubt African Americans' capacity for freedom (although he would later entertain such doubts when he assessed how his own freedmen fared). Yet he could see that unlike Meade and his family, Randolph had done nothing to prepare his slaves for freedom.[19]

Finally, there was the problem of Meade's position in the church. Bishop Moore was aging, and there had been questions at the time of Meade's election about whether he could succeed Moore as the diocesan bishop without a second election. Meade was popular as a person, and those questions seemed to have been settled. Yet some Virginia Episcopalians murmured that Meade's evangelical style was too enthusiastic, too much like the Methodists who had left to form a church of their own. John Randolph himself had once characterized Meade as a Methodist. "I give him credit for sincerity & piety," Randolph wrote. "But I have little doubt of his being to a certain extent &, on certain subjects, insane." A country mob west of Richmond built a bonfire for a Methodist book urging gradual emancipation, and Virginia clergymen who had once supported colonization published newspaper letters disclaiming it. All of that put an edge on Meade's participation in a lawsuit to free several hundred slaves.[20]

Although Meade did his duty as the slaves' trustee, he tried to avoid the spotlight. He and Frank Key regretted that the Tucker brothers were unwilling to reach a compromise on the "delicate matters" in the probate case. And six months before the first motions in the General Court, they told Beverley Tucker that they meant to leave all of the decisions about the case to their lawyers. Meade left for a trip through distant parishes in western Virginia just as the General Court convened, and in his response to a letter from Beverley Tucker five years later, he remained diffident about his involvement in the case. He had never done more than his lawyers asked him to do, he wrote, and he aimed to do as little as possible.[21]

．．．．

JOHN RANDOLPH LIKELY came to know Frank Key through Key's brother-in-law Edward Lloyd V, Randolph's colleague in Congress and one of the largest slaveholders in Maryland. Key was a small, slightly built man with a handsome face, curly brown hair, and disarming brown eyes. He first came to Washington from his family's plantation in western Maryland to study law with a distinguished uncle, and by the time he met Randolph about 1806, he was among the most promising young lawyers in the city. Key was also an enthusiastic Episcopalian who looked on slavery as one of the human evils that good Christians must strive to overcome.[22]

Like so many enslavers with qualms of conscience, Frank Key decried slavery without ever entirely renouncing it. Over the course of his thirty-year career in Washington, he argued more than one hundred cases for destitute men and women who claimed they were illegally enslaved, and his success in those cases won him a reputation among local African Americans as their lawyer. Yet he also helped slaveholders recover fugitive slaves, defended slaveholders against their slaves' claims for freedom, and held slaves of his own throughout his life. Although Key had freed seven slaves by the time Randolph's will went to court, he still owned at least eight others. Some of them were servants in his Georgetown house; others worked on his family's plantation.[23]

Key supported gradual emancipation not simply because he believed slavery was wrong, but because he believed it was dangerous. He had seen slaves around the Chesapeake Bay go over to British invaders during the War of 1812, just as they had done in the Revolutionary War. He worried that enslaved people were internal enemies of the American republic, and we can still hear the bravado prompted by his anxiety in two lines from the anthem for which he is famous. "No refuge can save the hireling and slave," he wrote, "from the terror of flight or the gloom of the grave."[24]

Key's hopes for an eventual end to slavery focused on African colonization, and he worked hard to get federal funding for the American Colonization Society. In 1819, Congress passed a law authorizing federal authorities to send illegally imported slaves back to Africa, and Key helped persuade President Monroe to use the funds appropriated for that purpose to establish Liberia. When a sensational court case put the law to its test, Key readily accepted the Monroe administration's invitation to argue the case before the Supreme Court.

The *Antelope* case had begun in 1820 when a federal revenue cutter stopped a ship lurking off Spanish Florida near a place that was often used to smuggle slaves into Georgia. When the revenue authorities climbed aboard the *Antelope*, they found the ship's hold crowded with 281 Africans in shackles. They brought the captives into Savannah and asked a federal judge to release them and send them to Liberia. Several Spanish and Portuguese slave traders claimed the captives and insisted they had been bound for legal slave markets in South America. It took five years of litigation to bring the case to Washington—years during which the captives worked and sometimes died on Georgia plantations.[25]

Key's argument for the *Antelope*'s captives "dazzled" the spectators who came to hear it in the Supreme Court's small chamber beneath the main floor of the Capitol. Key contended that a person found upon the seas could not be presumed a slave simply because he was an African. All men were free by the laws of nature, so the law of nations did not require the United States to surrender the captives to foreign slave traders unless the traders could prove that they had legally enslaved the Africans. The slave traders before the court, said Key, had failed to do that. The court accepted Key's basic position, and although it found that a trader who claimed one-third of the captives had proven legal enslavement, it authorized the government to send the rest of the *Antelope*'s survivors to Liberia.[26]

The *Antelope* decision could have been an important victory for the African colonization movement, yet by the time the Supreme Court issued its final orders in the case two years later, the federal money appropriated for Liberia was gone and support for further funding had dwindled. John Randolph was not the only member of Congress who had turned hostile. The Senate Foreign Relations Committee denied that the central government ever had the constitutional authority to establish an African colony, and the men who were aiming to make Andrew Jackson president in 1828 stigmatized colonization as a part of the intolerable nationalistic agenda championed by his opponent, Henry Clay.

Frank Key continued to support colonization, but he also backed Andrew Jackson. When Jackson became president, Key and his brother-in-law Roger B. Taney drifted into an informal circle of Jackson advisers often lampooned as the Kitchen Cabinet. Jackson appointed Key as United States attorney for the District of Columbia in 1833, and when the revered John Marshall died two years later, Jackson nominated Taney to be chief justice of the Supreme Court.[27]

Key had been United States attorney for only four months when John Randolph died, and slavery made his job difficult. The District contained a volatile mix of slave traders, free Blacks, working-class whites, slaveholders, fugitive slaves, foreign visitors, and contentious congressmen. Nat Turner's revolt two years earlier had shaken Washington as well as Richmond, and white anxieties about the Black population had risen sharply. The Black abolitionist David Walker's strident *Appeal to the Colored Citizens of the World* urged Black men everywhere to rise against their white oppressors, and the new American Anti-Slavery Society had just begun publishing a newspaper called the *Emancipator* to oppose colonization and push for immediate emancipation. Anxious whites believed those abolitionists and their message were a clear and present danger.

Key himself became the target of an antislavery newspaper editor soon after he took office. Benjamin Lundy had moved his *Genius of Universal Emancipation* to Washington in order to escape persecution in Baltimore, and he soon began to report on appalling abuses in the capital city. He said that the constables who worked for Key were robbing free Blacks and even selling them into slavery. "There is neither mercy nor justice for colored people in this district," he proclaimed, in an unmistakable slap at the new United States attorney.[28]

Simmering tensions boiled over in the heat of August two years later. A white mob assembled to lynch an enslaved man who had tried to murder the prominent woman who owned him, and when General Walter Jones summoned the militia to protect the prisoner, the mob went on a rampage. Over the course of two days, they burned Black-owned houses, businesses, churches, and schools. The outburst was one of more than a hundred race riots that broke out around the country in the summer of 1835 as racial fears led whites to prey on Black communities from New England through Pennsylvania to Mississippi.[29]

Key blamed abolitionists for creating these explosive tensions, and he took advantage of the excitement to attack the spread of abolitionist literature in the District. He had heard that a Quaker doctor named Reuben Crandall was distributing abolitionist pamphlets from his office in Georgetown, and he decided to make an example of him. He arrested the frail, studious young man, threw him in jail, and charged him with publishing seditious libels to incite Black insurrection. Key kept Crandall locked up all winter, and by the time Crandall came to trial in the spring, newspaper reporters could see that eight months in a damp prison cell had broken his health.

Key used Crandall's trial to defend African colonization as the only safe alternative to slavery. Abolition, he told the jury, could never eliminate the "great moral and political evil" associated with slavery because that evil was the presence of "the whole colored race." Without removal of the African population, emancipation would lead to "far greater evils" than slavery itself. Blacks would demand the same rights as whites, he said, and the races would eventually amalgamate. Crandall and abolitionists like him were treacherous men who had to be stopped before they destroyed the social order. The jury was sensible enough to reject Key's arguments and free the defendant, but Crandall died of tuberculosis two years later.[30]

Key's speech to the jury in Crandall's case makes it plain why he found his duty as trustee for Randolph's slaves uncomfortable. Thirty-five years of experience as a lawyer for slaves seeking freedom, Key explained to the jury, had nearly exhausted his enthusiasm for Black liberty. He had represented Black plaintiffs in more freedom cases than any other lawyer in the District, and he had always rejoiced when they won one. But over the years, he had learned that emancipation was "a perilous gift" to Black men and women in a country where the law made their freedom a "dangerous mockery." He could no longer rejoice in Black freedom unless those released from bondage went to "a land of their own."[31]

Key left most of the fight for the liberation of Randolph's slaves to Bishop Meade. When Beverley Tucker named Key a defendant in another challenge to Randolph's will a few years later, Key waived his right to participate in the case. "Notice to Bishop Meade," he told Tucker, "shall be considered as notice to me." Frank Key died from a quick bout of pneumonia while Randolph's will was still in the courts. Despite his reservations about emancipation, his will gave his own slaves their freedom on the death of his wife.[32]

• • • •

HENRY TUCKER GOT a surprise two months before the General Court heard the first motions on John Randolph's will. He was working in his office one day when prominent Richmond merchant Joseph Marx appeared with a codicil Randolph had written as he was leaving London in 1831. Marx did a large business for Virginia planters who shipped crops to Europe, and Randolph had left a packet of papers at his firm's London office with instructions to send it to America if he did not survive the voyage home. The London office was still holding the papers when its staff heard about the controversy over Randolph's will, opened the packet, and found this document.[33]

Henry dashed off a note to his brother Beverley as soon as he read the document. The first thing he noticed was that the codicil referred to provisions in the will it was amending that did not appear in any of the wills the brothers had found. Those references seemed to confirm their impression that there must be another will. That would not matter if the General Court upheld the last will, because the last will revoked all earlier wills. But if the court did not uphold the last will, they would have to decide what to make of a codicil to a missing will.[34]

The second thing Henry Tucker noted was that the London codicil significantly changed Randolph's earlier will. Instead of leaving almost the entire estate to Randolph's slaves and his friend William Leigh, the codicil made large bequests to two members of the Tucker family. Elizabeth Bryan got the Lower Quarter at Roanoke together with Randolph's silver and his library. Henry received the Bushy Forest plantation, Randolph's expectancy in some Bland family property, and all of Randolph's lots and houses in the small town of Farmville. Because those bequests shifted property away from the slaves, the codicil gave Leigh £3,000 on deposit with the London firms of Gowan & Marx and Baring Brothers to pay for the slaves' resettlement outside Virginia. It also granted "my faithful servant John, sometimes called John White" a $50 annuity and begged the legislature to let him and his family stay in Virginia.[35]

Whatever Beverley Tucker made of the legal issues raised by the London codicil, he could not have helped noticing how it further fractured the interests of different members of the Tucker family. Both Elizabeth Bryan and Henry Tucker might get greater shares of Randolph's estate under the codicil than they would receive if all of his wills were invalid. Shortly before the General Court convened, the Tucker family held a meeting to consider what they should do, and they agreed to put this latest codicil aside until the court ruled on the last will. They also accepted the contingent fee arrangement that encouraged their lawyers to prove Randolph had died intestate. Those decisions reassured Beverley that Elizabeth and Henry were not going to push for unequal shares of the estate. They could not, however, relieve his chagrin that he and St. George Coalter were the only family members who got nothing in Randolph's will yet again.[36]

Beverley got better news a week later when William and Mary appointed him to his father's old chair as professor of law. The distinguished appointment made it easier for Beverley to justify his presence in Virginia. Whatever he might say about the importance of defending his father's honor from the accusation in Randolph's will, remaining in Virginia with no visible purpose other than to break his brother's will was beginning to seem less than honorable. The faculty appointment also gave Beverley the sort of public recognition he always craved. Although he tried to be nonchalant about it when he shared the news with his wife, he later confessed to her how much the honor had meant to him. Beverley wanted—and emotionally needed—the "deference and respect" that he knew she expected her husband to command.[37]

Quiet and reliable William Leigh was a very different man from Beverley Tucker. After letting it be known that he would renounce his interest under Randolph's earlier will, Leigh had stepped aside to let the Tucker family decide what they were going to do. He knew very little about their intentions, he told a friend six months before the General Court heard the first motions in the case. When the whole Tucker family was in Richmond for the previous term of court, he reported, the only one of them who had done more than exchange "common civilities" with him was Henry. He really did not know what to make of Beverley, Leigh continued. The man was "so fond of distinction and notoriety" that he would do anything to get public attention. "I sometimes think, as his poor brother always maintained . . . , that he is a little disordered in his mind."[38]

The appearance of the London codicil changed Leigh's mind about what he himself should do. Although he remained determined to stay out of the will controversy, he decided not to renounce whatever he might receive under the will that the court eventually admitted to probate. The London codicil gave substantial property to the two members of the Tucker family whom Randolph favored, so Leigh no longer felt embarrassed about receiving whatever Randolph might have left to him. He thought a legacy would be appropriate recognition for his close friendship with Randolph and his many years of attention to Randolph's business affairs. He also convinced himself that the slaves did not really need his testimony to defeat Randolph's last will because there was so much other evidence of Randolph's insanity at the time he wrote it.[39]

A month before the trial in the probate case was scheduled to begin in 1835, Bishop Meade visited Leigh and asked him to reconsider. Leigh was the only white person who knew what had happened on the night Randolph made his last will, and Meade's lawyers believed that Leigh's testimony at the trial would be crucial. Meade asked Leigh to renounce his interest under all of Randolph's wills so that he could give that testimony. Meade was a persuasive man with abundant moral authority. And he spoke to Leigh not only of his religious duty, but also of his honor—of what "the publick expects."

Leigh took Bishop Meade's request seriously because he thought that Meade was asking no more than Meade himself would do. Still, Leigh struggled with the decision. Most of the lawyers in Richmond were saying they could not imagine testimony strong enough to overturn Randolph's last will. Leigh, on the other hand, remained convinced that there was already plenty of evidence to overturn it. In either case, Leigh asked himself, why should he renounce everything in order to give testimony that probably would not make any difference?[40]

Chapter 7

A CELEBRITY TRIAL

Francis Scott Key, by Joseph Wood, 1816

EVERYONE KNEW THAT THE TRIAL OF JOHN RANDOLPH'S will would be a major spectacle. At a time when speeches and debates were important forms of public entertainment, big trials were enormously popular. The drama of lawyers' arguments, the allure of witness confessions, and the unexpected twists and turns that came from each new revelation—they all combined to make trials great theater. The Randolph case promised all of those things and much more when it went to trial in the summer of 1835. It had the kind of special attractions that make some trials sensational even today.[1]

In the first place, there was John Randolph himself. He was not only a political celebrity, but a colorful character of the first order. Randolph had always craved public attention, and the slashing rhetoric and unforgettable theatrics that he used to get it continued to command attention even after his death. No man in America, wrote a British observer, had ever deployed biting sarcasm so unsparingly or left so many casualties on the field of debate. Although Randolph's critics said that made him a bad politician, even they conceded his virtuosity and the power of his most memorable phrases.[2]

Randolph's figures of speech defined political rhetoric long after his death simply because they were so striking. "Dough face" remained a choice term of derision for Northern Democrats who were soft on slavery as late as the Civil War because that is what Randolph had called them after the Missouri debates. The expression was not as inscrutable then as it is now, and it stung sharply enough to make many Northern politicians hesitate about compromising with slaveholders. The consummate compromiser Henry Clay claimed it had done "more injury than any two words I have ever known."[3]

Then there was the fascination with other people's money. Newspapers had speculated excitedly about the value of Randolph's estate at the time of his death, and public curiosity remained high two years later. Both his friends and his enemies said Randolph was a miser who had accumulated a great deal of money toward the end of his life. He had boasted that he would die as rich as Stephen Girard, the fabulously wealthy Philadelphia merchant and banker who left an estate worth about $7 million. And while no one thought Randolph had been nearly that wealthy, they found his property more interesting than Girard's. Girard was a self-made man who had owned the sort of mercantile and financial assets that Virginians professed to value only for their power to buy something worth having. Randolph was the heir to one of those extensive colonial plantations that gave a Virginian real standing. That he, unlike most other members of the old gentry, had preserved and even enlarged that patrimony made his estate especially intriguing.[4]

Next came scandal. Few men ever got into as many outrageous quarrels as John Randolph, and the challenge to his will was certain to expose them.

Well-connected Virginians had never forgotten Randolph's savage attack on Nancy Randolph, whose suspicious miscarriage brought disgrace to his brother Richard. Nancy moved to New York after Richard's death and became the housekeeper for Gouverneur Morris, a rich old rake who soon married her. John Randolph had not seen her for ten years when he arrived at her husband's fine mansion in 1814 to retrieve his nephew Tudor, who had collapsed there from a bout of tuberculosis.

Seeing Nancy Morris rich and happy drove John Randolph wild. Days after his visit, Randolph wrote her a scathing letter that recounted her past sins and accused her of poisoning Richard Randolph. Nancy was furious, and she sent copies of John's cruel letter along with her own wide-ranging response to her friends and his political enemies in Washington and Virginia. She ridiculed plain old Jack Randolph for styling himself John Randolph of Roanoke, and she took the opportunity to remind him that he had once tried to woo her himself. Copies of both letters swirled through polite society, and the old scandal morphed into a new one.[5]

As Virginians speculated about what else might come out at the trial, they reminded each other of many entertaining stories about Randolph's outrageous behavior. All of Charlotte County could tell how Randolph how fallen out with his neighbor Robert Carrington, barricaded the only road Carrington could take to a river crossing, and then posted a sign giving access to a long list of people that included everyone in the neighborhood except Carrington. Richmonders remembered the autumn when Randolph came to see his friend John Brockenbrough's elegant new house—and liked it so well that he stayed for seven months. Clerks at the Bank of Virginia recalled Randolph's announcement that he would sign his bank drafts in blood. And some of Randolph's friends had received letters from him begging for the milk of an ass because the devil would not let him drink anything else.[6]

The Tucker family's play for Randolph's estate was certain to bring other relatives into the fight. Richard Randolph's only surviving son St. George would get the largest share of the estate if his uncle's will proved invalid, and since the unfortunate St. George had few needs and no legal capacity to make a will of his own, his mother Judith's family stood to inherit much of the property when he died. Judith's brothers and sisters were already taking an interest in that possibility because they, like many other members of the Virginia gentry, had fallen on hard times.

Judith Randolph was one of ten children impoverished by agricultural decline, improvidence, and their father's late-life marriage to a woman less than half his age (who bore him a favorite son and went on to marry Randolph's friend John Brockenbrough). Even the most successful of Judith's three brothers, Thomas Jefferson's son-in-law Thomas Mann Randolph Jr., struggled to make ends meet, and Nancy Morris was the only sister who had married a prosperous man. The family had gotten legal advice about John Randolph's will, and their lawyers were in touch with St. George Randolph's legal representative, a Southside lawyer named Frederick Hobson. Nancy Morris, the only one of them who could afford to be so nonchalant, sneered at their scramble after "Jack [Randolph]'s leavings."[7]

The General Court trial might also bring new revelations about sex. Rehashing Nancy Morris's old misfortune would be titillating enough, but the story behind Randolph's failed courtship of Maria Ward had never been told. Ward was an especially beautiful young woman, and her close relationship with the boyish congressman John Randolph attracted considerable attention. Tongues ran away with themselves when the relationship abruptly ended in 1805, and Randolph fell into a fit of depression. The following year Ward married another Randolph, the son of a former governor of Virginia. By the time John Randolph died, she had been dead for seven years.[8]

Two hundred years of prying have never revealed what happened between Maria Ward and John Randolph. Some speculated that the two parted because he was impotent; others pointed to the relationship as proof to the contrary. Whatever had happened, the breakup publicly embarrassed Randolph and forever highlighted painful questions about his sexuality. His neighbors and other Virginians whispered that he was neither a man nor a woman. Those insinuations shadowed the beardless Randolph for the rest of his life, and his anxiety about his sexuality may have helped to shape him into the prickly, often savage, and sometimes cruel person he became. Some of Randolph's friends traced the onset of his madness to the broken relationship with Ward.[9]

The five lawyers assembled to prove all of this were another popular attraction. They were leading counsel, men whose forensic skills and political influence made them celebrities in their own right to the people of antebellum Virginia.[10]

From his perch as president of the Court of Appeals, Henry Tucker had chosen counsel quite well for the Bryan boy. Chapman Johnson—who made the first motion to probate Randolph's last will the previous summer—was a great favorite in the Virginia courts, and his colleague Robert Stanard was equally renowned. Stanard had served as Speaker of the Virginia House of Delegates and United States attorney for Virginia, and a few years later, he would become a judge on the Court of Appeals. While William Leigh's elegant brother Benjamin Watkins Leigh might have been an even more attractive choice as counsel, Henry Tucker could not ask him because of William Leigh's adverse interest in the case.[11]

Bishop Meade and Frank Key did even better than Judge Tucker when they got Walter Jones to represent Randolph's slaves. Johnson and Stanard had superb reputations in Virginia, but General Jones had a leading national reputation. He was one of the elite Washington lawyers who regularly appeared before the Supreme Court. Stephen Girard's heirs had hired him to break the will in which Girard left his huge estate to found a college, and while Jones was engaged on the Randolph case, he also worked on a New Orleans estate even bigger than Girard's that ultimately went before the Supreme Court seventeen times. Jones had retained two well-known Richmond lawyers to assist him. John Robertson had recently been elected to Congress after completing his term as attorney general of Virginia, and Samuel Taylor was the star pupil, nephew, and heir of the last chancellor in Virginia's old high court of chancery.[12]

On top of the trial's other attractions was the excitement aroused by controversies touching slavery and the racial order. Very few Virginians had ever written a will that freed over two hundred slaves. That dramatic act suggested that John Randolph had serious qualms about slavery—and many Virginians were eager to see the court dismiss that impression by upholding Randolph's last will.[13]

Virginia had drawn a line under free discussion about slavery after the General Assembly rejected gradual emancipation in 1832. White fears restrained free men as well as slaves. Arguments that had once been made openly were no longer tolerated. "The people of Virginia . . . were in favor of prospective abolition some years ago," lamented one newspaper editor; "*now* we are against its *consideration* under any circumstances." If a leading defender of the slave states' rights such as John Randolph had truly intended to free all of his own slaves, that would dent the self-justifications about Black incapacity for freedom that Virginia slaveholders needed to believe. If Randolph had ultimately changed his mind, on the other hand, they could use the progression in his thinking to validate the hardening of their own attitudes toward bondage.[14]

On its face, of course, there was no problem with the manumission provision in Randolph's earlier will. A man had the right to free his slaves. Virginia law was clear, and it had changed very little for thirty years. A slaveholder could manumit slaves by deed or by will as long as he provided for the support of those too young or too old to support themselves. The slaveholder's creditors could seize the prospective freedmen to satisfy debts that they could not recover from his other property, although the courts had stopped creditors from selling freedmen if the income from hiring them out could settle the debts within a reasonable time. Because Randolph had paid his debts and provided for his slaves, nothing in the law would prevent his slaves from going free if the court invalidated his last will and revived the earlier one.[15]

There was no danger that the slaves Randolph freed could become a disruptive presence because they would have to leave the state within one year. The legislature might give a few of Randolph's household servants permission to remain in Virginia, but it certainly would not make an exception for a large number. New laws had directed local authorities to pay more attention to the registration of free Blacks so that they could identify and remove freedmen who stayed illegally. Although enforcement remained lax, no one would overlook a prominently identified group of more than two hundred.[16]

White Virginians did not think that the liberation of a man's slaves under the terms of his will was a conceptual challenge to slavery. Although Anglo-American theorists might say that all men were free by the law of nature, English and American judges never doubted that positive law had decreed otherwise. And once the legislature had enslaved certain men, it could continue to restrict their freedom even after their owner released them from bondage. That was not an accurate description of how slavery emerged in Virginia, where planters had enslaved Native and African men and women under arrangements customary in the Atlantic world even before the colonial assembly passed laws to enforce those practices. But it did account for the way the law of manumission later developed.[17]

From the introduction of slavery until 1723, no law prevented Virginia slaves from gaining freedom, and some of them became free after a term of years, by self-purchase, or through outright release from bondage. The assembly then made it illegal to emancipate a slave except for exceptionally meritorious service, limiting the rights of both the enslaved and the enslavers in what the legislators believed to be the public interest. When the post-Revolutionary legislature decided to allow manumissions once more, no one doubted that it had the power to specify how they could occur.[18]

The manumission law that the Virginia assembly passed in 1782 gave slaves no rights. It simply gave slaveholders a new privilege. Slaveholders could free their slaves for whatever reason they pleased simply because the legislature had said so. Slaves, on the other hand, could not purchase themselves because any money they earned and anything else that they possessed already belonged to their owner. Even after they went free, the law set limits on their freedom. Manumission did not restore slaves to some natural state of liberty, and it could never give them the freedom enjoyed by white people. Freedmen had very few civil rights, and they would return to some form of bondage if they committed a crime or failed to pay their taxes.[19]

Yet despite the restrictions that the legislature had placed on manumissions, a manumission as large as Randolph's troubled some white Virginians. They could not explain it in any of the acceptable ways. It was much more than a gesture of gratitude or affection toward the few household servants Randolph sometimes called his "best friends." Although Randolph had made special provisions for Essex, John, Juba, and their families, those were lost in his much larger act. Nor did the manumission seem to be the result of deep religious conviction. Despite a burst of enthusiasm after his conversion experience, Randolph had never seemed to be a particularly devout man. He occasionally spoke of his Christian duty toward his slaves, but he did very little about it. The codicil in which he begged his executor not to send his slaves to Liberia had rejected the evangelical Episcopalian commitment to African colonization, and William Lloyd Garrison's *Liberator* exalted that this "*dying testimony of one of the founders of the Colonization Society"* exposed the moral bankruptcy of the whole enterprise.[20]

Casting Randolph's manumission as the honorable act of a good master was also unconvincing. Randolph would have liked the world to understand the manumission in that way. Randolph always stood on his honor. Throughout his life, he spoke of his slaves as a burden inherited from his ancestors that he had the duty to bear uprightly, and he repeatedly expressed the hope that they would "never know another taskmaster." If he did not free his slaves because of gratitude, affection, or religious conviction, his white contemporaries now asked themselves, why else would he have annihilated a third of his estate? But they could not quite conceive of Randolph as the sort of benevolent master who would free his slaves.[21]

Randolph had been too self-absorbed, too calculating, and in the end too mean. He never spoke of himself as a patriarch in the way a long line of Virginia planters from the colonial grandee William Byrd II to the republican Thomas Jefferson had done. He rarely used the sense of responsibility he felt toward his slaves as a paternalistic excuse for holding them in bondage. Instead, he described himself as a "Centurion" wielding the power to compel obedience. "I say to one go & he goes," Randolph told a friend in Boston, "to another do this & he doeth it." When Randolph was young, he had treated his slaves and the debt with which they came packaged as inextricable parts of a single economic equation, and even after he got a grip on the debt, he understood his relationship to the persons he enslaved mostly in economic terms. The nature of slave property, as he put it to a friend, obliged him to extort from the slaves fit to work enough profit to support them and their families and to leave him a fair return on his investment.[22]

Even if Randolph's manumission could be seen as a patriarchal act, it was still troubling. As the cotton boom pushed slave prices higher and abolitionist writers grew shriller, Virginia enslavers needed to believe that their slaves were better off in bondage than they would be in freedom. So the best they could say for an old man who freed hundreds of slaves was that he had been misguided, lost in the Revolutionary fantasies of his youth or the religious fears of his old age. And yet it was hard for them to dismiss John Randolph's case quite that easily. Randolph had indeed grown up with old-fashioned Revolutionary ideas about human freedom, but Virginians thought he had outgrown them thirty years ago. Even after his religious conversion, he had emphatically defended states' rights and slave property. To think that such a man might have wanted his own slaves to go free was unsettling. It forced slaveholders to ask themselves why, and it gave abolitionists a propaganda victory.[23]

The editor of the *Richmond Whig* saw an opportunity to put all of the excitement over Randolph's will to good use. John Hampden Pleasants was the son of a good Jeffersonian Republican who had served as governor and United States senator. But Pleasants himself had become a spokesman for the Whig Party, which opposed the establishment Democrats who backed Andrew Jackson. Pleasants supported democratic reforms at the Virginia constitutional convention, and he kept writing about the burden that slavery placed on Virginia's economy even after the legislature rejected gradual emancipation. Pleasants had always loathed John Randolph, and Randolph had no use for the quarrelsome young man. Encountering Randolph on the street one day, Pleasants blocked his path with the announcement that "I don't get out of the way of puppies." "I always do," replied Randolph as he stepped aside.[24]

Pleasants decided to publish transcripts of the testimony in the Randolph case. That was going to cost money, but it was a chance too good to miss. Transcripts from such an extraordinary trial would sell lots of newspapers and best his rivals at the *Richmond Enquirer*. Pleasants banged heads with that conservative Democratic paper every day, and although the *Enquirer* probably would reprint the transcripts if they proved as popular as Pleasants expected, the *Whig* would get credit for beating the *Enquirer* to the punch. Transcripts of the Randolph trial also could have political value for the Whig Party. The

testimony was almost certain to show that Randolph had been a madman, and that should embarrass the Jacksonian Democrats who had
backed him for years.[25]

Pleasants found just the person to report on the trial in Edward
Vernon Sparhawk, an experienced journalist who had reported congressional debates for the Whiggish *National Intelligencer* in Washington. Sparhawk's work for the *Intelligencer* had brought him a
moment of national attention a few years earlier when the pugnacious
Jacksonian editor Duff Green assaulted him in a Senate committee
room for misquoting (maliciously, Green said) a passage from one
of John Randolph's speeches. Sparhawk complained to the Senate,
which simply ignored him after Green insouciantly assured them that
he had pulled Sparhawk's ears and tweaked his nose "not to hurt, but
to disgrace him." Sparhawk later left Washington to edit a Richmond
magazine called the *Southern Literary Messenger,* but his position at
the magazine was unraveling and he needed another job. Sparhawk
was a careful reporter, and historians have him to thank for a surviving account of the trial. The General Court's own records vanished in
the flames that consumed much of downtown Richmond at the end
of the Civil War.[26]

The General Court's lofty courtroom with its sweeping view over
the city of Richmond made a grand stage for the drama Sparhawk was
about to record. The courtroom's position at the front of the state capitol signified the General Court's importance, and the eleven judges
arrayed across the high bench at the front of the room on court days
announced its authority. Although the court sometimes used juries,
there would be no jury in this probate case. A Virginia court sitting
to probate a will was exercising a jurisdiction that had belonged to
the church courts in England. Those were civil law courts in which
judges resolved all questions of law and fact, and probate courts in
Virginia followed similar procedures.[27]

Celebrity, money, scandal, and slavery were going to make the
Randolph trial sensational enough to sell many copies of the *Rich-*

mond Whig. But the legal question presented to the General Court judges was more specific. It was simply whether Randolph had been competent when he canceled his old will and made a new one on New Year's Day, 1832. If so, the new will would stand, most of Randolph's slaves would go to market (to put it in the plain terms of that time), and the rest of them would form part of a large inheritance for the Bryan child. If not, the new will would be invalid and Bishop Meade would get a chance to probate the old one and set the slaves free. The decision would turn on the General Court's view of the evidence and the legal meaning of madness.

Chapter 8

THE MEANING OF MADNESS

William Leigh, painting, c. 1845

JOHN RANDOLPH'S SANITY HAS BEEN A FOCUS OF FASCI-
nation for more than two centuries. His family, friends, and enemies wondered about it throughout his lifetime, and historians have
questioned it ever since. "Who can tell," asked a journalist who tried
to sketch the man, "in the close alliance between reason and madness, which were so strongly mixed up in his character, how much

his actions and words partook of the one or the other?" Some people thought him crazy, wrote Nancy Morris long after she and Randolph had exchanged vicious letters, but he seemed to her more like "those whom Satan entered in old times." Perhaps Randolph's cousin Anna Dudley, who lived with him in the household at Bizarre years earlier, gave the best short assessment when she said that Randolph "was at all times . . . very eccentric, and . . . at some times insane."[1]

The stories about Randolph's peculiarities were legion. His restless travels as a young man, his extravagant and wandering speeches, his dark moods and flashes of violence, his erratic religious fervor, his talks with the devil—there was no end to them. What emerged from the stories were several marked behavioral tendencies. An insatiable craving for attention was the most obvious, and with it came fawning attachments to some and malicious disregard for the feelings of others. Then there were the fluctuations between excitement and dejection, enthusiasm and gloom. Randolph's obsessive concern with his health and his property threaded through both those tendencies as a cry for attention and a companion in melancholy. Finally, there were Randolph's warm affections and his abiding resentments. Although Randolph made some lasting friendships, he drowned others in torrents of antipathy once he conceived the notion that someone had deceived or disrespected him. The dominant feature of his political life was an unbridled instinct for opposition, which deepened until he had alienated almost everyone. "Among all those with whom he has been associated during the last thirty years," wrote a Massachusetts senator who liked him, "there is scarcely an individual whom he can call his friend."[2]

Historians and their readers are tempted to use modern psychological concepts to construct intelligible understandings of past behavior. But a diagnosis of Randolph's mental condition in modern terms is extraordinarily difficult and ultimately unrevealing. The men and women who left descriptions of Randolph's behavior had a mindset different from our own. They saw what their experience prepared them to see, understood what they saw using the intellectual tools available to them, and described what they understood in terms that no longer mean what they intended to say. Even if we can retrieve enough from their accounts and Randolph's own writings to hazard a modern diagnosis, our characterization is necessarily ahistorical. The meaning of behavior depends on its context, and the historical implications of a man's behavior depend more on what his contemporaries made of it than on what we think about it. To understand how the courts dealt with John Randolph's will, we must look at the legal and medical framework within which they heard the evidence about his sanity.[3]

· · · ·

IN THE WORLD John Randolph inhabited, a free adult man had considerable freedom to dispose of his property by will as long as he knew what he owned, knew which persons should be the natural objects of his bounty, and understood how the provisions of his will would affect them. This test for determining whether a man possessed the mental capacity to make a will had emerged from decisions in the English and American courts. It was principally cognitive, intellectual; it turned on whether a man could remember things and think logically about them. The test was not meant to be demanding. The courts said even feebleminded and senile persons could meet it. The law had given men power to leave their property to someone other than their heirs at law, the courts explained, so that they could use that power to get the care and attention they needed when they were old and infirm. A man therefore could disinherit anyone except his wife, who had a right to claim a lifetime dower interest in a share of his real property. (The whole inheritance regime was decidedly masculine; women generally could not dispose of their property by will unless they were single.)[4]

An insane person lacked the capacity to make a valid will. This rule followed from the essentially cognitive nature of the basic test. The common law originally conceived of madness as a loss of reason or judgment. It described an insane person as *non compos mentis* because he had lost control over, or perhaps even access to, his rational faculties. The law denied an insane person the power to make a will in order to protect him and his family from the consequences of a disposition of his property that he might not have made if he had been able to think more rationally. This concern with protecting families added a moral or normative element to the law's understanding of madness. It tempted judges to treat a man's disinheritance of his family as evidence of insanity, and judges sometimes shrugged off warnings that what might appear to be normal bequests to family members were not by themselves sufficient evidence of sanity.[5]

In the two decades before John Randolph died, medical doctors had begun reshaping the law's understanding of insanity. Medical studies of the mind were part of a broader expansion in scientific inquiry, and the practical achievements of the new science fostered the belief that science could help to solve a wide range of human problems. Among them were problems that arose in legal cases. Doctors developed a new discipline they called medical jurisprudence, which brought scientific knowledge to bear on the detection of crime, problems of proof, and evaluations of sanity.[6]

As medical doctors searched for better ways to treat madness, they began to reconceptualize it. Insanity was not, they concluded, primarily an intellectual disorder. It had more to do with derangements in human emotions than impairments to rational thinking. Confused thinking was more often a consequence than a cause. What made a man mad was the absence or distortion of the feelings that men usually have about themselves and others. An otherwise rational man therefore could be insane on certain subjects. Most insanity was partial, a derangement of particular feelings rather than a disabling madness. The doctors spoke of insane persons as estranged or alienated. They referred to themselves as alienists, and they called the human phenomena they studied mental alienation.[7]

The new work on mental alienation complicated the work of the courts. It meant that men who appeared to be sensible could claim they were not sane and therefore not responsible for their crimes or accountable for their contracts. Disappointed heirs could contend that men who seemed rational had not been competent to make their last wills. Such arguments had the potential to undermine older understandings of fault and blame, obligation and liability. The arguments also tended to elevate the testimony of doctors. Because they knew more about the science of the mind, their expert opinions could crowd out the common wisdom of judges and juries on which the law had traditionally relied.[8]

Judges schooled in the old ways resisted at first, particularly in criminal cases. Anglo-American law had long recognized that a person who lacked *mens rea*—a mind or intention to do the thing—should not be held criminally responsible for an unlawful act. If the person did not know what he was doing, he was not morally blameworthy, and punishment could not deter him or set an example for others. A person who lost control of his rational mind therefore was excused. A person who lost control of his emotions was another matter entirely. Extreme provocation might justify certain crimes of passion, but if the criminal law excused a person who knew what he was doing in other cases, it would lose the ability to deter malicious behavior. Judges therefore insisted that insanity would not excuse a person from criminal responsibility for an intentional act unless he simply could not understand that it was wrong.[9]

In probate cases, judges were more receptive to the new ideas about insanity. Although Anglo-American law gave men considerable freedom to determine who would inherit their property when they died, it had always retained a bias toward keeping property in the family. Widows had dower rights in their husband's real property, and widowers retained control of their wife's property by curtesy after her death. Judges were suspicious of wills that disinherited a man's children, discriminated against unoffending family members, or squandered family property on charity. "*Families* . . . contain the foundation and primitive elements of all other social institutions," wrote one prominent Southern judge in a testamentary manumission case. "*Wills* . . . calculated . . . to set at nought this divine ordinance" therefore deserved no favor. When judges could find evidence of fraud, undue influence, imbecility, or madness in such cases, they used it to protect the heirs at law and what they regarded as the natural order of things.[10]

A broader and more flexible conception of insanity was welcome in this context. Partial insanity could explain why a man who appeared sensible had left an unaccountable will. The medical books about mental alienation gave the man's heirs a language in which to voice their disappointment. The books helped lawyers and witnesses show the connection between a man's behavior and some type of mental alienation that experts recognized. They gave judges greater confidence in the conclusions that they were already predisposed to reach in such cases.[11]

Monomania was the type of mental alienation most frequently alleged in probate trials, and although it was decided before that term came into use, the English case of *Dew v. Clark* became the leading precedent on both sides of the Atlantic. The case involved the will of a London doctor named Ely Stott who made a modest fortune by treating patients with electricity. Stott's first wife died shortly after the birth of his only child, Charlotte, and he conceived an irrational antipathy toward the small girl. He claimed she was perverse and immoral, banished her from his table, and beat her. He told his patients that she was "the special property of Satan." The way Stott spoke of her was so furious that patients tried to reason with him, and respectable families took Charlotte into their own care. Stott's will left the bulk of his estate to two nephews he scarcely knew. His daughter sued to prevent probate.[12]

The English probate court held for the daughter because it believed that Stott was mad. Although he was able to carry on a successful medical practice, Stott had lost touch with reality on the subject of his daughter. Most men who became insane did not lose their minds entirely, explained the court. They were insane simply because they clung to delusions on certain subjects despite plain evidence and reasonable arguments to the contrary. "A man who is very sober and of

a right understanding in all other things," therefore, "may in one particular be as frantic as any man in Bedlam." Other courts in England
and the United States readily accepted that conclusion in probate
cases, and by the 1830s, they were recognizing delusions and irrational antipathies like Stott's as the essence of monomania.[13]

Judges in Virginia were less inclined to look to Kentucky for legal
precedents, but a Kentucky case decided at about the same time came
closer to John Randolph's situation. George Moore was a miserly old
bachelor who hated his brothers. He mistakenly believed they had
tried to kill him when he was deathly ill twenty-five years earlier.
In the final years of his life, Moore stayed drunk, boasted of wealth
that he did not have, and ranted about his brothers. About two weeks
before he died, Moore wrote a will that completely disinherited them.
The will provided for an enslaved woman who lived with Moore
and went free at his death under the terms of an earlier deed, and
it left the rest of Moore's estate to men with whom he had no blood
relationship.[14]

Moore's brothers claimed that the will was invalid because Moore
had been insane. The county court judges agreed, and the Kentucky
appeals court upheld them. The appeals court recognized that Moore
had been competent to manage his own affairs despite his drunken-
ness. It nevertheless decided that his groundless hostility to his brothers was "a species of derangement" that had prevented him from
exercising free will when he disposed of his property. The last will
therefore could not stand, and all of Moore's property passed to his
brothers under the intestacy laws. Although the court said nothing
about Moore's decision to leave property to an enslaved woman, his
violation of racial norms may have influenced the decision.[15]

The lawyer who represented Moore's devisees was incredulous,
and his unsuccessful petition for rehearing made such an eloquent
case for testamentary freedom that the Kentucky court reporter took
the unusual step of printing it alongside the appeals court's opinion. What had medical doctors added to the stock of human knowledge about the mind, the petition demanded, except "a succession of

short-lived theories, founded on conjecture, and ending in the establishment of constructive madness!" Their theories did not justly distinguish between "*delusions of the mind*" and "*depravity of the heart*." George Moore may have been "selfish, capricious and unamiable—an unkind brother and an implacable enemy," but the matter put to the court was a question of legal privilege rather than moral duty. As long as a man was competent to manage his own affairs, he had a right "to play the fool" and scatter the property he had received from his ancestors however he pleased.[16]

Faced with similar collisions between testamentary freedom and claims of insanity, the courts in Virginia and elsewhere used procedural rules to help find resolutions. If a dead man's last will appeared regular on its face, the courts presumed he was sane when he made it. Once opponents of the will introduced some evidence of the man's mental alienation, however, the proponents of the will had the burden of proving his sanity. The evidence of alienation could take different forms. It might show that the man raved, saw demons, obsessed over his health, fixated on grievances, or insisted on things that simply were not true. Most frequent, of course, was evidence that the man bore unjustified grudges against his heirs at law.[17]

Proponents of the will could try to impeach evidence of insanity by showing that it was false or unreliable. If that failed, they could attempt to show that the testator's beliefs had a sensible basis (even if they were not true), his obsessions some plausible explanation, his visions a mystical or religious origin, and his ravings a sufficient resemblance to the talk of a mere fanatic. When the evidence of insanity was simply irresistible, the proponents of the will had to take a different approach. Two were available. The proponents could claim that the testator made his will during a remission or lucid interval in his insanity, or they could argue that the man's insanity had not affected his decisions about the disposition of his property because his will did what the man would have done if he had been sane. A common way to prove either one of those propositions was to show that the will was consistent with intentions the testator had expressed when he was sane.[18]

Judges asked to consider what a man *would* have done if he were sane easily drifted into thinking about what the man *should* have done. The subjective question about the man's intentions could elicit a normative response. Men who left their property to their natural heirs appeared sane enough; men who disinherited their heirs did not. The chancellor of New York expressed no more than the received wisdom when he said that an unreasonable disposition of property was "always proper evidence to be taken into consideration in judging the state of the testator's mind."[19]

Men like George Moore who left their entire property to strangers and enslaved women presented relatively simple cases because they flouted both kinship and racial norms. In most cases, the facts were more ambiguous and judges were more likely to overcome their biases. In Virginia, where the Court of Appeals was sympathetic to slaves in manumission cases, judges found it difficult to conclude that a testamentary provision for the manumission of slaves was evidence of the testator's insanity. In most of the reported cases where the freedom of slaves was at issue, judges quietly overcame whatever discomfort they felt and upheld the testator's will.[20]

. . . .

THE GENERAL COURT began the trial of John Randolph's last will on the first of July, 1835. Judge Leigh had recused himself, so another judge came to Richmond to provide the necessary quorum. Although the court's high-ceilinged courtroom overlooking the city was not as hot as it had been when Chapman Johnson offered the will for probate a year earlier, flies still attended through the windows left open for fresh air.[21]

Opening arguments made it clear that the trial was not going to be as wide-ranging as some observers had expected. Bishop Meade's lawyers carefully limited their attack on Randolph's sanity to the period when he made his last will in order to avoid any suggestion that he had been insane when he made the earlier will freeing his slaves. The Bryan boy's lawyers went through the motions of defending the last will, but they did not present a strong case. Although they nominally represented the now four-year-old heir, they were taking instructions from the whole Tucker family, and the family wanted the court to find Randolph intestate. The Tuckers had decided to present the last will for probate mainly to induce Judge Leigh to renounce his interest under the earlier will, so that the substantial property Randolph had left to Leigh would pass to the heirs at law if Meade should later convince the court to uphold that will. Frederick Hobson as the legal representative for St. George Randolph, who would take the largest share in intestacy, had the same interest as the Tuckers. All of the litigants therefore regarded this trial as just a preliminary step toward a trial of the earlier will.[22]

In his opening argument for Bishop Meade, Walter Jones said he would prove that Randolph had been insane ever since he returned from his diplomatic mission to Russia in the autumn of 1832. Although Jones conceded that Randolph might have had some lucid intervals, he insisted that Randolph did not make his last will in one of them. Whenever Randolph spoke of his will, including on his deathbed, the will he remembered as the true expression of his intentions was the earlier one that freed his slaves. Jones then read the earlier will and its codicils into the record.

Robert Stanard did not contradict Jones when he replied on behalf of the Bryan boy. Stanard simply claimed that the will Jones had read could not be the will Randolph canceled when he wrote his last will. It could not be the canceled will because it did not contain provisions to which some of the later codicils expressly referred. Randolph's penultimate will—the one the court should consider if the last will was invalid—therefore appeared to be missing. Although Stanard conceded that the missing will probably had emancipated Randolph's slaves, he questioned how the court could ever enforce it if it could not be found.[23]

Despite the parties' relatively limited objectives, the trial was a long one. The testimony alone took two weeks, with an adjournment for funeral honors to Chief Justice Marshall on the day his body came home to Richmond for burial. (Church bells tolled as a large procession accompanied the great man's body through the city, and among the pallbearers at the head of the procession were Henry Tucker and the two lawyers who represented the Bryan boy.) The court heard from more than twenty witnesses. Isaac Parrish, the Quaker doctor from Philadelphia, came to testify about what Randolph had said on his deathbed. "He appeared in the Court with his hat on," reported the *Richmond Enquirer*, "and expressed himself in the peculiar phraseology of his sect." The testimony that followed ranged from colorful to peculiar to plainly outrageous. John Hampden Pleasants, of the *Richmond Whig*, saw his investment in trial reporting pay off, and the editor of the rival *Richmond Enquirer* had to acknowledge that the witnesses were disclosing "many curious circumstances touching the conduct and character of this celebrated man."[24]

Bishop Meade's counsel tried to show a connection between the changes in Randolph's behavior after his return from Russia and the changes he made to his will. Randolph had picked a quarrel with nearly everyone after he came home. He offended his old constituents by giving a speech in which he told them they were not half the men their fathers had been. He had his overseer John Craddock arrested, and when Craddock applied to Randolph's neighbor Robert Carrington for help with bail, Randolph turned on Carrington. The two of them had been friends. Carrington witnessed Randolph's 1828 codicil, and he was visiting in Randolph's house when he got Craddock's request for assistance. But Randolph now violated their long-standing agreement about managing unfenced fields by turning livestock into his corn stubble while Carrington's oats were still stacked in the adjacent field. He denied Carrington a right-of-way that the whole community used, and on the day he wrote his last will, Randolph purchased land from Elisha Hundley so that he would own all of the land surrounding Carrington's plantation.[25]

Randolph also grew alienated from Judge Leigh, who had long

been his most trusted friend. He needled Leigh for neglecting Roanoke and mismanaging the slaves during Randoph's absence. He said that Leigh had sold a filly named Whistleberry too cheaply (although Leigh charged the price Randolph listed before he went away), and he tried to get her back from his Charlotte County lawyer John Marshall. He began to entrust his business affairs to Wyatt Cardwell, a parvenu to whom Randolph had never even spoken before he went to Russia. "There never was an angry or an unkind word between us," Leigh reflected in a letter to a friend soon after Randolph died, but Randolph's loss of confidence in him was obvious. Leigh attributed it more to "a perversion of his feelings" than some disorder in his rational mind.[26]

The most shocking trial testimony concerned Randolph's abuse of his slaves. Witnesses thought his gross mistreatment of them was "the strongest evidence" of his insanity. They said Randolph had been a sensible if demanding master before he went to Russia. When he came back, he was far otherwise. He told everyone that his slaves had produced short crops in his absence. He insisted that his foreman Billy had stolen wool from him, and he searched Billy's house, confiscated some of his household goods, and drove him out to the fields. (Randolph left a detailed account of this quarrel with Billy in his own letters.) His violent mistreatment of Essex and the other household servants was notorious, and the whole neighborhood took notice when field hand Moses replaced John as the driver of Randolph's carriage. Randolph told Leigh, Cardwell, and others that he had decided not to free his slaves because of their misconduct.[27]

Whatever their views on the subject of manumission, Randolph's friends and neighbors found the changes in his behavior toward his slaves unaccountable. They all said that the slaves at Roanoke had been diligent and reliable during Randolph's absence. "His slaves were remarkably good," Robert Carrington told the court; "they were the best negroes [that I] ever saw." Carrington did not believe they were thieves because they were too afraid of Randolph to steal.[28]

Fifty-two-year-old Judge Leigh testified last, and his appearance in the courtroom was highly charged. Leigh was a colleague of the judges, and he was the only white person who had been with Randolph and his servants on the winter night when Randolph wrote his last will. Leigh was also the popular hero of the trial. After Bishop Meade's entreaty to him, Leigh had finally decided to renounce all of his interest in the property Randolph left him so that he could take the stand for the benefit of the enslaved. That was the sort of high-minded, disinterested conduct that men and women in Virginia's honor society could applaud, whatever their views on slavery. "Among the witnesses is Judge Leigh," wrote the *Richmond Enquirer* on the day he was to appear. "He has nobly relinquished the fine Legacy which was bequeathed to him . . . in order to testify, as he believed, in behalf of truth and justice."[29]

Leigh gave the General Court the most detailed account of Randolph's disturbed behavior during his final years. His testimony was orderly, clear, and dispassionate, yet even though Randolph had been dead for more than two years, it carried an unmistakable tone of sadness. Leigh remembered many painful occasions, and he did not spare his own feelings.

Two months after the night when Randolph wrote his last will, Leigh happened to stop at Roanoke as Randolph, John Marshall, and one of Randolph's closest friends from Congress were sitting down for a dinner with many bottles of wine. Randolph did not welcome him. "We boys were going to have a frolic tonight," he told Leigh, "and here you have come with your grave judicial face to spoil it all." Randolph continued to tease Leigh throughout dinner for being a "kill joy," until Leigh at last apologized for coming and offered to leave. Randolph then came down the table, enfolded Leigh's hands in his, and assured him that he had not meant to hurt his feelings. For the next two days, Randolph would not let him leave. He said Leigh's horse had escaped from the barn, although the stable hands told Leigh that Randolph had ordered them to let the horse out.[30]

Henry Tucker was with Randolph when Leigh visited a few weeks later, and Randolph asked each of them to draft provisions for a new will that would benefit the other while he himself wrote the rest of the will. Randolph was obviously enjoying this game, although Leigh doubted he was competent to play it. When Leigh next visited, he found Randolph in bed with a bottle of brandy. Randolph said the house was full of devils that John could not chase out because he was too drunk. When Randolph tried to dictate a new will to Leigh later that day, he could not keep his mind on one thing long enough to finish.

Leigh continued to see Randolph regularly, but the visits grew increasingly difficult. Randolph's state of mind was unpredictable, and he sometimes asked Leigh to search for papers and do other small favors that made it nearly impossible for Leigh to leave. He became so "extremely parsimonious" that he "scarcely gave his guests food fit to eat." His servants put the same cold pudding on the table for two or three days running, and Randolph would comment when a guest cut off more meat than the servants had already sliced. Randolph's parsimony did not extend to the amount he drank. Although he consumed as much as a bottle of wine every day after dinner, said Leigh, "this did not make him drunk, for he could bear more than any man I ever saw."

Leigh had a clear view about Randolph's sanity and his feelings toward the Tucker family. He said Randolph was sane when he made his earlier will in 1821 and insane in the winter of 1831–32, when he wrote the last will. He told the court that Randolph had never expressed affection for any of his relatives other than Elizabeth Bryan. Randolph had complained for decades about St. George Tucker's appropriation of the Bland slaves, and he had claimed that it was St. George who advised Beverley Tucker to take the slaves Randolph gave him away to Missouri. Randolph told Leigh he would leave his blood relatives nothing because "they had treated him with no kindness."[31]

Beverley Tucker went to the springs in the Virginia mountains long before Leigh testified. He washed his hands of the way his brother Henry, John Coalter, and the Bryans were handling the case. Because he and his nephew St. George Coalter would get nothing under any of Randolph's wills, Beverley thought squabbling over particular wills was a waste of time. "I do not mean to quarrel about it," he wrote to his father-in-law from the springs, but he looked forward to the time when he and his nephew could bring a lawsuit of their own to establish a full intestacy. "When I take [the business] in hand," he continued, "there will be fewer counsellors, and less confusion, if there is less wisdom."[32]

By the time the evidence closed back in Richmond, Robert Stanard and Chapman Johnson had not made much of a case for Randolph's last will. They sharply questioned any testimony that disparaged the Tuckers and cast doubt on Randolph's earlier will whenever they got the chance, but they offered little resistance to claims that Randolph was insane. They were just trying to lay the groundwork for an attack on Randolph's earlier will in the next trial. They banked an important point when they got Judge Leigh to admit that Randolph never expressly acknowledged his intention to free his slaves until after he had abandoned it. They also got Leigh and other witnesses to recount Randolph's frequent late-life argument that enslaved laborers in Virginia were better off than the peasants and wage slaves in Europe and New England.[33]

What Stanard and Johnson never tried to explain was why Randolph might have wanted to leave his entire estate to John Coalter Bryan. That would not have been difficult. Although Randolph may have lost control of his emotions by the time he wrote his last will, he was not irrational. Old families, their land, and their independent way of living were bedrocks of his value system. The last will was in fact a testament to beliefs and prejudices that Randolph indulged for most of his life. It preserved the estate Randolph had inherited from his forebears as a rich legacy for a descendant of his beloved mother, and by granting the Bryan boy only a life interest, it aimed to keep the estate intact for at least one more generation.[34]

Randolph was proudly—and painfully—aware that he belonged

to a decayed gentry that was no longer in control of Virginia. The decline of his class was a recurring theme in conversations and letters throughout his lifetime, especially during the years surrounding the death of his nephew Tudor, and historians often draw on his descriptions of gentry decline because they are so evocative. He had spent a melancholy day visiting the graves of his forefathers, Randolph mourned to a New York friend as the dried leaves began to fall one autumn. They had "once owned all the country hereabout that was worth having," wrote Randolph, but now the land belonged to strangers, their great house was gone, and the church where they worshipped had become a stable. "Everything bears the mark of decay."[35]

"Before the Revolution," began the saga as Randolph told it, "the lower country of Virginia, pierced for more than a hundred miles from the seaboard by numerous bold and navigable rivers, was inhabited by a race of planters, of English descent, who dwelt on their principal estates on the borders of those noble streams." They were rich, well educated, and hospitable, trading freely with England and living in peace. But free living, bad agriculture, and the disruption of the Revolution had brought an end to all of that. After the war, their great mansions were left to ruin, their churches abandoned, and their fields deserted to the deer and wild turkeys. The most enterprising members of the old families dispersed from Georgia to Missouri, and those who remained in Virginia sank into obscurity. "They whose fathers rode in coaches and drank the choicest wine now ride on saddle-bags, and drink grog, when they can get it."[36]

Most historians have emphasized the debt incurred to pay for conspicuous consumption as the leading reason for the Virginia gentry's decline. The old gentry as a class had been living beyond their means since at least 1765, and the long economic depression that followed the Revolution toppled the most indebted of them. Some held on into the early nineteenth century by reducing their lifestyles and improving their plantations just as John Randolph had done, but many had to make their living in some other way or migrate to better land in Kentucky, Missouri, or the Cotton Belt. By the time Randolph made his last will, relatively few descendants of the old gentry still owned large ancestral properties like Roanoke.[37]

It seemed to Randolph that loss of ancestral land was the core reason for gentry decline, and he laid the blame "chiefly" on the Revolutionary legislature's changes to the laws of inheritance. Before the Revolution, many large Virginia estates were subject to entails, which were legal restrictions on title that made it difficult for the owner to sell or mortgage the land and required him to pass it on to the next generation. When a man died without making a will to provide otherwise, a primogeniture statute gave substantially all of his land to his eldest son. After the Revolution, the General Assembly swept those restrictions away. It abolished entails altogether and replaced primogeniture with a law that distributed an intestate man's property equally among his children.[38]

Randolph criticized Thomas Jefferson and the other republican idealists on Virginia's Revolutionary law revision committee for recommending those misguided changes to the inheritance laws. It was easy to see, he grumbled to a friend from the South Carolina planter class, that none of them ever expected to have a male heir. After they changed the law, freer borrowing and more land division had nibbled away the great estates. The children of the great landowners began to marry beneath themselves and disappear into the masses. That was the "inevitable conclusion to which Mr. Jefferson and his levelling system has brought us."[39]

Randolph was far from the only person who understood the Revolutionary changes to inheritance law in class terms. St. George Tucker explained to his law students that Virginia had abolished entails because the preservation of great estates was "utterly incompatible with the genius and spirit of our constitution." Foreign visitors attributed the abandoned great houses they saw in the Virginia countryside to the breakup of the estates needed to support them. That was just as it should be, according to the New York jurist Chancellor Kent. Once the law allowed property to circulate freely, "the steady laws of nature" would splinter great fortunes as quickly as they accumulated. In the decade after Randolph died, American reformers were still arguing that inheritance reform and more equal distribution of property were necessary for the advance of democracy.[40]

Randolph was proud of the land and slaves he had saved from the wreckage of his family's fortune. Roanoke was a good and extensive plantation; rescuing it from debt had taken most of his lifetime. Randolph also was intrigued by the legal devices still available for perpetuating large estates. He took particular interest in a famous English will that put a vast fortune in trust to accumulate for the testator's eldest male grandchildren, and he had considered leaving his slaves and his plantation in trust to endow a school. So once his slaves and Judge Leigh disappointed Randolph, it was not at all unnatural for him to think of leaving his entire estate to a young relative for life with the remainder to heirs who could use it to maintain what was left of his family's position in Virginia. Other Virginians readily understood that. The Virginia writer Edgar Allan Poe based one of his short stories on the English will case, and even though the Bryan boy's lawyers had not raised the point, a judge of the General Court asked Leigh to confirm for the court record that John Randolph's property was a "patrimonial estate."[41]

Torrents of rain washed Richmond the night after Leigh finished testifying, and the downpour continued the next day. The mail from the north could not get through, and a bridge washed out on the road west to Charlottesville. Samuel Taylor awoke too sick to begin the closing arguments for Bishop Meade, so he sent his notes to his co-counsel, John Robertson.[42]

Closing arguments took three days. Robert Stanard argued that Randolph's last will should stand because Bishop Meade had failed to show that Randolph was ever permanently insane. And even if Randolph had been insane, said Stanard, a will favoring the son of Randolph's favorite niece was so sensible that Randolph must have made it in a lucid interval. In his response for Bishop Meade, John Robertson claimed that the abrupt changes in Randolph's last will showed just the opposite. Randolph had long intended to free his slaves, and nothing but a "gross mental delusion" could explain his sudden decision to do otherwise. The English decision in Doctor Stott's case therefore was a good precedent for rejecting the will. Walter Jones made the final arguments for Meade, and on the third day—a Saturday—the trial ended with Chapman Johnson's long summation in support of the will.[43]

"We presume that few doubt what the judgment of the Court will be," jeered the *Richmond Whig* in what sounds like a parody of Johnson's summation. The law *presumes* that wills are valid, continued the paper, and most people were simply indignant *at the very idea* that John Randolph might have been insane. Perhaps that explained—and here came the editor's jab—why Johnson and Bryan's other lawyers had never bothered to present *any evidence* that Randolph was sane. The *Richmond Enquirer* huffed that the *Whig* was trying to "browbeat the Court" and tip the scales of justice.[44]

The *Whig*'s prediction may have been biting, but it was correct. Randolph's will leaving his ancestral property to the son of his favorite niece had enough normative appeal to survive Meade's challenge despite the Tucker family's scant effort to defend it. The General Court upheld the will by a vote of six judges to five. The judges delivered no opinions, and the court adjourned after having sat for "an unexampled session of three weeks." Randolph's will had excited more attention than any other will in Virginia history, said the *Enquirer*, so there was certain to be an elaborate appeal.[45]

. . . .

BEVERLEY TUCKER WROTE another novel while the Randolph will was on appeal. *The Partisan Leader* imagines Southern secession, and it is the thing for which Beverley Tucker is most often remembered. The Nullification Crisis three years earlier had turned many Southern Democrats against Andrew Jackson. Even though most of them did not support South Carolina's claim to nullify federal law, they thought that Jackson's belligerent response showed too little respect for state sovereignty. Beverley was among the extremists in that group who declared that secession was the true remedy for unconstitutional challenges to states' rights, slavery, and Southern economic interests. His novel was a tale of the future written to dramatize those views, and the story it told also revealed tensions simmering within the Tucker family.[46]

The Partisan Leader begins in the mountains west of John Randolph's Piedmont plantation. A band of partisans has assembled there to harass federal troops that are tightening their grip on the countryside. The troops have occupied Virginia to stop it from joining the Southern states that seceded from the Union over tariff issues in 1848 when the centralizing Jacksonian Democrat Martin Van Buren won a fourth term as president.

The partisan leader is a young soldier named Douglas Trevor. His father Hugh is a moderate Unionist and a prominent figure in the Richmond political establishment. The cautious old man temporizes in all things, and he has hesitated to oppose the federal invasion. Both of his sons were serving as officers in the federal army until Douglas, spurred by the insults a Van Buren sycophant offered to his beloved cousin Delia, resigned to join the partisans. Delia is the daughter of Hugh's younger brother Bernard Trevor. Bernard is an ardent secessionist, quite the opposite of his precautious brother. A man of noble convictions and firm resolution, Bernard lives quietly on a plantation in the rolling hills east of the mountains with his beautiful daughter, courageous wife, and loyal slaves. He, Douglas, and the slaves face down a federal contingent sent to corrupt local elections in which Bernard wins a seat in the legislature. Bernard and his family then flee to North Carolina, and Douglas marries Delia before riding off to the partisans' mountain hideout where the novel's action began.

It is perhaps no accident that the commander of a federal battalion sent to root the partisans out of the mountains is Douglas's brother, Owen. Van Buren has spies everywhere, and he takes delight in such things. The battalion occupies the foothill town of Lynchburg, but Owen has been promoted beyond his ability and he leads one of his regiments into a partisan trap. Douglas's men defeat the regiment and take Owen prisoner. In the act of protecting his brother from harm, Douglas reveals himself to Owen. The plot then pivots sharply. Owen escapes back to Lynchburg, gathers a few wily men, abducts Douglas from the partisan camp, and sends him off to prison in Washington. As the novel ends, Van Buren is plotting Douglas's condemnation in an unjust trial. A partisan's bullet has killed Owen, and a diminished Hugh Trevor comes to Washington to beg Van Buren for the life of his remaining son.[47]

The Partisan Leader appeared under a pseudonym with a false printer's imprint and a fictitious publication date of 1856. The author and his publisher, Duff Green (now as aggressively anti-Jacksonian as he had once been Jacksonian), may have hoped the book could help defeat Van Buren in the 1836 presidential election, but it came out too late in the year to gain a wide audience before the voting.[48]

Henry Tucker first heard of the book from friends who suspected that Beverley Tucker had written it, and what he heard did not please him. Others had recognized him as Hugh Trevor. Henry canceled his subscription to the *Southern Literary Messenger* when it gave the novel a favorable review, and he put off reading the book for almost a year. He was still reading it when he sent Beverley an abrupt letter. "That my own brother should have published such a libel on me and so flattering a panegyric of himself," he wrote, "I ought not to believe." Yet the book's reflections on his character were so severe that he felt justified in asking "whether you are or are not the author of the Partizan leader."[49]

Henry's letter found Beverley summering at a mountain spring with the ailing St. George Coalter, and Beverley took great pains with his response. He explained that he had written *The Partisan Leader* to show why Southern liberty depended on the active defense of old Republican principles now espoused by the States' Rights Party. He thought the men on both sides of the great question about Union were "sincere, honest, virtuous and firm," and he had meant to illustrate that in the characters of the two Trevor brothers. He confessed that Henry Tucker had been his model for Hugh Trevor, but only because he found it impossible to sketch a faultless man of sound Unionist opinions without thinking of his brother.[50]

Beverley was sharper when he sent a copy of this letter to his wife Lucy. Henry would not be satisfied with that explanation, he predicted, "simply because he is not satisfied with himself." Yet as Beverley later reflected on the friction in their relationship, he could see—although he could not plainly confess—that his own insecurities were part of the rub. Virginia had not received him home as the man of distinction he so much wanted to be, and he could not help feeling jealous of the distinction Henry had achieved. John Randolph's estate had become too important to him because he needed the money. Although he tried to put a good face on it, being a law professor was not really enough. "Necessity drove me into my present position," he told Lucy. "But were I foot loose, I would be in Missouri in six weeks."[51]

The great American historian and man of letters Henry Adams never met Beverley Tucker, but he knew men who were like him. Adams went to college with Robert E. Lee's son Rooney and other young white Virginians at a time when they were becoming alienated from their fellow citizens in the North. He was in Washington during the secession winter of 1861 when his father served as a Republican congressman from Massachusetts, and he watched with bemusement as Southern alienation burst into civil war. Adams went on to write a psychologically insightful biography of John Randolph that portrayed him as an avatar of the Southern delusion that led to the war. And when he reflected on what had happened in the winter of 1861 as he was writing his autobiography nearly fifty years later, Adams described it in psychological terms. "The Southern secessionists were certainly unbalanced in mind," he wrote, "fit for medical treatment, like other victims of hallucination—haunted by suspicion, by *idées fixes*, by violent morbid excitement." They had refused to learn enough about the wide world around them to understand their real place in it. Their grand delusion had been their undoing. What

Henry Adams saw in their "glaring . . . defiance of reason" was pure madness.[52]

. . . .

IN THE SPRING of 1836, the Court of Appeals in Richmond unanimously reversed the General Court's decision on John Randolph's will. There was no fanfare, and the court gave no explanatory opinion. It simply held that Randolph's last will and testament was void because he was "of unsound mind" when he made it. The court stressed that it was expressing no opinion on any other supposed will. The judges and everyone else knew that this appeal was just a way station in the contest over Randolph's estate.[53]

By the time the Court of Appeals announced its decision, the parties to the case were already preparing for a new trial. If the court had upheld the General Court's probate sentence, Bishop Meade's lawyers would have brought a new suit in the chancery courts to overturn Randolph's last will. Virginia statute allowed persons interested in an estate to bring such a challenge anytime within seven years after a will was admitted to probate. Because the Court of Appeals decision set aside the last will, Meade's lawyers instead returned to the General Court to probate the 1821 will in which Randolph freed his slaves.[54]

The General Court trial during July 1836 was wider-ranging than the first trial. Meade's lawyers set out to prove that except during a period of insanity after his return from Russia, Randolph always intended to free his slaves. Frederick Hobson, the representative for St. George Randolph, took the opposite position. He claimed that none of Randolph's wills could be valid because the man had been insane for decades. Henry and Beverley Tucker had planned to take the same line, but they had to trim their position because Elizabeth Bryan's husband insisted on protecting her claim to a larger share in the estate by defending the codicil Randolph made in London. Edward Vernon Sparhawk once again reported the case for the newspapers.[55]

John Brockenbrough was Meade's key witness. A doctor by training, Brockenbrough was president of the Bank of Virginia and one of Randolph's closest friends. Yet Brockenbrough had his own doubts about the wisdom of manumission, and what he told the court about Randolph's views did not unambiguously support Meade's case. In the early years of his friendship with Randolph, Brockenbrough testified, "I frequently heard him say no man should own his slaves." After he had seen the deplorable condition of free laborers in Europe, however, Randolph appeared to change his mind about slavery. Although he never expressly told Brockenbrough that he no longer intended to free his own slaves, he talked quite a lot about the relatively better condition of enslaved laborers in Virginia. He said that his brother Richard had been "maddened by the principles of the French Revolution" when he manumitted his share of the family's slaves, and he spoke of "the miserable condition" in which the freedmen lived on the land Richard had given them at Israel Hill.[56]

Benjamin Watkins Leigh appeared as a witness for Hobson. Watkins Leigh was Judge Leigh's older brother, and he had been Randolph's close friend since they were boys. He was a prominent lawyer, one of Virginia's United States senators, and a strikingly handsome and articulate man. He lived in the fashionable Court End of Richmond, just down the street from John Brockenbrough and within sight of the elaborate house his father-in-law John Wickham had built with the fortune he made by pursuing British creditors' claims against men like John Randolph.[57]

The confident eloquence that made Watkins Leigh one of Richmond's best lawyers made him a very compelling witness, and Hobson's lawyers used his testimony to plumb Randolph's quarrels with Nancy Morris and his estrangement from members of the Tucker family. Those things highlighted Randolph's propensity toward irrational antipathies, the evidence of mental alienation most likely to succeed in an American probate case. Randolph had always been irritable, Leigh told the court, and his anger was commonly quite out of proportion to whatever had provoked it. "He was—he seemed sometimes like a man without a skin," especially during his frequent periods of ill health.

But in some important respects, the testimony Watkins Leigh offered was unhelpful to Hobson. Leigh believed that Randolph had been sane, except in rare intervals, until after his return from Russia. He also believed that Randolph had meant to free his slaves. When Randolph spoke against emancipation late in his life, Leigh had predicted that he nevertheless would free his own slaves when he died, and Randolph never denied it. Leigh believed "he would not consent that any other man should be the master of his slaves."[58]

John Randolph's cousin Richard Randolph Jr. had stayed with Randolph at Roanoke during the six weeks before Randolph wrote his 1821 will, and he was the only person to witness it. Richard testified that Randolph had been genuinely concerned about what would happen to his slaves when he died. "I believe he said, that they could not be placed in a better condition than they then enjoyed, and that he would give five hundred pounds to know how they could be kept in as good a condition after his death." While that tended to confirm Randolph's emancipatory intentions, Richard's other recollections of the visit testified to Randolph's irrational antipathies. St. George Tucker's mishandling of Randolph's property during his minority had been "a subject of frequent conversation," Richard recalled, and Randolph "was in the habit of dwelling upon it."[59]

Dr. Thomas Robinson gave the clearest testimony to Randolph's insanity. Robinson had come to know Randolph during the time he practiced medicine in Prince Edward County and Randolph was still living at Bizarre. According to Robinson, Randolph's behavior changed markedly when his widely watched romance with Maria Ward ended. Randolph became sleepless, irascible, and morose. By the time Robinson moved to Petersburg a few years later, he had concluded that Randolph was insane, and when Randolph afterward consulted him in Petersburg, Robinson saw the same symptoms of madness.

Robinson said the most obvious symptoms were "incoherent conversations and other signs of disordered intellect." Randolph would burst unprompted into bitter complaints about St. George Tucker's mismanagement of his patrimony and Beverley Tucker's removal of family slaves to Missouri. He became "hopelessly deranged" on the subject of religion after his conversion experience in 1819, and he would ramble on about visions without ever actually saying whether he had seen one. His behavior was sometimes so bizarre that Robinson considered asking his relatives to seclude him so he would not embarrass himself. Robinson had never heard Randolph talk about emancipating his slaves, although he (like others) remembered Randolph saying that his brother Richard had freed his slaves under the influence of "a madness growing out of the exciting principles of the French revolution."[60]

The General Court's decision came after a whole week of such testimony and another week of oral argument. With only one of the eleven judges dissenting, the court upheld John Randolph's 1821 will and all of the codicils to it. The "most important feature" of the will, proclaimed the first press notices, was the emancipation of a large group of slaves.[61]

Reports of the General Court's decision quickly appeared in William Lloyd Garrison's *Liberator* and other leading antislavery newspapers. The papers reprinted Randolph's entire will, and they recounted a probably apocryphal story about Randolph chasing a slave trader off his property on horseback with drawn pistols. The papers also praised Judge Leigh for his sacrifice on behalf of the slaves' freedom. Although Leigh had renounced a legacy worth $150,000 so that he could testify, they said, the fine example of his "disinterested conduct" represented a much "more valuable inheritance to his descendants."[62]

It took the Court of Appeals a year to resolve appeals from the General Court's decision. All of Randolph's heirs had objected to the decision, and the arguments dragged on from early November into early December. The lawyers' speeches "are very much in detail," groused Henry Tucker as he listened from the sidelines. Walter Jones's argument for Meade "has already occupied 3 days. When he will finish 'who knows save heaven'? He does not I am sure." Soon after the lawyers did finish, the Court of Appeals lost its quorum.

Henry Tucker and Judge Francis Brooke had disqualified themselves from the outset because Tucker had a direct interest in the case and Brooke's young nephew Henry Laurens Brooke had just married Tucker's daughter Virginia. When a third judge fell mortally ill, that left only two judges on the case. Since the court needed at least three to proceed, it referred the case to a special court made up of the two remaining judges and a judge appointed from the General Court.[63]

Arguments on the Randolph case resumed before the Special Court of Appeals the following June, and again they took nearly a month. Legislators who were already complaining about long delays in the appeals court pointed to the time spent on the Randolph case as a clear demonstration of the need for judicial reform. Young St. George Coalter lost all patience as he listened to Walter Jones ramble on again, and he impetuously concluded there was absolutely nothing in anything Jones had to say. The wiser and more dispassionate Henry Tucker made a different assessment. He had no doubt, he wrote to Beverley, that the court was going to turn the slaves loose—and he pitied the poor wretch who would have to deal with the estate in that case.[64]

"By this Will all [Randolph's] slaves are liberated," proclaimed an early newspaper report on the special court's decision a few days later, and papers around the United States loudly applauded the news. Garrison's *Liberator* celebrated John Randolph for "this noble devise." If ever there was such a thing as a generous, high-minded slaveholder, wrote Garrison, Randolph probably was it. The *Liberator* also published a letter from a Quaker in upstate New York praising Judge Leigh for his disinterestedness. But amid all of the press celebrations, at least one Virginia newspaper was willing to state the obvious. "We do not suppose that this will be a final decision," it said, because the law gave Randolph's heirs the means to challenge his will in another court.[65]

Chapter 9

JOHN WHITE'S ROANOKE

Tobacco field in southern Virginia,
photograph by Bryan Pollard, 2022

JOHN WHITE BECAME THE FACE OF ROANOKE AFTER JOHN
Randolph died. For years, White had appeared with a smile to
greet Randolph's visitors as they emerged from the dense Southside forest surrounding his houses. Now he played host to the pil-
grims who came to see this strange place where Randolph had lived.
One of the overseers or the steward Wyatt Cardwell might also ride
over with travelers who had written ahead. Yet when visitors later
recorded what they saw on their pilgrimage to Roanoke, what they
remembered were the things White had shown them, and when they

told evocative stories about Randolph's life there, they were repeating what White had said.[1]

The main road going south passed by the gate into the Middle Quarter where Randolph's two houses stood, and travelers of all kinds used it. White men on horseback and farm wagons driven by enslaved laborers were the most common sight. Poor women in threadbare dresses and barefoot slaves on short errands walked. There were occasional two-wheeled gigs, and sometimes a passing carriage lifted a light cloud of dust. The stagecoach came that way too, carrying mail and strangers who did not realize they were passing Randolph's gate and his cropland in the river bottom below. A Washington journalist encountered Randolph quite by accident when her stage happened to pass as he was riding out on "a large pampered white horse." Slave coffles also walked that way on their forced march to markets in the cotton states. The men came shackled together in pairs on a long chain with the women behind them. "Some wuz singin' and some wuz cryin'," recalled a woman who saw them pass when she was a girl. "Some hed dey chillun and some didn't."[2]

Randolph's houses stood a mile off the road at the end of an overgrown lane through the forest. The first thing the visitors noticed when they came within sight of them was the undergrowth. Both buildings appeared to have been set down in untamed woodland. The vines, weeds, and scrub bushes grew right up to the doors as though the place had never been inhabited. There were a few patches of pounded earth around the outbuildings in the background, but nothing else broke the underbrush and no harsh light pierced the shadows cast by overhanging branches.

John White explained that Randolph had never suffered anything in the forest to be cut. While Randolph was away in Europe one summer, White and his father Essex had pruned the limb of an oak tree that was growing toward one of the windows. On his return, Randolph wanted to know why they had done such a thing. Because the swaying of the limb in the next storm could break the window, Essex told him. Then why, Randolph asked, did you not move the house?[3]

White left a strong impression on the visitors who retold such stories because he had presence. There was nothing distinctive about White's physical appearance. From what we can tell, he was a short man in his midfifties with a dark complexion, a high forehead, and hair that was beginning to turn gray. But White's manner and intelligence were arresting. He was, as a younger man put it many years later, "a very smooth kind of a fellow." White had been a favored household servant all his life. He knew how to engage people and put them at ease. His trips to Philadelphia, New York, London, and Saint Petersburg had shown him far more of the world than most white or Black Virginians ever saw, and he understood a good deal about how it worked. Through tough experience, White had found his place in that world—something many men never accomplish—and his bearing expressed that hard-won sense of himself.[4]

When White took visitors through Randolph's houses, he made certain that they saw what they were expecting to see. They went away believing that everything at Roanoke was just the way Randolph had left it on the day he and White set off on their last trip to Philadelphia. There were books everywhere, shotguns standing in corners, papers still lying on Randolph's desk. The gaming equipment piled on a table by the wall looked as though it had just been cleared from the center table. Decanters nearby sat ready for use. The visitors' accounts never mentioned that Beverley Tucker had lived there for a year after Randolph died. They said nothing about the riffling of Randolph's papers in search of another will.

Randolph's grave was an essential part of the pilgrimage. It lay beneath a tall pine tree near the frame house. At the head and foot stood the rough stones Randolph asked White to put there. Randolph had found the stones on the plantation many years earlier and brought them to the house for this purpose, White told visitors. He had used them as outdoor washstands while he lived. White did not say that some in Randolph's family thought the grave should be grander. (Elizabeth and Randolph Bryan envisioned a mound 60 feet in diameter and 20 to 30 feet high with a 12-foot stone monument on top. It would have dwarfed every building on the plantation. "I do not like the idea," Beverley Tucker had told them, "and am indisposed to interfere with [my brother's] own characteristic fancy. . . . He was unlike all other men, in life and in death, and common place honours are unappropriate to him.")[5]

White did not take visitors to the outbuildings, of course. Few had any interest in slave quarters or a blacksmith's shop. Some of them had heard that Randolph kept a preaching barn in the back. Whether it was just the shop or one of the other log buildings did not much matter to them. The relevant thing was that Randolph had controlled his slaves' religious meetings and required them to listen to white preachers, just as state law later came to require. Some visitors would have heard about all of that from the preachers. (One preacher came away shocked by the pious exegesis Randolph tried to put on his Sunday morning pronouncement that the hog-stealing Phil was a "damned rascal." It never occurred to the preacher that the enslaved congregation was probably more offended by his own harping on some ancient scriptures that enjoined slaves to obedience.)[6]

Some visitors went to see Randolph's deer park, an affectation in a thickly forested country full of deer that were doing plenty of crop damage. Whatever slave housing they saw along their way found no place in the accounts of their visits. The slave houses must have looked like the ones on other Southside plantations. That means they varied in structure and quality.[7]

A few favored slaves got decent quarters and cast off furniture. Not long before he died, Randolph complained that his foreman Billy's two-room cabin was about as good as Randolph's own log house. Billy even had a shed porch like Randolph's, although Billy used his to shelter hogs and a farm cart. Billy's furnishings included two beds and eight good blankets for a family of five and a pot big enough to boil a ham. He had a set of steel fire tools (which briefly had been fashionable thirty years earlier) that looked finer than the damaged iron tools Randolph despised in the taverns where he had to stop on his way to Washington.[8]

Others enslaved at Roanoke lived in far rougher places. A family or a group of singles got a cell measuring 12 by 12 or 12 by 16 feet that they had to furnish with whatever they could nail together. Many of them slept on the floor. Their cell was usually in a stand-alone or double-pen building put up near the part of the plantation where they worked. The oldest ones were just log shelters with hard dirt floors, mud-lined wooden chimneys, and a window with a plank shutter hung on rusting hinges. Some of the newer ones had simple timber framing, although the sills moldered on the ground and the floors were still dirt. A few stood on fieldstone pilings, and they had a rock or brick chimney and a rough plank floor. They might even have finished interior walls, but the wind that blew under the floor in winter could make them cold.[9]

Charlotte County was colder during the winters of the early nineteenth century than it is today, and the men, women, and children at Roanoke struggled to stay warm through the long dark nights. The fireplace in each cell was small, and most of the heat went up the chimney with the smoke. Randolph had given them essential woolen clothing and blankets each year as Christmas presents, in a charade practiced throughout the South until slavery ended. Women got shifts, men shirts and trousers, and both received shoes and short jackets. Occasionally, they got a hat. The clothes were made from the hard wool of old sheep, and once constant daily wearing compacted it, the coarse fabric held about as much chill as it turned away.[10]

In the will that freed them, Randolph provided annual suits of clothes for John White, his parents, and the other household slaves whom Randolph hoped could remain in Virginia. He also gave them a food allowance that he thought would make them "quite comfortable." It was enough for a daily ration of 1 pound of cornmeal, ¼ pound of pork, 2 tablespoons of brown sugar, and a tablespoon of coffee. The abolitionist press asked readers to imagine what this special arrangement for a few favorite servants said about the lot of ordinary field hands. Like those enslaved elsewhere, the slaves at Roanoke needed to keep a garden for vegetables, raise some chickens for eggs and meat, and forage for small game. When they stole hogs, hams, or other provisions, it was because they were hungry. "'Cose we knowed it was wrong to steal," a Virginian born in slavery told his Black interviewers many decades later, but slaves "had to steal to git somepin' to eat. I know I did."[11]

Agricultural work kept the enslaved warmer in daytime than they were at night, and the winter months were filled with plenty of hard labor. Once the tobacco was cured, stripped, and prized into casings, the corn had to be shelled, the remaining wheat threshed and winnowed, and the hogs butchered. The cattle needed fodder nearly every day. The best horses required constant attention, and the barn work was heavier in wintertime because the horses used more straw. Carting manure to the fields and working the dung into depleted soils was the dirtiest winter work of all. A disproportionate share of it fell to women. Clearing fallowed fields of briars and bushes so that they could be replanted was a snake-ridden, lacerating business. The more fortunate slaves got to work opening new tobacco plots in the forests. Felling trees and clearing underbrush was strenuous, but conditions were cleaner, and traps set to catch the fleeing wildlife could yield some small game for the pot. Fires stoked to burn the wood into potassium-rich ashes for fertilizer gave off welcome heat.[12]

Most white visitors to Roanoke saw more pleasant scenes because they came on nice days in spring and autumn. The spreading forest turned an idyllic green in early springtime, when white dogwood and pink redbud blossoms twinkled through the trees. Fresh pastures looked clean, and horses just released from winter confinement were not yet much troubled by flies. Although setting out the tobacco seedlings was backbreaking labor, their spicy aroma was pleasant and the task looked tidy from a distance. Visitors hardly noticed that the men overseeing the work carried lashes. By autumn, the tobacco had grown a bit weedy despite repeated hoeing, and some of the horses'

backs were welted with grubs. (Radical, the steed on whom Randolph
would have ridden down Nat Turner's rebels, died from grubs the
winter after Randolph's burial.) Yet no one mentioned those things
because they—like the lash—were so commonplace. What visitors
looked for as the countryside ripened were the size and color of the
tobacco leaves, the number of ears on the cornstalks, and the vigor of
the foals that had survived the summer.[13]

A visitor might have remarked on the use of the lash at Roanoke
if he thought it was being abused, although even men reared in the
North could be rather casual about such things. To a young Presbyterian minister from New Jersey, John Randolph's assault on Juba at an
1828 electoral rally in Charlotte Courthouse was just part of the scene.
"Mr. Randolph attended the assemblage," he told a friend, "dressed in
a coat of Virginia homespun, and leather breeches, whipped his servant in the public court-yard, and uttered some oracular predictions."
The way Randolph's slaves remembered their whippings was different. Freedom, Clem Clay testified many decades later, meant freedom
from "cow-hiding on the back. . . . I got some myself; I ought to know
something about it."[14]

• • • •

JOHN WHITE DEALT with visitors of all kinds at Roanoke. An aspir-
ing teenage journalist from Massachusetts named Ben Poore came
with Wyatt Cardwell in the spring of 1835. He wanted to see what
horses remained in Randolph's stud after the successful reduction sale
of the previous summer, and his report on the visit shows he believed
Cardwell's account of good stewardship. Poore said Cardwell had continued Randolph's practice of giving the slaves all of the corn, wheat,
beef, and pork raised on the place. "I will venture to say," he wrote in
what sounds like an echo of Cardwell's bluster, "that if certain offi-
cious '*brother Yankees*' succeed in their attempts so to construct his
will as to set them at liberty, every *soul*, before they enjoy freedom one
year, will wish themselves back." The young man's report concluded
with a vivid description of the places John White had shown him. It

was from those passages that he would create a fuller account fifty years later when he had become the *Boston Journal*'s famous Washington correspondent Perley Poore.[15]

Another teenager named Eliza Lavalette Barksdale came the following year on what her diary records as the 32nd of August. She was on a pleasure outing with friends from nearby Rough Creek. One of the party rode ahead to announce their arrival and ask White to chain up the dogs. Barksdale walked through Randolph's houses with some young beaux she emphatically claimed as her own exclusive property. Her knowledgeable eye caught details about Randolph's furnishings, right down to the fading satin on his sofas, the calico covers tied over his hair-bottomed chairs, and the summer rugs woven of rice straw. One of the dogs shed its chain when she was leaving the frame house, and Barksdale stepped on the hem of her dress as she scrambled back through the glassed doors. Although the deer park had the highest fence she had ever seen, all but three of the deer had jumped out.[16]

What did John White make of Poore, Barksdale, and the curious travelers who just dropped in because they had heard the place was not far off the main road? Although "we have irretrievably lost the thoughts, desires, fears, and perspectives of many whose enslavement shaped every aspect of their lives," White is not a complete cipher. The visitors and many others wrote about White throughout his life. His self-presentation affected their perceptions of John Randolph, and the decision White later would make about how to exercise his freedom reveals something about his personality. That the men and women enslaved with him liked White despite his favored position suggests that he was a man of perception and tact. While he must remain more impenetrable than some other men, we can imagine that White left an impression on visitors to Roanoke because he was quick to see who they were and wise enough to know what they needed.[17]

Tact was important at Roanoke in the years after John Randolph died. No one knew what would happen to the plantation and those who lived there, and everyone expected it would take a long time to find out. In the meantime, almost everything was unsettled. After the Tucker family tried to shoulder him aside, Judge Leigh vowed he would have nothing to do with the place until the courts established Randolph's will. That left the Tucker family as heirs in possession, although none of them ever qualified as administrator. Wyatt Cardwell continued with day-to-day oversight even though neither Leigh nor the Tuckers had complete confidence in him. By the time Leigh finally qualified as executor in December 1837 (at the first session of the General Court after the appeals court upheld Randolph's will), Randolph had been dead for more than four years.[18]

The uncertainty that haunted slaves after a slaveholder's death is a trope that can overshadow the complexity of particular situations. Slavery in one place was not like slavery in another, and the situation at Roanoke was out of the ordinary. Randolph left no wife or children, he had replaced his longtime steward Leigh with the upstart Cardwell, and he had run off his old overseers. Although Beverley Tucker lived on the place for the first season after Randolph died, Randolph's heirs were never more than occasional visitors after that. While courts in Richmond considered whether the slaves could go free, the speculative boom in the cotton states raised slave prices in Virginia more than 60 percent and drew thousands of Black Virginians into the slave markets. Randolph's slaves had every reason to think they were just as likely to be sold as freed. Certainly, no one took time to assure them otherwise, and their daily lives were clouded by the near certainty that families would be torn apart when some of them were sent to work elsewhere.[19]

Roanoke was overstocked. Wyatt Cardwell said so, and John Marshall and Randolph Bryan agreed. John Randolph had lost his grip on plantation management toward the end. Most of the young horses remained unsold, too many of them not even gelded. And although Randolph had kept buying more land as his slave population increased, there were too many slaves as well.[20]

The enslaved population on the plantation was pushing toward 300, and about 150 of them were fit for hard labor. Preparing the excess horses for sale would provide additional employment for the

ones qualified to do it. Some of the others could be put to work opening new fields for expanded tobacco production, a plan that seemed
attractive when tobacco prices rose in the mid-1830s and then became
necessary to cover expenses when prices plunged after the panic of
1837. The rest would have to go elsewhere, and since the estate could
not sell them until the courts resolved the dispute over Randolph's
will, they would have to be hired out.[21]

Hired slaves left each January for at least the next year. Wyatt
Cardwell managed to hire out many of them to planters in Charlotte
and neighboring counties, so they probably went on foot carrying
small bundles of clothing behind the horses of the white men sent
to collect them. Although proximity did not necessarily mean they
could come home for visits, it gave Cardwell more confidence that
they would not be misused. As the population of working-age slaves
at Roanoke increased, however, Cardwell probably had to march
some of the surplus slaves to the hiring markets at nearby courthouse
towns and watch them loaded onto their hirers' farm wagons to go
farther afield.[22]

White men who hired slaves tended to treat them more carelessly
than they would have treated their own property. A hire contract
might specify clothing, working conditions, and safe discipline, but
the hired slave had no effective way to complain if the hirer ignored
it. The slaveholder or his steward might never hear of malnutrition
and misuse until the slave ran away or returned home with injuries.[23]

Courts were reluctant to let a slaveholder recover damages for injuries inflicted by slave hirers even though the slaveholder had a right
to demand them, and the criminal law put scarcely any limit on what
the temporary master could do. One of the most notorious decisions
in the American law of slavery involves the prosecution of a man for
shooting an enslaved woman he had hired. The man had been beating her for some small offense, and when she managed to get away
from him, he shot her in the back. A North Carolina jury found him
guilty of criminal assault and battery, but the state's supreme court
released him. Even a hirer must have "uncontrolled authority" over

the slave's body, declared the court. "The power of the master must be absolute, to render the submission of the slave perfect." Virginia's highest criminal court never used such frank language, although it came to the same result.[24]

Enslaved workers were more likely to flee when their enslaver died, especially when the unsettled state of his affairs created new risks for them or their families. Slaves who were hired out and separated from their friends and families had even more reason to run, and they sometimes found opportunities to blend into the free Black communities that had grown up in cities such as Richmond, where urban households, livery stables, workshops, and factories created a steady demand for menial labor. Yet for the slaves in Randolph's estate, flight must have presented greater risks than those they faced at home.[25]

A man like John White had some chance of escaping. He knew how to travel on his own, he could find excuses for appearing at least as far north as Fredericksburg, where John Coalter lived, and the white population was likely to perceive him as a reliable fellow. Even White, however, had been taken up and jailed when he absconded toward Washington years earlier.[26]

Men and women who had never left southern Virginia were far less likely to make it across Mason and Dixon's line or even to camouflage themselves among free Blacks in the cities. And slaves caught running away frequently dropped into the maw of the domestic slave trade and disappeared into harsher slavery in the cotton states. Even if slaves managed to get to a free state, their prospects there were uncertain. They would have to live without their friends and families in a strange country where, everyone said, they were not welcome. Unless they went all the way to Canada, they could never escape the risk of being discovered, seized, and returned to slavery.[27]

While frustration over unfulfilled promises of manumission sometimes prompted slaves to risk leaving, the tantalizing possibility of safer, legal freedom could encourage slaves to stay. The slaves at Roanoke apparently stayed. The papers left by Randolph's heirs and administrators mention no escapes, and the number of slaves taxed to

Randolph's estate each year remained relatively stable until it began to rise as the number of children reaching taxable age exceeded the number of taxable slaves who died. Although Randolph's slaves dissembled to whites about their expectations as custom required them to do, both they and Randolph's heirs knew that their prospect for freedom had risen significantly when the General Court upheld the will that emancipated them. Henry Tucker was realistic about it. "The negroes are generally well, and express themselves anxious to get a master," he reported to his brother after a quick trip to Roanoke in 1837. "This I am sure they will not have speedily if they ever have which I much doubt."[28]

Household slaves could find it especially difficult to wait for freedom because the slaveholder's death profoundly changed their daily lives, especially when it left no other white person in the household. Men and women with little past experience of agricultural labor could find themselves sent to the fields. A good manager tried to minimize their discontent by giving them more responsible jobs. Juba, for example, was put in charge of a stallion named Wildfire, and Cardwell sent them out to other parts of the state during the first several breeding seasons after Randolph died.[29]

An abolitionist newspaper in New York claimed that Juba was in Canada a few years later, although the endorsements on letters he carried for Cardwell and the Tucker family show he was still in Virginia. Juba's ticket off the plantation was an invitation to work for Beverley Tucker in Williamsburg. Beverley had bought his childhood home from his father's estate after he began teaching at William and Mary. His household now teemed with young children and law students, and he and his wife needed more help. Cardwell said he would be glad to send Juba, his family, and the cook Queen down to Beverley. Juba "will be better off," Cardwell wrote, "and it will be great relief to me. . . . He will occasionally get drunk and get in difficulty with the Overseer and require my interference to get him out of the scrape." When the time came to leave for Williamsburg, however, Juba and the others refused to go.[30]

Perhaps the example of the free Black community at Israel Hill helped the enslaved community at Roanoke hold together. It had been thirty years since the slaves emancipated by John Randolph's brother Richard moved to Israel Hill, but the freedmen there were still in touch with friends and cousins who remained enslaved at Roanoke 40 miles away. Israel Hill was just outside the market town of Farmville, so slaves from Roanoke who ran errands or hauled tobacco to the warehouses there could stop at Israel Hill to visit even though their overseers tried to discourage it. Those visitors caught glimpses of what life could be like when a community gains freedom together.[31]

Although white newspaper writers continually disparaged the settlement at Israel Hill as a burden on its white neighbors, a celebrated study by historian Melvin Patrick Ely shows that the Hill's residents had overcome the odds that hostile whites stacked against them. They grew grain and tobacco, built comfortable houses, and established themselves as carpenters, masons, vegetable farmers, midwives, wagoners, and boatmen. They lent each other savings and successfully sued their white neighbors for unpaid debts. A resident named Phil White was able to turn a profit on lots in Farmville at the same time that one of Israel Hill's most vocal white critics was going broke.[32]

The sense of community at Israel Hill must have been important to slaves at Roanoke who lived in hope of their own group emancipation. Several generations of the same families lived on the Hill, bound together by long acquaintance and intermarriage. While they sometimes quarreled as kith and kin do, they mainly supported each other. Flight from slavery at Roanoke would mean estrangement, the loss of extended family and old friends. For men and women who grew up in a community that had lived together on the Randolph plantations for almost a century, that prospect must have been chilling.[33]

• • • •

WYATT CARDWELL ASSURED Randolph's heirs that he was making good profits for them at Roanoke. Last year's crop was the best in many years, he wrote to Beverley Tucker as the slaves finished setting out tobacco seedlings in 1835. He had just sent 120 hogsheads (about 168,000 pounds) of good quality tobacco to market, and he had more than enough grain to feed the horses and the slaves through the next harvest. Three years later, he pronounced his crop "the largest we have ever made." Cardwell used profits from crop sales to give the heirs substantial cash distributions in proportion to the shares they would take if Randolph had died intestate.[34]

Although favorable weather no doubt accounted for a good part of Cardwell's success, the rest of it must have come from expanding production and working the slaves harder. Randolph had expected his slaves to work "constantly, but moderately." Like other planters who knew that an exhausted workforce would become unhealthy, Randolph sometimes reduced the size of the crop he expected his overseers to produce so they would not overwork his slaves in order to increase their own remuneration. His neighbors believed that until he returned from Russia, Randolph's demands on his slaves had been reasonable.[35]

Charlotte County planters thought that an efficient field hand should work 2 to 3 acres of tobacco in addition to sharing in the production of enough corn and grain to feed the slaves, horses, and livestock on the plantation. That meant planters expected every field laborer to plant ten to fifteen thousand seedlings each spring and turn them into 1,500 to 2,000 pounds of tobacco.[36]

Whether the men and women enslaved at Roanoke hit that mark after Randolph's death is difficult to know. Cardwell left no accurate count of how many slaves he kept on the plantation each year. Surviving farm accounts and letters suggest, however, that the slaves at Roanoke did work to the mark. They also had to take care of the estate's large horse breeding business, which required more labor than the ordinary livestock operations on a typical plantation. The slaves at Roanoke therefore must have been working harder than most other slaves in the area.[37]

Cardwell remained steward at Roanoke after the courts upheld Randolph's 1821 will and Judge Leigh qualified as executor, but the management of Randolph's estate began to change. The codicil Randolph signed in London left Bushy Forest to Henry Tucker and the Lower Quarter to Elizabeth Bryan. With agreement from the other heirs, Henry Tucker sold Bushy Forest and kept the proceeds for himself pending final settlement of the estate. Randolph Bryan took possession of the Lower Quarter and began running it for his wife's separate account. Bryan hired slaves from the estate to work his wife's property, but the sale of Bushy Forest reduced the estate's need for labor and pushed more of the Roanoke slaves onto the hire market.[38]

Judge Leigh told Cardwell not to make distributions to Randolph's heirs without first accounting to the estate for the hire value of the slave labor he was using to make crops. While a dead man's real property passed directly to his heirs or those named in his will, his slaves and other personal property belonged to his estate until it was settled. Randolph's estate therefore had claims against the heirs for the use of its slaves to raise crops on their land. Leigh aimed to establish a credit for the value of those claims so that he could draw on it to satisfy the estate's liabilities, adjust accounts between the white heirs, and resettle the slaves outside Virginia. Leigh made the heirs sign bonds promising to refund any distributions in excess of their final shares.[39]

The financial arrangements left everyone feeling uncomfortable because no one's credit was sure. The country hit hard times after the panic of 1837. Crop prices collapsed, cash grew scarce, and more than a few of the banks failed. The young British writer Charles Dickens could still see the effects when he visited the United States five years later. The Philadelphia bank founded by Stephen Girard had just closed its doors, and work on the magnificent Greek Revival buildings for the college endowed by Girard's will had come to a halt because the state of Pennsylvania defaulted on the bonds in which his estate was invested.[40]

Given the times, the Tucker heirs worried about whether they ultimately could collect money due to the Randolph estate. St. George Randolph was going to get a much smaller share under the will than he had been receiving before the will was established, and his representative Frederick Hobson might struggle to refund the difference. "These are ticklish times [for] speculators such as Hobson," wrote Randolph Bryan. Even John Randolph's longtime tobacco factor had failed to pay the estate for the crop he had just sold, and "when he is found wanting what may not we fear from other men." The heirs also worried about the money passing through Cardwell's and Leigh's hands. It was common practice for a fiduciary to comingle the money he held for others with his own funds, and although he was liable for that amount to the full extent of his own assets, the heirs were unavoidably exposed to the fiduciary's credit.[41]

Randolph's nephew St. George Coalter died from tuberculosis shortly after his thirtieth birthday in the summer of 1839, leaving his wife and five young children in dire need of money. Beverley Tucker complained to his brother that Judge Leigh was holding back money that he should have distributed to them. Henry Tucker, who regularly saw Leigh in the courts, knew him better than that. "You do Leigh injustice," he told Beverley. "He has no reserves I am sure," and rather than mingling money as executors typically did, he "keeps the money of the estate in Bank separate from his own."[42]

The irrepressible Elizabeth Bryan had her own views about how the family ought to handle the Randolph estate's affairs. When Beverley Tucker took his complaint about Cardwell's money management to her husband, she responded with her usual candor. "Now it seems very strange to me," she told her uncle, "that these things should be so loosely attended to." Because Cardwell was obviously too busy to keep good accounts, it was up to the heirs to find someone else to keep them. Her uncles as the principal heirs should attend to that, she told him, instead of complaining to her husband. Sloppiness would only lead to "trouble & even bitterness" when they finally settled the estate. "So much for *Bet's* say," she concluded, "& you know I always will have my say."[43]

The Tucker heirs almost never mentioned Randolph's slaves in the many letters they exchanged about the management of his estate. They sometimes complained that Cardwell kept more slaves on the plantation than he needed, and they renegotiated the amount they paid to Leigh for slave hire each year. But they were entirely indifferent to the slaves themselves. None of their letters said a word about the slaves' freedom. None acknowledged the fears and uncertainties that the slaves must have suffered while the heirs squabbled over Randolph's will. None expressed relief that there had been no unrest of the sort enslavers expected when slaves lived in limbo for years.[44]

The widespread labor strikes that erupted in England during the summer of 1842 did grab the Tucker family's attention because they seemed to confirm the relative merits of a slave labor system. Half a million poor miners and mill hands across the Midlands had refused to work, marched to protest reductions in their wages, and clashed with the troops sent to suppress them. The Tuckers, like other American slaveholders, took the strikers' violent discontent as further proof that they were worse off than American slaves. Some slaveholders probably thought the strikes were fair comeuppance for British self-righteousness over the final abolition of West Indian slavery four years earlier. Elizabeth Bryan expressed sympathy for the strikers when she forwarded the latest English newspapers to Beverley Tucker. "It would be hard to starve in the midst of a nobility rolling in superfluous wealth," she wrote, "& the whole system must be *wrong* where such a thing is possible. How much more *free*, enlightened and happy are our slaves."[45]

Chapter 10

A DECADE IN CHANCERY

Petersburg Courthouse, stereographic negative, c. 1865

T HROUGH THE WAVY OLD GLASS IN THE FRONT WINDOWS of his house in Williamsburg, Beverley Tucker could look across the market green to the back of the James City County Courthouse. It was a moldering one-story brick structure with tall multipaned windows and the kind of hipped roof and cupola that had been standard on Georgian public buildings in the American colonies. The clerk's office sat crumbling beside it. Both buildings had decayed along with the rest of the city after Virginia moved its capital to Richmond during the Revolution, although they and some of the other buildings at the center of town still clung to a faded respectability.[1]

Tucker's rambling old frame house on the edge of the green was one of them. His father St. George Tucker had bought the house and its large garden when he moved to Williamsburg after John Randolph's mother died, and he gradually enlarged it to make room for his children, stepchildren, tutors, slaves, and the law students he taught there when he was home from court. Beverley Tucker and his young family had moved into the place a few years after he took his father's chair as professor of law at what everyone now called William and Mary College.[2]

William and Mary became the principal support of the town after the seat of government moved. Its glory days as the finest college in the state had passed, and it now drew most of its students from eastern Virginia. The faculty and the students nevertheless created a steady local market for housing, food, and services. Its professors were well-respected members of a small community of well-to-do landowners, professionals, and merchants who gave the rundown town an air of sophisticated repose. Renewed interest in the treatment of madness had more recently revived a large public asylum on the edge of town. Established some years before the Revolution, the asylum was the first hospital dedicated to the treatment of madness in the British American colonies, and its revival brought important new commercial opportunities to some of the ordinary townspeople.[3]

Beverley Tucker's life in Williamsburg was a telling variation on his father's. St. George Tucker had been a judge who taught law and ultimately gave up teaching to spend full time on the bench. Beverley was a committed teacher and fluent writer whose need for attention made him anything but judicious. His father had tried to warn white Virginians that they must gradually abolish slavery if they wanted their state to thrive. Beverley stridently defended slavery to anyone who would listen. His colleagues on the college faculty included other defenders of slavery—Thomas Roderick Dew became the most infamous because he wrote a long essay against abolition—but few went as far as Beverley Tucker.[4]

Williamsburg's "piquant air of decline" made Beverley positively giddy. It filled him with nostalgic longing for Virginia as he imagined it had been when the old gentry dominated its politics and society, and that longing gave emotional resonance to his belief that challenges to slavery were existential threats to what still remained from that past. Long before others took secession seriously, Beverley became a gadfly determined to prod white Virginians out of their complacent belief that slavery could survive if the slave states remained in the Union. He described Northerners as mercenary vulgarians of specious piety, and his scholarly commitment to states' rights and the compact theory of government quickly degenerated into political activism.[5]

Abel Parker Upshur was the judge who presided when the circuit superior court came to James City County each spring and autumn, and he was one of Beverley Tucker's closest friends. Upshur had grown up at his family's plantation on the Eastern Shore of Virginia, made his mark as a young lawyer in Richmond, and then moved back home to take the bench about ten years earlier. He and Tucker regularly exchanged letters, and Upshur sometimes stayed at Tucker's house when he held court in Williamsburg.[6]

The two men shared similar views on slavery and states' rights. Upshur grew up believing that slavery would wither away if abolitionists just had the patience to leave it alone, but Nat Turner's rebellion destroyed his sense of complacency. In the wake of the uprising, Upshur's court charged forty-two free Blacks on the Eastern Shore with remaining in Virginia illegally. Upshur eventually reenslaved twelve of them and at least two more women in the county west of Williamsburg, and he became an outspoken opponent of all proposals for emancipation. Upshur insisted that slavery was the best possible way to keep order in a biracial society and a sensible way to prevent otherwise inevitable conflicts between capital and labor.[7]

Upshur was not a secessionist, although he had given Beverley Tucker's *Partisan Leader* the favorable review in the *Southern Liter-*

ary Messenger that prompted Henry Tucker to cancel his subscription. Upshur did share Beverley's strong objections to the centralizing theories of government set out in Justice Joseph Story's popular new treatise on American constitutional law, and Beverley knew Upshur was writing a long scholarly essay to refute them. Upshur also backed the territorial expansion of slavery, and six years later when he became secretary of state in the administration of his good friend John Tyler, he would push aggressively for the American annexation of Texas.[8]

By the time the Court of Appeals upheld the will in which John Randolph freed his slaves, Beverley Tucker had been waiting more than four years to challenge it. He and his nephew St. George Coalter were the only members of the Tucker family who got nothing under any of Randolph's wills. The last will would have given Elizabeth Bryan's son substantially everything, and the London codicil to the earlier will, which the Court of Appeals had just upheld, gave Henry Tucker and Elizabeth Bryan working plantations worth substantially more than what they would receive in intestacy. Although the family originally agreed that all of them would cooperate to pursue an intestacy, it had always seemed clear to Beverley that he eventually would have to bring a suit to protect his own interests.[9]

Virginia law made it easy for Beverley to challenge Randolph's will even after it was admitted to probate. Anyone interested in a dead man's estate who did not participate in the probate case could contest the man's will by filing a suit in chancery. The law allowed such challenges because probate was usually a simple, uncontested procedure. It was designed to let executors and heirs take control of the decedent's property quickly so that they could protect its value. The person presenting a will for probate did not even have to notify other interested parties, so a chancery suit was often an heir's first opportunity to contest a will that had disappointed him.[10]

Chancery was an additional legal system that emerged in late medieval England when private individuals began turning to the king's chancellor for relief they could not get in other courts. By the middle of the nineteenth century, however, chancery had acquired a bad reputation. The English chancery's willingness to hear everybody and rectify everything led to complex procedures, high costs, and long delays. Although chancery courts in America experienced some of the same problems, they were usually more adept because their caseloads were lighter and their cases were simpler. In the same year when Charles Dickens's *Bleak House* sparked outrage over the costs and delays that consumed entire estates in the English chancery, a Virginia-born lawyer turned humorist thought American readers would simply chuckle when he wrote that a planter's property was melting away "like an estate in chancery under the gradual thaw of expenses."[11]

When John Randolph died, Virginia no longer had separate chancery courts. Chancery suits went to the circuit superior courts, where the judges dealt with them using the special rules developed in chancery. Although there was generally no jury in chancery, Virginia law did require one in suits that challenged a will. Wills could take land away from the heirs at law otherwise entitled to it, and landowners had a long-established right to defend their title before a jury of their peers. The judge had to accept the jury's verdict on the validity of a will unless he found grounds to order a new trial.[12]

Beverley Tucker had begun preparing for a chancery suit while Randolph's will was still on appeal, and after the appeals court upheld the will, he set to work in earnest. St. George Coalter agreed to join in the suit, Henry Tucker assured Beverley he would not oppose it, and Henry's new son-in-law—the young Richmond lawyer Henry Laurens Brooke—agreed to represent Beverley.[13]

Beverley was anxious to file suit as soon as Judge Leigh qualified as Randolph's executor. Once qualified, Leigh got full control of Randolph's personal property. The estate had few debts, so nothing except a chancery suit could prevent Leigh from freeing Randolph's slaves under the terms of his will and sending them out of the state.[14]

The Randolph estate held over three hundred men, women, and children in bondage, at least fifty more than there had been when Randolph died. The market value of slaves had risen on account of the insatiable appetite for enslaved labor in the new cotton states. And although the financial panic that began earlier that year was denting prices, the average price for a slave in Virginia was still more than $500. So the slaves in Randolph's estate were worth about $150,000, which was 60 to 100 percent more than they had been worth when the newspapers were dickering over the value of the estate four years earlier. Land in southern Virginia had not appreciated, so the slaves represented a larger part of the estate than ever, perhaps nearly half of it. Once the slaves went to a free state, Randolph's heirs would have no real hope of recovering them.[15]

Leigh qualified as executor in Richmond during the first week of December 1837, and on the following Monday, Beverley Tucker could watch from his front window as Henry Brooke walked across the market green in Williamsburg to file a bill of complaint with the clerk of Judge Upshur's court. The bill sought a fresh start in the Randolph will litigation. It claimed that John Randolph had not been of sound mind when he made any of the wills presented to the General Court. It offered to prove the terms of a lost will by which Randolph had given his heirs the same shares of his property that they would have received in intestacy. And it sought an injunction to stop Judge Leigh from liberating Randolph's slaves.[16]

As the courts back in Richmond prepared to adjourn, Henry Tucker handed Leigh a summons from Upshur's court and asked him to carry it to Halifax County so that the sheriff there could serve it on him when he got home. Although Leigh took the paper politely, Henry thought he would object to it, and he did. He was anxious to have the matter tried as soon as possible, Leigh wrote to Henry, but he had decided to refuse the summons because he thought the court in Williamsburg lacked jurisdiction. Randolph's slaves were *"the real defendants,"* and the case should be tried in a court convenient to them. "I will of course forward the process to the Sheriff of Halifax," Henry assured his brother Beverley, but Leigh's determination to resist trial before Judge Upshur was clear.[17]

Leigh knew Judge Upshur lacked sympathy for free Blacks. He also knew that Upshur and Beverley Tucker were close friends. He believed that was why Upshur had thought it proper not to participate in the General Court trials of Randolph's will. Although Upshur might try to perform his duty honorably in this new chancery case, his inclinations would weigh heavily against upholding a will that freed more than three hundred slaves. While a jury would ultimately decide the case, Upshur could determine what they heard and instruct them how to evaluate it.[18]

Beverley Tucker was just as determined that the case not be heard in Southside Virginia. Even though Judge Leigh's involvement in the case would push it out of Randolph's old district into an adjacent judicial circuit, the freeholders who sat on juries there would be the same sort of men who had reelected Randolph to Congress for decades. They had forgiven his foibles, pardoned his offenses, and consistently believed most of what he told them. If Randolph said he had disinherited St. George Tucker's descendants because Tucker had wronged him, they would take his word for it. If Randolph later decided to favor some of the Tuckers over others, they would not say that was mad. Many people in the Southside knew that Randolph had given Beverley Tucker a generous amount of his property at the time of Beverley's first marriage. Leaving the rest to other members of the family could seem entirely sensible. Although Southside jurors would think that freeing a large group of slaves was eccentric, they knew a few saner men had done it.[19]

Judge Upshur quickly gave Beverley Tucker the injunction he needed to stop Leigh from releasing the slaves, and the case puttered on in Upshur's court for almost two years. While the Randolph heirs took depositions, Leigh had to wait for the parties to file their answers so that he could make a motion to dismiss the case for lack of jurisdiction. St. George Coalter died in the meantime.[20]

By the time Leigh's motion to dismiss got a hearing in November 1839, Beverley Tucker's chancery suit had grown personal. Elizabeth and Randolph Bryan decided to support Leigh rather than Beverley in order to protect Elizabeth's claim to Randolph's Lower Quarter, and although everyone tried to remain on cordial terms,

Beverley and Randolph Bryan began exchanging testy letters. John Robertson—the seasoned lawyer who represented Meade and Key as the slaves' trustees—heightened tensions when he persuaded the parties backing Leigh's motion to argue that Judge Upshur should transfer the case because he was Beverley Tucker's close friend. The argument seemed to imply that Upshur's decision to hear the case in Williamsburg was dishonorable.[21]

That implication apparently rattled Judge Upshur, who wrote an unusually long opinion to justify his denial of Leigh's motion. Upshur began by protesting that judges themselves must dismiss a case if they lack jurisdiction, but having nodded to the rule, he ignored it. He said he was rejecting Leigh's objection to jurisdiction because Leigh had waited too long to raise it, and he insisted that the case would not get a fair hearing in the Southside. "John Randolph filled a large space in the eyes of that community for a long series of years," wrote Upshur. Voters there had long ago decided whether they thought he was sane or not, so a jury trial of that question would inevitably take on "a political character." The prospect for a "speedy, fair, and satisfactory trial" was better in Williamsburg.[22]

A special Court of Appeals gave Upshur's opinion short shrift. It noted that not even one of the defendants resided in Upshur's district, so his court clearly lacked jurisdiction to hear the case. Having given Beverley Tucker an injunction to protect him from immediate harm, Upshur should have transferred the case to the place where harm might occur. That place was Charlotte County, where Randolph's executor could free his slaves from bondage. Because Upshur had decided to hear the matter in his own court instead, the appeals court dismissed the case altogether.[23]

Undaunted by his failure as a plaintiff in chancery, Beverley Tucker tried again as a defendant. He persuaded St. George Coalter's executor to file a chancery complaint in Williamsburg against Beverley and everyone he and St. George Coalter had sued in the first case. Beverley's residence in Williamsburg would have been enough to give the court jurisdiction if Beverley had actually been adverse to the complaint, but since he was not, the ruse seemed obvious.[24]

Judge Leigh's answer emphasized that the real issue in the case was the "freedom of between three and four hundred human beings & their descendants forever," which had to be tried in the place where they lived. The only defendant in Williamsburg, Leigh wrote, was not truly a defendant at all because he and the plaintiff had precisely the same interest in overturning John Randolph's will. Bishop Meade's answer tweaked Judge Upshur's conscience by reminding him that he had once told Meade that he could not properly sit in judgment on Randolph's will because of his relationship with Beverley Tucker.[25]

Those answers embarrassed Beverley Tucker enough to make him drop his guard. In a long rambling response, he conceded that his interest was the same as St. George Coalter's, but he denied that he had colluded with Coalter's executor to bring the suit in Williamsburg. His objective since the day when he first read John Randolph's will, he said, had been to refute the "grave and dishonorable charge" that it made against his father, St. George Tucker. The only way he could do that without calling his dead brother a liar was to prove—what was indeed the fact—that his brother had been insane when he made the will. "If madness is a crime he has much to answer for," wrote Beverley. But honorable men should feel the same compassion for his brother's sad delusions as they felt when they beheld "the ravages of death on the cheek of beauty."[26]

When the suit came on for hearing a few days later, however, it was Beverley Tucker's credibility that looked ravaged. Leigh's lawyers forced all of the parties to admit that the summonses they had received from the court were in Beverley's own handwriting, that Beverley's lawyer was taking depositions in the plaintiff's name, and that Beverley was the only named defendant within the court's jurisdiction. That left Judge Upshur little choice. He declared that it would be improper for him to hear the case, and in May 1841, he transferred it to the circuit superior court in Petersburg.[27]

. . . .

THE BUSTLING CITY of Petersburg was the antithesis of Williamsburg. Although both places had roots in the colonial past, Petersburg had put the past well behind it. The westward shift that left Williamsburg to decline made Petersburg an important entrepôt, and the rebuilding that followed a devastating fire in 1815 gave the place a fresh look. The city sat along the south bank of the swift-moving Appomattox River, just 12 miles above its confluence with the wider James and 25 miles below Richmond. It had always been an important gathering place for agricultural commodities from the Southside, and with the opening of a 60-mile railroad link to the Roanoke River (one of the longest early railroads in the nation), it had begun to draw crops from a swath of counties across southern Virginia and down into North Carolina. Annual exports from Petersburg ran to 5,000 hogsheads of tobacco, 100,000 bushels of wheat, and 50,000 bales of cotton.[28]

Petersburg had also become an important manufacturing center. It sat beside a series of falls in the river, and the water tumbling over them powered six tobacco factories, six flour mills, three cotton plants, two cottonseed mills, and an iron foundry. Although enslaved African American workers made up most of the workforce, the growth of industry had also attracted more free Blacks to Petersburg than to any other city in the South. The city's overall population had grown by 40 percent in the previous decade. Over half of the inhabitants were Black, and about a third of those were free.[29]

Petersburg's free Black families lived in segregated neighborhoods on the fringes of the city. Women headed more than half of these families, and the property they acquired with their labor helped to anchor the Black community. Many of the men found work as skilled blacksmiths, carpenters, and bricklayers, and some of them accumulated enough money to live as comfortably as Petersburg's white artisans. The success of the free Black population made many whites uncomfortable, and a group of white citizens in Petersburg had recently urged the state legislature to appropriate more money to send free Blacks to Africa.[30]

On a rise near the middle of town stood Petersburg's eye-catching new courthouse. Its elegant windowless facade of tan stucco rose two stories from an earthen podium above Sycamore Street. The slender fluted columns of the front portico emphasized the loftiness of the building's design. And to complete the effect, the builders had added an octagonal clock tower with two tiers of columns and a neoclassical figure of Justice on the top.[31]

Just a block away at Sycamore's intersection with Bank Street stood a large stone that made no pretensions to justice. Slave dealers used it to auction off enslaved workers for the city's factories and the cotton fields farther south. The men, women, and children sold there usually came from farms and plantations in the surrounding countryside. "Some 'fused to be sol' lak dat," a Petersburg man remembered eighty years later. "I mean dey cried, Lord! Lord! I done seen dem young'uns fout an' kick lak crazy folks. . . . Den dey'd handcuff 'em and beat 'em unmerciful."[32]

James Gholson had been the circuit judge in Petersburg for less than two months when he received the Randolph will case, but he was a man of experience. Born into an established, slaveholding family in nearby Brunswick County, Gholson had earned undergraduate and graduate degrees at Princeton and then come home to start a law practice. Gholson served two terms in the legislature and a term in Congress, and he was practicing law in Petersburg when a leading lawyer and former circuit judge nominated him to the bench.[33]

Gholson had made a name for himself as a defender of the status quo in the General Assembly's debate over slavery after Nat Turner's rebellion. Reformers led by Jefferson's grandson Thomas Jefferson Randolph proposed a gradual emancipation plan under which children born into slavery after July 4, 1840, would go free at the age of majority unless their enslavers sold them out of state in the meantime. The state would then hire them out to pay for the cost of their removal from Virginia. Gholson thought this plan for uncompensated emancipation amounted to an unthinkable confiscation of private property.[34]

"Will you believe it," he asked the reformers, "when I tell you that [the] great men of the revolution *owned slaves*?" Those men fought the Revolution to defend their rights in slaves and other private property, and when the Virginia Declaration of Rights famously proclaimed that "all men by nature are equally free and independent," it definitely was not talking about slaves. Gholson said he felt "ridiculous" arguing about such things because they were not even debatable. When some future citizen of Virginia learns that the legislature actually did debate uncompensated emancipation in the year 1832, Gholson predicted, he will ask in utter amazement how such men could possibly have been "the sons of their fathers."[35]

Like it or not, Gholson declared, Virginians could not free enslaved children for the simple reason that they could not afford it. "Our slaves constitute the largest portion of our wealth, and by their value, regulate the price of nearly all the property we possess." Slave values depended on continued slave sales into the cotton states, and legislation that raised questions about the marketability of enslaved children born in Virginia would depress the value of slaves, land, and everything else. The inescapable fact was that slaves directly or indirectly accounted for "nearly all our wealth."

There was, however, one subject on which Gholson thought the General Assembly should act: "I allude to the removal of the FREE colored population." Nearly one-tenth of the state's Black residents were free, he said, and they were "the most depraved, dissolute, miserable, and dangerous portion" of its inhabitants. Their presence made slaves discontent. It would take everything the state could afford to spend for the next decade to remove them, and until that was done, what was the point of discussing the emancipation and removal of enslaved children?[36]

Gholson's rhetoric charmed the Virginia public, and historians still treat his speeches as piquant expressions of views that were common among whites in the parts of Virginia with large enslaved populations. But it is important for us to recognize that his opinions on emancipation and colonization were not inconsistent with respect, perhaps even sympathy, for manumission.

A slaveholder's decision to free his own slaves was altogether different from emancipation because it was an exercise of private property rights and (at least according to law) the new freedmen had to leave the state. In the decades following the legislature's debate on emancipation, the Virginia Court of Appeals continued to give a liberal construction to wills manumitting slaves. The judges even showed discomfort with an old precedent in which the court had refused to free children born while their mother was serving out her final years in bondage under the terms of a will that liberated her. The precedent was no more than a literal application of the general rule that slavery follows from the condition of the mother, but the judges grew sensitive to its harshness. The General Assembly reversed the precedent by statute in the late 1840s, and even though legislators and judges in other slave states had begun resisting manumissions decades earlier, it was not until the late 1850s that the Virginia appeals court stopped construing emancipatory wills with a bent toward freedom.[37]

Well-trained Virginia circuit judges therefore had no reason to resist manumissions at the time Randolph's will came before Judge Gholson, and although a statistical analysis of Virginia circuit court decisions remains to be done, case studies suggest they did not. One intriguing study involves a Halifax County case heard by Judge Leigh himself.[38]

Young Philip Vass was in prison for murder when he wrote his will in 1831, and he died there about a year later. His will freed the six slaves he had inherited from his father and set aside $2,000 to buy them 250 acres in North Carolina. Vass's only heirs were his brothers and sisters, and they fell to squabbling about the division of their father's estate. That put Vass's title to the six slaves in question, so his executor did the expedient thing and kept them in bondage until the passage of seven years put both wills beyond challenge. The following year, the five surviving slaves brought suit in Judge Leigh's court for freedom and $2,000. Leigh set them free as the will directed, but the monetary bequest was a problem. North Carolina did not allow free Blacks to settle there, so Vass's heirs claimed that the bequest had failed and the money belonged to them. Although Leigh agreed, the appeals court reversed him. When the four freedmen who were still alive left Virginia years later, their legacy had grown to about $5,000, and they used it to go to Ohio.[39]

Judge Gholson tried to bring order to the Randolph case after it landed in his court. He designated Beverley Tucker as a plaintiff rather than a defendant, in exchange for which the other defendants agreed to accept his court's jurisdiction. He made Henry Brooke the guardian of John Randolph's nephew St. George for purposes of the case. And he pushed the parties to complete their pleadings so the case could proceed.[40]

Novelists and law reformers have given the pleadings practice in nineteenth-century Anglo-American courts a bad name. They described legal pleadings as arcane traps for unwary litigants and causes of expensive delay, and *Bleak House* painted an enduring picture of the resulting human suffering. Although there are strokes of truth in that portrayal, it has drawn attention away from the usual reasons for the long delays in litigation at the time.[41]

Most delays in the mid-nineteenth-century Virginia courts arose from scarce personnel. The same judges had to hold court in many different places. Superior court judges sat with the General Court in Richmond and then rode circuit through the multiple counties in their home districts. They spent much of their time living out of their saddlebags, and they were unable to hear cases in any one locality for more than a few weeks twice a year.[42]

Although most places where the judges held court had plenty of lawyers, many of those lawyers lacked the training and capacity to handle novel or complicated cases. They were scrappy fellows who knew more about cajoling witnesses, befriending judges, and playing to juries than they did about the law. Proceedings in big cases frequently had to be postponed from one term of court to the next because the better-trained lawyers responsible for them were busy with cases somewhere else. That was especially likely to happen when the parties had hired leading counsel, such as General Walter Jones, who was in wide demand.[43]

The result was litigation that kept to the slow beat of a metronome set by the biannual terms of court. If a lawyer was not available to try a case when the judge came to town, he could just seek a postponement. And if the parties needed time to respond to a substantive motion, the judge had no choice but to defer the case until he came back to town half a year later. More than two years passed in this way before Judge Gholson was able to schedule a trial in the Randolph will case.[44]

The long delay did not go unnoticed. "What Has Become of the Slaves of the Late John Randolph?" ran a headline in the American Anti-Slavery Society's *Emancipator*. Newspapers in the South were reporting that the slaves still worked on Randolph's plantation even though the courts had established his will years ago. "How is this?" the *Emancipator* demanded. "For whom is their labor, (worth perhaps $10,000 a year,) bestowed? Where are their earnings since the death of their master?"[45]

A newspaper in Petersburg put the same dollar figure on the slaves' labor and lamented the repeated delays in the Randolph case. Just as some great lawyers had left wills others could not unravel, it said, "so the Roanoke Orator, in the matter of his Will, had displayed less practical wisdom than belongs to many a plain farmer that whistles in his furrow." A Presbyterian minister from New Jersey who was visiting his old congregants in Charlotte County reported that clerks there were busy copying the voluminous depositions taken from Randolph's friends and neighbors. "Meanwhile," he wrote to a friend, "the proceeds of the immense estate go to the Tuckers and Coalters and Bryan."[46]

Pretrial motions in the Randolph case revealed that Judge Leigh's capacity to testify for the defendants was the most contentious issue. Leigh was the best witness for Randolph's intention to free his slaves, and Leigh's decision to renounce Randolph's large bequest to him so that he could testify for the slaves' freedom gave him special credibility. Leigh's haunting description of Randolph's madness on the night when he canceled his emancipatory will was a dramatic moment in the General Court trials, and Beverley Tucker meant to stop Leigh from telling that story to the jury in the chancery case. He thought he had hit on a way. He let Leigh qualify as Randolph's executor before he sued him.[47]

Leigh may have renounced the bequest Randolph left him, but once he qualified as Randolph's executor, he had other interests in the case. He became a necessary party to any litigation because he as executor held legal title to Randolph's personal property. He also could be liable in his personal capacity if he mishandled the property or failed to file good accounts. He was entitled to fees and commissions for his work as executor. Beverley Tucker believed that those personal exposures should prevent Leigh from qualifying as a disinterested witness in the case even if his formal role as a party was not enough.[48]

Judge Gholson took a different view. His pretrial order dismissed all claims against Leigh in his personal capacity and reserved decision on whether Leigh could testify. Reserving decision suggested that he was not going to exclude Leigh's testimony simply because Leigh was a party, and dismissing the personal claims against Leigh seemed to remove any other likely grounds for exclusion.[49]

Beverley Tucker and the other opponents of Randolph's will appealed that order in the summer of 1843, and Judge Leigh took advantage of the appeal to renew his claim that Randolph's slaves should be named defendants in the case. The appeal delayed the case for nearly a year. Not until the following spring did the Court of Appeals uphold Judge Gholson's decision and send the case back to Petersburg for trial.[50]

The appeals court had no doubt that Leigh was a competent witness because an executor had no real interest in the validity of the will he administered. His job was to protect the estate and distribute it to whomever the courts ultimately recognized as the rightful heirs. His liability for anything he did in the meantime would be the same no matter who got the property. While it was true that the executor's fees could be smaller if the court invalidated the will and appointed someone else to administer the estate, that was no loss to the executor because fees were nothing more than compensation for the work he had to do.[51]

The court brushed aside Leigh's attempt to bring the slaves into the case with language that echoes through many antebellum decisions on the law of slavery. "The race of people to which those persons belong is, by our laws, *prima facie* in a state of bondage here, and none but physical means can be necessary to enforce the rights of owners." Slaveholders, in other words, could never be required to answer to slaves in court. Although the "humanity of the law" had given slaves the privilege of suing for their freedom, they could only come into court under the special procedure the legislature had provided for that limited purpose. To let slaves appear in any other way whatsoever, the court held, would derogate from the power of masters and cause "much inconvenience" in "the administration of justice."[52]

. . . .

IT UNSETTLES US not to know what the slaves at Roanoke thought about their exclusion from the suit over John Randolph's will and their long retention in bondage. Similar feelings have tempted generations of historians to construct the lost thoughts and emotions of the enslaved from the relatively little evidence that survives. But those reconstructions reveal more about the mindset of each generation of historians than they tell us about the slaves themselves, and historians today look back with dismay and sometimes horror at the historical accounts their predecessors believed to be accurate. For all of their earnestness about redressing past errors, even revisionist attempts to describe the lived experiences of the enslaved have tended to generalize, flatten, and thus diminish the diversity and complexity of their actual human existence. Slaves in one place lived different lives than slaves in another, and individual slaves were no more likely to think like each other than individual free men.[53]

We know that the slaves held by John Randolph's brother Richard became restive after waiting more than ten years for the freedom Richard had promised them in his will. Richard's widow Judith
pressed John Randolph to free them because she believed they were
becoming ungovernable. It is tempting to believe that John Randolph's own slaves felt the same way when they learned that two pro-
tracted probate trials for their freedom had led to nothing more than
two interminable chancery suits about the same thing.[54]

But John Randolph left his slaves in a very different position than
Richard Randolph left his. Richard's will promised his slaves homes
on 400 acres of the plantation where they and their ancestors had lived.
John's will could promise his slaves nothing better than exile to some
undetermined place far away. How that affected their feelings about
the long delays in chancery is more than we should presume to know.

Historians can use the relatively few surviving autobiographical
accounts of lives in slavery to imagine the feelings of the millions of
enslaved men and women who left no testimony of their own. Narratives written by refugees who successfully escaped bondage have
even gained a popular audience, and statements given to the Freedmen's Bureau after the Civil War and to researchers such as the
Works Progress Administration writers during the Great Depression
have proved to be enormously rich sources for scholars. Yet like all
first-person stories, these accounts have limitations. Refugees who
managed to escape slavery were obviously unusual, applicants to the
Freedmen's Bureau focused on their claims for relief, and survivors
alive in the 1930s had been young children when slavery ended. By
analyzing the accounts carefully, however, historians have been able
to shed light on otherwise unanswerable questions. And one of the
refugee narratives comes from a Virginian whose freedom depended
on a contested will.[55]

Peter Randolph was nineteen years old when Carter Edloe died in
1844, leaving a will that freed Randolph and the other seventy-two
slaves on his large plantation near Petersburg. Randolph remembered
with quiet indignation that no one told the slaves about Edloe's will.

Randolph found out about it six months after Edloe's death only because he had somehow learned to read, and when he and the others tried to claim freedom, their lawyer cheated them of their share in the estate's income. The slaves did manage to go free three years later with the help of a neighboring planter who thought Edloe's executor was treating them unjustly. Two of the older slaves chose to remain in slavery, and a woman who had lived with Edloe decided to move to Philadelphia with the four children she had borne him. The other freedmen went to Boston, where Randolph became a minister in a Baptist church that was active in the antislavery movement.

Peter Randolph's account of his life in slavery, written eight years after he reached Boston, is fresh and unsparing. He describes the deficient diet, hard labor, and harsh floggings meted out to slaves on Virginia plantations. He laments the fate of his brother Benjamin, whose refusal to take a whipping eventually consigned him to the auction block down the street from the Petersburg Courthouse. Randolph and his family never heard from Benjamin again. Randolph's narrative pointedly names the dishonest lawyer and the just-minded planter who figured in his bid for freedom under Edloe's will, but it says nothing in particular about the three years he remained in bondage after Edloe died. That wait for justice—at least as Randolph chose to tell the story—seems no worse than the other enormities of slave life.[56]

. . . .

FROM BEVERLEY TUCKER's point of view, it was he who had been waiting many years for justice, and Beverley worked hard to take advantage of his opportunity when Judge Gholson finally tried the chancery case in late January 1845. Beverley's lawyers took depositions from the Randolph relatives who had joined the Virginia diaspora to other states, from Randolph's friends in Richmond and the Southside, and from his political acquaintances in Washington. Although many of the witnesses had already testified in the probate trials, Beverley and his lawyers took pains to sharpen their accounts of Randolph's behavior and to pin particular episodes of madness to the periods when Randolph wrote his wills.

Theodorick Bland Dudley vividly described a derangement that began in the summer of 1818, a few months before Randolph wrote the earliest of the wills presented to the General Court. Dudley was Randolph's cousin and one of the young men Randolph had helped to educate. He lived at Roanoke for a time after he finished medical school, and Randolph had treated him like a son until the spring of 1822, a few months after Randolph wrote the codicil that pointedly cut Dudley out of his will.[57]

According to Dudley, Randolph had confessed that his mind grew disordered after his love affair with Maria Ward ended and that "he knew he had alienated almost all his nearest friends by his unhappy temper." When Randolph's derangement burst into the open, he would ride over his plantation by moonlight, rousing slaves and over-seers to resist neighbors he believed were cutting down the boundary trees along his property line. Randolph went from being "generous & liberal" to "parsimonious & miserly," and he showed no inclination to free his slaves. He said manumission would only aggravate their unfortunate condition.[58]

Senator Thomas Hart Benton, whose many late-night conversations with Randolph at their Washington boarding house had made the two of them close friends, said he had seen signs of mental aberration during the winter of 1821–22, when Randolph wrote his next will. Randolph became increasingly sleepless and prone to give "undue or even mysterious importance to trifles." Although Randolph seemed to recover his equilibrium the following year, Benton thought he showed the same signs of derangement in the winter of 1825–26, when he wrote a codicil to the 1821 will. Randolph grew so insistent on stopping the Baltimore mail coach as it passed by their boarding house that the driver changed his route.[59]

Randolph's friends in Southside Virginia had witnessed many bouts of madness during the years when Randolph wrote his final codicils and his last will. A neighbor named Henry Watkins received a note from Randolph in the spring of 1832 begging him to come to Roanoke at once. "I write with a blotting pen upon greasy paper," Randolph had scrawled, "unclean and offensive in the eye of God—because I am under the powerful influence of the Prince of Darkness who tempts me with a beautiful Mulatto girl and a bottle of ice Champaigne." Watkins found Randolph reading his Bible in a high state of excitement when he arrived, and Randolph had insisted that if it were not for the guns he kept close at hand, " 'my negroes would kill me.' "[60]

Randolph's good friend William Barksdale did not want to say that Randolph had been mad, but he acknowledged having seen some odd behavior. Although the codicil cutting Dudley out of Randolph's will said that Barksdale knew the reason, Barksdale confessed that Randolph had never mentioned the matter. Barksdale said Randolph's inherited debts had oppressed him, and he thought Randolph had never considered his property his own until he paid them. Yet in the years after he paid them, Randolph grew more miserly and more suspicious of his friends.[61]

John C. Calhoun was never on very friendly terms with Randolph, but they had known each other through the many years they served in Congress. Randolph opposed Calhoun when he was a nationalist and scorned his praise when Calhoun later turned to the defense of states' rights. Yet it was the iron-faced, gray-haired Calhoun rather than the flighty Randolph who would enter national memory as the greatest champion of Southern rights, and Calhoun could say with some justification that Randolph's thinking on slavery had shifted more than his own. "Mr. Randolph," Calhoun said, "was more excited at some periods than at others; more so than is usual with most men." During the 1816 debates about slave trading in the District of Columbia, Randolph seemed "adverse to negro slavery." After he returned from his first trip abroad in 1822, however, Randolph regularly maintained in debate and conversation "that the slaves of the south were in a better condition than the operatives of Europe."[62]

Randolph's friends and neighbors thought changes in his behavior toward his slaves were the clearest indication of his late-life madness. His lawyer John Marshall described how well Randolph had treated his workforce during his early life, and he remembered with pain and reluctance the vile things Randolph had done to them toward the end. A Fredericksburg lawyer who had known Randolph since college and served a few terms with him in Congress attributed the change to the deterioration of Randolph's mind. Whenever Randolph fell into one of his states of excitement, the man testified, he became indecently obsessed with two topics—"negro slavery & . . . religion."[63]

Testimony on Randolph's beliefs about slavery could have swayed the Petersburg jury who heard the case. Virginia jurors had to be white men who owned enough property to give them a stake in the good order of the community. The twelve Petersburg residents empaneled for the Randolph case included tobacconists, druggists, bank cashiers, a grocer, and one fairly successful merchant. Like most of the middle-class freeholders in Petersburg, nine of them owned slaves, and four of them owned at least half a dozen. Although these men had different economic and social interests than slaveholding planters, they would not have questioned the importance of slavery to the continued prosperity of their city and their own businesses.[64]

The jurors listened to the evidence and the lawyers' arguments for two weeks. That was a very long time for a jury to sit in antebellum Virginia, so long that the legislature promptly exempted them from service on another jury for four years. The jury heard so much about different wills and numerous codicils that it was difficult for them to decide what they should do. Was Randolph mad when he freed his slaves and disinherited his whole family? Was he thinking more clearly when he left plantations to Elizabeth Bryan and Henry Tucker but excluded the other heirs? Might there actually have been another will in which Randolph treated all of them alike? Only two things seemed clear to the jury. Randolph had lost his equilibrium at some points in his life, and the rest of the time he had meant to free his slaves.[65]

It probably was Judge Leigh's testimony that tipped the jurors toward that conclusion, just as Beverley Tucker had feared. Although no transcript survives, we can find the story Leigh told in his deposition and his earlier testimony before the General Court. Judge Leigh knew how to handle juries. He was sincere, plain-spoken, and self-effacing. As they heard him describe two pivotal scenes, the jury could easily imagine them.[66]

In the first, an emaciated old man leans toward his fire on a dark winter evening with his will in his hand as his best friend begs him not to burn it. Perhaps John White or one of the other enslaved servants stands frozen in the next room listening through the door. The old man's black eyes flash with madness, but his friend maintains a calm voice. The man finally agrees to cancel the will by cutting out his signatures instead. Why, his friend then suggests, must he do anything at all? Why not wait until he has written another will to replace this one? "You know what my feelings towards my slaves have been," the man replies, "but they have behaved so badly during my absence they are all changed." He takes out scissors and cuts.

Then it is July eighteen months later. The friend sits with the man's handsome half-brother in the shaded room of a village tavern. They are sifting through crumpled clothes in the man's traveling trunk in search of a will, and they find the cut papers. The brother reads them, and his face flushes. He hands them to the friend. The friend reads them and looks up. The will they contain frees the man's slaves and provides for their support, pointedly disinherits his whole family, and leaves his friend the rest of the man's large estate. The friend stares at the whitewashed wall as he comes to grips with what he must do. There are other men in the room, so he says nothing. When he is alone with the brother that evening, he says he will release his interest under the will if the man's family will release the slaves.[67]

Judge Leigh's renunciation of the legacy Randolph left him helped the Petersburg jury to find a Solomonic solution. It allowed them to free Randolph's slaves without disinheriting Randolph's family. On February 11, 1845, the jury found that the papers Leigh had rescued from the flames were John Randolph's "only true last will and testament." With those simple words—and after thirteen long years of waiting—Randolph's slaves gained legal title to their freedom.

The jury's verdict was a serious disappointment to the Tucker family. Henry Tucker would have to give up the money he had received when he sold Bushy Forest years earlier, Elizabeth Bryan might have to give up the Lower Quarter, and all of them would have to account for the significant annual profits they had received from the plantations while the case was in chancery. The family would lose about half of their inheritance on account of the manumission. And the clause in the will that expressly disinherited them because of wrongs attributed to St. George Tucker would go on record as the sane opinion of John Randolph. The Tuckers' lawyers asked Judge Gholson to poll the jury, and after each of the twelve men affirmed his verdict in open court, the lawyers moved for a new trial.[68]

It took two days of discussion, but Judge Leigh finally persuaded the Tuckers' lawyers to acknowledge the slaves' freedom and settle the case. The settlement agreement had four parts. Leigh would not require Randolph's heirs to account for the annual profits they had received from his plantations, and he would support their motion to strike those parts of Randolph's will that disparaged St. George Tucker. In return, Randolph's heirs would accept the rest of the jury's verdict, and they would give Leigh $30,000 out of the estate for the benefit of the freedmen and pay them reasonable wages for the coming year.[69]

Thirty thousand dollars was a large amount of money, perhaps a fifth of what remained in the estate after freeing the slaves. It significantly exceeded the value of the property Randolph had left to the slaves in his will. The heirs' agreement to pay such a sum was a remarkable moral and legal victory for Judge Leigh. The long litigation over Randolph's will had kept over three hundred persons in bondage for more than ten years, years during which the heirs profited from their labor. The costs of litigation had whittled into the amount Randolph left for the slaves' benefit. It seemed to Leigh that Randolph's heirs owed the slaves compensation for all of that.[70]

But the law was not in the slaves' favor. Virginia courts had repeatedly held that slaves who won their freedom were not entitled to receive anything for the labor extracted from them while they were unlawfully enslaved. Judges said that the profits from slavery were just too difficult to calculate. The slaveholder had housed, fed, and clothed the slave, and there was no way of telling whether the slave had produced enough to cover those costs. In disputes between free men, of course, the courts had no difficulty determining the hire value of a slave's time. To extend the same principle to freedmen, however, would have undermined the core principle that those who enslave other men and women must never be accountable to them.[71]

The slaves who worked for a dead man's estate during a dispute over his will had an even weaker claim because, no matter what the will said, the slaves were not entitled to freedom until the man's executor released them. Henry Tucker made that point in an opinion he wrote for the Court of Appeals about the time John Randolph died, and another judge on the court later expounded it. The slaves held by a decedent's estate, the judge wrote, received protection, support, and other benefits that would not be available when they were free. Freedom was a benefit to them in name only because it could not increase their "respectability, comfort, or happiness." "No practical injustice" therefore would be done, he said, by striking the balance due to them at zero.[72]

A man named Lewis Clarke who escaped from slavery in Kentucky at about this time struck the balance differently. He reckoned the expenses of maintaining a slave amounted to $11.51½ per year, while a working slave's labor was worth $100. Even if only half of the slaves on a plantation were able to work, the average annual deficit in the enslaver's account with each slave was $44.24¼. "The account stands unbalanced thus," wrote Clarke, "till the great day of reckoning comes."[73]

Leigh was able to recover what the slaves themselves could not because he had claims that the law recognized. As Randolph's executor, he was the legal owner of the slaves in Randolph's estate. He had a right to the value of their labor, and he had been careful to negotiate hire agreements with the Randolph heirs who used the slaves to work their land. Although the hires he collected were part of the property he had to distribute when the estate settled, Leigh had a right to hold the heirs accountable for them in the meantime. The liquidation of Leigh's claims for hires and the slaves' claims under Randolph's will into the $30,000 lump sum settlement gave the freedmen a benefit that the law otherwise would have denied them.[74]

. . . .

TWENTY-ONE-YEAR-OLD John Randolph Tucker brought the news from Petersburg to his ailing father at the University of Virginia the day after the case settled. Henry Tucker had retired from the Court of Appeals a few years earlier to become the university's professor of law. He suffered a mild stroke shortly after he moved to Charlottes-ville to take his new position, and although he appeared to have recovered, frequent fainting sensations made him anxious about how little time he had left to settle his financial affairs.

"How unexpected I need not say," Henry Tucker wrote to Beverley when he learned of the jury's verdict. He had never imagined losing so much of the estate to Randolph's slaves, and the amount that he would now have to refund to the other heirs staggered him. Because it would take him time to raise the money, he thought Beverley might prefer to receive some property instead. "Let me hear from you," he urged in a follow-up letter the next day, "for this *slam* has overwhelmed me & made me desirous to adjust every thing while the breath is [still] in my nostrils."[75]

Beverley got a more spirited note from Elizabeth Bryan a few days later. She had been managing the uneasiness between Beverley and her husband ever since Randolph Bryan helped to get the chancery case removed from Williamsburg, so she was glad the family could put the matter behind them. "I must congratulate you that this vexatious case is disposed of at last," she wrote, "tho' in a way that was unexpected & undesired by all concerned." She had always feared that

"Lawyers, Managers, Executor & finally the Servants" would make off with everything, so she was thankful the family would have some property left to divide among themselves.[76]

Whether the men and women enslaved at Roanoke were surprised to learn of their freedom is more than we can tell. We cannot even tell how they first heard the news. We do know that someone—perhaps it was Wyatt Cardwell or even Judge Leigh—must have told them they would spend another year planting tobacco, tending crops, and working for hire in Virginia before they had to leave. Perhaps someone also explained that they were not legally free to go anywhere until Judge Leigh actually released them. The wages they earned in the meantime were for their own benefit, of course, but the money would belong to John Randolph's estate.[77]

News of the slaves' freedom quickly appeared in newspapers throughout the United States. "The Negroes get their liberty and thirty thousand dollars, and the rest of the property goes to the heirs at law," reported the *Richmond Whig*. That seemed "about as fair an adjustment of the contest as could have been made." The *Richmond Enquirer* speculated that the estate would buy land for the freedmen in Texas, and papers from Maine to Mississippi and western Ohio repeated that story.[78]

A Whig newspaper in Boston published a histrionic account that called the Randolph will case "an extraordinary drama on the Theatre of Justice." Randolph was "one of the most singular men of the age," it said, and his will "one of the most and longest contested." The paper declared the verdict a victory for the American Colonization Society, which it thought had joined forces with Randolph Bryan to rescue Randolph's will from the rest of his relatives. Even a Cincinnati newspaper with proslavery sympathies ran an item applauding the outcome of the case. "Upwards of 380 slaves are rendered *free* by the will of John Randolph!" it proclaimed. "They will receive . . . $30,000 and a year's wages. Justice is slow but sure!"[79]

Cincinnati from Covington, Kentucky,
by Robert S. Duncanson, 1850

Part Three

. . . .

FREEDOM
AND
LOSS,
1845–46

Chapter 11

PROMISED LAND

Map of Ohio, *The Cerographic Atlas of
the United States*, 1845

THE BURGEONING YOUNG CITY OF CINCINNATI WAS A
captivating sight in 1845. Its fine brick buildings stretched for
miles along a high bluff on the north bank of the Ohio River, and
from the other side of the river in Kentucky, viewers could see the
city's street grid spreading back toward a low range of hills in the

distance. Brightly painted steamboats with tall smokestacks lined the riverbank to deposit and take on cargo, and a sparkling channel of water cutting straight north through the street grid marked the Miami Canal's pathway into Ohio's rich agricultural interior.

Founded scarcely sixty years earlier, Cincinnati was the sixth largest city in the United States. Its position on the Ohio River had made it the emporium of the American West, and its rapid emergence was a testament to the tremendous economic vitality of the great crescent heartland that swept from the head of the Ohio at Pittsburgh to the mouth of the Mississippi at New Orleans. Goods to develop this vast American interior poured through Cincinnati, and thousands of hogs walked into town each year to become the staple meat for the whole region. An extension of the Miami Canal had just opened all the way to Lake Erie—giving Cincinnati a thrilling new water connection up the lake to Buffalo and then across upstate New York on the Erie Canal to the Hudson River and New York City.[1]

Cincinnati was also becoming an important center for building boats and manufacturing everything from agricultural implements to textiles. Even the depression that followed the panic of 1837 had barely slowed its expansion, and the city was full of new European immigrants. A population that numbered 25,000 in 1830 had soared to 75,000 by 1845. Only half of the adult males were American-born, and fewer than 10 percent of them had been born in Ohio or other parts of the West. A third came from the German states, and most of the rest from Great Britain and Ireland. Although Cincinnati's trade with the cotton states was a vital part of its business, only 14 percent of the city's population came from a slave state. Fewer than 3 percent of its residents were Black.[2]

Charles Dickens enjoyed Cincinnati when he visited on his first American tour in 1842. He described the booming city as "cheerful, thriving, and animated." He found the streets and sidewalks well paved, the shops well stocked, and the buildings remarkable for their neat elegance. Other visitors, however, thought that the city's residents were neither hospitable nor interesting because they were too harried by business. All agreed that the city had mushroomed far beyond any-one's imagination.[3]

At eight o'clock on a July morning in 1845—five months after the Petersburg jury gave its verdict on John Randolph's will—Judge Leigh was in Cincinnati boarding the stagecoach to Columbus. He had arrived by steamboat the previous morning only three days after leaving Baltimore, and the speed of the trip amazed him. So did the bustle in Cincinnati.[4]

The restless activity swirling all around him was what most struck Judge Leigh. The people in Ohio seemed "to have but one object—to be moving," he told his wife. The "anxious faces of the crowd" depressed him, and he felt glad that he himself lived "in a quiet and retired Country, where the propensity to travel has not seized on all classes of Society."[5]

Leigh was not the first traveler to be struck by this difference between Ohio and the Southern states. Alexis de Tocqueville attributed it to slavery. Society slumbered where slavery made the white part of the population scorn labor, he wrote, while "the confused hum" of Ohio proclaimed "the presence of industry." Yet Leigh's age and tradition-alism probably had more to do with his reaction than anything else. Another French visitor to the United States thought the main effect of faster travel was "to reduce the distance not only between places, but between different classes," and a conservative former mayor of New York from Leigh's generation bemoaned the consequences. Even the winds go faster now-a-days, he grumbled in his diary; "everything goes ahead but good manners and sound principles."[6]

It took the big red stagecoach carrying Judge Leigh some time to work its way out of the busy city. Even after the coach got on the main road to the northeast, the driver kept a restrained pace. The road was macadam and the uphill grade rather gentle, but with the temperature already in the eighties, the driver did not want to exhaust his horses before he got to the next station. So the 28 miles east to Lebanon, where Leigh planned to get off, were going to take longer than the usual five hours. The hard-faced driver let the passengers figure that out for themselves. He kept his eyes on the road and his tobacco-stained mouth shut except when he needed to spit.[7]

The land sweeping out to the horizon was some of the best land Leigh had ever seen. Here and there were a few hills and now and then a little village, but the rest of the countryside was a level expanse of rich woodland and crop fields studded with small farmsteads. The soil was dark, the clearings flat, and the fields abounding with the gracious undulation of ripe wheat and the stiff ranks of new corn. The ubiquitous split-rail fences, which spoiled the scene for Europeans accustomed to more careful agriculture, did not bother a man used to the sloppy farming in Southside Virginia. Nothing he saw gave Leigh any pause about Ohio agriculture. The question on his mind was different. Would the inhabitants of this fine country allow John Randolph's slaves to settle here?[8]

. . . .

OHIO EXISTS IN American memory as a free state where the victims of slavery could find refuge. The mighty stream separating Ohio from the slave states becomes the River Jordan, and Harriet Beecher Stowe's heart-stopping depiction of Eliza Harris crossing the river on broken ice in *Uncle Tom's Cabin* remains one of the most indelible images in American literature. Ohio in fact does have a proud antislavery heritage, but history is always knottier than it seems, and to understand Ohio as Judge Leigh encountered it when he came seeking a home for the Roanoke freedmen, we must set aside our preconceptions.

Although Ohio was a free state, race and slavery played an outsized role in Ohio life. It could hardly have been otherwise. The state had extensive connections with the slave states on its borders and vital economic ties to the rich plantation markets down the Mississippi River. The resulting concerns about race and slavery cut in different directions. Fugitive slaves made it impossible for Ohioans in the southern counties to close their eyes to the humanitarian horrors of slavery, and refugees attempting to move on to Pennsylvania, New York, or

Canada received covert assistance from good people throughout the whole state. Yet most white Ohioans stoutly resisted Black settlement within the state. Some claimed that they too had come to Ohio to escape the slave system, which subordinated ordinary white folk to slaveholders, and they conflated the presence of slavery's victims with the evils of the institution itself. Others, including some of the foreign immigrants in the poor parts of Cincinnati, simply resented Black competition for menial work. And even in northeastern Ohio where outspoken antislavery settlers from New England predominated, there were almost no Black residents.[9]

A few African Americans had been coming to Ohio ever since the central government opened it to settlement after the Revolution, but they were generally unwelcome and sometimes not even free. Although the Northwest Ordinance of 1787 prohibited slavery north of the Ohio River, some of the early white settlers from Virginia brought along their slaves as long-term indentured servants. Among those settlers were men who figured prominently in the organization of Ohio as a new state in 1802.

While the Ohio state constitutional convention continued the prohibition on slavery, there had been significant debate before the convention agreed to restrict the use of indentures. The constitution specifically denied Blacks the right to vote. The following year, the new state legislature picked up a provision that the convention had almost adopted and excluded Blacks from the militia. The legislature also passed the first in a series of laws designed to discourage African Americans settlers.[10]

The Ohio Black Law of 1804 focused on fugitives from slavery. It prohibited any person of African descent from settling in Ohio unless he produced a judicial certificate of freedom, and it required persons of color already living in the state—of whom there were only a few hundred—to obtain a certificate of freedom from the clerk of court in their home county. Anyone who hired an undocumented Black person could be fined up to $50. State judges had to order the arrest of fugitives upon satisfactory proof from slaveholders, although anyone who abducted a purported fugitive without obtaining a court order could be fined $1,000.[11]

Three years later in 1807, the Ohio legislature adopted another Black law with a different focus. Virginia had just enacted its statute requiring newly emancipated slaves to leave the state. Many of the Virginia freedmen were likely to come to the neighboring state of Ohio, and legislators from Ohio border counties where the Black population had already started to grow were especially concerned about that. They claimed that slaveholders would free old or injured slaves in order to spare themselves the cost of supporting them, and they feared that many Blacks who reached Ohio would require relief from the public purse.[12]

Poor relief was the obligation of each locality, and taxpayers generally accepted their responsibility to relieve indigents in their own community. The exclusion of paupers from elsewhere, however, had been an important feature of Anglo-American poor laws for centuries. Ohio's laws already allowed the overseers of the poor to remove anyone without means of support who tried to take up residence in their township. Fear and racial prejudice nevertheless prompted a more drastic response to the anticipated influx of free Blacks.[13]

The Black Law of 1807 prohibited any person of African descent from settling in the state unless two Ohio landowners posted a $500 bond for the person's support. If a Black person settled without obtaining a bond, the local overseer of the poor could order him out of the township. Anyone who hired an unbonded Black was liable for a fine of $100 and the entire cost of his maintenance. Having protected taxpayers from Black migrants, the law went on to codify a harsh customary rule of evidence. It denied Black persons the right to testify in any civil suit with a white party or in any criminal prosecution against a white defendant.[14]

Few freedmen could satisfy the bond requirement. Five hundred dollars was more than the cost of most Ohio farms, and even landowners who could afford to expose themselves to such a penalty certainly would not do it for a Black stranger. The American

Anti-Slavery Society sharply highlighted the bond law when it called Ohio preeminent "among all the free States . . . for the wickedness of her statutes" against Blacks. The sole purpose of the law, it claimed, was "to prevent colored emigrants from remaining within the state." Frederick Douglass tried to be more forgiving. He said the "shameful laws" were just "the servile work of pandering politicians" who wanted to conciliate slaveholders. "There is nothing mean, narrow, or churlish about a true Buckeye."[15]

In fact, the bond requirement did not stop African Americans from coming to Ohio because local authorities rarely enforced it. By 1830, Blacks represented more than 1 percent of the population, and the Black population edged toward 2 percent as the overall population surged during the next two decades. The Black laws did, however, allow whites to take advantage of Black workers, deny them public relief, and banish them whenever local prejudice required it. Blacks had to live in fear of expulsion and without judicial protection from the wrongs that whites did to them in the meantime.[16]

Some Blacks with education, connections, extraordinary perseverance, or good luck made comfortable livings as barbers, seamstresses, small merchants, and builders. A few accumulated substantial property. But their success set them apart. White prejudice and fear of wage competition generally kept Black workmen out of the best-paying jobs. Men trained as blacksmiths, carpenters, coopers, and masons were obliged to work as farmhands, day laborers, janitors, and brick carriers. They frequently had to shift from place to place in order to find employment. And as African Americans from the countryside began moving into the cities in search of factory jobs, working-class whites—often immigrants who themselves faced discrimination—made it clear to their bosses that they would not work alongside Blacks.[17]

A free Black Virginian named John Malvin who came to Cincinnati in 1827 described the consequences. "I thought upon coming to a free State like Ohio, that I would find every door thrown open to receive me," he wrote, "but from the treatment I received by the peo-

ple generally, I found it little better than in Virginia." Some refugees from slavery who fled to Ohio moved on to one of the British
provinces in Canada. "I would about as lief live in the slave States as
in Ohio," declared one woman who had been in Ohio for ten years
before leaving for Canada. The loss of community was her main complaint. "In the slave States I had protection sometimes, from people
that knew me—none in Ohio."[18]

Two years after Malvin arrived, the Ohio Supreme Court dismissed
a constitutional challenge to the bond requirement, and white officials in Cincinnati warned unbonded Blacks to leave. A white mob
attacked the city's Black neighborhoods, and about a thousand Black
residents emigrated to Upper Canada. David Walker's resounding
Appeal to the Colored Citizens of the World used the incident to rally
Black resistance to slavery and colonization. Another riot erupted
seven years later when James G. Birney moved the offices of his abolitionist newspaper to Cincinnati. This time, Black residents fired on
the whites who ransacked their shops and houses. A third riot in 1841
was the largest racially motivated confrontation between free people
that any American city had seen at the time. A white mob of seven to
eight hundred men marched on a Black neighborhood of fewer than
a thousand men, women, and children, and when Black defenders
shot at them, the mob brought out a cannon.[19]

A young Irish traveler ruminated on the race problem in Ohio after
he encountered two wagonloads of Blacks from Cincinnati on their
way to Canada in 1829. He took pains to tell his readers that Ohio's
Black laws surely violated the federal Constitution, yet he understood the unremitting nature of the racial antipathy behind them. He
thought that even the Canadian authorities were beginning to question the stream of African American immigration. "Where then can
the unfortunate African find a retreat?" he wondered. His answer
was darkly pessimistic. "The most probable finale . . . will be that the
Christians must at their own expense ship them to Liberia . . . , and
there throw them on barren shores to die of starvation or to be mas-
sacred by the savages!"[20]

Despite the prejudice against Blacks in Ohio, Judge Leigh believed it was still the most promising place to settle the men and women freed by John Randolph's will. His choices were limited. Randolph had expressed a strong desire not to send them to Liberia, and the cost of transporting so many of them there would have been prohibitive. Most African Americans rejected the idea of going to Liberia anyway if anyone bothered to ask them. Sending the freedmen to one of the Canadian provinces would have been just as difficult to arrange and probably no more acceptable to them. A few Virginia freedmen had gone to Pennsylvania, but buying enough land to support this large group in Pennsylvania would cost more than Leigh could afford. The obvious destination was somewhere in the free states northwest of the Ohio River where good land was still plentiful and cheap.[21]

The more distant states in the West were no more attractive than Ohio. Indiana had a statute almost identical to the Black laws in Ohio, and the state supreme court had recently upheld it. Illinois had a similar law that doubled the bond requirement to $1,000. The territorial legislatures in Iowa and Michigan had followed the same path, and they kept their restrictions in place when they became states. Although the laws in those states were hardly better enforced than the Black laws in Ohio, agitation against Black immigration was growing in all of them. Within a few years of Judge Leigh's trip, Indiana, Illinois, and Iowa adopted laws that excluded Black immigrants altogether.[22]

Leigh thought he could settle a large group of freedmen in Ohio because another Virginian already had done that. William Fanning Wickham was a Richmond lawyer and a brother-in-law of Judge Leigh's older brother Watkins. Wickham had succeeded his father, Randolph's old creditor John Wickham, as testamentary trustee for an Englishman named Samuel Gist who left a will freeing more than three hundred Virginia slaves.[23]

Samuel Gist was a storybook character. An orphan educated at English charity schools, Gist came to Virginia as shop boy for a merchant's agent in 1739, married a rich older widow, and acquired large plantations and slaveholdings across three counties. He joined George

Washington, William Byrd, and other leading Virginians in a large speculation on land and timber in the Great Dismal Swamp. Before the Revolution, he moved to London where he invested in marine insurance and slave trading. Gist was no stranger to sharp practices, and through some slick transfers of title, he managed to prevent Virginia's Revolutionary government from confiscating his plantations as the property of an enemy alien. When he died in 1815 and for reasons that he never explained, Gist left substantially all of his Virginia estate to the people he had enslaved there.[24]

Gist wanted the emancipated slaves to live on his Virginia plantations, and the statute that required freedmen to leave Virginia did permit exceptions. But an exception for such a large group was scarcely imaginable, and when the General Assembly passed a special act to implement Gist's will, it assumed that the freedmen would have to go to Africa because people anywhere in America would have "just objection . . . to the residence of the negroes among them." It was with the help of antislavery Quakers in Ohio that Wickham managed to send the freedmen there. The Quakers persuaded him that people in Ohio would accept a group of free Blacks, and they helped him buy the necessary land. In 1819, Wickham settled more than a hundred freedmen on 2,200 acres about 50 miles east of Cincinnati, and as he resolved claims against Gist's estate over the next twelve years, he sent the rest of the freedmen to live on that land and an additional tract nearby.[25]

Although Wickham capably discharged his trust, he had significant doubts about the freedmen's prospects in Ohio. Wickham was a slaveholding planter himself, and he accepted the dogma that African Americans were better off under the good management of white slaveholders than they could be on their own. Wickham retained title to the Ohio land in trust for the freedmen so that less honorable men could not cheat them out of it. That limited the settlers' options and forced many of them to remain on the relatively unproductive soils that Wickham's agents had selected. So the Ohio settlements continued to require financial support from Samuel Gist's estate for many years, which only confirmed Wickham's doubts about the wisdom of the manumission.[26]

Others also were prepared to see failure when they looked at the Gist settlements. Before the first freedmen even left Virginia, an Ohioan who happened to be in Richmond warned newspaper readers back home of what they should expect. "I am told," he wrote, that the migrants "are perhaps as depraved and ignorant a set of people as any of their kind." He predicted that Ohioans would suffer from Virginia's "iniquitous policy . . . in driving all their free negroes upon us." An account of the settlements in a Cincinnati paper fifteen years later smugly confirmed that prediction. "The experiment was to test the merits of the negro race under the most favorable conditions for success," it said, and the result had been a complete failure. Although the land used for the settlements was not of the best quality, the settlers could have made it sufficiently productive with good management and hard work. Instead, they sank "into laziness and poverty and filth" and "their only produce is children."[27]

An English traveler with abolitionist sympathies who visited the settlements in 1834 agreed that the settlers lived in miserable conditions. Most of them were still in "the Camps" they established when they had to live in tents. Yet the Englishman did not think the fault lay with them. Their land was too wet for cultivation, he said, and the whites in the area regularly took advantage of them. "All of the whites with whom I conversed upon the subject admitted that [the Black settlers] had been defrauded—but then their color! What right had they to remain where they were—they were marked as a distinct people—they could never associate with the chosen race—they must go to Liberia." No wonder, the traveler reflected, some of the settlers thought that "death, or even slavery, seemed preferable to their lot in the wilderness."[28]

Judge Leigh now found himself in the same position as William Wickham, and he responded in much the same way. He did his duty with diligence even though he questioned the wisdom of what his duty required. Years of litigation over John Randolph's will had taxed

Leigh's time and his emotional energy. Executing the will now that it had been established was going to involve at least as much trouble. Why, he had asked himself in recent months, was he doing this? His obligation to his friend Randolph was the obvious answer. There must never be any doubt in anyone's mind that he would honor that obligation. But as honor led him down a path that seemed endless, Leigh needed a more satisfying answer for himself, and his doubts about manumission made it difficult for him to find one. Qualifying as Randolph's executor was "the most imprudent act of my life," he confessed to his son. "I doubt whether the slaves will be benefitted by obtaining their freedom, and so I am harassed beyond measure to attain an object, which at last may produce no good."[29]

Leigh was on his way to the small town of Lebanon to get advice from Thomas Corwin, one of the most important men in Ohio. Corwin had served five terms in Congress and a term as governor, and the legislature had just returned him to Congress as a member of the Senate. He was a prominent figure in the Whig Party that opposed the Jacksonian Democrats. Like most Whigs, Corwin wanted the central government to emphasize internal improvement and economic development instead of territorial expansion. He was also an outspoken advocate for what were then regarded as moderate policies on race and slavery. He supported repeal of the Ohio Black laws at the same time he backed the removal of Black Americans to Liberia. The important thing in his opinion was to eliminate causes for strife between white Americans and chances for division of the Union.[30]

Corwin had grown up with the state of Ohio. His parents brought him from Kentucky to a farm just outside Lebanon in 1798 when he was four years old. They were modest people like other early settlers in the area, and although Corwin's father later served in the legislature, he could afford to educate only one son. That was Tom's elder brother Matthias. But Tom Corwin gave himself an education, and he discovered that he had a gift for speaking in public. By the time he turned twenty-six, he was a practicing lawyer with his own seat in the state legislature. Nearly everyone liked Corwin, and he was generous to a fault. Despite being the best paid lawyer in the county, he had little money because he so often adopted the misfortunes of others.[31]

The temperature stood above ninety when Judge Leigh's six or seven hour journey finally brought him to Tom Corwin's frame house in midafternoon. Leigh probably spent the night there before catching a stage out of town the next day. What the two men discussed is not difficult to imagine. Corwin must have reassured Leigh that the bond requirement in the Black laws was indeed a dead letter. He thought the legislature would repeal it, a prediction that came true four years later in 1849. And he believed it was particularly unlikely that local officials would use the law to exclude settlers who owned enough land to support themselves. Leigh probably asked Corwin about the Gist settlements and other existing communities of Black farmers. He also inquired about antislavery activists who might be willing to help him. The two men undoubtedly discussed an eccentric abolitionist named Augustus Wattles and a Black settlement on the raw western fringe of Mercer County.[32]

· · · ·

MERCER COUNTY SITS at the midpoint of Ohio's western border astride a summit in the state's Till Plains. The wide plateau at the top of the summit stretches away in all directions, broken only by a few hillocks that look like wooded islands in the flat landscape. This summit has long been important. Its south face marked the line excluding white settlement from Native American territory agreed at Fort Greenville in 1795, and Mercer County did not become a white political jurisdiction until 1824. A dozen years later, builders of the Miami Canal extension decided to use a shallow fold in the plateau to capture the enormous amount of water they would need to lift boats over the summit through a new series of locks. When completed in the year of Judge Leigh's visit, the Grand Reservoir created there was said to be the largest artificial lake in the world. Nine miles long and up to 4 miles wide, it had flooded more than 17,000 acres.[33]

The earliest white settlers in Mercer County bought land in the townships south and east of what became the reservoir. They were from Virginia, Kentucky, Pennsylvania, and more settled parts of Ohio, but a second wave of settlement in the 1830s brought mostly German immigrants. The Germans usually came in groups and settled in clusters near others from the same part of Germany or others of the same religious faith. The result, as two scholars have so vividly noted, was more a checkerboard than a melting pot. Although German Protestants established the canal town of New Bremen, most of the Germans in Mercer County were Catholic. They included merchants, teachers, and tradesmen as well as farmers.[34]

Mercer County was on the frontier of agricultural settlement. Most of the land remained uncleared, and a farmer's life there was hard. Whether he bought prairie or woodland, he needed three to five years to tame it into a self-sustaining farm. Felling trees and plowing around massive roots was only somewhat more difficult than trying to break up deep prairie sod. It could take a man and his family ten years to clear three or four 10-acre crop fields.[35]

One settler long remembered that the native grasses on his land were so thick and tall that he had to begin by pulling them out by hand to make enough room to swing a mattock. The wolves creeping through the dense cover made him nervous. But his alarm at the sound of movement vanished one day when he looked up to see "the loveliest picture on earth, my young wife coming towards me holding her first born in her arms and smiling so kindly . . . to encourage me in my work."[36]

The diaries kept by immigrant farmers are less sentimental accounts of constant toil. "Wirking on Cleering" is the ceaseless refrain throughout one of them, occasionally relieved by the notion that it was "a fine day." The diarist plowed a small field for corn in the late springtime. When summer came, he made hay, and by July, he was cutting and tramping wheat. He plowed and replanted his wheat field in the autumn, and when the standing corn finally dried out, he cut it and began husking the ears. Christmastime found him butchering and threshing rye, although he apparently did not work on the feast day itself when he noted that a neighbor came to visit and it "Rained all Day."[37]

Misfortunes are just simple facts in the diary of another immigrant farmer. His family caught malaria during their first autumn in Ohio, his sister died, and the fever recurred even after the ground had frozen. Temperatures rose to 100 degrees the following summer, and his grain withered from drought. His widowed brother-in-law died the next spring before they had finished building a house. Two years later, his entire corn crop blew down in a violent thunderstorm. "Considerable fever" continued to infect the area every autumn. His family and farmhands got sick, although a decade's experience taught him that his wife's fevers were usually "not very serious."[38]

Construction of the Grand Reservoir had riled nearby settlers because of their fear of disease. Damp places in southern Mercer County were already breeding grounds for malaria, and a cholera outbreak had severely depopulated the whole region just five years earlier. As shallow brown water started to accumulate behind the embankment, settlers feared new infections. They also complained that speculators with inside information had made off with the compensation available for flooded land, while adjacent landowners whose property was damaged got nothing. They held protest meetings and elected local farmer Robert Linzee to take their grievances to the canal commissioners. When the commissioners ignored them, settlers took matters into their own hands. Over the course of two days, more than a hundred of them breached the earthworks to release the brackish water. At least thirty were arrested, but a local grand jury returned no indictments. That gave countenance to the sort of vigilante violence these white settlers would soon bring to bear on their Black neighbors.[39]

African Americans were among the early settlers in Mercer County. They included freedmen from Virginia, Kentucky, North Carolina, and Alabama. Most of them bought uncleared land on the cutting edge of settlement in the western part of the county. The forest canopy there was thick, and sounds quickly got lost in the undergrowth.

Days could pass when a man clearing land heard nothing except the sound of his own blows, bird calls, wolves in the underbrush, and the distant voices of his family. The next house was more than a quarter mile away somewhere among the trees. Although it took time for the dank land to dry out after he had cleared it, a small field could yield good crops. Getting in the crops was often difficult, however, because malarial fevers hit hardest at harvest time.[40]

About a hundred Black families lived in two townships southwest of the reservoir by the mid-1840s. They had cleared around 1,000 acres and put up a gristmill, sawmill, meetinghouse, and school. Charles Moore, a freedman from Kentucky, laid out a small village to support the growing community. He called it Carthagena after the ancient North African city of Carthage. The place soon had a wagonmaker, blacksmith, mason, and tanner as well as weavers, shoemakers, barbers, and even a hatter. Black and white settlers in the area patronized these tradesmen, and Black men trudged to work on the reservoir alongside white immigrants who needed to earn more money to pay for land.[41]

The thriving settlement around Carthagena quickly doubled the number of African Americans in Mercer County. Where there had been only 204 in 1840, there were now nearly 400. Although Black settlers represented less than 4 percent of the county's overall population, they accounted for almost 20 percent of the residents in the two townships where virtually all of them lived.[42]

Augustus Wattles, a Quaker from Connecticut not quite thirty years old, bought about 1,100 acres near Carthagena in 1837. He had been educated at the Oneida Institute in New York, the most influential of the manual labor colleges founded during the previous decade to instill egalitarian ethics by mixing study and toil. Oneida was an early hotbed of abolitionism, and there Wattles met a man who would become one of the most influential abolitionists of all, Theodore Dwight Weld. Wattles followed Weld to Lane Seminary outside Cincinnati in 1833, and soon after Weld and others began agitating for the seminary to get involved in the abolition movement, Wattles

left to open a school for Blacks in Cincinnati. While his new wife
Susan Lowe managed the school, Wattles started traveling as one of
the early agents for the American Anti-Slavery Society.[43]

Wattles believed that enslaved Americans had the right to more
than emancipation. He thought they deserved viable opportunities
for education and self-support. The racial prejudice that he saw in
Cincinnati and other cities convinced him that free Blacks could
best find those opportunities by forming communities of their own
in the countryside. What the Black inhabitants of Mercer County
had already achieved made it an appealing place for more settlement,
and Wattles decided to open a manual labor school at Carthagena to
attract and educate Black settlers who could work the land while they
raised the money to pay for it.[44]

Within a few years, reports in the abolitionist press were praising
Wattles's efforts. Other newspapers reprinted the stories and brought
the Black settlement in Mercer County to national attention. Trustees
for the estate of a New Jersey Quaker named Samuel Emlen offered
to buy the manual labor school from Wattles, and he used their funding to expand it as the Emlen Institute. Even men with relatively conservative outlooks could approve of what Wattles was doing. "Instead
of merely spouting pretty words like the other abolitionists," wrote
one foreign observer, Wattles "had taken hold of the matter by the
right end and, without getting involved in the quarrel about slavery, had taken steps to improve the *free* colored and thus emancipate
them from the scorn that rests upon them in the North with the same
weight as does servitude in the South."[45]

There were dozens of rural Black settlements in Ohio at the time,
but the success of the community around Carthagena brought it particular notice. When the National Convention of Colored Citizens
met at Buffalo in 1843, the Carthagena settlers offered themselves as
role models for free African Americans everywhere. They trumpeted
the independence achievable in a rural community, and they urged
Blacks doing menial jobs in the cities to leave them. "Would you not
be serving your country and your race to more purpose," they asked,

"if you were to . . . go out into the country and become a part of the bone and sinew of the land?"[46]

Carthagena probably caught Judge Leigh's attention for two reasons. In the first place, the size and growth of the community seemed to indicate that whites were willing to accept Black settlement in the area. Blacks had been living there for a decade, and whites had not contested their presence. What was more, the Black community was welcoming new settlers. Established farmers helped new ones, tradesmen took apprentices, and the Emlen Institute offered a few young men the chance for more formal education. Because neither Leigh nor John Randolph had prepared the freedmen at Roanoke for their new lives, they had much to gain from this kind of support.[47]

Quaker support for the settlement at Carthagena was also important. The Society of Friends had opposed slavery since the eighteenth century, and it was Quakers seeking to cleanse themselves from their own involvement with slavery who pushed for Virginia's post-Revolutionary manumission law. The Friends in Virginia had freed their own slaves and encouraged other manumissions. Quakers believed it was their religious duty to help the needy and the outcast, and their humanity toward Black Americans was legendary. His great hope when he was a slave boy in Maryland, the abolitionist Samuel Ringgold Ward later remembered, was "to reach a Free State and to live among Quakers."[48]

In border states such as Ohio, Quakers succored, sheltered, and sometimes hid refugees from slavery. But most Quakers who did those things were not outspoken abolitionists. They sought quietly to follow the Inner Light in their own lives, to do good to others, and to shun the evils of this world. They believed that true religion should not give rise to strife, and they thought it was wrong to undermine civil government. They rejected the use of force. That meant most Quakers shied away from abolitionist agitation for immediate universal emancipation. It was evangelical Protestants from more militant religious traditions who sparked the abolition movement in the 1830s, and the Quakers who became important leaders of the movement were dissident "come-outers" who rejected their own faith's quietist tradition.[49]

Uncle Tom's Cabin drew a cherished image of the activist Quakers in Ohio who helped Eliza Harris and her family escape pursuing slave catchers, and such people actually did exist throughout the antebellum period. By the time Judge Leigh visited, however, the Ohio Yearly Meeting of Friends had disowned them. Although Ohio Quakers abhorred slavery and sympathized with its victims, the majority believed they should resist the temptation to join the abolitionist tumult. William Lloyd Garrison's claim that moral suasion alone could lead to the abolition of slavery strongly appealed to them, and they understood his fiery argument that the Constitution of the United States was an evil compact with slaveholders. Yet they could not accept his call for open disobedience to the law. Even Quakers who supported Cincinnati abolitionist James G. Birney as presidential candidate for the antislavery Liberty Party in 1840 were mildly suspect among their more traditional brethren.[50]

A Garrisonian editor named J. Elizabeth Hitchcock who was trying to drum up support from Friends in eastern Ohio responded to their concerns by keeping her focus on moral persuasion. A few pennies spent on an antislavery pamphlet could do wonders, she insisted. A three-penny tract sent to North Carolina had persuaded a slaveholder there to free nineteen men and women who were now rejoicing with Augustus Wattles in Mercer County. "How many slaves did the political action of the Liberty Party ever free? How many is it ever likely to free? Not one." Moral action, she assured her Quaker readers, could do the work that "political action . . . only retards." It was antislavery Ohioans like Hitchcock's readers who conducted refugees to freedom on the Underground Railroad, schooled Black children, and integrated Oberlin College.[51]

Judge Leigh's views on Quakers were probably the same as John Randolph's. From his earliest days in public life, Randolph had strongly objected to the antislavery petitions that Quakers presented to Congress. He said the Quaker testimony against slavery was just as dangerous as the abolitionist agitation of less admirable men, and he insisted that Congress must completely ignore their petitions. Yet Randolph never doubted the purity of Quaker intentions. The Friends in Virginia were upright, law-abiding people known for their charity and fair dealing. They were willing to work with African Americans, and free Blacks trusted their Quaker employers to hold onto their wages until they needed the money. While Virginia Quakers might give food and shelter to refugees from slavery, they would not entice another man's slaves to flee. Randolph praised Quaker goodness on his deathbed, and he entrusted his own last testament for manumission to his Quaker doctors. Faced with the task of settling hundreds of newly manumitted men and women in a strange country, Leigh welcomed help from the Friends.[52]

. . . .

JUDGE LEIGH CAUGHT a stagecoach to the boom town of Dayton after his meeting with Thomas Corwin. Situated on the east bank of the Miami River about 50 miles north of Cincinnati, Dayton had been the northern terminus of the Miami Canal for more than a decade before the canal opened to Lake Erie. Canal traffic brought the city great prosperity, and its population had tripled during those years to almost 10,000. Leigh stopped there to consult a respected lawyer named Peter Odlin whom Corwin had recommended. From Dayton, it was 57 miles up the canal to New Bremen, the canal port nearest Carthagena. Most canal boats made about 3 miles an hour, so a trip straight through would have taken a day. Leigh probably proceeded in slower stages so that he could talk to other people Corwin had recommended along the way.[53]

The locks on the Miami Canal extension must have intrigued Leigh because canal locks in eastern Virginia were not nearly so massive. When a boat entered one of the new canal's high stone chambers, great wooden gates swung shut behind it and water came rushing down through wickets in the closed gates at the other end. Once the rushing water had lifted the boat to the level of the water beyond the far gates, the wickets closed, the far gates opened, and the mules on the towpath resumed pulling the boat north.

Leigh's slow passage up the Miami Canal gave him plenty of time to look at the surrounding country. Beside some of the locks were small villages, the kind of places with a mill, a few warehouses, a general store, and some locals who had time to watch boats pass. In the busier towns of Troy and Piqua, Leigh saw factories, distilleries, and large lumberyards. Between the towns were forests, crop clearings, and open fields where native grasses grew taller than a man's head. Dusk brought clouds of mosquitoes, and passengers had to reach for the netting rolled up in cloth beds tied overhead.[54]

Although Judge Leigh was discreet about his business in western Ohio, he needed to be forthright enough to test local reactions to a large group of Black settlers, and the story he had to tell was soon big news. Within months after his return to Virginia, newspapers from Cincinnati to New York and Boston were carrying a full report.[55]

The papers said that Leigh had $25,000 available to settle nearly four hundred slaves liberated by John Randolph's will. He was looking for a place in Ohio where they could find "legal protection, social and educational privileges, and the means of support." He planned to give each family 40 acres, a cabin, and the tools they would need to start farming. Leigh hoped those arrangements would assure locals that the new settlers could support themselves.

On its face, Judge Leigh's plan seemed realistic. There were about eighty families in the Roanoke community, so 40 acres for each of them would require 3,200 acres. The federal government was selling uncleared land in western Mercer County for $1.25 per acre, the state of Ohio offered canal land for $2.50, and good land already in private hands was available for $3 to $4. At those prices, Leigh could buy 3,200 acres for about $8,000 to $9,000. That would leave $200 per family for travel expenses, housing, and farm tools.[56]

Forty acres was enough to support a family on the agricultural frontier. It was the typical size of a farm in western Mercer County, and most families could farm no more than that because clearing, planting, and harvesting 40 acres took the work of two to four adult laborers. An ambitious farmer with a big household or a man who aimed to speculate on rising land values might buy a larger farm, but ordinary folk did not. (The average size of a farm in the area around Carthagena was 46 acres as late as 1900.)[57]

Leigh emphasized the Black settlers' ability to support themselves when he spoke to the newspapers because he feared that some Ohioans were not going to welcome them. Although everyone had assured him that the state's Black laws were not being enforced, he told the papers, he had seen enough "unkindness toward the negro" as he traveled through the state to give him concern. He had expected that Northerners who opposed slavery would show more compassion for "the suffering slave."

A few months earlier, young John Mercer Langston had experienced the sort of unkindness that Leigh must have witnessed. Langston (who later became a lawyer, congressman, educator, and diplomat) had been traveling through eastern Ohio on his way to study at Oberlin College, and he left an account of the trip in his autobiography. He said that innkeepers refused to let him through their doors, and but for the intervention of another passenger, the driver of the public stagecoach would have compelled him to ride on the roof.[58]

Race and slavery were becoming increasingly divisive political issues in the spring of 1846 as the nation tensed for a war with Mexico over the American annexation of Texas. Andrew Jackson's political heir James Polk had made sweeping appeals for territorial expansion during the 1844 presidential contest, and after his election, Polk did not even wait for the Texans to ratify annexation before sending American troops into Texas territory. Polk's move had wide support in the slave states, where the value of more cotton land and more proslavery voters was obvious. But working-class white men in all parts of the country also found Polk's aggressive expansionism thrilling, and the leading Jacksonian magazine in New York famously described annexation as a fulfillment of the growing white population's "manifest destiny to overspread the continent."[59]

Most of Polk's Whig opponents argued that the seizure of Texas was an unjust provocation that would lead to a costly war, and the prospect of going to war for slave country strengthened the hand of antislavery elements in the party. Among the most outspoken antislavery Whigs were men such as Congressman Joshua R. Giddings, who came from the part of northeastern Ohio where settlers with roots in New England upheld a high moral tone. Even the moderate Tom Corwin, who feared the war would dangerously exacerbate sectional differences over slavery, seemed to be tilting toward his antislavery colleagues.[60]

Northern Democrats thought this tendency toward abolitionism made Whig candidates vulnerable. Abolition was not popular because it threatened the existing order of things. It also seemed to put the interests of Black slaves ahead of the interests of hard-laboring white men, and populist Democrats found it easy to exploit economic fears with the rabble-rousing claim that abolition would lead to racial amalgamation.[61]

Race-baiting had powerful political potential in Ohio. So Jacksonian Democrats in the state legislature seized on early reports that Judge Leigh had bought a large tract of land in a part of Mercer County where—according to the newspapers—persons of color already owned nearly all of "three or four townships." Many Ohio Whigs had spoken out for repeal of the state's Black laws, and the prospect of a large influx of freedmen was just what Democrats needed to swing racial prejudice into play against their Whig opponents in the autumn election.[62]

Days after news of Leigh's land purchases appeared in the newspapers, a Democratic member of the legislature proposed an inquiry into whether Ohio could ban "the colonization of emancipated negroes from other States." He said Leigh's plans made him fear that Ohio otherwise would become a dumping ground for "all the superannuated slaves" of adjoining states. "As we have no participation in the subject of slavery," he declared, "we ought not to be subjected to any of its evils." A prominent Whig member begged to remind him that

Ohio had "*agreed* to submit to many of the evils of slavery" when it joined the Union. The Constitution gave men the right to own slaves, he said, and it gave freed slaves the right to go where they pleased. The Ohio House nevertheless resolved to consider a ban on Black migrants, and the Senate adopted an identical resolution by the overwhelming vote of twenty-six to six.[63]

The sensational news about Leigh's large land purchase was in fact premature. Leigh was still collecting money from the sale of John Randolph's property in Virginia when the Ohio legislature acted, and Leigh's son Thomas did not come to Ohio to conclude land purchases until three months later. But the gist of the news was correct. Leigh had retained a Quaker named Samuel Jay to help him assemble about 3,000 acres in Mercer County, and negotiations for that much land were impossible to hide in a place where land generally sold in small tracts.[64]

Thomas Leigh got to Cincinnati on the last Monday in April and took a boat up the Miami Canal to meet Samuel Jay near Piqua. The "fine hearty old quaker" immediately impressed the young lawyer from Virginia, who appreciated Jay's assurances that he would stay with Leigh in Mercer County until the two of them had finished their business. That business was going to take much longer than Leigh had anticipated, however, and he told his wife not to expect him home until the first of June. Although that meant they would be separated for a long time, he thought they could take comfort in knowing that it was all for the benefit of John Randolph's "poor negroes." If Thomas Leigh had any inkling of what lay ahead, he failed to mention it.[65]

Chapter 12

ANOTHER CANAAN

Procession of the Roanoke freedmen in Cincinnati,
sketch by Edward Henry Knight, July 1846

INSTEAD OF PUTTING OUT TOBACCO SEEDLINGS AS THEY HAD
done every spring for as long as anyone could remember, the 383
people enslaved at Roanoke spent the spring of 1846 preparing to leave
Virginia. On the last Wednesday in April, they set out for Charlotte
Courthouse to get their freedom papers. A farm wagon carried some
of the old people. The rest of them walked the 15 miles into town.[1]

The central green in Charlotte Courthouse looked much the same
as it does today. The two-story brick courthouse with its pleasing Pal-
ladian proportions and columned porch was elegant enough to sustain the memory that Thomas Jefferson had designed it. A handsome
Greek Revival office building for the clerk of court stood behind it,
and to the left was a stout new jailhouse of hewn stone. On the far side

of the green was Wyatt Cardwell's tavern, where Judge Leigh and Beverley Tucker had met thirteen years earlier to search John Randolph's trunks for another will. A second tavern, a few law offices, a handful of houses, and a new Presbyterian church stood along the surrounding streets.[2]

The clerk of court had reckoned he could register the people from Roanoke over the following two days so the county court could approve their papers at its monthly session on Monday. Winslow Robinson was forty-seven years old. He had worked in the clerk's office since he was fourteen, and he had been the clerk of court for more than twenty-five years. He had a firm hand on the business. Yet as he watched hundreds of men, women, and children with bedrolls stream into the green late that afternoon, he must have had second thoughts about this job.[3]

Robinson had never done anything like this. He did not know anyone who had. Although Virginia law required him to register all free Blacks in the county, that task had never required much work. Other manumissions had involved but a few slaves, and Blacks who were born free generally ignored the registration requirement. Robinson usually registered people one or two at a time, and many of them simply needed to replace lost papers. Only one slaveholder in Charlotte County had ever registered the manumission of more than four slaves, and he was a Methodist minister who had freed just eleven over the course of two decades. The previous federal census listed only 305 free Blacks in the whole county.[4]

Virginia law made the free Black registration process sound simple enough. It directed the clerk to take down each person's name, age, color, and height together with "any apparent mark or scar, on his or her face, head or hands." The clerk was then to prepare a certificate of freedom containing that information. The object was to describe the individual well enough to prevent someone else from using the certificate as a ticket out of slavery.[5]

Winslow Robinson had probably not planned to begin registering the Roanoke slaves until the next morning, but as he looked over the crowd outside his window, he decided that he and the deputy clerk had better enroll a few people that afternoon just to get themselves organized. He called in two young men who happened to be near his door. Frank Brown was slightly under 6 feet, one of the tallest men in the crowd, and Robinson measured him to the eighth of an inch. He never did that again. The rest of his measurements stopped at the half or quarter inch. Robinson noted a small scar on Brown's forehead and a patch of discolored skin on the hand of Johnson Crowder, the man Robinson had called in with him.[6]

The clerks took a couple with a small child next. Phil White appeared to be about forty-five years old. Robinson thought his wife Sylva looked twenty years younger. Their daughter was old enough to walk. Robinson recorded that neither of the adults had apparent scars or marks. He never made a notation like that again either. After the Whites came a tall dark man named Alec who had been standing with a woman and two children. Alec had a scar behind his right ear, and the woman whose name was Sally had an injured hip. Robinson described her as a mulatto. The children, whose complexions he called bright, were hers.[7]

The clerks registered a young man named Willis before they quit for the day. Robinson must have worried about how long those ten entries had taken because he stopped looking for identifying marks. In entries for the nearly four hundred people he registered over the next two days, he recorded only four more marks. He noted that a man named Freeman had suffered frostbite and burns on both hands. He identified six of the women as pregnant.

Robinson need not have worried about getting the job done on time. He registered well over three hundred people the next day, and by Friday evening, he and his deputy had a list ready for the court's meeting on Monday.[8]

John Randolph's long-suffering manservant Juba never got a certificate of freedom. He and about thirty other adult members of the

Roanoke community died while Randolph's will was stuck in the courts. Juba's fifty-year-old widow Celia appeared in Robinson's register with three daughters, a son-in-law, and two grandchildren. But Randolph's manservant John White did survive the wait for freedom. The sixty-three-year-old man and his wife Betsy entered the register with three sons and a daughter, a granddaughter, and the four-year-old son of John's dead sister Nancy. The field hand Moses, who had sometimes worked as a manservant when Randolph turned on White, also survived to freedom. He was sixty years old. He had a wife, three grown children, a daughter-in-law, and one grandchild.[9]

Winslow Robinson's record of the Roanoke slaves on the eve of their emancipation is an important historical document. It describes a large enslaved community that had been together for nearly a century. The living members of the community were descended from the slaves John Randolph's grandfather sent to the Piedmont in the mid-eighteenth century, and unlike the slaves on so many other Virginia plantations, they had not been divided by estate settlements or sales to the slave trade for thirty-five years. Eighty-four of them descended from just nine of the people Randolph inherited. At least twenty-one traced to an elderly woman registered as Old Milly, another sixteen to seventy-year-old Essex and his wife Caty Brown, thirteen to Peter and Jenny Johnson, and ten to Sampson and his wife Lucinda. Robinson's record reveals a great deal about this community, but it can be difficult to interpret.[10]

Too much has been made, for example, of the absence of marks on the slaves' bodies. The free Black registration law was concerned with marks for purposes of identification, and it specified only marks on faces, heads, and hands. So even if Winslow Robinson had examined the Roanoke slaves more carefully than he did, he would not have looked at their backs. The small number of recorded marks therefore says nothing about the Roanoke slaves' experience with whippings or other abuse. Both Black and white people in Charlotte County knew that Randolph's overseers whipped them—Randolph had beaten a few of them himself—and the absence of recorded marks does not belie that.[11]

Color presents a more treacherous puzzle. Winslow Robinson used nine different terms to describe the complexions of the Roanoke slaves: black, dark, dark brown, brown, light brown, light, bright, very bright, and mulatto. Other county clerks across Virginia used forty-five terms in their free Black registers, including words such as "copper," "chestnut," and "olive." This language obviously reflects racial constructs, and modern historians can be tempted to sift it for evidence about racial mixing. But the evidence to be found here has limitations because Robinson and the other clerks were using the words for a different purpose. They were simply trying to establish personal identity, in the same way that passport clerks in the time before photography described white men as "pale," "ruddy," or "dark."[12]

No one recorded how the men and women from Roanoke felt about leaving their lifelong home. Probably no white person asked them. Judge Leigh almost certainly never consulted them before selecting Ohio as their destination. The law required them to leave Virginia, and he thought it was his responsibility to decide where they should go. Other whites might have been afraid to know what the freedmen actually thought. White Virginians needed to believe that their slaves were better off with them than they could be anywhere else. That made some of them ashamed to sell slaves, and it encouraged them to tolerate the continued presence of emancipated slaves who were supposed to leave. If they did ask the Roanoke freedmen whether they were sorry to leave Virginia, the answer they would have expected was yes.[13]

• • • •

THE VIRGINIA PIEDMONT grows wide south of Richmond, and Charlotte County lies about 50 miles east of the mountains that dominate the western part of the state. Until they began walking to Ohio in early June 1846, few of the Roanoke freedmen had ever seen those

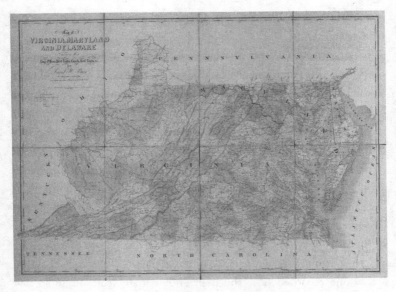

Map of Virginia, Maryland, and Delaware,
The American Atlas, 1839

mountains. It probably was not until the third day of their westward migration that the freedmen and the wagons carrying their baggage passed the upcountry town of Lynchburg and entered the first ridges. After that, it must have seemed to them that the mountains went on forever.

Although we have no record of the Roanoke freedmen's route, we can reconstruct it from antebellum road maps, the accounts of other travelers, and surviving references to places the freedmen passed. The westward road that the freedmen would have taken through the Blue Ridge Mountains followed a forest trail along the James River, so the walkers and the wagons could cross into the Shenandoah Valley without much difficulty. But as soon as they emerged from the forest, the freedmen saw a tall range of mountains on the other side of the valley that stretched into the distance as far as they could see. An excellent turnpike, which slave traders often used to drive coffles from Washington, took the travelers north through the valley to the small town

of Lexington. There they turned onto a narrower road that headed
west into the Allegheny Mountains.[14]

The freedmen spent more than a week in the endless Allegheny
ridges. A large group of all ages moved slowly, and the steepness of
the road hindered their wagons. Although progress was slow, the
journey was well conducted. Wyatt Cardwell, the longtime steward
of Randolph's plantation, had provided a tent for each family and
stocked the wagons with cooking equipment and basic staples. The
travelers bought fresh vegetables and meat along the way. Quite a few
of the men were experienced wagon drivers, and they all knew how
to take care of themselves in rough conditions. They had been doing
that all their lives. A white relative of the steward named Thomas
Cardwell came along to conduct them through a country where such
a large crowd of Black people could easily have sparked fears among
the white people they encountered.[15]

Clem Clay, who made the trip as a boy of twelve or fifteen, testified a half century later that the old people rode in the wagons while
everyone else walked. In the evenings, the families made a large camp
in the forests by the road, and the adults sometimes held religious services using hymns they remembered or extemporized. A lead soloist
would alternate lines with powerful refrains from the whole assembly. Two hymns that survivors of the migration were still singing in
Ohio decades later provide our only glimpse into what they were feeling. "*Stand back, Satan, an' let me come by*," rang the opening solo line
of one of them.

> *Stand back, Satan, an' let me come by*
> *Then I'll shout glory, glory!*
> *You whipped ole Sal, an' you'll whip her again*
> *Stand back, Satan, an' let me come by*
> *Then I'll shout glory, glory hallelujah!*

And a second hymn expressly melded celebrations of human freedom
and spiritual redemption.

Glory, glory, free at last
I'm new-born again!
We've been a long time talkin' 'bout trials here below
I'm new-born again.[16]

From where the freedmen turned west out of the Shenandoah Valley to the falls of the Kanawha River in what later became West Virginia is a stretch of about 140 miles. Modern drivers see the dramatic peaks and valleys on this route as they speed along Interstate 64, and drivers who take the back roads can still see the sharp elevations of the nineteenth-century road. "Now and then," wrote one antebellum gazetteer, the road "courses along the margin of some rocky and stupendous precipice, often several hundred if not a thousand feet in depth," and "you feel an involuntary shuddering at the slender barrier which separates you from eternity." The greatest thrill of all came at a peak above the New River called Hawk's Nest, where travelers could peer over a sheer cliff and watch the hundreds of hawks nested in its crevices as they hunted for fish in the water 1,200 feet below.[17]

Not far beyond Hawk's Nest, the road descended to a picturesque valley where the Gauley River tumbled into the New River to form the Great Kanawha. The roar from a 22-foot waterfall downstream told weary travelers they had reached the head of navigable water on the western side of the mountains. The Kanawha flattened beyond the falls, the valley gradually widened, and travelers began to see signs of commerce. Clouds of smoke rose from the soot-stained furnaces that were boiling salt out of brine pumped from beneath the river. Busy boat landings dotted the riverbanks. And heavily laden steamboats churned by them with cargoes of salt, coal, and timber for Cincinnati and other ports down the Ohio and Mississippi Rivers. For men and women who had never before gone beyond the quiet plantation country of Southside Virginia, these sights and sounds must have been astonishing.[18]

On the last day of June, the freedmen boarded a small stern-wheeler named the *Yucatan.* They had been on the road for almost a month and walked nearly 300 miles. Then with the modern miracle of steam locomotion, the boat whisked them another 300 miles down the Kanawha and Ohio Rivers in little more than a day.[19]

. . . .

THE SIGHT OF nearly four hundred free Blacks walking up Main Street on July 1, 1846, made a big impression on the people of Cincinnati. But no one was surprised to see them. The newspapers had been buzzing about their arrival since the beginning of June. That was when the recordation of Judge Leigh's large land purchases in Mercer County formally alerted white residents that the Black population there was about to double. At a meeting held about the time the freedmen left Roanoke, white men in the affected townships resolved to resist the new settlement. They warned that they would exclude any Black settler who did not post the hefty $500 bond required by the Ohio Black laws—using "force and arms" if necessary.[20]

Reports of the Mercer County meeting struck raw nerves. The main Democratic paper in Cincinnati claimed that the citizen reaction illustrated "the practical consequences" of the abolitionists' "extreme dogmas." "No, sir," objected the antislavery Liberty Party's paper; such troubles were just "the practical consequences of the existence of Slavery in the South, and the encouragement given to it by . . . the Democratic Party." Free Blacks would not come to Ohio if slaveholders did not drive them from home.[21]

The editor of Cincinnati's leading Whig newspaper agreed. "The emigration of John Randolph's negroes," he wrote, proved that the free states were more involved in slavery than Ohio Democrats wanted to admit. "And evidently, the people of Virginia think so too." For whenever death's dark call awakened their withered conscience, they freed their slaves and sent them to live in Ohio. Yet this good Whig could not resist ending his editorial on a racially inflected note of outrage. "What right have they," he demanded, "to be pouring in upon us their helpless, new made free?"[22]

The Roanoke freedmen's arrival may not have surprised anyone, but their appearance drew considerable attention. No one had ever seen so many Black people in one group, and the whole crowd had to walk through the middle of town to get from the steamboat landing up to the turning basin where boats took on passengers for the Miami Canal. The editor of the evening paper scooped the story because the crowd walked right past his office. "They are of all ages and condition," he reported, "from the infant upon the breast, to the old man tottering under the weight of time and infirmities." They had their baggage wagons with them, and although they wore coarse slave cloth, he thought they had a much more "comfortable appearance" than the newly emancipated slaves he was accustomed to seeing. An English engineer who saw them walk by his office in the next block made a sketch of the procession.[23]

The Miami Canal was only 40 feet wide, and boats on it moved no faster than a team of mules could pull them. The sides of the narrow boats stood wide open in warm weather. So passengers got a good view of the countryside, and people along the way got a very good look at them. There were not many people in the woods and farmland north of Cincinnati, of course. Men working in the nearby fields must have looked up to watch the boatloads of Black families pass, and some of the curious might have waited along the canal path if they got word that "John Randolph's negroes" were coming. The freedmen saw more of the local people in the canal towns, where word of their arrival spread faster and their boats had to wait for water to rise in the locks. Onlookers took a particular interest in Randolph's famous man John, and newspapers reported that John White bowed politely to those who identified him.[24]

What the freedmen heard about the protest in Mercer County would not have surprised them any more than their arrival surprised the people in Cincinnati. Endemic prejudice had permeated their lives since they were born. It also pervaded the lives of the free Blacks they knew in Virginia, such as the families John Randolph's brother had settled at Israel Hill. It was prejudice enshrined in law that had compelled them to leave Virginia. Although they hoped to find less prejudice in a free state, they had doubts about that. A newspaper writer who spoke with some of them as they moved north on the canal shared those apprehensions. "We have no idea that they will be permitted to remain in Mercer county," he wrote. "How unfortunate that these poor blacks had not at once been sent to Liberia! There they would have enjoyed those privileges of 'liberty and equality,' which it is not their lot to meet with save in the land of their fathers."[25]

The three boats carrying the settlers from Virginia reached the Mercer County canal town of New Bremen just before dawn on Sunday, July 5. The captain of the lead boat moved it into the lock, the massive wooden gates swung shut behind it, and as the water rose, the first morning light began to reveal the surroundings. Alongside the right of the lock was an open landing flanked by a long row of warehouses and grain mills, and on the other side of the canal were the scattered buildings of a small town. Most of them were constructed of logs, many of the ones built with sawn timber remained unpainted, and all of them looked fairly new.[26]

German immigrants had established the town just fifteen years earlier. They were farmers, tradesmen, teachers, and ministers who had found it difficult to maintain their middling standard of living under unstable economic conditions in the German states. Many of them met on the Atlantic crossing or during their progress across Pennsylvania and down the Ohio River. What they had found in common besides their language and culture was their religion. They were Protestants, and the charter they signed when they founded the town declared that it would be an enclave for "Germans of Protestant faith." They thought it was important to say so. Their religion was part of their identity, and they had heard that most Germans in the rest of Mercer County were Catholic.[27]

When the water had lifted the first of the Black settlers' boats to the top of the lock chamber, the tender lashed it in place and threw down planks so the passengers could unload. Families assembled on the landing, organized baggage, and then took a swinging bridge across the canal to the town side. Their land lay in scattered tracts 8 to 15 miles farther west. They were planning to set up camp outside town and wait for Judge Leigh to meet them before going further. But news of their arrival spread quickly, and as the morning sun rose, a white mob gathered to stop them.[28]

Members of the mob came from all over Mercer County. Farmers from the western townships where Leigh was buying land had time to ride into town. Some of the townspeople also joined in, and they silenced a stouthearted young townsman named Charles Boesel who tried to dissuade them. A boatload of armed men came down the canal from the old county seat of Saint Marys to lend their weight to the growing assembly. By noon, the mob's leaders were ready to make demands.[29]

Assuming the Mercer County citizens who later signed resolutions against Black settlement were representative, the members of the mob appear to have been men of modest means like most other residents of the county. Some of them had small farms, others apparently were tradesmen or landless youths. Some had been living in the county at the time of the previous federal census, others had not. About half of them used British surnames; the rest of the names were German. An abolitionist editor in Cincinnati who took the trouble to look them up in the tax records mordantly observed that the combined value of their property was about $2,000, far less than the value of the land that belonged to the freedmen arriving from Virginia.[30]

The mob demanded that Tom Cardwell, the white man they took to be in charge, either post the $500 bond for each immigrant that the Black laws required or remove the whole lot of them by ten o'clock the next morning. Cardwell asked the mob's leaders to deal with Judge Leigh, who was expected to arrive within the next three days, and he offered to deposit $1,000 as security for the settlers' good behavior in the meantime. The mob claimed that the delay would just give Cardwell time to run away and leave the immigrants behind. Cardwell said they could lock him up in the county jail until Leigh got there, but even that failed to satisfy them. They insisted that Cardwell post bonds or remove everyone the next day. In the meantime, they arrested him, unloaded the remaining settlers, and set an armed guard around their camp.[31]

The Quaker land agent Samuel Jay came up the canal from Piqua the next morning, but he had no authority to post the bonds the mob demanded. So Cardwell bowed to mob pressure and hired two southbound boats to take the settlers back down the canal. White men armed with muskets and bayonets walked along the towpath beside the boats until they crossed the Mercer County line. There they left Tom Cardwell, reported the Saint Marys newspaper, "in full possession of his sable cargo and in the enjoyment of his liberty." The paper said not a word about the distress inflicted on hundreds of men, women, and children.

"Every reflecting man must see," urged the paper's Democratic editor, that a large Black settlement in the county would wither "the brightest hopes" of "an honest and industrious people who have endured the privations and hardships of opening farms and establishing themselves homes in an unbroken wilderness." The Black settlement would render their farms worthless just as surely as "the settling of a cloud of locusts upon the fair fields of Egypt." A Columbus paper ran the story under a headline that read *Great excitement in Mercer county—the importers of the slaves compelled by the people to reship them.*"[32]

Racist violence was common in the United States during the 1830s–40s. The riots that erupted in Washington during Francis Scott Key's years as the federal prosecutor and the repeated attacks on Black neighborhoods in Cincinnati were part of a pervasive pattern. Philadelphia alone saw five major race riots during those decades, and few large American cities were spared. One particularly vicious riot in New York lasted for nearly a week until the mayor raised additional troops and officials of the American Anti-Slavery Society publicly disclaimed any support for marriage between persons of different races. Both the violence and the disclaimer appalled European witnesses, and the plot of a novel that Alexis de Tocqueville's traveling companion wrote about American racial prejudice features a couple whose wedding provokes the riot.[33]

Although mobs were more unusual in rural areas, there was plenty of vigilante violence. The checkerboard pattern of settlement in Ohio encouraged people who had settled with others of their own kind to protect their turf from outsiders, and the exclusionary provisions of the Black laws—which entrusted enforcement to each township—gave them a ready justification for taking matters into their own hands whenever the intruders were African American.[34]

The racial violence was an expression of white fears that permeated all parts of the United States. The spread of abolitionism was a threat to the established order of things everywhere. The number of slaves in the United States had risen sharply during the early nineteenth century. They represented an enormous capital investment, and their output was a principal driver of economic expansion in the North and West as well as in the South. Slave-grown cotton represented more than half of the value of American exports. It supported Northern shipping, commerce, finance, and textile manufacturing as well as the boom in Southern agriculture. The economic expansion drove the demand for agricultural production in the West, and the prosperity of Cincinnati and its hinterland depended on trade with the cotton South. Threats to all of that sparked insecurities, and insecurities ignited fear.[35]

When fear burst into violence, abolitionists and free Blacks were the natural targets. Abolitionists were disturbing the peace. They said so themselves. So to frightened people, silencing them seemed to be a sensible thing to do. Free Blacks were the living embodiment of the change abolitionists advocated. So excluding them (by terror as well as colonization) was another obvious reaction. Just as free Blacks had long been unwanted in slave states because whites feared they would disrupt the binary social order, emancipated Southern Blacks became unwelcome in free states because whites feared the consequences of racial diversity. Either the immigrants would fail to support themselves and become a burden on society, ran white thinking, or they would work for too little and drag down white wages. No matter what, they would attract more Blacks and eventually—the argument always climaxed with lurid images—"mongrelize" American society.[36]

Historians have struggled to explain the behavior of antebellum mobs. Did mobs erupt in reaction to troubling events or did designing people orchestrate them to achieve their own purposes? Were they led by "gentlemen of property and standing" or by working-class agitators? Was it economic anxieties or racial prejudice that made the violence so virulent? Whatever the answers to those questions, two things are clear. Whites of all classes participated in mob violence, and many white politicians used the racial prejudice on display in the mobs to rally political support. Recent European immigrants uncertain about their own place in American society were particularly susceptible to political appeals based on white solidarity, and in ways that varied from place to place, populist Democrats in the free states used racism to justify their opposition to abolitionism.[37]

William Sawyer, the Democratic congressman who represented Mercer County, was a good example. He had grown up outside Dayton, worked as a blacksmith, and then served several terms in the Ohio legislature as an outspoken friend of the white working man. After twice failing to win election to Congress from Dayton, he moved to Saint Marys in 1843 and won the congressional seat there the following year. The Whigs detested Sawyer, and just months before the Roanoke freedmen reached New Bremen, the Whig press had ridiculed Sawyer's vulgarity.[38]

"Every day at 2 o'clock he feeds," began a front-page item in the *New-York Tribune*. It described how Sawyer ate sausages in a window seat of the House chamber, wiped his greasy hands in the sparse hair on his bald head, and picked his teeth with a jackknife before returning to his duties as lawmaker. The satiric piece aimed to amuse, and when Sawyer rose to tell the House that he would not stand for such abuse, he made the mistake of asking the clerk to read it into the record. Amid the resulting peals of laughter, the Democratic majority made the further mistake of voting to expel the *Tribune*'s correspondents. That prompted stories in other newspapers and broadcast Sausage Sawyer's embarrassment to the entire country.[39]

Whig sneers at Sawyer's sausages had a nativist undertone. Sawyer's congressional district was more distinctly German than the district that had twice rejected him before he moved to Mercer County. The immigrant preference for Democratic candidates was both a cause and an effect of the Whigs' disdain for poor, ignorant foreigners. Although the German farmers and tradesmen in Sawyer's district differed from the urban laborers Whigs particularly despised, most of the Germans outside of New Bremen felt stigmatized for another reason. They were Catholic.[40]

Evangelical Protestants claimed that Catholicism was a "political religion" led by a foreign despot. Anti-Catholicism had a long heritage in Puritan New England, and the influential Presbyterian preacher Lyman Beecher fanned the embers that Yankee settlers brought with them to Ohio when he moved to Cincinnati in 1832. His *Plea for the West* warned that foreign Catholic immigration into the heartland was a threat to American democracy. Beecher's plea resonated with many American Protestants, and their hostility drove immigrant Catholic voters into the arms of Democratic candidates who emphasized the equality of all white men. In cities where white immigrants competed with Blacks for work, Democrats could triangulate religious and racial prejudices to solidify white working-class support.[41]

Sawyer was still in Washington when the Roanoke freedmen reached Mercer County, but when he campaigned for renomination to Congress a few months later, he took credit for raising the mob that met them in New Bremen. He had seen "the Randolph negroes . . . coming at a distance," he told crowds back home, and he "kept the boys advised and told them to be ready and not let them land!" Whigs pounced on the possibility that Democrats might pick another candidate for Sawyer's seat, and their newspapers made merry about the Democrats' reduced appetite for sausages. But Sawyer's race-baiting got him reelected, and his reelection emboldened him.[42]

"There was very little difference between Abolitionists and Whigs in Ohio," Sawyer told Congress shortly after the election. The Whigs wanted to repeal Ohio's Black laws and "mix up negroes and whites at the ballot-box." That must never happen, he said. The Black laws were what stood between his constituents and an invasion by free Blacks and escaped slaves. That was why the men of Mercer County "rose in their might" to enforce the law against the manumitted slaves John Randolph's estate had sent into his district. He was willing to admit that free Blacks had the same political rights as whites—just as long as they were not in Ohio. "In Ohio the people were white, and chose to be governed by white men," he proclaimed. "Let the negroes go where they can govern themselves."[43]

The two boatloads of Virginians that Sawyer's constituents had expelled from Mercer County reached a place called Lockport late in the day they left New Bremen. The massive stone canal lock there filled the side of a hill about 10 miles north of Piqua and just 4 miles above Colonel John Johnston's farm on the Great Miami River. Johnston had come to Pennsylvania from Ireland when he was eleven and eloped to Ohio about sixteen years later with a teenage Quaker named Rachel Robinson. He had served as a federal Indian agent for thirty years and hosted many large Native encampments on his broad river bottom. So Samuel Jay naturally thought of the farm as a good place for the Virginians to camp while Judge Leigh sorted out the problem in Mercer County.[44]

Four hundred strangers camped a few miles out of town were bound to attract a lot of attention in Piqua, and they did. The attention increased when some of them moved to an open field beside a slaughterhouse that was even closer to town. The white townsfolk came out in the evenings to see "the songs and dances of the new colonists," as one newspaper patronizingly put it. "It was quite a show," one white man recalled many years later. "I never saw so many colored people in my life." The "colonists" in their turn used the occasion to raise popular sympathy and sell some corn bread to the crowd.[45]

A Methodist minister was so taken by the scene that he described it

Miami Canal lock at Lockport (now Lockington),
Ohio, photograph, 1933

in a newspaper letter about church business. He said he had not seen such mouthwatering hoecakes since he left Southside Virginia, and he felt "compassion" for a local Yankee who swore fire-singed corn bread was just too ugly to eat. The minister's digression ended with reflections on the troubled life of John Randolph. "I will talk about him before the Lord," the good man concluded, "and if it does him no good, it may soften my own heart."[46]

While the settlers camped outside Piqua, Judge Leigh spent weeks looking for places to settle them. At first, he was led to believe that opposition in Mercer County might not be widespread. He went to Saint Marys with a delegation that included Colonel Johnston and other notables from Piqua as well as Peter Odlin, the Dayton lawyer Leigh had consulted the previous year. They took rooms in a local hotel and invited the citizens to call on them, but those consultations soon ended.

The Saint Marys newspaper explained why. It was indeed "a hard case" to turn away "80 families of black slaves" worn out by "labor-

ing to build up princely fortunes for their task-masters," wrote the
editor, but it was "a harder case" to accept "a colony of manumitted
slaves, whom Virginians admit to be a dangerous nuisance in *their*
community." Mercer County farmers did not want to live surrounded
by "negroes fresh from the slave plantations of Virginia," and if the
Blacks were allowed to settle, the farmers would not even be able
to sell their land and leave because "no man would buy it." Other
newspapers sharply reminded whites in Mercer County that they had
managed to take a great deal of the freedmen's money for the purchase of land and the construction of houses before coming to this
conclusion.[47]

Judge Leigh next tried to settle the freedmen in the first county to
the southeast. Shelby County already had several small Black communities, and Leigh hoped some of the Virginia families could join each
of those communities without raising much opposition. He told local
officials that he had spent only $9,000 to $10,000 of the freedmen's
money, so he could afford to buy some additional land and cover the
freedmen's expenses for eighteen months. The plan initially appeared
acceptable. Leigh contracted for some land near a place called Rumley, and he found employment for some of the freedmen on farms
around the county seat in Sidney. But after armed whites tried to
intercept settlers headed for Rumley, it became apparent that Shelby
County could not absorb many of the freedmen without inviting a
stronger backlash. Only a score of the families camped at Piqua were
able to go there.[48]

Leigh was unprepared for this kind of resistance. Thomas Corwin, Augustus Wattles, and the others he consulted the previous year
had led him to believe that the $500 bond requirement in the Black
laws would not be a problem. He had not enlisted abolitionists to help
him because he thought their support would alienate other citizens,
and nothing in his own experience prepared him to face down racial
prejudice. His lawyerly inclination toward discussion and compromise completely misled him. He even spoke openly about sending the
freedmen to Liberia, which was precisely the wrong thing to say in

a state where the American Colonization Society had more branches than anywhere else but Virginia. Although Judge Leigh was "a gentleman and a worthy man," concluded one abolitionist observer, he lacked the "firmness and decision" necessary to deal with the problem he now faced.[49]

That Leigh eventually found places for the rest of the Roanoke freedmen in Miami County was due to their own persistence and the help of his land agent Samuel Jay. Miami County lies immediately south of Shelby, and white settlers had lived there longer than in the counties to the north. Piqua and the county seat of Troy were thriving towns with a demand for domestic help and hired workmen. Quaker farming communities in western parts of the county needed farmhands. Domestic help and farmhands typically got room and board. Jay used his connections in the county to help the freedmen find jobs that could sustain them until Leigh came up with another plan.[50]

This approach seemed to restore a measure of calm. "The Farmers around Troy and Sidney have taken possession of the negroes and given them quarters," reported a Cincinnati paper. The employers said the freedmen could remain until Judge Leigh found a permanent place for them. "The excitement has nearly subsided." Most whites seemed to accept the arrangements on the understanding that they were temporary and in the hope that the freedmen would eventually go to Liberia.[51]

But there was still resistance. One group in Piqua threatened to mob anyone who hired the Black settlers, until another group announced they would put down such a mob by force. Some of the freedmen were still on Colonel Johnston's farm at the end of August when he wrote about the situation to his son-in-law in Dayton. "The Quakers were here yesterday . . . visiting the Black people," he said, and he had spoken to them about finding a freedwoman who would be willing to go to Dayton as a house servant. Johnston thought that would not be difficult. Some people in Miami County, he explained, were using the Black laws to prosecute local employers for hiring the unbonded Roanoke freedmen.[52]

Worse things were happening up in Mercer County. Johnston reported that citizens there had just warned "all of the coloured people in the County to prepare and leave in 6 or 9 months." Newspapers throughout Ohio carried the story a few days later.[53]

A meeting at New Bremen had resolved that every African American in the county was settled in violation of the bond requirement in the Black laws and "contrary to the wishes of the white population." "We will not live among negroes," the meeting proclaimed, and as white people had settled Mercer County first, they were determined to resist Black settlement by every means, "the bayonet not excepted." If Blacks did not leave by the first of March, white vigilantes would remove them. In the meantime, white citizens were not to employ them, trade with them, or grind their grain.[54]

The New Bremen meeting also called for tighter Black laws. Those laws should "absolutely prevent for all time to come" the immigration of any Black person into Ohio. God himself required it, the meeting declared, because he had made "undeniable distinctions" between "different races of men." The meeting denounced the abolitionists' attempts "to fasten disgrace upon the laboring classes of this country by means of their miscalled philanthropy." The men who signed these resolutions were the middling fellows with German and British surnames whose combined property was worth less than the Virginia freedmen's land. (A newspaper in Philadelphia noted that Congressman Sawyer "of sausage notoriety" was among them.)[55]

The resolutions imperiled everything the Black community at Carthagena had accomplished, and the next day, Augustus Wattles wrote to Whig governor Mordecai Bartley for help. Wattles claimed that only a few of the residents in affected townships had objected to Judge Leigh's land purchases. Most of the purchased land adjoined property owned by other African Americans, and the Virginia freedmen could settle it without making any white man "a neighbor to a black" who was not one already. Wattles said that the "feeling of the Germans" toward the Black residents in the area had always been friendly, and the townspeople at New Bremen had said nothing against the new Black settlers before they arrived. In fact, he had not heard one respectable man speak against Black settlement. Yet unless Governor Bartley intervened, he had no doubt the rabble would do what they said.[56]

The Black residents around Carthagena drafted their own appeal to the governor. "We came to the county when it was new and unsettled about eleven years ago," they asserted, and bought 25,000 acres of land. They had cleared the land, built good roads, and paid hundreds of dollars in taxes. None of them had ever been convicted of a crime or "been insolent or uncivil with the whites," yet "for some reason unknown to us unless it be the unreasonable prejudice that exists against color, our lives and property have been threatened."[57]

Governor Bartley was no friend of vigilante violence, but the Black laws were an issue in the upcoming autumn election, and he did not want to jeopardize the Whig Party's chances with moderate voters by taking too strong a position. So the proclamation he issued to the people of Mercer County was measured. He called on local officials to maintain the peace and relieve him of "the unpleasant duty of resorting to more summary measures." If any of the Black residents had violated the law, he said, law-abiding citizens should seek their legal remedies. The Whig candidate to succeed Bartley was just as cautious. He had already come out against the Black laws, yet when he campaigned in Mercer County, he disappointed some of his abolitionist supporters. He told voters there that he did not believe Blacks should vote or own land.[58]

• • • •

BY AUGUST 1846, the expulsion of John Randolph's slaves from Mercer County had become national news. Newspapers everywhere ran the story alongside reports on the war with Mexico that had broken out a few months earlier. The same columns also carried news of renewed sectional debate over the expansion of slavery into new territories, a debate that gave special resonance to the story about racial exclusion coming out of Ohio.

A Democratic congressman from Pennsylvania named David Wilmot had reignited the sectional debate when he proposed to ban slavery in any territory ultimately conquered from Mexico. By making the ban a proviso in critical war legislation, Wilmot thought Northern Democrats could protect themselves from the charge that President Polk had led their party into the war for the benefit of Southern slaveholders. The proposal passed the House despite nearly unanimous Southern opposition, and although it failed in the Senate, Wilmot's proviso provoked unquenchable discord. It pitted the slaveholders' demand for new slave country against white working men's desire for access to free soil—land where they could farm free from the competition of enslaved labor. The confrontation would roil American politics for almost two decades until civil war finally ended it.[59]

The versions of the Roanoke freedmen's story that appeared in newspapers around the country reflected the outlines of the national dilemma. The Ohio newspapers naturally took a Western perspective. Democratic papers insisted that Black settlement would destroy the value of white farmers' land and cheat white laborers of an honest living. The Liberty Party paper claimed that was "all wrong." Even if the Virginia freedmen stayed in Ohio rather than going to Liberia, it said, their presence would cause "no serious inconvenience" to white citizens. Southerners should not colonize their emancipated slaves in Ohio, "but we are decidedly opposed to any and every movement . . . for maltreating or in any way molesting those already here." Some of the abolitionist papers were sharper. They said the Ohio legislature was responsible for "the outrages" against John Randolph's slaves because it had failed to repeal the Black laws.[60]

A correspondent for the *New-York Tribune* took a more sweeping antislavery view. Not only had Mercer County stopped John Randolph's slaves from settling together as a community, he wrote, the adjoining counties had even prevented them from settling in small groups. Now Judge Leigh would have to send them away to Liberia. "O my country!!" he wailed. "Soil of the free!!—refuge of the persecuted and oppressed, where all men are of right and ought to be free and equal, what a sad commentary is this on thy boasted liberty!" *Tribune* editor Horace Greeley ran the story on the front page, and William Lloyd Garrison reprinted it for the readers of his *Liberator*.[61]

The advocates of African colonization who wrote for the American Colonization Society's journal drew a starkly different picture. What had happened to Randolph's freedmen, they said, was the result of pervasive racial prejudice—and the demonstrable failure of all efforts to change it. The settlement of emancipated slaves in Africa was the only possible solution, and events like those in Mercer County ought to have a good influence on the minds of "sensible, reflecting colored people." Such scenes "speak about as plain as common preaching that the free colored people of the United States are not exactly *free* to make a home where they please, and we think they will begin to have a *realizing* sense of this by-and-by."[62]

What the Southern papers presented was a nasty caricature. "These negroes did not act smart," snickered an editor in Natchez. If they had just pretended to be runaways, Ohioans would have welcomed them with open arms. An editor in the Piedmont region of Virginia was almost as mean when he wrote that Northerners who wept for the "imaginary" suffering of slaves would "laugh in your face" if you asked them to help relieve it. Other Virginia papers said much the same thing a bit more politely. For all of their great interest in runaway slaves, claimed one, the people in Ohio had no real compassion for the free Black man. "He is but a 'poor negro,' not fit for a good neighborhood anywhere" in their state.[63]

The men and women from Roanoke who walked west for freedom could not read the newspapers, and the whites who wrote for the newspapers did not bother to talk to them. But what the freedmen could have told was the plainest story of all. Freedom had rendered them homeless. It had dispersed the community in which they and their parents and their grandparents once lived. It was about to leave them, as one Black refugee put it, without protection from anyone who had ever known them. Perhaps that explains why one of their most abiding memories of the confrontation at New Bremen features

Tom Cardwell mounting an overturned crate to lecture the white mob about their right to settle in Mercer County.[64]

Although John White had seen a good deal of the world, he had not experienced this kind of hatred. He had been jailed, beaten, and abused, but never discarded. He had a firm sense of who he was and how the world ought to treat him. And his first month in Ohio convinced him that the people there would never respect him. If he had to be hired out, he would work for someone who valued him and not for some trifling white man who treated him as a broken-down old slave. He decided to go back to Virginia.[65]

That decision involved risks. Virginia law said that emancipated slaves who returned to the state would be whipped and sold back into slavery. Laws like that had gone largely unenforced for years, of course. Whites in the Virginia countryside usually countenanced or even encouraged the quiet persistence of freed slaves they had known all their lives. Return from a free state was different from mere persistence, however, and racial regulation in Virginia was becoming harsher. Governor William Smith was about to ask the legislature for a law removing all free Blacks from the state. "Extra Billy" Smith, as the governor was called, was a wheeler and dealer. He had gotten his name by milking the central government for extra payments on his postal delivery contracts. He surely knew that the legislature would not enact such a law and that local officials could not enforce it if they did. Yet his proposal was not pointless. He thought many voters would like it, and he wagered that it would encourage them to enforce existing laws.[66]

John White believed he could win the other side of that bet. "They have no feeling for colored people in Ohio," he told a Virginia newspaper writer as he and his family made their way back to Charlotte County. If the legislature would not grant them permission to live free in Virginia as John Randolph's will requested, then they would return to slavery as Virginia law required.[67]

White knew that slaveholding Virginians would expect him to say that, but he certainly did not think it would happen. Although the legislature typically gave scant attention to petitions for permission to remain, his fame, his age, and Randolph's wishes gave White better odds than most freedmen. Five years later, he and his wife Betsy did register with the clerk in Charlotte County as free Blacks with permission to remain in Virginia, and an entry made a few months after that listed every member of their family except for their son Moses, who had remained with a wife in Ohio. John White himself would die in Ohio the following year while he and Betsy were visiting Moses.[68]

John White's words about race relations in Ohio were what most white Americans wanted to hear. They believed that Blacks could never find true freedom in the United States because the toils of racial prejudice would long outlast the shackles of slavery. They thought Judge Leigh should have set an example by sending this highly visible group of freedmen to Liberia. Now that Leigh had spent so much of their money buying land in Ohio, lamented the Colonization Society's journal, the group was stuck there. "We have been informed that many of the rest of them would come back to Virginia and be slaves . . . *if they could get back*. And yet they are now free and in a free state! But what does it all amount to?"[69]

EPILOGUE

Randolph freedmen's reunion, photograph, c. 1902–05.
Fountain Randolph stands eighth from the left (with cane),
and Goodrich Giles stands tenth from the right.

THE ROANOKE FREEDMEN NEVER DID GET THEIR LAND in Mercer County, and their story took on a fraught meaning after the Civil War. Those who seek lessons from the past often shape their accounts of historical events in order to suit their present purposes. And what white men overwhelmed by universal emancipation found in the Roanoke freedmen's story was proof that they did not owe four million newly emancipated slaves anything more than their freedom.

There had been a moment toward the end of the Civil War when emancipated slaves believed the Union might give them 40 acres and a mule. Historians often trace the idea to William Tecumseh Sher-

man's Special Field Order Number 15, which distributed abandoned
rebel land along the Georgia and South Carolina coast to freedmen
during the final months of armed conflict. The order came at the
urging of local Black leaders, who knew that land was the essential
basis for personal independence in a rural society. "The way we can
best take care of ourselves is to have land," they told Sherman, "and
turn it and till it by our own labor." Union officers allocated 40 acres
to each adult male worker, and many of the workers got informal
access to the army's cast-off mules.[1]

The 40-acre benchmark reflected American agricultural experience in the West. Forty acres was a quarter of a quarter section, a
sixteenth part of the square-mile sections into which the central government had surveyed the Western territories. It was the typical size
of a small family farm in Sherman's home state of Ohio and the other
free states in what we now call the Midwest. Those states contained
the nation's principal agricultural frontiers when the war began, and
the opportunities available there shaped notions about what a free
man working on the margin of American agriculture had a right to
expect. Forty acres was as much land as he and his family could work,
and it could produce enough food and cash income to support them.

Congress debated the systematic redistribution of Southern land
as the war ended. The act establishing the Freedmen's Bureau authorized federal officials to assign up to 40 acres of abandoned or confiscated land to each emancipated male worker, and rumors about 40
acres and a mule swept through Black communities across the South.
A land confiscation bill introduced by the Radical Republican congressman Thaddeus Stevens two years later fanned the flame. "The
opinion *generally* entertained by the reflecting freedmen," wrote a
Freedmen's Bureau officer stationed in Southside Virginia, "is that
the property held by their employers has been forfeited to the Government by the treason of its owners, and it is liable to be confiscated
whenever Congress demands it."[2]

Proposals to confiscate rebel property soon died, however, and
Union commanders had to claw back the land they had allocated to

emancipated slaves along the Southern coast. Although Congress did pass a law that reserved public lands in the South for sale to home-steaders, the freedmen they hoped to benefit lacked the capital to buy it. Timber companies persuaded Congress to repeal the law ten years later. Still, the idea that a freedmen should receive 40 acres and a mule did not die. Emancipated people continued to talk about it—at first as a fading hope and then as a lingering call for justice.[3]

The call still resounded in a memoir that Henry Clay Bruce published at the end of the nineteenth century. Bruce had struggled to make a living after he escaped from slavery during the Civil War, and although he himself had ultimately prospered, he held the federal government responsible for the continued struggle of many others.

"History does not record," wrote Bruce, that slavery had robbed the four million men and women emancipated by the war of all knowledge about how to support themselves. For two hundred years, they and their ancestors had labored entirely for others. They cleared vast regions of the continent and delivered mighty streams of gold into the pockets of white people North and South. Yet the government set them free "without a dollar, without a foot of land, and without the wherewithal to get the next meal even." It seemed to Bruce that "a Christian nation" made wealthy by the work of "a subjugated people" owed them a better start. "Justice seems to demand one year's support, forty acres of land and a mule each."[4]

William Mungen, who represented Mercer County in Congress after the war, did not have to look far for a counternarrative to dismiss such calls for reparation. He said that the experience with John Randolph's slaves in his own district proved it was pointless to give land to emancipated slaves. When Randolph freed his slaves, Mungen told Congress, he sent them to one of the most fertile parts of Ohio and gave them "teams, cattle, farming utensils, provisions, and money." What was the result? "There is not a Randolph negro on any of those lands," Mungen declared, because they were "too lazy" to farm them. "The negro always has been a failure," he concluded, "and always will be a failure when thrown entirely upon his own resources."[5]

That story became the accepted narrative among whites in Mercer County and then in the rest of the country. It conflated the attempted settlement of the Roanoke freedmen with the Black farming community around Carthagena and concealed the white violence against Black settlers. A man named A. J. Linzee, whose family had been among Mercer County's early white settlers, recited the tale to a local newspaper over twenty years later. Linzee claimed that the Roanoke freedmen had settled on their land in Mercer County after whites grew reconciled to the idea. He said each family got 80 acres, a house, a team of horses, farm implements, and a year's provisions. Yet only forty-eight adult Black males remained in the whole county. "And so it was with these people," concluded Linzee. Although they had been "so well provided for," they could not open new farms and cultivate new crops in a cold climate.[6]

The people once enslaved by John Randolph told a more honest story. They told it to curious farm boys while they worked in the summer heat on crop fields in western Miami County. They told it to other workmen through swirls of dust as they swept out factories in Piqua. They told it to masons on the construction sites in Troy, where they carried countless loads of brick. And when their listeners were called to testify in an Ohio courtroom decades later, what each of them remembered hearing was the same. The Roanoke freedmen had gone up the canal to Mercer County to settle their land, but "the Dutch out there" had refused to let them stay. At first, the freedmen thought there must have been some mistake. They had heard Ohio was "a free country," where they could "go any place they wanted to go without having any papers." Yet they found that was not so because "they couldn't go to their own land."[7]

· · · ·

JUDGE LEIGH HAD done what he could to repair the Roanoke freedmen's loss. Once it became clear that they could not settle in Mercer County, Leigh decided to sell the land he had bought there and use the money to buy land for them in Miami and Shelby Counties. By the time Leigh returned to Ohio to execute that plan in July 1847, his agent in Mercer County had already sold several hundred acres to white farmers. Sales continued at a measured pace for the next six years, and Leigh ultimately sold all of the land for about $1,000 more than he had paid for it. After subtracting land taxes, sales commissions, and expenses, the Randolph estate probably broke even.[8]

Leading abolitionists back East remained concerned about the fate of the Roanoke freedmen, and when most of the land was gone, some of them claimed the sales had been unnecessary. Four hundred Blacks still lived in Mercer County at the time, and the well-connected New York abolitionist Lewis Tappan heard there was no longer any objection to Black settlement there. Tappan thought every person in the mob that drove off the Roanoke freedmen had "left the county . . . or is dead." If Leigh had enlisted support from abolitionists more aggressive than the Quakers, he wrote, "there never would have been any difficulty."[9]

William Sawyer had indeed left Mercer County when the township where he lived became part of Auglaize County two years after the Roanoke freedmen arrived, but he was far from dead. He still represented Mercer County in Congress, and whenever the subject came up in debates, he continued to defend the Mercer County mob. He went even further. Congressmen who wanted to keep slavery out of territory conquered from Mexico, he warned them, should pause to consider the consequences. "It would be that Virginia, and Maryland, and Kentucky, and the rest would shove off their free negroes and settle them on the people of Ohio." His constituents would never submit to that. If he had it in his power, he said, "there should be no slavery under the canopy of heaven." Yet if he were asked whether bondage should continue or Blacks should come to Ohio, he would unhesitatingly opt for slavery.[10]

Although Judge Leigh's surviving papers do not show exactly what he did when he reached Ohio in the summer of 1847, other evidence makes it apparent. Days after his arrival, he met with his lawyer Peter Odlin in Dayton. He told his wife that he "anticipated a great deal of disagreeable and troublesome business," but he thought they could arrange things so that he would not have to come back again. He said the work was going to take two or three weeks.[11]

The Roanoke freedmen began to buy land that summer. One of the earliest recorded purchases came a few weeks after Leigh's arrival. Gabriel White paid $100 for a 12-acre lot across the Great Miami River from Piqua. The following year, his brother Shadrack bought the eastern side of the same parcel for $200, and Sam Rial paid $125 for an adjacent lot. The three lots were part of a newly sub-divided area called Rossville.[12]

Two months after Gabriel White bought his lot in Rossville, six Roanoke freedmen purchased adjacent parcels west of Troy from Leigh's land agent Samuel Jay. Meshack Jones paid $175 for 35 acres, and two others paid about $100 for 20- to 25-acre parcels. The other three purchasers bought 5 to 15 acres for $25 to $75. Four more fami-lies bought almost 200 acres on the far western side of Miami County for $400 the following month. They called their settlement Mar-shalltown. Over the next two years, another eight families bought an additional 80 acres in the county for $1,130, and a freedman named Theodorick Randolph who lived in Shelby County recorded the pur-chase of three lots in Sidney for $120.[13]

The Roanoke freedmen made other land purchases in the wake of Judge Leigh's visit that are more difficult to identify. Some of the transactions simply went unrecorded. The purchasers received deeds, but did not take them to the county courthouse to be entered in the public land records. Some of those unrecorded transactions found their way into the records years later when subsequent purchasers recorded earlier deeds in order to perfect their chain of title. Johnson Crowder and his father Armstead, for example, bought 26 acres out-side Piqua while Leigh was in Ohio, yet their deed only entered the record when they sold part of the land five years later.[14]

In other cases, the Roanoke freedmen did not take title in their own names. They bought land through trustees who held title for the freedmen's benefit. This was a fairly common way for free Blacks to hold property in both the slave and the free states. Even though the trust might be unenforceable where Blacks were not allowed to own real property, it could give them workable access to land. And a trustee could help them protect their land in states like Virginia and Ohio, where Blacks did not have all of the legal rights that they needed to defend their own property (such as the right to testify against white wrongdoers).[15]

Protection against crimes committed by whites was important. When it became clear that the Roanoke freedmen were going to remain in Miami and Shelby Counties, new white resistance emerged. One notable incident involved a settlement southwest of Piqua on land some of the freedmen had bought from Samuel Jay (in one of the transactions that never entered the public records). The settlers had nearly finished building three cabins there in September 1847 when a gang of whites came by night and tore them down. When the settlers rebuilt the cabins, the whites felled three large trees on top of them, shattering the logs and scattering the broken pieces in every direction. "The fact is," wrote a white man who reported the incident to a Cincinnati newspaper, "that our Anti-slavery friends do not do their duty." They "shrink from defending these poor blacks" because they fear that by supporting Black settlers, they will give themselves a bad reputation.[16]

Even some Quakers did not want Roanoke freedmen to settle near them. When a dozen freedmen who were working southwest of Troy deposited $1,150 with three of their Quaker neighbors, other Friends warned the three not to buy land for Blacks in that area. One of the three apparently heeded the warning, but Elijah Coate and Andrew Stevens did not. They bought about 120 acres in trust for the twelve men at a place just outside West Milton. The community that the men and their families established there came to be called Hanktown. Coate and Stevens never recorded the deeds they received for the land. Even the deed they made to a successor trustee did not enter the public record until eighteen years later, when the freedmen and their heirs filed suit to divide the land and take title in their own names.[17]

Recorded deeds alone show that at least twenty-four Roanoke freedmen bought land within a few months of Judge Leigh's return visit. That accounts for almost a third of the Roanoke families. The average purchase was 12 acres, and the average transaction price was $106. In ten additional transactions recorded over the following two years, the average acreage fell to 7 and the average price rose to $117. The size and timing of these purchases suggest that Leigh had begun distributing the freedmen's share of the Randolph estate. They also show that what Leigh delivered fell far short of his original plan to give each family 40 acres.[18]

Leigh's initial distribution to the freedmen might have amounted to as much as $8,000. Divided among about eighty families, it would have given each of them enough to pay the average purchase price in the land transactions recorded at the time. Leigh probably could not have distributed more than $8,000 because he did not have the money. He had used most of the Randolph estate's available cash to send the freedmen to Ohio and purchase the land in Mercer County. He also had arranged for the freedmen to receive periodic subsistence payments until they got settled. The rest of the $30,000 due to them was still tied up in obligations owed to the estate.[19]

It took Leigh nearly as long to collect amounts due to the Randolph estate as it took him to sell the Mercer County land. The buyer of the Charlotte County land that Leigh sold for the freedmen's account was paying for it on installments, and the Randolph heirs took years to pay Leigh their shares of the remaining amount promised to the freedmen. Leigh repeatedly dunned Beverley Tucker by pointing out that he could not pay the lawyers who had represented the slaves in court until Beverley paid him.[20]

The Roanoke freedmen could not have bought so much land after only a year in Ohio without distributions from the Randolph estate. The annual wage for a white adult male farmhand was $100 to $120 plus room and board. Female domestic help received much less. It was not legal to hire unbonded Blacks until the Ohio legislature repealed the Black laws several years later, so some employers surely underpaid them. And the Roanoke freedmen may have had to accept lower wages simply because so many of them were seeking jobs at the same time. Freedmen who bought land needed to have more than just the purchase price. They had to buy tools, seed, and building material. Even if a man and his family saved all of their earnings (which would have been difficult for families with children too young to work), they could scarcely have accumulated enough money to make a homestead in such a short time.[21]

The Black abolitionist Martin Delany met some of the Roanoke freedmen at Troy in 1848, a year after the first land purchases. In a letter to Frederick Douglass's abolitionist newspaper, he reported that they "generally are very ignorant, though some of their children have learned to read during the short time they have been in Ohio." He took particular note of the ethnic appearance of Juba's sixteen-year-old daughter Susan because she was said to resemble her father. "If so," wrote Delany, "Juba was a pure Guinean, small features and intelligent expression." Delany himself had been born in Virginia, but his free mother took him to Pennsylvania as a child so that he could get an education. When white fellow students forced Delany out of the Harvard Medical School four years later, he would publish a Black nationalist manifesto urging African Americans to escape white persecution by settling in West Africa.[22]

A white man who saw the same group of freedmen at Troy sent a derogatory report to a Baltimore newspaper, and quite a few Southern papers reprinted it. It read like a typical white account of a free Black community in the slave states. The writer claimed that "these once valuable servants" had become a burden on society. Their poverty was "a sad commentary on the miserable policy of emancipating negroes and allowing them to remain in this country." Several of the freedmen expressed "an ardent wish" to return to Roanoke, he said, where "they did not know what it was to suffer for want." The leading Democratic paper in Richmond published the report as "an illustration of the *blessings* of freedom to the negro in the fertile State of Ohio."[23]

In fact, the men and women freed by John Randolph's brother Richard had found greater security in Virginia. Whites often complained about their settlement at Israel Hill, but no one ever tried to drive them away. When historian and civil rights activist W. E. B. Du Bois studied Israel Hill almost a century after its formation, he reported that all but three of the twenty-five families living there owned their own houses. Although generations of subdivision had made most of their farms too small to support a family, the residents were able to supplement their incomes by working at nearby farms and tobacco factories. Those who worked as masons and carpenters had made enough money to build new houses with three or four rooms. A recent study by historian Melvin Patrick Ely has shown that the Israelites (as they called themselves) were integral participants in the white-dominated economy of the area. Even Israelite families who lost their land for failure to pay taxes often remained on it because the whites who bought it wanted to keep hardworking laborers in the community.[24]

While most of the Roanoke families eventually obtained land in Ohio, they never got the fair start Judge Leigh meant them to have. Instead of living in a community where they could help each other, they found themselves scattered across two counties. Few got enough land to support themselves, and the work available to them as farmhands, day laborers, and domestic servants was marginal and insecure. Some had to move to town where menial jobs were more plentiful. Those left working in the fields sang the same sorrow songs they had sung in slavery. An old white man who heard them when he was a boy could no longer remember the words, yet the resonant hum of their blended voices still haunted him a half century later.[25]

For this group of freedmen, 40 acres and a mule had been more than a dream. It was a promise from their master's executor. But their land was gone, and the money Judge Leigh gave them had failed to repair the loss. They felt dispossessed for the simple reason that they had been.[26]

. . . .

FIFTY-NINE YEARS after the mob met them at New Bremen, the surviving Roanoke freedmen and their descendants sued to reclaim the land in Mercer County. They had filed a test suit against a German farm couple named Anna Maria and Bernard Dewell the previous year, which must have alerted some of the neighbors. But the notices Sheriff Joseph Hinders served on fifty-six Mercer County farmers in the spring of 1905 were still startling. They demanded that each farmer surrender his land and all of the profits he had ever made from it to the beneficiaries of John Randolph's will. The notices threw a cloud on the titles to more than 3,200 acres of farmland. A local newspaper said they came "like a bolt from the clear sky."[27]

There actually had been rumbles of thunder. The Roanoke freedmen and their descendants—who called themselves "the Randolphs" regardless of their surnames—started holding annual picnic reunions in 1902. Goodrich Giles organized the first one with the help of Fountain Randolph, and it drew more than four hundred people from farms and towns throughout Miami and Shelby Counties. By the time of the second reunion, talk about a lawsuit to recover the land in Mercer County surfaced in local newspapers. The test suit against the Dewells came a year later.[28]

Goodrich Giles was the son of Roanoke freedman Archer Giles and a woman named Sallie. At the time of the first reunion, he was fifty-five. He had built a successful stable and livery business in Piqua and then run as a Republican candidate for city council. He owned 425 acres of farmland as well as shares in several commercial ventures around town, and he was said to be worth more than $50,000. Booker T. Washington pointed to him as a conspicuous example of the success some Black men were achieving in Ohio.[29]

Fountain Randolph was altogether different. He had been a laborer all his life, and when his house in Piqua burned down a few years earlier, the newspapers had described him as "a poor colored man." At sixty, he was beginning to lose his eyesight, but his memory was prodigious. Randolph knew more about the survivors of the trek from Virginia and their descendants than anyone else, and he nurtured a sense of community among them. When the crowd attending the first reunion formed the Randolph Ex-Slave Association, they elected Fountain Randolph as president.[30]

Talk about a lawsuit began after Black law student John Beam brought the Randolphs' claim to the attention of William Henderson, a respected Black lawyer in Indianapolis. Beam had heard about the lost land while he was teaching at the segregated school for Black children in the Piqua subdivision of Rossville. Henderson thought the matter seemed worth pursuing, and he contacted Goodrich Giles. Once the Roanoke descendants decided to sue, probably with financial backing from Giles, Henderson brought a white lawyer and state senator from Mercer County named James Johnson into the case as local counsel.[31]

Race relations in Ohio had deteriorated tragically by this time. The Ohio legislature allowed Blacks to vote in 1870, and it repealed laws requiring segregation in schools and marriages seventeen years later. Yet the hope that those changes in law signaled a change in white mores was soon lost in a haze of reactionary violence. Blacks faced sustained discrimination and de facto school segregation even in the eastern parts of the state, where antislavery sentiment had been strongest.[32]

Lynchings became a grim fact of life throughout the state. Although the Ohio legislature passed a law making local taxpayers financially accountable to the victims' families, white violence against Black Ohioans continued into the opening decade of the twentieth century. A white mob in the northeastern city of Akron rioted when officials stopped them from abducting a Black prisoner accused of raping a white child, and white mobs in Springfield lynched Black prisoners and set fire to the Black part of town. John Beam himself might have been a victim of racist violence. He was convicted of killing a white woman several years after he set up a law practice east of Mercer County, and guards claimed that he hanged himself in prison a month later.[33]

Repression strengthened bonds among Black families in Ohio.

Driven back on their own resources, they redoubled their commitment to mutual support. That commitment found expression in the growth of churches, better schools, new newspapers, and organizations like the Randolph Ex-Slave Association. It also sparked a keener interest in the protection available to African Americans under the law. The liberal laws that had provoked the white backlash were meant to give Black citizens basic legal and political rights and improve their access to economic opportunities. William Henderson was part of a new generation of professionally trained Black lawyers who set out to help Black people realize the promise of those laws.[34]

Early civil rights organizations such as the Niagara Movement looked for opportunities to contest the infamous separate-but-equal doctrine that the federal Supreme Court had announced in the *Plessy v. Ferguson* decision of 1896. About the time that the Roanoke freedmen filed their suits in Ohio, lawyers in the movement were helping a woman named Barbara Pope test whether the doctrine could apply to interstate transportation. Pope was a fifty-two-year-old writer and teacher in the District of Columbia whose once-enslaved parents had a proud history of resistance to oppression. In the summer of 1906, she bought a first-class ticket on a southbound train and refused to move to the Jim Crow car when the train entered Virginia. State authorities arrested her, and the circuit court imposed a fine. But the Virginia attorney general confessed error rather than confront Pope's constitutional challenge to segregated interstate railcars, and the state supreme court reversed her conviction. Pope then brought a suit against the railroad in the District of Columbia for $50,000 in damages. Although she recovered only $1, the twin victories by this forerunner of Rosa Parks showed that the *Plessy* doctrine could be challenged successfully.[35]

Other Black activists demanded compensation for the millions of African Americans impoverished by slavery. In the 1890s, several white Republican congressmen from the Western states had proposed giving federal pensions to former slaves. They claimed that the pension payments would help revive the war-damaged economy of the

Southern states, and they convinced a few Democratic congressmen from the South to back the proposal. Black leaders organized associations to support the idea, and some of the organizations began raising money from their working-class members to provide for mutual relief. These movements for reparation were active when the Roanoke freedmen sued for their lost land, and they continued while the freedmen's suits were in the courts.[36]

Joseph Moton and York Rial were the named petitioners in the freedmen's lawsuits, each representing a different class of individuals. Moton represented the descendants of freedmen who were more than forty years old when they went free. They were the ones for whom John Randolph's will specifically provided 10 acres each. Moton was the grandson of Moses, the field hand who sometimes served as John Randolph's manservant. His surname suggests that his ancestors were among the enslaved pioneers who had cleared Roanoke in the eighteenth century for the Randolph's steward Joseph Morton. This Joseph Moton was born free in Ohio to Moses's daughter Margaret. He had fought in the Union army during the Civil War, returned to Miami County, and settled in Troy. He became a Baptist minister and supported himself by working as a janitor at the county courthouse.[37]

York Rial was one of several dozen survivors of the migration to Ohio. He represented the class of freedmen who were forty or younger when they left bondage. Rial called Piqua his home, although like many other Black laborers, he had spent years living elsewhere in order to find work. His house stood on a lot in Rossville beside the Great Miami River. He had inherited the place from an uncle who bought it in an unrecorded transaction soon after the Roanoke freedmen came to Ohio.[38]

The man who became the lead defendant in the lawsuits might never have heard the thunder that preceded them. Gerhard Kessens did not read English-language newspapers. His spoken English was so bad that his lawyer had to translate for him when he testified at trial. Kessens had grown up in the German kingdom of Hanover and immigrated to Cincinnati in 1860. He moved to Mercer County about ten years later when he had scraped together enough money to buy a 40-acre farm. He paid another German farmer $1,250 for the place. Kessens lived there with his wife, two adult children, and a German-speaking hired hand. They also worked 80 acres across the road that Kessens bought some years later. When Sheriff Hinders served notice on him in 1905, Kessens was sixty-nine years old.[39]

The petitioners' claim against Kessens and scores of his neighbors was relatively simple. They said Judge Leigh had purchased the land in Mercer County with money that belonged to the men and women freed by John Randolph's will. Leigh therefore held the land in trust for them, and he had no authority to sell it without accounting to them for the sales proceeds. The petitioners claimed that Leigh had never made such an accounting. His conveyances of the land therefore were fraudulent. They had not extinguished the freedmen's equitable interest in the land, and all subsequent owners took the land subject to a constructive trust for the freedmen's benefit.[40]

Those claims must have seemed unbelievable to Kessens and the other defendants. Land was the basis for everything in a rural county. It was home, neighborhood, and livelihood. It was the most valuable asset these farmers would ever possess. They thought they had bought their farms fair and square, and they knew they had worked hard to improve them. Kessens did admit that he had never checked the title to his land; he just accepted the seller's assurance that the title was good. Yet foolish as that was, it was not the reason for his problem.[41]

A title search in the Mercer County records would not have alerted Kessens to the freedmen's claim. The search would have revealed that Leigh bought and sold the land as executor for the estate of John Randolph. But executors have the power to buy and sell property, and title records say nothing about what they do with the sale proceeds. Even a buyer who knew that a mob had driven Randolph's heirs from the county years earlier would have had no reason to think that created a defect on land titles. If anything, the mob's action justified Leigh's decision to sell the land.[42]

The problem facing Kessens arose from the tension in the Anglo-

American legal system between law and equity. The common law aimed to keep the peace and encourage material progress by protecting settled expectations. A farmer's legal right to his land gave him the benefit of his labor. He could make a safe home on the land because no one had a right to oust him or his family. He could plant corn there in confidence that the crop would belong to him. He could build barns and fences with assurance that the improvements would profit him and his lawful heirs.[43]

Equity, on the other hand, aimed to right wrongs the law could not remedy. The beneficiaries of a will could force the dead man's executor to deliver property that he had purchased with money left to them. If the executor sold the property in the meantime, they could claim it from the buyer if he knew or should have known that the executor had failed to settle accounts with the beneficiaries. Equity would accept the damage done to the buyer's expectations because the beneficiaries' rights arose first, the executor had done wrong, and the buyer was complicit in his misconduct.[44]

But Moton and Rial also had a problem in this case. Equity imposed time limits on petitions for justice because delay could cause injustice. A farmer who worked the land invested his life and labor in it. Over time, his interest in the land could outgrow the interest of wronged prior owners who failed to reclaim it. So equity refused to help petitioners who had slept on their rights. It acknowledged that the statute of limitations and the doctrine of adverse possession could extinguish dormant claims on land after twenty years.[45]

Delay was excusable if there was a good reason for it. Because a minor had no right to sue, for example, the statute of limitations did not run against him until he came of age. A victim of fraud could not know that he had a claim until he discovered the wrong, so time did not run against him until he had an adequate chance to learn of it. A person who lacked education or practical experience could reasonably take longer to discover a fraud than someone who did not suffer from those disadvantages. But sixty years was more than most lifetimes in the early twentieth century, so the excuse for such a long delay had to be enormously compelling.[46]

The excuse that Moton and Rial offered was profound ignorance. They said that the Roanoke freedmen and their descendants had not known about the land Leigh purchased for them because they suffered under the disabilities of slavery. Their illiteracy and inexperience prevented them from discovering their claim until John Beam, the law student teaching school in Rossville, began to investigate. This excuse played to white preconceptions about the simplicity of emancipated slaves. And it built on the recognition that many Black children in nineteenth-century Ohio were poorly educated because their schools remained effectively segregated and significantly underfunded.[47]

The lawyers that Kessens and the other farmers had hired said those claims of ignorance were not credible, and the Mercer County court of common pleas agreed. It refused to believe that the freedmen could have come all the way to western Ohio without knowing where they were to settle when they got there. The court therefore dismissed Moton's case without trial.[48]

The appeals court reversed. It agreed that the freedmen must have understood they were going to settle land in Ohio. But it did not follow, explained the court, that illiterate men and women "emerging from the condition of slavery" would have understood their legal rights to the land. And what they did not understand, they could not have imparted to their children and grandchildren. The appellate court ordered the court of common pleas to hold a trial.[49]

The petitioners failed to prove their case when it came to trial. The farmers gathered Black and white witnesses to testify that the freedmen had been talking about their lost land for decades, and the surviving freedmen's testimony to the contrary was unconvincing. The farmers also found a country lawyer who said that he had given freedmen at Hanktown a copy of John Randolph's will more than twenty years earlier. The petitioners fell back on the argument that Judge Leigh had concealed the true nature of their rights, but the judge found no evidence of fraud. He held that the petitioners had waited too long. After thirty-six years of "unremitting toil and industry," wrote the judge, Gerhard Kessens's land belonged to him.[50]

The petitioners got a new trial before the appeals court in 1914, and they used it to expand on their claim against Judge Leigh. Numerous witnesses testified that Leigh had never given the freedmen any money. By failing to pay them anything at all, the petitioners' lawyers argued, Leigh had concealed their rights in John Randolph's estate altogether. The man who had given up a large inheritance in order to free Randolph's slaves became the villain in their descendants' story.[51]

Kessens's lawyers showed that Leigh actually had distributed money to the freedmen, but they could not prove that he gave them the entire net proceeds from selling their land. Leigh's accounts to the Virginia courts were missing. The court in Petersburg had sent the Randolph will case to the chancery court in Richmond some years before the Civil War, and the records kept there vanished in flames at the end of the war. The Confederate soldiers who evacuated Richmond set fire to tobacco warehouses and military papers, and the uncontrolled blaze destroyed the center of town before Union troops could put it out.[52]

The dramatic sweep of the petitioners' story was not lost on the appeals court. If one of the lawyers were to publish it for the public, wrote the judges, it "would at once take deserved rank with the noteworthy productions" of American literature. A prominent African American lawyer turned writer agreed that the briefs read "like a novel." But a good story is one thing, the law is another. And the judges were not beguiled into a happy ending.[53]

The story as the appeals court finally told it in 1916 was a complete tragedy. The court agreed that the terms of John Randolph's will had given the freedmen an equitable interest in the land Judge Leigh bought for them. But it thought Leigh had a right to sell the land after he concluded that the freedmen could not settle in Mercer County. And it found plenty of evidence that Leigh had distributed money among the freedmen. Absent any proof to the contrary, the court had to presume that Leigh had done his fiduciary duty and used the proceeds from land sales for the freedmen's benefit. In any event, the court held, the petitioners' claims against subsequent owners of the land came too late. The freedmen had known about their land ever since they came to Ohio. They and their descendants had talked about it for decades. If they had any remaining claims to it, they should have raised them long ago.[54]

The Ohio Supreme Court affirmed the decision a year later. And in May 1917, the court in Mercer County confirmed the land titles of Gerhard Kessens and fifty-six other defendants. Joseph Moton and York Rial were dead. Kessens was eighty-one years old. The legal battle had lasted for twelve years.[55]

．．．．

THE GREAT WAR for a free Union had taken Joseph Moton to Southside Virginia in 1864. He enlisted in the Twenty-Seventh Regiment of the United States Colored Infantry, one of two Black regiments raised in Ohio after state authorities overcame their reluctance to arm African American men. Moton was eighteen years old at the time. A thirty-year-old freedman from Rossville named Philip White joined the same regiment. Paul Crowder and four other Roanoke freedmen had already enlisted in the Fifty-Fifth Massachusetts Volunteer Infantry Regiment when it came recruiting in Ohio a year earlier, and several of the freedmen at Hanktown joined the Fifth Regiment of the United States Colored Infantry about the time Moton and White volunteered. They were among more than five thousand Black Ohioans who served in the Union armies, armies in which 15 percent of the troops were Black by the end of the war.[56]

Moton's regiment was part of the army that besieged Petersburg during 1864–65 in order to break through defenses protecting the Confederate capital in Richmond. From the encircling trenches, they could see the female figure of Justice atop the tower of the Greek Revival courthouse. Union gunners used it to set the range on the artillery they deployed to shell the city. Justice sustained some damage in the barrage, and one Union soldier joked that she had compromised her anatomy as well as her virtue by consorting with Confederates. Yet the figure somehow survived. It was there when Union soldiers set off a massive explosion in tunnels they had dug under the Confederate lines. It gazed impassively as brutal fighting erupted between Black attackers and white defenders when Moton's regiment entered the blast crater. It still stood when the fall of Petersburg opened the door to Richmond in early April 1865. Moton probably never knew that the figure marked the place where a jury had upheld John Randolph's will twenty years earlier.[57]

By the time Richmond fell a few days later, Moton and his regiment were in North Carolina. They went to support William Tecumseh Sherman's attack on the Confederacy's largest army, commanded by Joseph Johnston. It was planting time in the bright green Carolina Piedmont, where the war had not yet ravaged the countryside. Union troops could see hundreds of the men and women liberated by the Emancipation Proclamation still laboring under the lash. But those laborers were to reap the crop in freedom. Johnston sealed the Confederate defeat when he surrendered his army to Sherman at the end of April, two weeks after Robert E. Lee's battered army had laid down their arms at Appomattox.[58]

Joseph Moton made it back to Ohio after the war. So did Philip White, Paul Crowder, and the other Roanoke freedmen who fought in Union armies. The new birth of freedom that Abraham Lincoln prophesied at Gettysburg came hard, and these men felt the birth pangs even in a free state. Ohio initially refused to give its Black citizens political rights, so they could not vote until the Fifteenth Amendment was ratified five years later. It took another ten years to elect a Black man to the Ohio legislature, and only a dozen Black men won seats over the next twenty years. Racial discrimination and segregation persisted throughout the state, but as the laws that sanctioned them began to fall away, African Americans gained some leverage against white oppression. Well-trained Black lawyers took their cases to the courts. And although white judges might discount what Black litigants had to say, they knew they had to hear them.[59]

John Randolph could never have imagined any of that. He did not believe in universal emancipation. He freed his own slaves to suit himself. Apart from funding their expatriation and resettlement, Randolph gave their futures almost no thought at all. He expected them to replicate in some free territory the sort of agricultural community that their ancestors had created in Virginia. He never prepared them for anything else because anything other than that was beyond him.

The manumission of his slaves nevertheless earned Randolph a measure of redemption in his own times. The Quaker abolitionist poet John Greenleaf Whittier wrote a touching elegy to him after the Virginia courts upheld his will. While Whittier did not spare Randolph's many faults, he asked the Almighty to rescue him from remorse and the reproach of others. "*Breathe over him forgetfulness,*" he wrote,

> *Of all save deeds of kindness,*
> *And, save to smiles of grateful eyes,*
> *Press down his lids in blindness.*[60]

Boston politician Josiah Quincy, whose father of the same name knew Randolph well, forgave him in a different register fifteen years after the Civil War. Whites throughout the reconstituted nation were seeking sectional reunion. Northerners like Quincy found it expedient to agree that Southerners had fought for a cause worthier than slavery. John Randolph—the champion of states' rights who freed his own slaves—was just the sort of man they wanted to commemorate. "The time has not yet come to estimate with impartiality the class of Southern gentlemen to which Randolph belonged," wrote Quincy at the end of a sketch of Randolph's character. Accept their premises, Quincy said, and they were "knightly figures" fighting to protect their families and their civilization. In retrospect, of course, they all seemed mad. Yet Quincy declined to dwell upon "their errors or delusions," which every schoolboy now thought himself competent to expose.[61]

Another 140 years have passed, and the descendants of Quincy's schoolboys freely condemn all enslavers. Some of them spare a kind word for a few, such as Randolph, who freed the men and women they once enslaved. Randolph would have liked the special attention. Yet he would have scorned the narrowness of the reason for it.[62]

The character of slaveholders who did or did not free their slaves is not the issue anyway. To understand the story of John Randolph's will, we need to delve much deeper. History is a process propelled by many wills. Praise and condemnation shed little light on the jumble of human motives, and they explain almost nothing about the workings of the historical process. We already know that slaveholders did great evil. We must think beyond that to understand why those who chose to free their slaves made so little difference.[63]

Before every person had a legal right to freedom, the gift of freedom was not liberating. Because manumission was just an exercise of the giver's rights, it changed almost nothing. It did not challenge the law or the social order. It gave the recipient no more than the law and social mores were prepared to concede. A prominent man's decision to free his slaves might set an example, but there was no particular reason for anyone else to follow it. To those who lived in a world built on slavery, manumission was not necessarily more honorable than the alternative. A man who released the workforce his family needed was more likely to be called mad than righteous.

Most whites in antebellum America had no particular interest in Black freedom, and freed slaves were almost universally unwanted neighbors. Virginia and other Southern states aimed to expel them. Ohio and other Western states tried to exclude them. Well-intentioned whites everywhere thought they would be better off in Africa. As most white Americans saw it, a vast continent cleared of Native peoples and rich lands cleared by Black labor were an inheritance ordained for freeborn white people. Their essential concern was not whether Black men and women could someday go free, but whether—as historian W. E. B. Du Bois put it—white men would own the earth "forever and ever, Amen!"[64]

ACKNOWLEDGMENTS

Everyone who writes history incurs debts, and many of mine are to the people of western Ohio. Hadley Drodge graciously shared work she had done for an outstanding exhibit about the Roanoke freedpersons at the National Afro-American Museum and Culture Center in 2017, and her colleague James McKinnon helped me use the museum's related collection. Historian Larry Hamilton showed me around Piqua, and Paisha Thomas (a descendant of Roanoke freedman Johnson Crowder) took time to talk with me about the community at Rossville. Angie Fair told me it would be fine to read court records in the Mercer County clerk's office, and thanks to her great efficiency, it was. The recorders' offices in Mercer, Auglaize, Shelby, and Miami Counties provided friendly access to their meticulous land records, and the historical societies in those counties shared their collections and publications. Jill Beitz, at the Cincinnati History Library and Archives, nearly took my breath away when she showed me the sketch of the Roanoke freedmen's procession through Cincinnati (which appears on the jacket of this book).

The papers of John Randolph, his family, and his contemporaries are widely scattered, but thanks to the generosity of the Tucker family and the efforts of generations of researchers, the Special Collections Research Center of the William and Mary Libraries and the Albert and Shirley Small Special Collections Library at the University of Virginia hold a great many of them. The Library of Virginia has created an invaluable digital database of eighteenth- and nineteenth-century Virginia chancery cases. Without the expert assistance of the archivists and librarians at all three of those institutions, I could not have assembled the material needed for this book. I also received much valuable assistance from the Library of Congress, the Virginia Museum of History and Culture, the Ohio History Connection Archives and Library, the Cincinnati History Library and Archives, and the Special Collections and Archives at Wright State University.

For their permission to use illustrations in this book, I thank the Cincinnati Museum Center, the College of William and Mary, the Colonial Williamsburg Foundation, CourtHouseHistory.com, the Handley Regional Library, the Historical Society of Pennsylvania, the Huntington Library, the Library of Congress, the Library of Virginia, the National Afro-American Museum and Cultural Center, the National Gallery of Art, Bryan Pollard, and the Walters Art Museum. I am especially indebted to Joan Gates, Katharine Gates, Elizabeth Leigh, and Ned Leigh for their kind permission to reproduce privately owned portraits and to Travis Fullerton and Neil Steinberg for creating digital images of those portraits.

Generous friends and historians have helped me throughout this project. David O. Stewart always took time to talk, read manuscripts, and offer unsparing criticism. Megan Kennedy was wise enough to see what I should have done better and frank enough to tell me about it. Julia May provided insightful suggestions and important technical assistance. John O. Peters shared his great knowledge of Virginia courthouses and introduced me to Mark Greenough, whose deep understanding of Virginia's capitol made its lost courtrooms reappear. Andrew Burstein, Nancy Isenberg, John Ruston Pagan, Chip Pottage, John Ragosta, Alan Taylor, Elizabeth Dowling Taylor, Billy L. Wayson, and Paula Tarnapol Whitacre offered helpful insights and support along the way. Annette Gordon-Reed's comments on the manuscript pointed the way toward important improvements.

Good fortune brought this book the superb editorial attention of

Robert Weil, who has significantly improved it. I am enormously grateful to him, assistant editor Haley Bracken, and everyone at Liveright for bringing the book to life. Another stroke of good fortune gave me the wise guidance of Lisa Adams at the Garamond Agency, and I remain greatly indebted for her careful attention and never-failing assistance.

Anna Baldwin May has been my essential partner in everything. Her sense of proportion rescued me from many alluring digressions, and without her unfailing good humor during times of pandemic and isolation, I could not have finished this book.

Peter Onuf's generous encouragement was crucial throughout this project. His penetrating observations at an early stage prompted me to reshape the book, and by bringing the manuscript to the attention of others, he helped it to find a good home. As a token of my very great appreciation, I have dedicated the book to him.

PEOPLE AND PLACES

Barksdale, William. Planter in Amelia County, Virginia, and John Randolph's friend.

Benton, Thomas Hart. United States senator from Missouri and John Randolph's close friend.

Bizarre. Plantation in Prince Edward County, Virginia, inherited by John Randolph's brother Richard.

Brockenbrough, John. Richmond banker and John Randolph's close friend.

Brooke, Henry Laurens. Husband of Henry St. George Tucker's daughter Virginia; represented Beverley Tucker in chancery suit over John Randolph's will.

Bryan, Elizabeth Tucker ("Betty" or "Bet"). John Randolph's favorite niece; Frances and John Coalter's daughter.

Bryan, John Coalter. Elizabeth and John Randolph Bryan's first child; principal heir under John Randolph's last will.

Bryan, John Randolph ("Randolph"). John Randolph's godchild and Elizabeth Tucker Bryan's husband.

Bushy Forest. Plantation in Charlotte County, Virginia, purchased by John Randolph.

Cardwell, Wyatt. Steward of John Randolph's plantations during the litigation over his will.

Carthagena. Village founded by Black settlers in western Mercer County, Ohio.

Celia. Wife of John Randolph's enslaved manservant Juba.

Coalter, Elizabeth Tucker. See Elizabeth Tucker Bryan.

Coalter, Frances ("Fanny"). John Randolph's half-sister; mother of Elizabeth Tucker Bryan and St. George Coalter.

Coalter, John. Husband of John Randolph's half-sister Frances; lawyer and judge.

Coalter, St. George Tucker. John Randolph's nephew; Frances and John Coalter's son.

Essex. Enslaved man in charge of John Randolph's household at Roanoke.

Hetty. Enslaved house servant at Roanoke; Essex's wife.

Hobson, Frederick. Legal representative for John Randolph's disabled nephew John St. George Randolph; named defendant in second probate trial of John Randolph's will.

Israel Hill. Community in Prince Edward County, Virginia, established by slaves freed under the will of John Randolph's brother Richard.

Jay, Samuel. Judge Leigh's agent to buy land in Ohio for the Roanoke freedmen.

Johnson, Chapman. Lawyer for the Tucker family in the litigation over John Randolph's will.

Jones, Walter ("General Jones"). Lawyer for John Randolph's slaves in the litigation over his will.

Juba. John Randolph's enslaved manservant.

Key, Francis Scott ("Frank"). Trustee for the slaves freed under John Randolph's will.

Leigh, Benjamin Watkins ("Watkins"). Judge Leigh's elder brother; lawyer and politician.

Leigh, William ("Judge Leigh"). John Randolph's executor; lawyer and judge.

Meade, Richard Kidder ("Uncle Kidder"). Husband of John Randolph's paternal aunt; later Bishop Meade's father.

Meade, William ("Bishop Meade"). Episcopal priest and bishop of Virginia; son of John Randolph's Uncle Kidder and his second wife.

Middle Peninsula. Region of Virginia lying between the Rappahannock and York Rivers.

Morris, Ann Cary ("Nancy"). Judith Randolph's sister; later wife of Gouverneur Morris.

Morton, Joseph. Steward for John Randolph's grandfather, Richard Randolph of Curles.

Moses. Enslaved field hand at Roanoke; sometimes John Randolph's manservant.

Moton, Joseph. Named plaintiff in Ohio suits to recover the Roanoke freedmen's land; son of freedwoman Margaret Moton and grandson of Moses.

Nancy. Enslaved house servant at Roanoke; Essex and Hetty's daughter.

Odlin, Peter. Lawyer in Dayton, Ohio; advised Judge Leigh on settling the Roanoke freedmen.

Queen. Enslaved cook at Roanoke.

Randolph, Ann Cary. See Ann Cary Morris.

Randolph, Frances. See Frances Tucker.

Randolph, John, Sr. John Randolph's father; died young and indebted.

Randolph, John St. George ("St. George"). Judith and Richard Randolph's son; disabled and later mad.

Randolph, Judith. Cousin and wife of John Randolph's brother Richard.

Randolph, Richard. John Randolph's eldest brother; Judith Randolph's husband.

Randolph, Theodorick. John Randolph's brother; died young.

Randolph, Tudor. Judith and Richard Randolph's son; died young.

Rial, York. Roanoke freedman; plaintiff in Ohio suits to recover the freedmen's land.

Roanoke. John Randolph's plantation on the Staunton and Little Roanoke Rivers in Charlotte County, Virginia.

Robertson, John. Lawyer for John Randolph's slaves in the litigation over his will.

Southside Virginia. Region of Virginia south of the James River and east of the Blue Ridge Mountains.

Stanard, Robert. Lawyer for the Tucker family in the litigation over John Randolph's will.

Taylor, Samuel. Lawyer for John Randolph's slaves in the litigation over his will.

Till Plains. Fertile plains in western Ohio formed by ancient deposits of glacial till.

Tucker, Frances. John Randolph's mother; later married St. George Tucker.

Tucker, Frances (the younger). See Frances Coalter.

Tucker, Henry St. George. John Randolph's half-brother; lawyer, judge, and law professor.

Tucker, Nathaniel Beverley ("Beverley"). John Randolph's half-brother; lawyer, judge, and law professor.

Tucker, St. George. John Randolph's stepfather; lawyer, judge, and law professor.

Upshur, Abel P. Judge of the Williamsburg circuit court; later navy secretary and secretary of state under John Tyler.

Wattles, Augustus. Quaker abolitionist who established a school at Carthagena, Ohio.

White, Betsy. Enslaved house servant at Roanoke; John White's wife.

White, John. John Randolph's enslaved manservant; Essex and Hetty's son and Betsy White's husband.

Wickham, John. Lawyer for John Randolph's British creditors; Benjamin Watkins Leigh's father-in-law.

Appendix B

CHRONOLOGY

1833

May	John Randolph dies
June	Randolph's burial
July	Randolph's papers searched for his will

1834

July   General Court hears motions in first probate case (*Bryan v. Meade*)

1835

July   General Court trial of first probate case

December   Court of Appeals reverses General Court decision

1836

July   General Court trial of second probate case (*Meade v. Hobson*)

1837

July   Court of Appeals affirms second General Court decision

December	William Leigh qualifies as Randolph's executor
	First chancery suit filed in Williamsburg (*Tucker v. Randolph's Executor*)

1840

March	Court of Appeals dismisses first chancery suit
April	Second chancery suit filed in Williamsburg (*Coalter's Executor v. Bryan*)
May	Second chancery suit removed to Petersburg

1842

December	Petersburg court enters pretrial order

1844

May	Court of Appeals upholds pretrial order

1845

February	Jury verdict in Petersburg frees slaves

1846

April	Freedmen register at Charlotte Courthouse
June	Freedmen leave for Ohio
July	Freedmen arrive in Ohio

Appendix C

MANUMISSION REGISTER[1]

Cert. No.	Name	Relationship	Complexion	Age	Ht.	Marks
215	Frank Brown		Dark	25	5'11⅝"	Small scar in forehead
216	Johnson	Son of Armestead	Dark	22	5'6"	Whitish appearance on one hand
217	Phill White		Dark	45	5'5"	No apparent scar or mark
218	Sylva	Wife of Phill	Dark	25	5'	No apparent scar or mark
219	Agness Jane	Daughter of Phill	Dark	2	2'6"	
220	Ellick		Dark	24	5'10¾"	Scar behind right ear
221	Sally		Mulatto	28	5'1"	Lame in the hip
222	Craddock	Son of Sally	Bright	7	3'6½"	
223	Jim	Son of Sally	Bright	4	2'6¾"	
224	Willis	Son of Queen	Dark	22	5'7"	Wart on middle of forefinger of left hand
225	Nero		Dark brown	26	5'4"	
226	Edy	Wife of Nero	Black	20	5'1"	
227	Fountain[2]	Son of Edy	Black	3	2'6"	
228	Hiram	Son of Nancy who is dead	Very bright	12	4'6"	
229	Mack	Son of Nancy	Very bright	10	4'3"	
230	Watkins Leigh	Son of Nancy	Very bright	8	4'	
231	John	Son of Nancy	Very bright	6	3'7½"	
232	Susan Ann	Daughter of Nancy	Very bright	5	3'4½"	
233	St. George	Son of Nancy	Very bright	3	3'	

1 Register of Free Negroes and Mulattoes, 1794–1865, Charlotte County, VA, certs. 215–596, reel 146, LVA. An imperfect transcription appears in Record of Black and Mulattoe Persons, Miami County, OH, 1834–46, Special Collections (Local Government Records), Wright State University Libraries, available at https://corescholar.libraries.wright.edu/cgi/viewcontent.cgi?article=1000&context=local_government. Shading indicates the family groups denoted in the register, but several persons denoted as separate individuals actually belonged to families.

2 Fountain Randolph, first president of the Randolph Ex-Slave Association.

234	Pugh Price	Son of Nancy	Very bright	1	2'4½"	
235	Doctor		Dark brown	45	5'5½"	
236	Edmund		Brown	55	5'5¾"	
237	Suckey	Wife of Edmund	Black	24	5'1"	
238	Giles	Son of Suckey	Mulatto	8	3'8"	
239	Nancy	Daughter of Edmund by another wife	Black	20	5'6"	
240	Jane	Daughter of Edmund	Brown	18	5'1"	
241	Susan	Daughter of Edmund by Hetty	Black	14	5'4"	
242	Martha	Daughter of Edmund and Hetty	Brown	12	5'3"	
243	Granny Nancy		Black	65	5'3"	
244	Meshack[3]		Black	42	5'3½"	
245	Cloe	Daughter of Meshack (mother dead)	Black	13	4'10"	
246	Crawford	Son of Meshack	Black	11	4'3½"	
247	Armistead	Son of Meshack	Black	7	4'1"	
248	John	Son of Meshack	Black	4	3'0½"	
249	Sindy	Daughter of Meshack	Black	1	2'3"	
250	Amelia		Black	22	4'11"	Now pregnant
251	Sampson		Black	65	5'5"	
252	Lucinda	Wife of Sampson	Mulatto	46	5'7"	
253	Patience	Daughter of Lucinda	Bright	26	5'1"	
254	John	Son of Patience	Bright	1	2'	
255	Patsy	Daughter of Lucinda	Light	24	5'4"	
256	Henrietta	Daughter of Patsy	Mulatto	6	3'10¼"	
257	Elizabeth	Daughter of Patsy	Light	4	3'3"	
258	Jane	Daughter of Patsy	Light	2	2'5"	
259	William	Son of Lucinda	Light	20	5'7"	
260	Queen	Daughter of Lucinda	Light	18	5'4"	
261	Little Sampson	Son of Lucinda	Light	16	5'7"	
262	Peyton	Son of Lucinda	Light	13	4'8"	
263	Old Milley		Black	68	5'5"	
264	Fanney	Daughter of Milley	Brown	29	5'2"	
265	Clem[4]	Son of Fanney	Mulatto	12	4'7"	
266	Delpha	Daughter of Fanney	Light	10	4'4"	
267	Barnett	Son of Fanney	Mulatto	8	3'11"	
268	Wyatt Cardwell	Son of Fanney	Mulatto	6	3'6"	
269	Nathan		Brown	27	5'6"	
270	Granny Hannah		Brown	100	5'	
271	Roger Billey		Black	66	5'7"	
272	Christian	Wife of Roger Billey	Black	48	5'5"	
273	John	Son of Billey and Christian	Black	20	5'5½"	
274	Harry	Son of same	Black	18	5'6½"	
275	Ryall	Son of same	Black	16	5'6"	
276	Jacob	Son of same	Black	14	5'1"	
277	Juba	Son of same	Black	12	4'9"	
278	Stephen		Black	30	5'10"	
279	Effy	Wife of Stephen	Black	27	5'4¼"	
280	Spencer	Son of Stephen and Effy	Black	12	4'11"	
281	Maria	Daughter of same	Black	10	4'4"	
282	Jack	Son of same	Black	8	4'1"	

3 Meshack Jones, who purchased land west of Troy, Ohio.
4 Clem Clay, a witness in *Moton v. Kessens*.

283	Saluda	Daughter of same	Black	6	3'6½"	
284	Dick	Son of same	Black	4	3'2½"	
285	John[5]		Black	63	5'2"	
286	Betsey	Wife of John	Black	48	5'4"	
287	John	Son of John and Betsey	Black	14	4'8¼"	
288	Aaron	Son of same	Black	20	5'8½"	
289	Moses	Son of same	Black	18	5'7½"	
290	Polly	Daughter of same	Black	17	5'	
291	Lucy	Daughter of Polly	Dark brown	2	2'4½"	
292	Charles[6]	Son of John and Nancy	Black	4	3'	
293	Queen		Mulatto	38	5'5"	
294	Essex	Son of Queen	Brown	18	5'1"	
295	Abel		Black	40	5'7"	
296	Anakey	Wife of Abel	Mulatto	35	5'2"	
297	Sally	Daughter of Anakey	Mulatto	22	5'3½"	
298	Patrick	Son of Sally	Light	4	2'11½"	
299	Catherine	Daughter of Sally	Light	0	1'7½"	
300	Robert	Son of Abel and Anakey	Brown	19	5'1"	
301	Betsey	Daughter of same	Brown	17	5'2"	
302	Tom Ellis	Son of same	Brown	15	5'0½"	
303	Letsey	Daughter of same	Light	12	4'3"	
304	Peter	Son of same	Brown	10	4'	
305	Nick Davis	Son of same	Brown	6	3'4"	
306	Charity	Daughter of same	Brown	3	2'8½"	
307	Frederick	Son of same	Brown	8	3'9½"	
308	Abram		Black	37	5'10"	
309	Judy	Wife of Abram	Black	30	5'	
310	Essex		Brown	38	5'7"	
311	Louisa	Wife of Essex	Black	35	5'1½"	
312	Clarissa	Daughter of Essex and Louisa	Brown	12	4'6½"	
313	Mildred	Daughter of same	Brown	10	4'5"	
314	Watson	Son of same	Dark brown	8	3'10"	
315	Rhoda	Daughter of same	Brown	6	3'9"	
316	Minton	Son of same	Dark brown	4	3'10½"	
317	Harriott	Daughter of same	Dark brown	2	2'3½"	
318	Phill		Black	60	5'3½"	
319	Lucy	Wife of Phill	Light	35	5'5"	
320	Martha	Dauger of Phill and Lucy	Light	20	5'1½"	Now pregnant
321	Isaac	Son of same	Black	17	4'11"	
322	Elvitell	Daughter of same	Brown	8	3'7½"	
323	Silas	Son of same	Dark brown	6	3'1½"	
324	Lethey	Daughter of same	Dark brown	2	2'3"	
325	Sam		Black	40	5'10"	
326	Dicey	Wife of Sam	Brown	40	5'3½"	
327	Peggy	Daughter of Sam (mother dead)	Black	18	5'2"	
328	Martha	Daughter of same	Black	16	4'11¼"	
329	Essex	Son of same	Black	11	4'4½"	Blemish in right eye
330	Solomon	Son of same	Black	9	4'2½"	
331	Jeter		Dark brown	26	5'7½"	
332	Mary	Wife of Jeter	Dark brown	20	4'8¾"	Now pregnant

5 John White, one of John Randolph's principal manservants.

6 Son of John White's deceased sister Nancy and her husband John.

333	Eliza	Daughter of Jeter and Mary	Dark brown	2	2'6½"	
334	Freeman		Dark	40	5'1½"	Lame in right leg; both hands much injured by a burn and frost bite
335	Milley	Wife of Freeman	Brown	40	5'	
336	Reener	Daughter of Freeman and Milley	Brown	18	5'0½"	
337	Biddy	Daughter of same	Black	14	4'9½"	
338	Anney	Daughter of same	Brown	11	4'5"	
339	Malinda	Daughter of same	Brown	9	3'11½"	
340	Beverley Tucker	Son of same	Brown	7	3'6½"	
341	Agness	Daughter of same	Brown	5	2'9½"	
342	Ceasar		Black	70	5'7"	
343	Bartlett		Black	50	5'3"	
344	Aggy		Black	45/50	5'4"	
345	Dolley	Daughter of Aggy	Black	26	5'3½"	
346	Madison	Son of Dolley	Light	7	4'1"	
347	Emilly	Daughter of same	Light	4	3'2"	
348	Kitty	Daughter of same	Brown	1	2'3"	
349	Fanney	Daughter of Aggy	Black	20	5'4"	
350	Phillis	Daughter of same	Dark brown	17	5'5"	
351	Bryan	Son of same	Black	12	4'11"	
352	Theodorick[7]		Mulatto	38	5'11"	
353	Rose	Wife of Theodorick	Mulatto	37	5'5"	
354	Wilson	Son of Rose and Archer	Light	17	5'1½"	
355	America	Daughter of Rose and Theodorick	Mulatto	14	5'3"	
356	Jackson	Son of Rose and Archer	Light	12	4'8½"	
357	Suckey	Daughter of Rose and Theodorick	Mulatto	9	4'2"	
358	Hillery	Son of same	Mulatto	7	3'9½"	
359	Viney	Daughter of same	Mulatto	4	3'	
360	Nancy	Daughter of same	Mulatto	1	2'1"	
361	Moses[8]		Brown	60	5'7"	
362	Pheobe	Wife of Moses	Brown	50	5'4"	
363	Margaret[9]	Daughter of Moses and Pheobe	Black	20	5'6"	
364	Diver	Son of same	Brown	18	5'2"	
365	Syphax		Mulatto	45	5'4½"	
366	Hannah	Wife of Syphax	Light	36	5'4"	
367	Albert	Son of Hannah	Brown/black	19	5'4"	
368	Letsey	Daughter of Syphax and Hannah	Mulatto	16	4'11"	
369	Eliza Monroe	Daughter of same	Light	13	4'5"	
370	Aggy	Daughter of same	Light	11	4'1"	
371	Maria	Daughter of same	Light	9	3'8½"	
372	Stephen Davis	Son of same	Light	7	3'4½"	
373	Henry	Son of same	Light	2	2'8"	
374	Old Quasha		Black	90	5'5"	
375	Mulatto Nancy	Wife of Quasha	Mulatto	80	5'	
376	Jeffrey		Black	80	5'2½"	

7 Theodorick Randolph, who purchased lots in Sidney, Ohio.

8 Moses Moton, a field hand sometimes John Randolph's manservant.

9 Margaret Moton, whose son Joseph Moton became the lead plaintiff in *Moton v. Kessens*.

377	Granny Pheobe	Wife of Jeffrey	Black	75	5'4"
379[10]	Siller	Granddaughter of Jeffrey (mother dead)	Brown	25	5'1"
380	James	Son of Siller	Light	2	2'7"
381	Lot		Black	30	5'5½"
382	Titus		Black	25	5'5¼"
383	Ellender	Sister of Titus	Black	20	4'11"
384	Hetty	Sister of Ellender	Black	10	4'11½"
385	Jamey	Brother of Ellender	Black	8	3'8½"
386	Thomas	Nephew of Ellender	Dark brown	9	3'10½"
387	Toney		Black	39	5'8"
388	Beckey	Wife of Toney	Black	35	5'½"
389	Gracey	Daughter of Toney and Beckey	Black	22	5'
390	Dolly	Daughter of Gracey	Black	2	2'3"
391	Sarah Anne	Daughter of Toney and Beckey	Black	17	4'10"
392	Elisha	Son of same	Black	10	4'3½"
393	Washington	Son of same	Black	8	3'10"
394	Dick	Son of same	Black	6	3'4"
395	Nelson	Son of same	Black	4	3'1"
396	Caty	Daughter of same	Black	3	2'9½"
397	Isham		Black	55	5'9"
398	Nancy	Wife of Isham	Dark brown	35	5'2"
399	Hampton	Son of Isham and Nancy	Black	15	5'1"
400	Isaac		Dark brown	45	5'6¼"
401	Issey	Wife of Isaac	Black	35	5'
402	Reener	Daughter of Isaac and Issey	Black	13	4'10½"
403	Mitchell	Son of same	Black	10	3'11"
404	Anderson	Son of same	Black	8	3'9"
405	Salley	Daughter of same	Black	3	3'2"
406	Billey	Son of same	Black	2	2'8½"
407	Jane	Daughter of same	Black	0	22"
408	Ryall		Brown	35	5'11"
409	Cook Jenny		Black	64	5'2"
410	Simon		Black	20	6'½"
411	Abram		Black	60	5'5½"
412	Nancy	Wife of Abram	Dark brown	27	5'3 ½"
413	Mary	Daughter of Abram and Nancy	Black	12	4'10½"
414	Savarey	Daughter of same	Black	11	4'8"
415	Guy		Brown	33	5'9"
416	Esther	Wife of Guy	Black	30	5'9½"
417	Elizabeth	Daughter of Guy and Esther	Black	10	4'4"
418	Lot		Black	30	5'11"
419	Fanney	Wife of Lot	Black	23	5'5½"
420	Rebecca Ann	Daughter of Lot and Fanney	Bright	2	2'11"
421	Carter		Black	33	5'9½"
422	Pheobe	Wife of Carter	Black	22	5'3"
423	Clemina	Daughter of Carter and Pheobe	Black	6	3'2½"
424	Betsey	Daughter of same	Black	4	3'
425	Suckey	Daughter of same	Black	0	2'

10 Recording clerk skipped number 378.

426	Isbell		Black	60	5'5"
427	Sam		Black	57	5'10"
428	Henry		Black	57	5'6"
429	Dosha	Wife of Henry	Black	40	4'11½"
430	Dinah	Daughter of Henry and Dosha	Black	15	4'10"
431	Hillery	Son of same	Black	12	4'5½"
432	Lethey	Daughter of same	Black	10	4'6"
433	Harriott	Daughter of same	Black	1	2'2"
434	Israel	Son of same	Black	5	3'
435	Anderson	Son of same	Black	10	4'4½"
436	Carpenter Phill		Brown	80	5'7"
437	George		Black	42	5'11½"
438	Mary	Wife of George	Black	30	4'11½"
439	Oliver	Son of George and Mary	Black	18	5'4"
440	Sarah Gould	Daughter of same	Black	7	4'2"
441	Phill		Black	57	5'8¾"
442	James	Son of Phill	Black/brown	22	5'5"
443	Dick	Son of same	Black	18	5'8½"
444	Phill[11]	Son of same	Black	15	5'
445	John	Son of same	Brown	10	4'5"
446	Frances	Daughter of same	Brown	8	4'5"
447	Charlotte	Daughter of same	Brown	7	3'8¾"
448	Solomon	Son of same	Brown	4	3'2"
449	Bob		Black	40	5'5"	Dark appearance on left breast
450	Hannah	Wife of Bob	Black	30	5'2"
451	Thomas	Son of Bob and Hannah	Black	15	4'6"
452	Jesse	Son of same	Black	13	4'1"
453	Abram	Son of same	Black	10	3'11"
454	Louisa	Daughter of same	Black	5	3'7½"
455	Hercules	Son of same	Black	3	2'11½"
456	Ceasar		Black	30	5'10"
457	Aaron		Black	43	5'8"
458	Vicey	Wife of Aaron	Brown	36	5'3"
459	Keziah	Daughter of Aaron and Vicey	Brown	15	4'10½"
460	Shadrack	Son of same	Brown	10	4'7¼"
461	Kitty	Daughter of same	Light brown	8	4'2"
462	Ursey	Daughter of same	Brown	7	3'6¾"
463	Jugurtha Sandmies (Sandy)		Black	30	5'6"
464	Quasha		Black	57	5'4"
465	Sally	Wife of Quasha	Black	40	5'4"
466	Fanney		Black	40	5'2½"
467	Hercules	Son of Fanney	Black	24	5'6¼"
468	Braxton	Son of same	Black	18	5'3"
469	Parthena	Daughter of same	Black	13	4'9¾"
470	Yarmer	Daughter of same	Black	10	4'9¾"
471	Joanna	Daughter of same	Black	8	3'10½"
472	Louisa	Daughter of same	Black	4	3'7¾"
473	Harry		Black	40	5'10"
474	Effy	Wife of Harry	Black	40	5'9½"
475	Othello		Mulatto	79	5'6½"
476	Sylla	Daughter of Othello	Brown	26	5'2½"

11 Philip White, who enlisted in the 27th Regiment of United States Colored Troops during the Civil War.

477	Clem	Son of Sylla	Light brown	11	4'4"	
478	Claiborne	Son of Othello	Brown	17	5'6"	
479	Theodorick		Light brown	23	5'7"	
480	Tamer	Wife of Theodorick	Black	19	5'1½"	
481	Phillis		Black	20	5'	
482	Dilcey	Daughter of Phillis	Black	5	3'4¼"	
483	Jackson	Son of same	Black	3	3'	
484	Angelina	Daughter of same	Black	1	2'2"	
485	Jordan		Black	38	5'6¾"	
486	Suckey	Wife of Jordan	Black	30	5'5½"	
487	Billey (Blacksmith)		Black	67	5'8"	
488	Maria	Wife of Billey	Black	40	5'5"	
489	Seymour	Son of Maria	Black	18	5'6"	
490	Jincey	Daughter of Maria	Black	16/14	5'2"	
491	Charles	Son of Maria	Black	16	5'1"	
492	Maria	Daughter of Maria	Black	6	3'9"	
493	Littleton	Son of Billey	Black	18	5'2"	
494	Mary Baker	Daughter of Billey	Black	16	5'	
495	Buck Smith	Son of Billey	Black	12	4'7½"	
496	Amey		Black	35	5'1¼"	
497	Syphax (Sye)		Mulatto	30	6'½"	
498	Lizzy	Wife of Syphax	Black	28	5'3"	
499	Celey[12]	Mother of Lizzy	Black	50	5'2"	
500	Paulina	Daughter of Celey	Black	22	5'4½"	
501	Fanney	Daughter of Paulina	Mulatto	3	3'9"	
502	Julia Ann	Daughter of Paulina	Mulatto	0	1'11"	
503	Susan	Daughter of Celey	Black	15	4'10¾"	
504	Amos		Black	65	5'10"	
505	Ned	Son of Amos	Black	26	5'8½"	
506	Matilda	Daughter of Amos	Black	22	5'5"	
507	Gabriel[13]		Black	57	5'	
508	Dolley	Wife of Gabriel	Black	40	5'	
508[14]	Lucretia	Daughter of Gabriel and Dolley	Black	20	5'2½"	
509	Moses	Son of same	Black	18	5'4¾"	
510	William	Son of same	Black	16	5'1"	
511	Polly	Daughter of same	Black	14	4'10½"	
512	John	Son of same	Black	10	4'2½"	
513	Jimmey	Son of same	Black	12	4'5"	
514	Shadrack[15]		Black	50	5'3½"	
515	Polly	Wife of Shadrack	Black	40	5'6½"	
516	Little Othello		Brown	44	5'8½"	
517	Patience	Wife of Othello	Black	30	5'2½"	Now pregnant
518	Amey	Daughter of Othello and Patience	Black	11	4'2"	
519	Agness	Daughter of same	Black	9	4'2½"	
520	Mickey	Daughter of same	Black	7	3'3"	
521	Alice	Daughter of same	Black	3	3'½"	
522	Isabella	Daughter of same	Black	2	2'7"	
523	Essex		Black	70	5'8"	
524	Caty	Wife of Essex	Black	50	5'3½"	

12 Widow of John Randolph's manservant Juba.

13 Gabriel White, who purchased land in Rossville, Ohio, in 1847.

14 Recording clerk used number 508 twice.

15 Shadrach White, brother of Gabriel White (cert. 507) who purchased land in Rossville.

525	Lobinda	Daughter of Essex and Caty	Black	20	5'4"	
526	Ephraim	Son of same	Black	22	5'9"	
527	Julius	Son of same	Black	15	4'6"	
528	Bull Abram		Black	40	5'5½"	
529	Patience	Wife of Abram	Black	25	5'2½"	
530	Lotty	Daughter of Abram and Patience	Black	4	3'5"	
531	Linder	Daughter of same	Black	2	2'9"	
532	Paul		Black	26	5'8½"	
533	Hetty	Wife of Paul	Black	25	4'11"	
534	Susanna	Daughter of Paul and Hetty	Black	8	3'11½"	
535	John Foster	Son of same	Black	6	3'5"	
536	Calomine	Daughter of same	Black	3	3'2"	
537	Michael		Black	27	5'5"	
538	Queen	Wife of Michael	Brown	25	5'	
539	Drucilla	Daughter of Michael and Queen	Mulatto	3	2'6"	
540	Betsey	Daughter of same	Black	1	2'	
541	Tennessee Isaac		Brown	50	5'7"	
542	Jeffrey		Brown	30	5'7"	
543	Jimmey		Brown	35	5'9"	
544	Davy	Son of Quasha	Black	45	5'5½"	
545	Thompson		Brown	38	5'6"	
546	Nelson		Black	33	5'2½"	
546[16]	Pagey	Wife of Nelson	Black	28	5'2"	Slight scar over right eye
547	James	Son of Nelson and Pagey	Black	3	2'11"	
548	Charlotta	Daughter of same	Black	2	2'2"	
549	Jenny	[Mother of Nelson]	Black	60	5'3"	
550	Jane	Daughter of Jenny	Black	18	5'3¼"	
551	Phill	Son of same	Black	14	5'¾"	
552	Thomas	Son of same	Black	10	4'9¼"	
553	Ben		Black	58	5'11½"	
554	Patsey[17]	Wife of Ben	Black	35	5'1¼"	
555	Milley	Daughter of Ben and Patsey	Black	13	4'10"	
556	Nancy	Daughter of same	Black	12	4'4½"	
557	Fanney	Daughter of same	Black	10	3'11"	
558	Spencer	Son of same	Black	2	2'7"	
559	Meshack (Buffalo)		Black	40	5'4¼"	
560	Mary	Wife of Meshack	Black	30	5'1"	
561	Roger		Black	40	5'8¾"	
562	Julia	Wife of Roger	Black	31	5'3"	Now pregnant
563	Robert	Son of Roger and Julia	Black	14	4'4¾"	
564	Abraham	Son of same	Black	7	4'½"	Left hand deformed
565	Billy	Son of same	Black	4	3'3¾"	
566	Diannah		Black	40	5'2½"	
567	Albert	Son of Diannah	Black	9	4'5"	
568	William	Son of same	Black	7	3'9½"	

16 Recording clerk used number 546 twice.

17 Ben and Patsey White recorded their manumission certificates as deeds in Ohio during 1852. Miami County Deed Book, 27:283, Recorder's Office, Miami County Safety Building, Troy, OH.

569	Hannah	Daughter of same	Black	5	3'5"	
570	Amanda Ann	Daughter of same	Black	25	5'2½"	
571	Queen	Daughter of Amanda Ann	Mulatto	4	3'7"	
572	Paul[18]	Son of same	Black	1	2'4"	
573	Amey	Daughter of Diannah	Black	30	5'1"	Now pregnant
574	Louisa	Daughter of Amey	Mulatto	7	3'10½"	
575	Armistead Crowder		Black	45	5'5"	
576	Teeney	Wife of Armistead	Black	38	5'2½"	
577	Dudley	Son of Armistead and Teeney	Black	19	5'6"	
578	Joe Minton	Son of same	Black	14	5'	
579	Suckey	Daughter of same	Black	10	4'7"	
580	Edward	Son of same	Black	8	4'1"	
581	Frederick	Son of same	Black	6	3'7"	
582	Tamer	Daughter of same	Black	4	3'1½"	
583	Armistead	Son of same	Black	0	2'2"	
584	Tiller		Black	40	5'5¼"	
585	Camilla	Daughter of Tiller	Black	14	4'9¾"	
586	Peggy	Daughter of same	Black	10	4'8½"	
587	Jacob	Orphan nephew of Tiller	Black	12	4'11¾"	
588	Martha	Daughter of Sam	Black	30	5'3"	
589	York[19]	Son of Martha	Black	9	4'4½"	
590	John		Black	65	5'5"	
591	Solomon	Grandson of John	Black	18	5'5¾"	
592	Dick		Mulatto	42	5'6½"	
593	Archer[20]		Brown	45	5'6"	
594	Austin	Son of Bushy Forest John	Black	37	5'9"	
595	Peter Johnson		Dark	66	5'1¾"	
596	Jenny	Wife of Peter Johnson	Black	55	5'3"	

18 Paul Crowder, son of Johnson Crowder (cert. 216); enlisted in the 55th Massachusetts Infantry Regiment during the Civil War.

19 York Rial, later a plaintiff in *Moton v. Kessens*.

20 Archer Giles, father of Goodrich Giles, who helped to organize the Roanoke freedmen's reunions and lawsuits in Ohio.

NOTES

Persons

ETB	Elizabeth Tucker Bryan
HSGT	Henry St. George Tucker
JR	John Randolph
JRB	John Randolph Bryan
NBT	Nathaniel Beverley Tucker
SGT	St. George Tucker
SGTC	St. George Tucker Coalter

Cases

Bryan v. Meade	John Coalter Bryan v. William Meade (Va. Gen. Ct., 1835)
Coalter's Ex'r v. Bryan	Executor of St. George Tucker Coalter v. John Randolph Bryan (Cir. Super. Ct., Petersburg, VA, 1845), Chancery Records Index no. 1857-039, Virginia Memory, LVA, https://www.lva.virginia.gov/chancery/case_detail.asp?CFN=730-1857-039 [pp. in digital file]
Meade v. Hobson	William Meade v. Frederick Hobson (Va. Gen. Ct., 1836)

Moton v. Kessens	Joseph Moton v. Gerhard Kessens, No. 304 (Ohio Ct. App., 3rd Cir., 1916), Mercer County Clerk of Courts, Legal Division, Mercer County Courthouse, Celina, OH [pp. in transcript attached to bill of exceptions dated 12 August 1916]
Tucker v. Randolph's Ex'r	Nathaniel Beverley Tucker v. Executor of John Randolph (Cir. Super. Ct., Williamsburg, VA, 1839), in TCP, box 86, and available at https://digitalarchive.wm.edu/handle/10288/17233 [pp. in original document]

Institutions

LC	Library of Congress
LVA	Library of Virginia
OHC	Ohio History Connection State Archives
UVA	Albert and Shirley Small Special Collections Library, University of Virginia
VMHC	Virginia Museum of History and Culture
W&M	Special Collections Research Center, William and Mary Libraries

Collections and Other Sources

BCRTP	Bryan, Coalter, Randolph, and Tucker Family Papers, UVA
BCTP	Brown-Coalter-Tucker Papers, W&M
BFP	Bryan Family Papers, LVA
Bruce	William Cabell Bruce, *John Randolph of Roanoke, 1773-1833*, 2 vols. (New York: G. P. Putnam's Sons, 1922)
Charlotte Free Register	Register of Free Negroes and Mulattoes, 1794–1865, Charlotte County, VA, reel 146, LVA
Dudley	[Theodore Dudley], ed., *Letters of John Randolph to a Young Relative* (Philadelphia, 1834)
Garland	Hugh A. Garland, *The Life of John Randolph of Roanoke*, 2 vols. (New York, 1850)

GFP-89	Grinnan Family Papers, VMHC, Mss1 G8855 d-89
GFP-90	Grinnan Family Papers, VMHC, Mss1 G8855 d-90
JR MSS	John Randolph Papers [Manuscripts], 1781-1860, UVA
JR MSS–MS 5273	John Randolph Papers [Manuscripts], 1781-1860, UVA, MS 5273, 2 typescript vols.
JRCD	John Randolph Correspondence and Diaries, 1803-1834, LC
JRP	John Randolph Papers, 1801-1830, VMHC, Mss1 R1554 b
Quincy	Edmund Quincy, *Life of Josiah Quincy of Massachusetts* (Boston, 1867)
RTFP	Randolph-Tucker Family Papers, 1723–1901, Brock Collection, Huntington Library, available on misc. reels 4222–4225, LVA
TCP	Tucker-Coleman Papers, W&M
WCBP	William Cabell Bruce Papers, LVA
WLL	William Leigh Letters, 1825-36, LVA

PREFACE

1. Edward Henry Knight, "The above procession . . . ," [July 1846], Campbell-Knight Family Papers, 1703-1973, pen and wash on paper, Cincinnati History Library and Archives, MS 895, box 15, vol. 5, p. 10; *Daily Cincinnati Chronicle*, 1 July 1846; *Cincinnati Daily Enquirer*, 2 July 1846; *Daily Cincinnati Gazette*, 2 July 1846; *Tri-Weekly Ohio Statesman* (Columbus), 3 July 1846; *Cincinnati Weekly Herald*, 8 July 1846; *Xenia Torch-Light* (OH), 9 July 1846; Charles Cist, *Sketches and Statistics of Cincinnati in 1851* (Cincinnati, 1851), 29-32; Charles Fontayne and William S. Porter, *Cincinnati Panorama of 1848*, daguerreotypes, Public Library of Cincinnati and Hamilton County, https://1848.cincinnatilibrary.org.

2. *New Monthly Magazine* (London), 1834, pt. 3:165; *Waldie's Select Circulating Library* 2, no. 25 (16 December 1834): 386–90. Randolph styled himself John Randolph of Roanoke after he moved to his plantation on the Little Roanoke River in 1810. He said he wanted to distinguish himself from relatives of the same name, but his false assertion that his father—who never lived at Roanoke—had also been known as John Randolph of Roanoke sustains the suspicion that the suffix was mainly an affectation.

3. Cong. Globe, 29th Cong., 2nd sess., 90-91 (William Sawyer and Joshua R. Giddings), 427 (Sawyer), 348 (Thomas H. Bayly and Giddings), app. 83-84 (Sawyer); ibid., 30th

Cong., 1st sess., 612 (Bayly and Giddings), app. 727-28 (Sawyer); *Emancipator* (Boston), 14 January, 1 July, and 5 August 1846; *Liberator* (Boston), 16 January, 7 August, and 21 August 1846; *Times and Compiler* (Richmond), 17 and 21 July 1846; *Richmond Enquirer*, 4 August 1846; *Cincinnati Weekly Herald*, 29 July 1846; *Mississippi Free Trader and Natchez Gazette*, 30 July and 8 September 1846; *African Repository and Colonial Journal* 22, no. 9 (September 1846): 270-72, and no. 10 (October 1846): 321-23; *Boston Daily Atlas*, 12 December 1846.

In other notable manumissions, Robert Carter III had freed 400 to 500 slaves, Robert Pleasants 400 to 440, Samuel Gist 350 to 400, Joseph Mayo 176, George Washington 156, and John Randolph's brother Richard 155. Julien Poydras manumitted 570 slaves and William Henry Fitzhugh about 200, but their wills deferred freedom for decades and ultimately liberated far fewer. All of these men except William Henry Fitzhugh made their decision before sectional antagonism congealed in the 1820s–30s. Philip J. Schwarz, *Migrants against Slavery: Virginians and the Nation* (Charlottesville: University Press of Virginia, 2001), 122-48 (Gist); Melvin Patrick Ely, *Israel on the Appomattox: A Southern Experiment in Black Freedom from the 1790s through the Civil War* (New York: Alfred A. Knopf, 2004), 20-47 (Richard Randolph); Andrew Levy, *The First Emancipator: The Forgotten Story of Robert Carter* (New York: Random House, 2005), 146-70; Eva Sheppard Wolf, *Race and Liberty in the New Nation: Emancipation in Virginia from the Revolution to Nat Turner's Rebellion* (Baton Rouge: Louisiana State University Press, 2006), 114–15 (Mayo); Kimberly M. Welch, *Black Litigants in the Antebellum South* (Chapel Hill: University of North Carolina Press, 2018), 176-80 (Poydras); Mary V. Thompson, *"The Only Unavoidable Subject of Regret": George Washington, Slavery, and the Enslaved Community at Mount Vernon* (Charlottesville: University of Virginia Press, 2019), 295-314, 340; William Fernandez Hardin, "'This Unpleasant Business': Slavery, Law, and the Pleasants Family in Post-Revolutionary Virginia," *Virginia Magazine of History and Biography* 125, no. 3 (2017): 210-45; Curtis L. Vaughan, "Freedom Is Not Enough: African Americans in Antebellum Fairfax County" (PhD diss., George Mason University, 2014), 65-70 (Fitzhugh).

4.   Ta-Nehisi Coates, "The Myth of Jefferson as 'a Man of His Times'," *The Atlantic*, 2 December 2012, www.theatlantic.com/national/archive/2012/12/the-myth-of-jefferson-as-a-man-of-his-times/265816/u.s; JR to James Mercer Garnett, 1 November 1823, JR MSS; Paul Finkelman, *Slavery and the Founders*, 2nd ed. (Armonk, NY: M. E. Sharpe, 2001), 134–36, 152–62, 189–90.

5.   *Liberator*, 1 January 1831; Dwight A. McBride, *Impossible Witnesses: Truth, Abolitionism, and Slave Testimony* (New York: New York University Press, 2001), 54–58, 78–84; Walter Johnson, "Agency: A Ghost Story," in *Slavery's Ghost: The Problem of Freedom in the Age of Emancipation*, ed. Richard Follett, Eric Foner, and Walter Johnson (Baltimore: Johns Hopkins University Press, 2011), 8–30. A leading journalist claimed at least three-quarters of the Northern public opposed emancipation at the beginning of the Civil War, and Ralph Waldo Emerson said Abraham Lincoln had been right to withhold the Emancipation Proclamation until "an audience hitherto passive and unconcerned" was "kindled" to support it. [Charles Creighton Hazewell], "The Hour and the Man," *Atlantic Monthly* 10, no. 61 (November 1862): 628; [Emerson], "The President's Proclamation," ibid., 639.

6.   Robert Elder, *The Sacred Mirror: Evangelicalism, Honor, and Identity in the Deep South, 1790–1860* (Chapel Hill: University of North Carolina Press, 2016), 177–82; Orlando Patterson, "Three Notes of Freedom: The Nature and Consequences of

Manumission," in *Paths to Freedom: Manumission in the Atlantic World*, ed. Rosemary Brana-Shute and Randy J. Sparks (Columbia: University of South Carolina Press, 2009), 18–21.

7.   Eugene H. Berwanger, *The Frontier against Slavery: Western Anti-Negro Prejudice and the Slavery Extension Controversy* (Urbana: University of Illinois Press, 1967), 32–33, 43–45; Joe William Trotter Jr., *River Jordan: African American Urban Life in the Ohio Valley* (Lexington: University Press of Kentucky, 1998), 24–25, 30; Samantha Seeley, *Race, Removal, and the Right to Remain: Migration and the Making of the United States* (Chapel Hill: University of North Carolina Press, 2021), 235–43.

8.   James Baldwin, "The Devil Finds Work" (1976), in *James Baldwin: Collected Essays*, ed. Toni Morrison (New York: Library of America, 1998), 510; Kendra Taira Field, *Growing Up with the Country: Family, Race, and Nation after the Civil War* (New Haven, CT: Yale University Press, 2018), 10–14. Over the last twenty years, a burst of studies has shown how microhistorical methods can contribute to a less essentialist understanding of slavery. Among the most recent are Jeff Forret, *Williams' Gang: A Notorious Slave Trader and His Cargo of Black Convicts* (Cambridge, UK: Cambridge University Press, 2020); W. Caleb McDaniel, *Sweet Taste of Liberty: A True Story of Slavery and Restitution in America* (New York: Oxford University Press, 2019); Joshua D. Rothman, *The Ledger and the Chain: How Domestic Slave Traders Shaped America* (New York: Basic Books, 2021); Christopher Tomlins, *In the Matter of Nat Turner: A Speculative History* (Princeton, NJ: Princeton University Press, 2020).

CHAPTER 1: A DEATH IN PHILADELPHIA

1.   William C. Allen, *History of the United States Capitol: A Chronicle of Design, Construction, and Politics* (Washington, DC: Government Printing Office, 2001), 132–33, 159, 182.

2.   John C. Fitzpatrick, ed., "The Autobiography of Martin Van Buren," *Annual Report of the American Historical Association for 1918*, 2 vols. (Washington, DC: Government Printing Office, 1920), 2:205.

3.   Robert Dawidoff, *The Education of John Randolph* (New York: W. W. Norton, 1979), 168–88; David Johnson, *John Randolph of Roanoke* (Baton Rouge: Louisiana State University Press, 2012), 42–47, 54–67, 99–105.

4.   Annals of Cong., 9th Cong., 1st sess., 555–74 (quoted at 561, 563), 770–76; Everett Somerville Brown, ed., *William Plumber's Memorandum of Proceedings in the United States Senate, 1803–1807* (New York: Macmillan, 1923), 444.

5.   JR to Joseph Scott, 12 January 1807, JR MSS; Norman K. Risjord, *The Old Republicans: Southern Conservatism in the Age of Jefferson* (New York: Columbia University Press, 1965), 50–95.

6.   JR to Josiah Quincy, 23 May 1813, Quincy, 330; JR to Thomas Robinson, 9 July 1813, Duke University Library, available on microfilm 7513, UVA; Nathaniel Macon to Joseph H. Nicholson, 1 February 1815, 12 February 1816, Joseph Hopper Nicholson Papers, LC; Dawidoff, *Education of John Randolph*, 198–243.

7.   JR to David Parish, 25 October 1813, JRCD; JR to John Brockenbrough, 30 January 1826, Garland, 2:265; Aaron Scott Crawford, "John Randolph of Roanoke and the Politics of Doom: Slavery, Sectionalism, and Self-Deception, 1773–1821" (PhD diss., University of Tennessee, 2012), 270–79.

8.   Annals of Cong., 17th Cong., 1st sess., 820; ibid., 18th Cong., 1st sess., 2361; Reg. Deb.,

19th Cong., 1st sess., 131. Some measure of the public perception of Randolph as a prophetic defender of states' rights appears in the frequency of published references to "John Randolph" and "John Randolph of Roanoke," which fell after his death and then peaked quite dramatically during the sectional crisis of the 1850s. Google Books Ngram Viewer, https://books.google.com/ngrams/graph?content=John +Randolph&year_start=1800&year_end=2019&corpus=26&smoothing=3&direct_ url=t1%3B%2CJohn%20Randolph%3B%2Cc0 and https://books.google.com/ngrams/ graph?content=John+Randolph+of+Roanoke&year_start=1800&year_end=2019 &corpus=26&smoothing=3&direct_url=t1%3B%2CJohn%20Randolph%20of%20 Roanoke%3B%2Cc0#t1%3B%2CJohn%20Randolph%20of%20Roanoke%3B%2Cc0.

9.   Arthur Singleton [Henry Cogswell Knight], *Letters from the South and West* (Boston, 1824), 46–47.

10. Andrew Burstein, *America's Jubilee: How in 1826 a Generation Remembered Fifty Years of Independence* (New York: Alfred A. Knopf, 2001), 193–203.

11. Fitzpatrick, "Autobiography of Martin Van Buren," 2:418–19.

12. JR to Andrew Jackson, 18 March 1832, Daniel Feller et al., eds., *The Papers of Andrew Jackson*, 12 vols. to date (Knoxville: University of Tennessee Press, 1980–), 10:174–76; *Lynchburg Virginian*, 1 April 1833.

13. *Lynchburg Virginian*, 4 March 1833; F[rederick] W[illiam] Thomas, *John Randolph of Roanoke and Other Sketches of Character* (Philadelphia, 1853), 15; W[illiam] H[enry] Sparks, *The Memories of Fifty Years* (Philadelphia, 1870), 226-27. For Randolph's tubercular symptoms, see JR to John Brockenbrough, 27 May 1828, 30 May 1828, 29 November 1828, 21 April 1829, Garland, 2:307–09, 314, 322.

14. Reg. Deb., 22nd Cong., 2nd sess., 750-98 (26 February 1833); Harry L. Watson, *Liberty and Power: The Politics of Jacksonian America* (1990; New York: Hill and Wang, 2006), 116-18, 126-29.

15. JR to Andrew Jackson, 26 March 1832, Feller, *Papers of Andrew Jackson*, 10:188 (quoting Shakespeare, *The Tempest*, act 5, sc. 1, l. 296); unknown to Henry Clay, 31 May 1833, John F. Hopkins et al., eds., *The Papers of Henry Clay*, 11 vols. (Lexington: University Press of Kentucky, 1959-92), 8:645-46; *Lynchburg Virginian*, 11 February 1833 (resolutions), 28 February 1833; Nicholas Wood, "John Randolph of Roanoke and the Politics of Slavery in the Early Republic," *Virginia Magazine of History and Biography* 120, no. 2 (2012): 112-13.

16. Garland, 2:369-70; Henry Clay to Francis T. Brooke, 11 March 1833, Hopkins, *Papers of Henry Clay*, 8:631; Robert V. Remini, *Henry Clay: Statesman for the Union* (New York: W. W. Norton, 1991), 78–83, 292–95, 431–33. For John Randolph's duel with Henry Clay, see chapter 5.

17. Samuel Johnson, "The Vanity of Human Wishes" (1755), John H. Middendorf et al., eds., *The Works of Samuel Johnson*, 23 vols. to date (New Haven, CT: Yale University Press, 1958–), 6:106; Thomas Hart Benton, *Thirty Years' View . . .*, 2 vols. (New York, 1854), 1:473–75; Annals of Cong., 18th Cong., 1st sess., 1301 (30 January 1824) (Randolph recited same verses).

18. *Boston Courier*, 24 May 1833; *Lynchburg Virginian*, 27 May 1833.

19. *Niles' Weekly Register* (Baltimore), 48:407 (8 August 1835); George B. Wood, *A Memoir of the Life and Character of the Late Joseph Parrish, M.D.* (Philadelphia, 1840), 35. Randolph objected to Quakers' antislavery petitions to Congress. Crawford, "John Randolph of Roanoke and the Politics of Doom," 264–67.

20. Henry E. Watkins to HSGT, 23 May 1833, RTFP, misc. reel 4223, frame 249; Ethelbert Algernon Coleman, Diary, [25] May 1833, WCBP, transcript vol. 6, p. 85, misc.

reel 3322; Condy Raguet, "The Last Moments of Mr. Randolph," *Examiner and Journal of Political Economy* 1 (4 September 1833): 45-46.

21. *Niles' Weekly Register*, 48:407–08; *Centennial Anniversary of the Pennsylvania Society for Promoting the Abolition of Slavery* (Philadelphia, 1875), 61.

22. Certificates of Isaac Parrish (quoted), Joseph Parrish, Francis West Jr., and Edmund Badger, 24 May 1835, WCBP, transcript vol. 5, pp. 212-18, misc. reel 3322; Memorandum of Francis West Jr., n.d., ibid., pp. 207-10; *Richmond Whig*, 28 July 1835; *New-York Spectator*, 30 July 1835; *Daily National Intelligencer* (DC), 5 August 1835.

23. Elizabeth Bryan endorsed Randolph's last note as "Sacred to his Memory!" and it became a family relic. JR, Last words, box 7, folder 72, JR MSS; Last writing of J.R. of Roanoke, BFP, ser. 1, box 1, folder 4 (lithograph with accompanying note by ETB's grandson John Stewart Bryan); ETB to NBT, 18 July 1833, TCP.

24. *National Gazette* (Philadelphia), 24 May 1833.

25. *National Gazette*, 28 May 1833; *Providence Patriot and Columbian Phoenix* (RI), 8 June 1833 (from *New-York Journal of Commerce*); *Niles' Weekly Register*, 44:357 (27 July 1833); *Lynchburg Virginian*, 10 June 1833. Randolph's half-brother Nathaniel Beverley Tucker valued the estate at $250,000 when he estimated that the fifth he would receive in intestacy was worth $50,000. NBT to Thomas A. Smith, 11 September 1833, 2 October 1833, TCP. The $250,000–$300,000 estimates were reasonable, but the value of Randolph's estate was probably closer to $350,000. Randolph owned about 8,400 acres of land at $160,000, 240 slaves at $80,000, 155 horses at $45,000, three town lots at $1,500, an unsold crop of tobacco, bank stock, bank deposits, a library containing over 1,100 titles, silver plate, sporting guns, furnishings, wines, and a carriage taxed at $600. Thomas A. Morton to JRB, 12 December 1833, Grinnan Family Papers, UVA, box 3; Wyatt Cardwell to NBT, 27 October 1834, TCP; Entries for JR, 1830 United States Federal Census and 1840 United States Federal Census, Charlotte County, VA, Ancestry.com; Entry for JR, Charlotte County Commissioner of Revenue Memorandum Books, 1833, reel 158, LVA; Entry for JR, Virginia Auditor of Public Accounts, Personal Property Tax Books, Charlotte County, 1833, reel 82, LVA; [JR], Book list, n.d., WCBP, transcript vol. 5, pp. 1–28, misc. reel 3322; [Wyatt Cardwell], List of wines, n.d., RTFP, misc. reel 4225, frame 75; *American Turf Register and Sporting Magazine* 6, no. 5 (January 1835): 248-50; WCBP, transcript vol. 6, pp. 70-78, misc. reel 3322; Bruce, 2:357.

26. Susan B. Carter et al., eds., *Historical Statistics of the United States: Earliest Times to the Present*, millennial ed., 5 vols. (New York: Cambridge University Press, 2006), 2:2-381–2-382, table Bb212; Daina Ramey Berry, *The Price for Their Pound of Flesh* (Boston: Beacon Press, 2017); Berry, "'In Pressing Need of Cash': Gender, Skill, and Family Persistence in the Domestic Slave Trade," *Journal of African American History* 92, no. 1 (Winter 2007): 22-36.

27. *National Gazette*, 28 May 1833; *New-York Spectator*, 5 June 1833 (from *Richmond Enquirer*), 13 June 1833; *Lynchburg Virginian*, 6 June 1833 (from *Morning Courier and New-York Enquirer*, 13 June 1833); *Poulson's American Daily Advertiser* (Philadelphia), 8 June and 13 June 1833; *Niles' Weekly Register*, 44:236 (8 June 1833), 44:255-56 (15 June 1833); *United States Telegraph* (DC), 14 June 1833; *Globe* (DC), 15 June 1833.

28. JR, Will, 1 January 1832, in Coalter's Ex'r v. Bryan, 42 Va. (1 Gratt.) 18, 29-31 (1844); *Evening Post* (NY), 1 July 1833; *National Gazette*, 1 July 1833; *Richmond Enquirer*, 4 July 1833; *New-York Spectator*, 8 July 1833, 25 November 1833; *Liberator* (Boston), 17 August 1833 (two items); Act of 3 March 1819, ch. 104, sec. 9, Va. Rev. Code (1819),

1:377. Whether a nuncupative will could manumit slaves in any event was debatable, although the better view was that it could. Winn v. Bob, 30 Va. (3 Leigh) 140, 146 (1831); Page v. Page, 41 Va. (2 Rob.) 424 (1843); Phoebe v. Boggess, 42 Va. (1 Gratt.) 129 (1844).

CHAPTER 2: BURIAL AT ROANOKE

1. Edward E. Baptist, *The Half Has Never Been Told: Slavery and the Making of American Capitalism* (New York: Basic Books, 2014), 173–82; Damian Alan Pargas, *Slavery and Forced Migration in the Antebellum South* (New York: Cambridge University Press, 2015), 19–32.

2. Judith Randolph to SGT, 27 January 1810, TCP; JR to Elizabeth Tucker Coalter, 19 July 1828, JR MSS-MS 5273; Complaint of JR, January 1810, John Randolph v. Judith Randolph (Charlotte County Ct., 1811), Chancery Records Index no. 1811-001, Virginia Memory, LVA, http://www.lva.virginia.gov/chancery/case_detail.asp?CFN=037-1811-001, pp. 21–24.

3. JR to ETB, 16 November 1831, JR MSS; JR to JRB, 11 February 1832, ibid.; Testimony of John Marshall, Bryan v. Meade, in *Richmond Enquirer*, 4 August and 7 August 1835; Powhatan Bouldin, *Home Reminiscences of John Randolph of Roanoke* (Richmond, 1878), 107–08.

4. Henry E. Watkins to John Brockenbrough, 24 May 1833, in *Lynchburg Virginian*, 3 June 1833; Bruce, 2:46–47.

5. Joseph Martin, *A New and Comprehensive Gazetteer of Virginia and the District of Columbia* (Charlottesville, VA, 1835), 148; Henry Howe, *Historical Collections of Virginia* (Charleston, SC, 1845), 223–24.

6. *Paulson's American Daily Advertiser* (Philadelphia), 27 May 1833; *Lynchburg Virginian*, 10 June 1833; "Grave of John Randolph," *Littell's Living Age* 11, no. 128 (24 October 1846): 195 (from *American Beacon*, Norfolk, VA).

7. Howe, *Historical Collections of Virginia*, 223; Bouldin, *Home Reminiscences*, 264; Simon Gikandi, *Slavery and the Culture of Taste* (Princeton, NJ: Princeton University Press, 2011), 10, 150, 168–74.

8. JR to Harmanus Bleecker, 15 July 1818, JR MSS, box 8; [JR], Book list, n.d., WCBP, transcript vol. 5, pp. 1–28, misc. reel 3322; Richard Beale Davis, *Intellectual Life in Jefferson's Virginia, 1790–1830* (Knoxville: University of Tennessee Press, 1972), 108–13; Hugh Blair Grigsby, "The Randolph Library," *Southern Literary Messenger* 20, no. 2 (February 1854): 76–79. An improving planter's library would have contained material about agriculture. Randolph's had virtually none.

9. Thomas Anburey, *Travels through the Interior Parts of America*, 2 vols. (London, 1789), 2:322–25, 337–40, 389–90; Lorena S. Walsh, *From Calabar to Carter's Grove: The History of a Virginia Slave Community* (Charlottesville: University Press of Virginia, 1997), 19–20, 102–03.

10. Gerald Steffens Cowden, "The Randolphs of Turkey Island: A Prosopography of the First Three Generations, 1650–1806" (PhD diss., College of William and Mary, 1977), 421–39. John Randolph identified several of the slaves he inherited as African and another as a victim of the tropical disease yaws. JR, Commonplace Book, [1808–32], p. 90, WCBP, misc. reel 3320.

11. Timothy S. Ailsworth et al., *Charlotte County, Rich Indeed: A History from Prehistoric Times through the Civil War* (Charlotte County, VA: Board of Supervisors, 1979),

47–48, 284–86; Philip D. Morgan and Michael L. Nicholls, "Slaves in Piedmont Virginia, 1720–1790," *William and Mary Quarterly,* 3rd ser., 46, no. 2 (April 1989): 211–51.

12. Wyndham Robertson, *Pocahontas, Alias Matoaka, and Her Descendants* (1887; Baltimore: Genealogical Publishing, 1993), 32, 33, 37; Robert S. Tilton, *Pocahontas: The Evolution of an American Narrative* (New York: Cambridge University Press, 1994), 28–32, 172–74; Cowden, "Randolphs of Turkey Island," 471–84.

13. Phillip Hamilton, *The Making and Unmaking of a Revolutionary Family: The Tuckers of Virginia, 1752–1830* (Charlottesville: University of Virginia Press, 2003), 41–44. The name "Bizarre" has intrigued historians, but it is just one of those references to agricultural risk-taking (such as "chance," "hope," and "folly") often found in plantation names. "Bizarre" came into English from a French word meaning brave or—more to the point—rash. Edward C. Carter II and Angeline Polites, eds., *The Virginia Journals of Benjamin Henry Latrobe, 1795–1798,* 2 vols. (New Haven, CT: Yale University Press, 1977), 1:142; *Oxford English Dictionary,* 1st ed. (1933), s.v. "bizarre."

14. William Bentley to F[rancis] Watkins, 12 April 1799, in *Virginia Gazette and Daily Advertiser* (Richmond), 23 April 1799; Carl Anthony, "The Big House and the Slave Quarters: African Contributions to the New World," in *Cabin, Quarter, Plantation: Architecture and Landscapes of North American Slavery*, ed. Clifton Ellis and Rebecca Ginsburg (New Haven, CT: Yale University Press, 2010), 180–84.

15. *Book of Negroes,* bk. 1, 29 July 1783 (passenger lists for ships *L'Abondance* and *Clinton*), "Black Loyalists: Our History, Our People," Canada's Digital Collections, http://blackloyalist.com/cdc/index.htm; William Withers to SGT, 20 May, 10 August, and 5 November 1781, TCP; Frances Tucker to Theodorick Bland [Jr.], 4 June 1781, TCP; SGT to Theodorick Bland Jr., 21 January 1781, in Charles Campbell, ed., *The Bland Papers,* 2 vols. (Petersburg, VA, 1840), 2:55; Stephanie E. Smallwood, *Saltwater Slavery: A Middle Passage from Africa to American Diaspora* (Cambridge, MA: Harvard University Press, 2007), 198–202.

16. *Book of Negroes,* bk. 1, 29 July 1783 (*L'Abondance*); Frances Tucker to SGT, 14 July 1781, TCP; Ailsworth, *Charlotte County,* 119–20; Robert G. Parkinson, *The Common Cause: Creating Race and Nation in the American Revolution* (Chapel Hill: University of North Carolina Press, 2016), 507–26.

17. Emory G. Evans, *"A Topping People": The Rise and Decline of Virginia's Old Political Elite, 1760–1790* (Charlottesville: University of Virginia Press, 2009), 116–20; Cowden, "Randolphs of Turkey Island," 472–77.

18. Inventory of Richard Randolph's estate, 1 September 1798, Prince Edward County District Court Will Book, 1:10, reel 19, LVA; Jones v. Bland and Randolph [1794], U.S. Cir. Ct., 5th Cir., D. Va., restored case files, LVA; Jones v. Randolph [1794], ibid.; Jones v. John Randolph's Ex'r [1797], ibid.; Randolph v. Hanbury [1801], ibid.; Lloyd v. Randolph [1829], ibid.; Bouldin, *Home Reminiscences,* 22–23.

19. JR to SGT, 30 January 1798, 9 May 1801, Randolph College, available on microfilm 567, UVA; JR to Tudor Randolph, 13 December 1813, JR MSS. Richard Randolph's share of his father's slaves could not go free until his father's estate satisfied its creditors, but a suit for freedom could have prevented the sale of slaves to settle the estate. Patty v. Colin, 11 Va. (1 Hen. & M.) 519 (1807); Paup's Adm'r v. Mingo, 31 Va. (4 Leigh) 163 (1833).

20. JR to SGT, 18 July 1796, Bruce, 1:132; Deposition of Anna Dudley, Coalter's Ex'r v. Bryan, p. 388; Robert Dawidoff, *The Education of John Randolph* (New York: W. W. Norton, 1979), 110–12.

21. JR to SGT, 24 January 1797, 30 January 1798, 15 January 1802, Randolph College, available on microfilm 567, UVA; JR to Daniel Call, 30 May 1798, JR MSS; JR to Joseph Scott, 29 December 1806, Huntington Library, available on microfilm 7513, UVA; JR to John Wickham, 1 April 1820, JR MSS; Randolph's Ex'r v. Randolph's Ex'r, 6 Va. (2 Call) 537 (1801); Randolph's Ex'r v. Randolph's Ex'r, 11 Va. (1 Hen. & M.) 180 (1806).

22. Judith Randolph to SGT, 28 September and 18 October 1801, TCP. For Judith Randolph's household slaves, see Entries for Judith Randolph, Virginia Auditor of Public Accounts, Personal Property Tax Books, Cumberland County, 1811–16, reel 93, LVA.

23. JR, Diary, 1805–15, entries for 11–18 November 1809, WCBP, misc. reel 3320; Judith Randolph to JR, 22 August, 27 August, [October], and 3 November 1809, JR MSS; Judith Randolph to JR, n.d. [1809], ibid., box 8.

24. Judith Randolph to SGT, 27 January 1810, TCP; Judith Randolph to SGT, 3 November 1809, Randolph College, available on microfilm 567, UVA; Cynthia A. Kierner, *Scandal at Bizarre: Rumor and Reputation in Jefferson's America* (Charlottesville: University of Virginia Press, 2004), 96, 100–01, 131–34.

25. Commissioners' report, 6 October 1810, John Randolph v. Judith Randolph, pp. 7–15; Orders of 1 January, 5 March, and 7 November 1810, 7 January and 3 December 1811, John Randolph v. Judith Randolph, Charlotte County Order Bk. 17, pp. 40, 53, 151–53, and Order Bk. 18, p. 99, reels 29 and 30, LVA; Judith Randolph to Creed Taylor, 17 March 1810, WCBP, misc. reel 3325; JR, Commonplace book, [1808–32], p. 90, WCBP, misc. reel 3320 (slave sales); JR to Judith Randolph, 12 February 1812, JR MSS.

26. JR to Theodore Dudley, 22 September 1811, Dudley, 104–05; Entry for JR, 1830 United States Federal Census, Charlotte County, VA, Ancestry.com; Entry for JR, Commissioner of Revenue Memorandum Books, 1833, Charlotte County, VA, reel 158, LVA; Entry for JR, Virginia Auditor of Public Accounts, Personal Property Tax Books, Charlotte County, 1833, reel 82, LVA.

27. Allan Kulikoff, *Tobacco and Slaves: The Development of Southern Cultures in the Chesapeake, 1680–1800* (Chapel Hill: University of North Carolina Press, 1986), 157–61; Pargas, *Slavery and Forced Migration*, 25–27.

28. Adam Rothman, *Slave Country: American Expansion and the Origins of the Deep South* (Cambridge, MA: Harvard University Press, 2005), 177–203; Gavin Wright, *Slavery and American Economic Development* (Baton Rouge: Louisiana State University Press, 2006), 85–88; Sven Beckert, *Empire of Cotton: A Global History* (New York: Alfred A. Knopf, 2015), 103–20.

29. Bureau of the Census, *Statistical View of the United States* (Washington, DC, 1854), 82; Douglass C. North, *The Economic Growth of the United States, 1790–1860* (New York: Prentice-Hall, 1961), 124; Paul W. Gates, *History of Public Land Law Development* (Washington, DC: Government Printing Office, 1968), 165; David F. Weiman, "Peopling the Land by Lottery?: The Market in Public Lands and the Regional Differentiation of Territory on the Georgia Frontier," *Journal of Economic History* 51, no. 4 (December 1991): 835–60.

30. Joel Chandler Harris, *Stories of Georgia* (New York, 1896), 216; Daniel Walker Howe, *What Hath God Wrought: The Transformation of America, 1815–1848* (New York: Oxford University Press, 2007), 356–57, 703–08; Joshua D. Rothman, *Flush Times and Fever Dreams: A Story of Capitalism and Slavery in the Age of Jackson* (Athens: University of Georgia Press, 2012), 2–13.

31. William Dusinberre, *Strategies for Survival: Recollections of Bondage in Antebellum Virginia* (Charlottesville: University of Virginia Press, 2009), 73–74; Calvin Schermerhorn, *Money over Mastery, Family over Freedom: Slavery in the Antebellum Upper South* (Baltimore: Johns Hopkins University Press, 2011), 13–16; Pargas, *Slavery and Forced Migration*, 123–24.

32. JR to Richard Kidder Randolph, 4 July 1810, JRCD. Contemporary estimates of annual capital increase from slave reproduction ranged from 2 to 5 percent, and abolitionists cited them as evidence that Virginia planters had become slave breeders. Theodore D. Weld, *American Slavery As It Is: Testimony of a Thousand Witnesses* (New York, 1839), 181–83; Gregory D. Smithers, *Slave Breeding: Sex, Violence, and Memory in African American History* (Gainesville: University Press of Florida, 2012), 20–43; Caitlin Rosenthal, *Accounting for Slavery: Masters and Management* (Cambridge, MA: Harvard University Press, 2018), 130–33, 153.

33. JR to James Mercer Garnett, 20 February 1820, JR MSS; ETB to NBT, 11 March 1846, TCP; Frederick F. Siegel, *The Roots of Southern Distinctiveness: Tobacco and Society in Danville, Virginia, 1780–1865* (Chapel Hill: University of North Carolina Press, 1987), 101–02, 123; William G. Shade, *Democratizing the Old Dominion: Virginia and the Second Party System, 1824–1861* (Charlottesville: University Press of Virginia, 1996), 33, 44.

34. Entries for JR, Land Tax Books, Charlotte County, VA, 1820–1833, reels 72–73, LVA; Testimony of William Leigh, Bryan v. Meade, in *Richmond Enquirer*, 30 October 1835.

35. JR to Joseph Scott, 23 August 1807, Huntington Library, available on microfilm 7513, UVA; JR to Josiah Quincy, 1 July 1814, Quincy, 356; Joseph Clark Robert, *The Tobacco Kingdom* (1938; Gloucester, MA: Peter Smith, 1965), 32–38.

36. Ibid., 38–46, 249–50; Drew A. Swanson, *A Golden Weed: Tobacco and Environment in the Piedmont South* (New Haven, CT: Yale University Press, 2014), 37–39.

37. Booker T. Washington, *Up from Slavery: An Autobiography* (New York: A. L. Burt, 1901), 11. For more about the daily lives of those enslaved at Roanoke, see chapter 9.

38. JR, Diary, 1808–1815, entries for 25 December 1810, 28 September 1813, WCBP, misc. reel 3320; JR to Theodore Dudley, 22 December 1813, Dudley, 148.

39. Reports from lawyers to William Cabell Bruce, WCBP, transcript vol. 6, pp. 70-78, misc. reel 3322 (real property); Abstract of the Returns of the Fifth Census, 22nd Cong., 1st sess., 1832, HR Doc. 263, 16; William Scarborough, *Masters of the Big House: Elite Slaveholders of the Mid-Nineteenth Century South* (Baton Rouge: Louisiana State University Press, 2003), 6, 454–55 (1850 slave census); Richard S. Dunn, *A Tale of Two Plantations: Slave Life and Labor in Jamaica and Virginia* (Cambridge, MA: Harvard University Press, 2014), 68–72.

CHAPTER 3: RUMORS

1. Garland, 1:63; Cynthia A. Kierner, *Scandal at Bizarre: Rumor and Reputation in Jefferson's Virginia* (Charlottesville: University of Virginia Press, 2004), 1–7, 20–25, 71–72; Chad Vanderford, *The Legacy of St. George Tucker: College Professors in Virginia Confront Slavery and the Rights of States, 1771–1897* (Knoxville: University of Tennessee Press, 2015), 76–79.

2. John Marshall, Notes of evidence, Commonwealth v. Randolph, [April 1793], Charles T. Cullen et al., eds., *The Papers of John Marshall*, 12 vols. (Chapel Hill: University

of North Carolina Press, 1974–2006), 2:161–78; William Waller Hening, *The New Virginia Justice* . . . (Richmond, 1795), 90; Alan Pell Crawford, *Unwise Passions: A True Story of a Remarkable Woman and the First Great Scandal of Eighteenth-Century America* (New York: Simon and Schuster, 2000), 75–80; John Ruston Pagan, "Poor Babes, Desperate Mothers: Concealment of Dead Newborns in Early Virginia," *Huntington Library Quarterly* 84, no. 2 (Summer 2021): 271–72.

3. SGT, Broadside to the Public, 5 May 1793, BCRTP, box 1; JR to SGT, 25 May 1793, St. George Tucker Papers, 1776–1818, LC; Inventory of Richard Randolph's estate, 1 September 1798, Prince Edward County District Court Will Book, 1:10, reel 19, LVA (secretary).

4. Will of Richard Randolph, 18 February [1795], Prince Edward County District Court Will Book, 1:4–7. Richard Randolph's sneering reference to pampered sensuality refers to his uncle Ryland Randolph's long-term relationship with an enslaved woman named Aggy to whom he had bequeathed freedom for herself and their children, all of his household furniture, passage to England, and £3,000. Gerald Steffens Cowden, "The Randolphs of Turkey Island: A Prosopography of the First Three Generations, 1650–1806" (PhD diss., College of William and Mary, 1977), 462, 469–70.

5. SGT, *A Dissertation on Slavery: With a Proposal for the Gradual Abolition of It, in the State of Virginia* (Philadelphia, 1796), 76–96.

6. Ibid., 94; SGT to Robert Pleasants, 29 June 1797, Charles F. Hobson, ed., *St. George Tucker's Law Reports and Selected Papers, 1782–1825*, 3 vols. (Chapel Hill: University of North Carolina Press, 2013), 1:10–12.

7. SGT, *Blackstone's Commentaries*, 5 vols. (Philadelphia, 1803), Note H, 2:A31–85; Ellen Holmes Pearson, *Remaking Custom: Law and Identity in the Early American Republic* (Charlottesville: University of Virginia Press, 2011), 129–35.

8. W[illiam] Bentley to the public, *Virginia Gazette and General Advertiser* (Richmond), 23 April 1799 (esp. attachment 5); Ann C[ary] Morris [Nancy Randolph] to JR, 16 January 1815, Bruce, 2:286–87.

9. JR to editor, *Virginia Gazette and General Advertiser*, 5 April 1799.

10. Annals of Cong., 9th Cong., 2nd sess., 626–27, 635–37; Adam L. Tate, *Conservatism and Southern Intellectuals, 1789–1861* (Columbia: University of Missouri Press, 2005), 117–20; Nicholas Wood, "John Randolph of Roanoke and the Politics of Slavery in the Early Republic," *Virginia Magazine of History and Biography* 120, no. 2 (2012): 106–43.

11. JR to Harmanus Bleecker, 10 October 1818, JR MSS, box 8; JR to Joseph H. Nicholson, 26 September 1800, Joseph Hopper Nicholson Papers, LC; JR to Josiah Quincy, 18 October 1813, Quincy, 339; Douglas R. Egerton, *The Virginia Slave Conspiracies of 1800 and 1802* (Chapel Hill: University of North Carolina Press, 1993), 93–115. Randolph's early library was lost in a fire at Bizarre in 1813; at the time he died, his library contained no books about abolition. [JR], Book list, n.d., WCBP, transcript vol. 5, pp. 1–28, misc. reel 3322.

12. JR, Will, 17 November 1800, TCP, available at https://digitalarchive.wm.edu/handle/10288/16293.

13. Richard Beale Davis, ed., *Jeffersonian America: Notes on the United States of America Collected in the Years 1805–6–7 and 11–12 by Sir Augustus John Foster, Bart.* (San Marino, CA: Huntington Library, 1954), 153, 57–58, 163–66; William Benemann, *Male-Male Intimacy in Early America: Beyond Romantic Friendships* (New York: Harrington Park Press, 2006), 168–74, 183–84; Marilyn K. Parr, "Chronicle of a British Diplomat: The First Year in the 'Washington Wilderness,'" *Washington History* 12, no. 1 (Spring/Summer 2000): 84.

14. Davis, *Jeffersonian America*, 307, 163; Kenneth S. Greenberg, *Honor and Slavery* (Princeton, NJ: Princeton University Press, 1996), 9–12, 15–16, 31–32; Simon Gikandi, *Slavery and the Culture of Taste* (Princeton, NJ: Princeton University Press, 2011), 160–74. A poet and minor aristocrat who later died in a duel caught the essence of honor culture: "So there it is—the mob's opinion! / The spring with which our honour's wound! / The god that makes this world go round!" Alexander Pushkin, *Eugene Onegin: A Novel in Verse*, trans. James E. Falen (Oxford, UK: Oxford University Press, 1995), ch. 6, stan. 11, lines 12–14.

15. Daniel P. Jordan, *Political Leadership in Jefferson's Virginia* (Charlottesville: University Press of Virginia, 1983), 7–10, 63, 69–80, 197–99; William G. Shade, *Democratizing the Old Dominion: Virginia and the Second Party System, 1824–1861* (Charlottesville: University Press of Virginia, 1996), 128–29, 160–61. For doubts about the role of deference, see Michael Zuckerman, "Tocqueville, Turner, and Turds: Four Stories of Manners in Early America," *Journal of American History* 85, no. 1 (June 1998): 13–42; John M. Murrin, "In the Land of the Free and the Home of the Slave, Maybe There Was Room Even for Deference," ibid., 86–91.

16. F. Thornton Miller, *Juries and Judges versus the Law: Virginia's Provincial Legal Perspective, 1783–1828* (Charlottesville: University Press of Virginia, 1994), 2–7; William G. Shade, "Society and Politics in Antebellum Virginia's Southside," *Journal of Southern History* 53, no. 2 (May 1987): 163–93.

17. Tate, *Conservatism and Southern Intellectuals*, 103–07; James L. Huston, *The British Gentry, the Southern Planter, and the North American Family Farmer: Agriculture and Sectional Antagonism in North America* (Baton Rouge: Louisiana State University Press, 2015), 178–83; Padraig Riley, *Slavery and the Democratic Conscience: Political Life in Jeffersonian America* (Philadelphia: University of Pennsylvania Press, 2016), 98–100.

18. SGT, *Blackstone's Commentaries*, 2:A31–34, 51–54; William Waller Hening, *New Virginia Justice . . .*, 2nd ed. (Richmond, 1810), 539; Morris Birkbeck, *Notes on a Journey in America from the Coast of Virginia to the Territory of Illinois*, 4th ed. (London, 1818), 16; Samantha Seeley, *Race, Removal, and the Right to Remain: Migration and the Making of the United States* (Chapel Hill: University of North Carolina Press, 2021), 192–97.

19. Robert McColley, *Slavery and Jeffersonian Virginia* (Champaign: University of Illinois Press, 1964), 115–26; Lacy K. Ford, *Deliver Us from Evil: The Slavery Question in the Old South* (New York: Oxford University Press, 2009), 35–38, 46–47, 54–65.

20. Eva Sheppard Wolf, *Race and Liberty in the New Nation: Emancipation in Virginia from the Revolution to Nat Turner's Rebellion* (Baton Rouge: Louisiana State University Press, 2006), 28–37; Peter J. Albert, "The Protean Institution: The Geography, Economy, and Ideology of Slavery in Post-Revolutionary Virginia" (PhD diss., University of Maryland, 1976), 129–36.

21. Acts of 6 May 1782, ch. 21, William Waller Hening, ed., *The Statutes at Large . . . of Virginia*, 13 vols. (Richmond and Philadelphia, 1819–23), 11:39–40; Act of 17 December 1792, ch. 41, secs. 36–42, Samuel Shepherd, ed., *The Statutes at Large of Virginia*, 3 vols. (Richmond, 1835), 1:127–28; Spencer v. Dennis, 8 Gill 314, 318–19 (Md. Ct. App., 1849) (manumission statute enacted not to benefit slaves, but to enlarge the privileges of slaveholders).

22. Anon. to Robert Carter III, 5 August 1796, in Louis Morton, *Robert Carter of Nomini Hall* (Williamsburg, VA: Colonial Williamsburg, 1941), 266–67; Michael L. Nicholls, "Passing through This Troublesome World: Free Blacks in the Early Southside," *Virginia Magazine of History and Biography* 92, no. 1 (January 1984): 62–63.

23. Act of 25 January 1806, ch. 63, sec. 10, Shepherd, *Statutes at Large*, 3:252; Kirt von Daacke, *Freedom Has a Face: Race, Identity, and Community in Jefferson's Virginia* (Charlottesville: University of Virginia Press, 2012), 77–81; Alejandro de la Fuente and Ariela J. Gross, *Becoming Free, Becoming Black: Race, Freedom, and Law in Cuba, Virginia, and Louisiana* (Cambridge, UK: Cambridge University Press, 2020), 159–62.

24. JR to Theodore Dudley, 27 December 1814, Dudley, 170; Commonwealth v. Ned of Campbell, 33 Va. (6 Leigh) 607 (Gen. Ct. 1835); Melvin Patrick Ely, *Israel on the Appomattox: A Southern Experiment in Black Freedom from the 1790s through the Civil War* (New York: Alfred A. Knopf, 2004), 70–74.

25. JR, Will, May 1819, in *Richmond Enquirer*, 26 July 1836 (partial text in Garland, 2:149–50); JR, Will, [1 December] 1821, and four codicils, in Coalter's Ex'r v. Bryan, 42 Va. (1 Gratt.) 18, 20–29 (1844).

26. JR to Harmanus Bleecker, 26 July 1814, JR MSS, box 8; JR to David Parish, 30 October 1815, JR MSS; Testimony of William Leigh, Bryan v. Meade, in *Richmond Enquirer*, 30 October 1835 (St. George Randolph's income); Eric Burin, *Slavery and the Peculiar Solution: A History of the American Colonization Society* (Gainesville: University Press of Florida, 2005), 37, 48; Loren Schweninger, *Appealing for Liberty: Freedom Suits in the South* (New York: Oxford University Press, 2018), 81–82; Sean Condon, "The Slave Owner's Family and Manumission in the Post-Revolutionary Chesapeake Tidewater," in *Paths to Freedom: Manumission in the Atlantic World*, ed. Rosemary Brana-Shute and Randy J. Sparks (Columbia: University of South Carolina Press, 2009), 342–43, 351.

27. JR to Francis Scott Key, 3 May 1819, Garland, 2:106 (Randolph wrote his 1819 will the next day); JR to Bleecker, 4 February 1816 and 22 May 1819, JR MSS, box 8; JR to [NBT], 15 April 1816, TCP; JR to Henry Middleton Rutledge, 3 May 1819, JRCD; Testimony of John Brockenbrough, Meade v. Hobson, in *Richmond Enquirer*, 26 July and 12 August 1836.

28. JR to James Mercer Garnett, 3 July 1806, JR MSS; JR to Joseph H. Nicholson, 7 July 1806, Joseph Hopper Nicholson Papers, LC; JR to John St. George Randolph, 6 September 1806, Duke University Library, available on microfilm 7513, UVA; Bruce 1:330–31.

29. JR to Bleecker, 26 July 1814, JR MSS, box 8; Testimony in Bryan v. Meade by Robert Carrington, *Richmond Enquirer*, 7 August 1835, and William Leigh, ibid., 3 November 1835.

30. JR to unknown, 31 January 1826, quoted in Garland, 1:11; Hugh Blair Grigsby, Memorandum about JR, n.d., excerpted in Michael O'Brien, *Conjectures of Order: Intellectual Life and the American South, 1810–1860*, 2 vols. (Chapel Hill: University of North Carolina Press, 2004), 2:668–71; Bertram Wyatt-Brown, *Southern Honor: Ethics and Behavior in the Old South*, 25th anniv. ed. (New York: Oxford University Press, 2007), 34, 289–97; David Johnson, *John Randolph of Roanoke* (Baton Rouge: Louisiana State University Press, 2012), 28–29, 131; Thomas A. Foster, *Rethinking Rufus: Sexual Violations of Enslaved Men* (Athens: University of Georgia Press, 2019), 102–12.

31. JR, Diary, 1808–1815, entries of 25 December 1810, 28 September 1813, WCBP, misc. reel 3320; JR, Commonplace book, [1808–32], entries for "Negroes" and "Overseers," ibid.; JR, Diary, 1 January 1818–1 January 1819, entries of 21, 26, 27, and 28 July 1818, JRCD; JR to James Mercer Garnett, 7 October 1811, 17 October 1813, 13 July 1818, JR MSS; JR to Josiah Quincy, 18 October 1813, JRCD; JR to Theodore

Dudley, 22 December 1813, Dudley, 148; John Randolph v. John Pentecost (Charlotte County Ct., 4 July 1818), in WCBP, transcript vol. 6, p. 3, misc. reel 3322; Powhatan Bouldin, *Home Reminiscences of John Randolph of Roanoke* (Richmond, 1878), 28, 126–28; 126–28; William E. Wiethoff, *Crafting the Overseer's Image* (Columbia: University of South Carolina Press, 2006), 75–77.

32. Charles Ball, *Slavery in the United States: A Narrative of the Life and Adventures of Charles Ball* (New York, 1837), 66, 68–69; [Joseph Holt Ingraham], *The South-West*, 2 vols. (New York, 1835), 2:287–88 (whips); William L. Andrews, *To Tell a Free Story: The First Century of Afro-American Autobiography, 1760–1865* (Urbana: University of Illinois Press, 1986), 63, 81–86.

33. JR to John Brockenbrough, 20 February 1826, 30 January 1826, Garland, 2:266, 265; JR, Diary, 1 January 1818–1 January 1819, entry for 30 August 1818, JRCD; JR to James Mercer Garnett, 16 November 1818, JR MSS.

34. JR to James Mercer Garnett, 24 and 25 November 1832, ibid.; Testimony of William Leigh, Bryan v. Meade, in *Richmond Enquirer*, 3 November 1835; Act of 2 March 1819, ch. 111, secs. 15–16, Va. Rev. Code (1819), 1:424–25; Act of 7 April 1831, ch. 186, secs. 4–6, Va. Rev. Code Supp. (1833), 245; Act of 15 March 1832, ch. 187, ibid., 246–48; Randall M. Miller, ed., *"Dear Master": Letters of a Slave Family* (Ithaca, NY: Cornell University Press, 1978), 33–36; Annette Gordon-Reed and Peter S. Onuf, *"Most Blessed of the Patriarchs": Thomas Jefferson and the Empire of the Imagination* (New York: Liveright, 2016), 57–71.

35. [John Randolph Clay], Notes, 7 September 1830, JRCD; JR to John Randolph Clay, 23 November 1830, ibid.; JR to Joseph Vance, 20 December 1831, JR MSS; JR to Andrew Jackson, 18 March 1832, Daniel Feller et al., eds., *The Papers of Andrew Jackson*, 12 vols. to date (Knoxville: University of Tennessee Press, 1980–), 10:174–76; *Lynchburg Virginian*, 1 April 1833.

36. Patrick H. Breen, *The Land Shall Be Deluged in Blood: A New History of the Nat Turner Revolt* (New York: Oxford University Press, 2015), 1, 92, 122, 130; Kay Wright Lewis, *A Curse upon the Nation: Race, Freedom, and Extermination in America and the Atlantic World* (Athens: University of Georgia Press, 2017), 83–102.

37. Testimony of Robert Carrington, Bryan v. Meade, in *Richmond Enquirer*, 7 August 1835; Testimony of John Brockenbrough, Meade v. Hobson, ibid., 12 August 1836.

38. JR to Andrew Jackson, 26 February 1832, Feller, *Papers of Andrew Jackson*, 10:127; Testimony in Bryan v. Meade by Wyatt Cardwell, *Richmond Enquirer*, 23 October 1835, and William Leigh, ibid., 30 October 1835, 3 November 1835; Deposition of Henry A. Watkins, Coalter's Ex'r v. Bryan, pp. 425–26.

39. JR to ETB, 16 November 1831, JR MSS; *Richmond Enquirer*, 2 December, 6 December, and 28 December 1831; *Liberator* (Boston), 10 March 1832; Testimony in Bryan v. Meade by William M. Watkins, *Richmond Enquirer*, 4 August 1835; John Marshall, ibid., 7 August 1835; Wyatt Cardwell, ibid., 23 October 1835; William Leigh, ibid., 30 October and 3 November 1835; [George Tucker], *Letters from Virginia* (Baltimore, 1816), 33.

40. JR to JRB, 11 February 1832, JR MSS; Testimony in Bryan v. Meade by John Marshall, *Richmond Enquirer*, 4 August and 7 August 1835; William Berkeley, ibid., 7 August 1835; John J. Flournoy, ibid.

41. William Leigh to John Randolph Clay, 10 August 1833, JRCD; Testimony of William Leigh, Bryan v. Meade, 30 October and 3 November 1835; Deposition of William Leigh, Coalter's Ex'r v. Bryan, pp. 488–92.

42. Orlando Patterson, *Slavery and Social Death: A Comparative Study* (Cambridge,

MA: Harvard University Press, 1982), 211–14, 223–26; Charles F. Irons, *The Origins of Proslavery Christianity: White and Black Evangelicals in Colonial and Antebellum Virginia* (Chapel Hill: University of North Carolina Press, 2008), 139–42; Howard Bodenhorn, *The Color Factor: The Economics of African-American Well-Being in the Nineteenth-Century South* (New York: Oxford University Press, 2015), 76–81.

43. JR to William Leigh, 1 January 1832, WCBP, transcript vol. 5, pp. 201–05, misc. reel 3322; Testimony of William Leigh, Bryan v. Meade, 3 November 1835; Deposition of John Marshall, Coalter's Ex'r v. Bryan, pp. 445, 454–55. Under Virginia law, removal of the testator's signature canceled a will, and a will entirely in his own handwriting required no witness. Bates v. Holman, 13 Va. (3 Hen. & M.) 502, 504–05 (1809); Act of 3 March 1819, ch. 104, sec. 1, Va. Rev. Code (1819), 1:375.

CHAPTER 4: HEIRS AT LAW

1. William Leigh to Peachy R. Gilmer, 25 June 1833, WLL; *Evening Post* (NY), 1 July 1833; *Richmond Enquirer*, 4 July 1833.

2. William Lee [Sr.] to SGT, 29 October 1778, TCP; NBT to SGT, 25 July 1801, 22 March 1807, ibid.; HSGT to JR, 20 April 1831, Huntington Library, available on microfilm 7513, UVA; William Meade, *Old Churches, Ministers, and Families of Virginia*, 2 vols. (1857; Baltimore: Genealogical Publishing, 1995), 1:450–51.

3. Powhatan Bouldin, *The Old Trunk, or Sketches of Colonial Days* (Danville, VA, 1896), 65; William Leigh to Peachy R. Gilmer, 24 April 1831, 25 November 1832, WLL; Entries for William Leigh, 1830 United States Federal Census, Halifax County, VA, and 1840 United States Federal Census, Halifax County, VA, North District and South District, Ancestry.com; James B. Longacre, Portrait of Benjamin Watkins Leigh, 1835, watercolor on board, VMHC; William Leigh [III], "Judge William Leigh," *Virginia Law Register* 2, no. 5 (September 1896): 316–20.

4. JR to William J. Barksdale, 16 April 1824, John Randolph Letters, 1816–1828, LVA; JR to Theodore Dudley, 15 July 1811, 24 January 1814, Dudley, 90, 131; JR to John Brockenbrough, 15 July 1814, 24 July 1824, Garland, 2:42, 226; William Leigh to JR, 15 April and 17 April 1820, TCP; Testimony of William Leigh, Bryan v. Meade, in *Richmond Enquirer*, 30 October 1835, 3 November 1835.

5. Leigh to John Randolph Clay, 10 August 1833, JRCD; Leigh to Peachy R. Gilmer, 3 March 1834, WLL.

6. Leigh to Clay, 10 August 1833.

7. Leigh to Gilmer, 18 August 1833, 21 September 1833, 30 September 1833, WLL; Testimony of John Marshall, Bryan v. Meade, in *Richmond Enquirer*, 4 April 1835; Act of 10 March 1819, ch. 96, secs. 4, 15, and 16, Va. Rev. Code (1819), 1:355, 357.

8. JR to NBT, 3 January 1822, TCP.

9. SGT to Richard Rush, 27 October 1813 (draft), in *Virginia Magazine of History and Biography* 42, no. 3 (July 1934): 211–18; SGT to William Wirt, 25 September 1815, in *William and Mary Quarterly*, 1st ser., no. 4 (April 1914): 252–53; Phillip Hamilton, *The Making and Unmaking of a Revolutionary Family: The Tuckers of Virginia, 1752–1830* (Charlottesville: University of Virginia Press, 2003), 17–29; Christopher Leonard Doyle, "Lord, Master, and Patriot: St. George Tucker and Patriarchy in Republican Virginia, 1772–1851" (PhD diss., University of Connecticut, 1996), 47–49.

10. Emory G. Evans, *"A Topping People": The Rise and Decline of Virginia's Old Political Elite, 1760–1790* (Charlottesville: University of Virginia Press, 2009), 134–76.

11. John Randolph [Sr.], Will, 25 July 1774, and codicil, 23 October 1775, Chester-field County Will Book, 2:328–33, reel 26, LVA; Hamilton, *Making and Unmaking*, 31–56. After coverture gave him possession of Frances Randolph's property, St. George Tucker was just off Jackson Turner Main's list of Virginia's wealthiest one hundred men, in company with James Madison and Richard Henry Lee. Jackson T. Main, "The One Hundred," *William and Mary Quarterly*, 3rd ser., 11, no. 3 (July 1954): 364n19.

12. Hamilton, *Making and Unmaking*, 73–87, 93; Robert Dawidoff, *The Education of John Randolph* (New York: W. W. Norton, 1979), 81–85.

13. John Randolph [Sr.], Will, 2:331; Richard Randolph to Frances Tucker, 12 April 1787, TCP; Dawidoff, *Education of John Randolph*, 87–93.

14. SGT to Theodorick Randolph and John Randolph, 29 June 1788, JR MSS; F. Thornton Miller, *Juries and Judges versus the Law: Virginia's Provincial Legal Perspective, 1783–1828* (Charlottesville: University Press of Virginia, 1994), 38–43.

15. JR to Henry Middleton Rutledge, 24 February 1791, 29 April 1797, quoted in Bruce, 1:91–92; JR to SGT, 25 May 1793, St. George Tucker Papers, 1776–1818, LC; John Marshall to SGT, [December 1794], TCP; JR to Daniel Call, 30 May [1798], JR MSS; Jones v. Bland and Randolph [1794], U.S. Cir. Ct., 5th Cir., D. Va., restored case files, LVA; Jones v. Randolph [1794], ibid.; Jones v. John Randolph's Ex'r [1797], ibid.

16. JR to Dudley, 13 October 1811, 30 December 1813, 13 March 1817, Dudley, 107, 146, 200; JR to Littleton Waller Tazewell, 27 February 1826, University of North Carolina Library, available on microfilm 7513, UVA; Entry for JR, Charlotte County Commissioner of Revenue, Memorandum Books, 1815, reel 156, LVA; Deposition of William Barksdale, 14 July 1841, Coalter's Ex'r v. Bryan, p. 397.

17. JR to James Mercer Garnett, 4 March 1826, JR MSS; JR to Joseph Scott, 23 August 1807, Huntington Library, available on microfilm 7513, UVA; JR to R[ichard] Kidder Randolph, 25 August 1810, 14 August 1820, JRCD; JR to Benjamin Watkins Leigh, 25 September 1813, JR MSS; JR to Josiah Quincy, 1 and 4 July 1814, Quincy, 356; JR to Harmanus Bleecker, 26 July 1814, 27 October 1816, JR MSS, box 8; JR to David Parish, 30 October 1815, JR MSS; David Silkenat, *Scars on the Land: An Environmental History of Slavery in the American South* (New York: Oxford University Press, 2022), 7–15.

18. JR to Brockenbrough, 24 July 1824, Garland, 2:224; JR to Dudley, 15 April 1816, 31 December 1816, Dudley, 177, 181; Order of 3 December 1829, Randolph v. Lloyd [1829], 5th Cir., D. Va., restored case files, LVA; Entries for JR, Auditor of Public Accounts, Personal Property Tax Books, Charlotte County, 1810–34, reels 80–82, LVA.

19. JR to Brockenbrough, 6 February 1826, Garland, 2:266; JR to Dudley, 30 December 1821, Dudley, 232; Cynthia A. Kierner, "'The Dark and Dense Cloud Perpetually Lowering over Us': Gender and the Decline of the Gentry in Postrevolutionary Virginia," *Journal of the Early Republic* 20, no. 2 (Summer 2000): 185–217.

20. [NBT], Notes for argument in *Coalter's Ex'r v. Bryan*, [1844–45], TCP, box 86; Deposition of Anna Dudley, Coalter's Ex'r v. Bryan, p. 388; *Lynchburg Virginian*, 1 April 1833; Testimony of John Brockenbrough, Meade v. Hobson, in *Richmond Enquirer*, 12 August 1836; Testimony of John Marshall, Bryan v. Meade, ibid., 4 August and 7 August 1835; Anna Dudley to NBT, 7 January 1840, TCP; Lemuel Sawyer, *A Biography of John Randolph of Roanoke* (New York, 1844), 124.

21. JR to Tudor Randolph, 13 December 1813, GFP-90; Testimony of Richard Randolph Jr., Meade v. Hobson, in *Richmond Enquirer*, 9 August 1836; Testimony of Thomas Robinson, Meade v. Hobson, ibid., 12 August 1836; Lisa Wilson, *A History*

of Stepfamilies in Early America (Chapel Hill: University of North Carolina Press, 2014), 26–34; Allan Kulikoff, "'Such Things Ought Not to Be': The American Revolution and the First Great National Depression," in *The World of the Revolutionary American Republic: Land, Labor, and the Conflict for a Continent*, ed. Andrew Shankman (New York: Routledge, 2014), 134–64.

22. JR to SGT, 14 April 1814, TCP; JR to [SGT], 28 February 1817, JR MSS (draft); Turner v. Turner, 1 Va. (1 Wash.) 139 and 8 Va. (4 Call) 230 (1792); Jordan v. Murray, 7 Va. (3 Call) 85 (1801); Acts of April 1757, ch. 6, sec. 1, William Waller Hening, ed., *The Statutes at Large . . . of Virginia*, 13 vols. (Richmond and Philadelphia, 1819–23), 7:119; Acts of September 1758, ch. 5, sec. 2, ibid., 7:238; Act of 31 December 1787, ch. 22, sec. 2, ibid., 12:506.

23. SGT to HSGT, 10 March 1816, TCP; John Woodson to SGT, 3 January and 6 January 1792, ibid.; Theodorick Bland [Sr.], Slave deed to Frances Tucker, 1 June 1784, ibid. (twenty slaves); SGT, Slave deed to JR, 27 November 1796, ibid.; JR and SGT, Endorsements canceling bond, 27 November 1796, ibid.; Testimony of Benjamin Watkins Leigh, Meade v. Hobson, in *Richmond Enquirer*, 2 August 1836; Suzanne Lebsock, *The Free Women of Petersburg: Status and Culture in a Southern Town, 1784–1860* (New York: W. W. Norton, 1984), 60–61, 66–67.

24. JR to [SGT], 28 February 1817; SGT to John Coalter, 1 November 1813, exhibit to testimony of John Coalter, Meade v. Hobson, in *Richmond Enquirer*, 9 August 1836; SGT to JR, [15 April] 1814, TCP; JR to Littleton Waller Tazewell, 8 November 1814, Littleton Waller Tazewell Papers, University of North Carolina, available on microfilm 7513, UVA; Tazewell to JR, 14 March 1815, ibid.; ETB to Lelia Tucker, 19 September 1833, BCRTP.

25. JR to Harmanus Bleecker, 22 August 1813, 28 March 1813, JR MSS, box 8; JR to Benjamin Watkins Leigh, 25 September 1813, JR MSS; JR to Josiah Quincy, 19 April 1813, 22 May 1814, JRCD; Charles F. Hobson, "St. George Tucker: Judge, Legal Scholar, and Reformer of Virginia Law," in *"Esteemed Bookes of Lawe" and the Legal Culture of Early Virginia*, ed. Warren E. Billings and Brent Tarter (Charlottesville: University of Virginia Press, 2017), 206–09.

26. JR to Tudor Randolph, 13 December 1813; JR to Bleecker, 10 October 1818, JR MSS, box 8; Dawidoff, *Education of John Randolph*, 80–82, 87–88, 95–97.

27. JR to Tudor Randolph, 13 December 1813; Frances Tucker to SGT, November 1787, TCP; JR to [SGT], 28 February 1817; JR to Brockenbrough, 24 July 1824, Garland, 2:224; David Johnson, *John Randolph of Roanoke* (Baton Rouge: Louisiana State University Press, 2012), 10–15.

28. HSGT to John Coalter, 12 February 1816, 4 March 1816, TCP; SGT to HSGT, 10 March 1816, 19 March 1816, ibid.; HSGT to SGT, 30 April 1820, ibid.

29. JR to Bleecker, 10 October 1818; Hamilton, *Making and Unmaking*, 109–112; Chad Vanderford, *The Legacy of St. George Tucker: College Professors in Virginia Confront Slavery and the Rights of States, 1771–1897* (Knoxville: University of Tennessee Press, 2015), 80–81.

30. HSGT to SGT, [1802], 10 October 1803, 5 November 1803, in Mrs. George P. Coleman [Mary Haldane (Begg) Coleman], ed., *Virginia Silhouettes: Contemporary Letters Concerning Negro Slavery in the State of Virginia* (Richmond: Dietz Printing, 1934), 7–8, 11; E. Lee Shepard, "Breaking into the Profession: Establishing a Law Practice in Antebellum Virginia," *Journal of Southern History* 48, no. 3 (August 1982): 393–410.

31. HSGT to SGT, 17 February 1804, 1 March 1804, in Coleman, *Virginia Silhouettes*, 9–10.

32. J. Randolph Tucker, "The Judges Tucker of the Court of Appeals of Virginia," *Virginia Law Register* 1, no. 11 (March 1896): 796–812; David M. Cobin, *Henry St. George Tucker: Jurist, Teacher, Citizen: 1780–1848* (Stephens City, VA: Commercial Press, 1992), 3–7; W. Hamilton Bryson, "The Winchester Law School, 1824–1831," *Law and History Review* 21, no. 2 (Summer 2003): 393–409.

33. HSGT, *Commentaries on the Laws of Virginia*, 3rd ed., 2 vols. (Richmond, 1846), 1:74; Elder v. Elder's Ex'r, 31 Va. (4 Leigh) 252, 261 (1833); Betty v. Horton, 32 Va. (5 Leigh) 615 (1833); Nicholas v. Burruss, 31 Va. (4 Leigh) 289 (1833); Eugene D. Genovese and Elizabeth Fox-Genovese, *Fatal Self-Deception: Slaveholding Paternalism in the Old South* (New York: Cambridge University Press, 2011), 4; Vanderford, *Legacy of St. George Tucker*, 91. Judge Tucker was not always on the side of freedom. When his court granted habeas relief to a freedman who was seized by his former master's creditors after he had purchased his freedom, Tucker dissented on the doctrinaire ground that the self-purchase was impossible because a slaveholder owns his slave's wages. Ruddle's Ex'r v. Ben, 37 Va. (10 Leigh) 467, 479–80 (1839).

34. Manns v. Givens, 34 Va. (7 Leigh) 689, 709 (1836); Parks v. Hewlett, 38 Va. (9 Leigh) 511, 521–24 (1838); Timothy S. Huebner, *The Southern Judicial Tradition: State Judges and Sectional Distinctiveness, 1790–1890* (Athens: University of Georgia Press, 1999), 86–95, 146–53; Alfred L. Brophy, *University, Court, and Slave: Pro-Slavery Thought in Southern Colleges and Courts and the Coming of the Civil War* (New York: Oxford University Press, 2016), 256–67; A. E. Keir Nash, "Reason of Slavery: Understanding the Judicial Role in the Peculiar Institution," *Vanderbilt Law Review* 32, no. 1 (January 1979): 127–84; Catherine Wisnosky, "The Will of the Master: Testamentary Manumission in Virginia, 1800–1858" (MA thesis, University of Nevada, Las Vegas, 2015), 8, 66.

35. JR to HSGT, 6 January 1828, JRCD; HSGT to NBT, 8 February 1829, 19 July 1833, TCP; HSGT to JR, 3 March 1829, ibid.; Frederica H. Trapnell, ed., *Virginia Tucker–Henry L. Brooke Correspondence, 1831–1869* ([Richmond], 1978), 6; Hamilton, *Making and Unmaking*, 112–13; Department of the Interior, National Park Service, National Register of Historic Places, Nomination Form for Woodbury, Jefferson County, West Virginia, 5 April 1974 (estimates completion in 1834–35), available at https://npgallery.nps.gov/NRHP/AssetDetail?assetID=7cdb46f9-25a5-46cc-aa73-545d7aa0726e.

36. JR, Codicil, 29 August 1831, in Coalter's Ex'r v. Bryan, 42 Va. (1 Gratt.) 22, 28 (1844); JR, Will, 1 January 1832, ibid., 29.

37. HSGT to SGT, 30 April 1820, TCP.

38. Robert J. Brugger, *Beverley Tucker: Heart over Head in the Old South* (Baltimore: Johns Hopkins University Press, 1978), 6–19 (quoted at 12), 21–33; Hamilton, *Making and Unmaking*, 114–15; Bertram Wyatt-Brown, *Hearts of Darkness: Wellsprings of a Southern Literary Tradition* (Baton Rouge: Louisiana State University Press, 2003), 38–40.

39. NBT to SGT, 5 September 1805, 28 February 1807, 22 March 1807, TCP; Hamilton, *Making and Unmaking*, 114–18.

40. SGT to NBT, 28 July 1807, quoted ibid., 121.

41. NBT to SGT, 6 October 1808, quoted ibid., 121–22.

42. JR to [NBT], 15 April 1816, TCP; David Hackett Fischer and James C. Kelly, *Bound Away: Virginia and the Westward Movement* (Charlottesville: University of Virginia Press, 2000), 138–40, 177–80.

43. Brugger, *Beverley Tucker*, 43–46; John Craig Hammond, *Slavery, Freedom, and*

Expansion in the Early American West (Charlottesville: University of Virginia Press, 2007), 56–62.

44. NBT to SGT, 19 January 1819, quoted in Brugger, *Beverley Tucker*, 59.

45. Adam L. Tate, *Conservatism and Southern Intellectuals, 1789–1861: Liberty, Tradition, and the Good Society* (Columbia: University of Missouri Press, 2005), 212–13; Hammond, *Slavery, Freedom, and Expansion*, 67–69.

46. Brugger, *Beverley Tucker*, 70–75.

47. NBT to Lucy Tucker, 8 July 1834, 9, 13, 18, and 27 October 1835, 17 September 1837, 1 June 1842, 23 April 1843, TCP; NBT to Thomas A. Smith, 2 October 1834, ibid.; Lucy Tucker to NBT, 25 April 1836, ibid. Beverley Tucker's novel gives affectionate tributes not only to his wife, but also to her father, the adroit and commanding General Thomas Smith. [NBT], *George Balcombe*, 2 vols. (New York, 1836), 1:15–16, 125–29, 242–43, 259, 271–73.

48. William Leigh to JR, 15 April 1820, TCP; HSGT to SGT, 30 April 1820, ibid.; JR to NBT, 3 January 1822, ibid.; Deposition of John Marshall, Coalter's Ex'r v. Bryan, pp. 459–60; Deposition of William Leigh, ibid., pp. 530–31.

49. JR to NBT, 3 January 1822, TCP.

50. Hamilton, *Making and Unmaking*, xii, 178.

51. Ibid., 130–31, 177–78; C. Dallett Hemphill, *Siblings: Brothers and Sisters in American History* (New York: Oxford University Press, 2011), 108–23, 153–70, 196–204.

52. Catherine W. M. Rudnicki, "In Her Words: The Historically Edited Diary of Elizabeth Tucker Coalter Bryan, in the Context of the History of Southern Antebellum Women" (MA thesis, Youngstown State University, 2008), 13 (quoted), 41; Frances Coalter to SGT and Lelia Tucker, 17 August 1809, quoted in Hamilton, *Making and Unmaking*, 175; NBT to ETB, 29 June 1833, 26 July 1833, 7 September 1840, 23 March 1846, BCRTP; HSGT to NBT, 16 September 1842, TCP; Anya Jabour, *Scarlett's Sisters: Young Women in the Old South* (Chapel Hill: University of North Carolina Press, 2007), 36–39.

53. JR to Elizabeth Tucker Coalter, 12 June 1821–25 April 1824, JR MSS, box 3 (letter book); JR to Elizabeth Tucker Coalter, 2 December 1824–19 February 1831, JR MSS (letter book); JRB to editor, *Daily Dispatch* (Richmond), 20 May 1878; Deposition of John Marshall, Coalter's Ex'r v. Bryan, p. 468.

54. Elizabeth Tucker Coalter to JR, 3 March 1829, JR MSS; JR to Elizabeth Tucker Coalter, 30 March 1828, 12 February 1826, JR MSS–MS 5273; JR to Elizabeth Tucker Coalter, 10 January 1828, 16 January 1828, JRP.

55. *Proceedings and Debates of the Virginia State Convention of 1829–30* (Richmond, 1830), 321, 858, 556; Alison Goodyear Freehling, *Drift toward Dissolution: The Virginia Slavery Debate of 1831–1832* (Baton Rouge: Louisiana State University Press, 1982), 58–81.

56. JR to Elizabeth Tucker Coalter, 7 October 1828, JR MSS–MS 5273; JR, Diary, entries for 22 February and 7 March 1830, WCBP, transcript vol. 5, pp. 40–51, misc. reel 3322; Dickson D. Bruce Jr., *Violence and Culture in the Antebellum South* (Austin: University of Texas Press, 1979), 188–89.

57. JRB to JR, 24 September 1830, BFP, ser. 1, box 1, folder 4; JRB to JR, 9 December 1830, Grinnan Family Papers, box 3, UVA; JR to JRB, 29 December 1830, in *New-York Daily Times*, 20 April 1854.

58. JR to JRB, 11 February 1832, JR MSS; ETB to Lelia Tucker, 16 March 1831, Grinnan Family Papers, box 3, UVA; JR to John Randolph Clay, 16 April 1831, JRCD.

59. ETB to NBT, 18 July 1833, TCP.

60. NBT to ETB, 29 June 1833, BCRTP; NBT to Thomas A. Smith, 12 June 1833, 22 June 1833, TCP.
61. JR to NBT, 26 October 1832, ibid.; Brugger, *Beverley Tucker*, 78–86.
62. Beverley D. Tucker, *Nathaniel Beverley Tucker: Prophet of the Confederacy, 1784-1851* (Tokyo: Nan'un-do, 1979), 245-54.
63. NBT to ETB, 26 July 1833, BCRTP; John Brockenbrough to NBT, 1 July 1833, TCP; NBT to Thomas A. Smith, 11 October 1833, ibid. Randolph shifted his Bank of Virginia deposits to the Bank of the United States, which was a sensible step in preparation for travel because BUS notes were more widely accepted. Randolph had brushed aside John Brockenbrough's reminder that the withdrawal would prevent the Bank of Virginia from honoring Beverley Tucker's drafts. Testimony of John Brockenbrough, Meade v. Hobson, in *Richmond Enquirer*, 12 August 1836.

Chapter 5: Search for the Will

1. *Richmond Enquirer*, 23 July 1833; Testimony of Wyatt Cardwell, Bryan v. Meade, in *Richmond Enquirer*, 23 October 1835. The courthouse village was named Marysville in honor of local landowner Mary Read, but residents at the time commonly referred to the place as Charlotte Courthouse. Timothy S. Ailsworth et al., *Charlotte County, Rich Indeed: A History from Prehistoric Times through the Civil War* (Charlotte County, VA: Charlotte County Board of Supervisors, 1979), 304–06.
2. Testimony in Bryan v. Meade by Winslow Robinson (clerk of court), *Richmond Enquirer*, 28 July 1835; John Marshall, ibid., 4 August and 7 August 1835; William Leigh, ibid., 30 October 1835.
3. JR, Testamentary drafts, [9 April 1832], appended to deposition of John Marshall, Coalter's Ex'r v. Bryan, pp. 465–67. For Randolph's boasts about descent from Pocahontas, see JR to *National Gazette* (Philadelphia), 2 December 1811, reprinted in *Richmond Whig*, 4 June 1833; JR to Josiah Quincy, 22 May 1814, JRCD; JR to Harmanus Bleecker, 15 July 1818, JR MSS, box 8.
4. Testimony of John Marshall, Bryan v. Meade, in *Richmond Enquirer*, 4 August 1835; JR to John Randolph Clay, 16 December 1827, JRCD; JR to John Brockenbrough, [August or September 1832], Garland, 2:349.
5. Deposition of William Leigh, Coalter's Ex'r v. Bryan, p. 520.
6. JR, Will, [1 December] 1821, in Coalter's Ex'r v. Bryan, 42 Va. (1 Gratt.) 18, 20–21 (1844); JR to NBT, 3 January 1822, TCP.
7. JR, Will, 1821, *Coalter's Ex'r*, 42 Va. 21–22; JR, Codicil, 5 December 1821, ibid., 22. For Francis Scott Key and William Meade, see chapter 6.
8. JR, Codicils, 31 January 1826, 6 May 1828, *Coalter's Ex'r*, 42 Va. 22–25 (quoted at 23), 25–29 (quoted at 27); NBT to Thomas A. Smith, 2 October 1833, TCP; Testimony of Winslow Robinson, Bryan v. Meade, in *Richmond Whig*, 28 July 1835.
9. ETB to Lelia Tucker, 19 September 1833, BCRTP; JR to Tudor Randolph, 13 December 1813, in *American and Commercial Daily Advertiser* (Baltimore), 8 August 1833 (from *New York Commercial Advertiser*); *New-York Spectator*, 8 August and 19 August 1833; *Daily National Intelligencer* (DC), 9 August 1833.
10. HSGT to NBT, 27 August 1833, TCP; ETB to NBT, 10 September 1833, ibid.; Peter W. Bardaglio, *Reconstructing the Household: Families, Sex, and the Law in the Nineteenth-Century South* (Chapel Hill: University of North Carolina Press, 1995), 5–7, 106.

11. NBT to ETB, 26 July 1833, BCRTP; NBT to Thomas A. Smith, 11 September 1833, TCP.

12. HSGT to NBT, 12 November 1837, TCP ("stranger"); Cartwright v. Cartwright, (1793) 161 Eng. Rep. 923, 1 Phill. Ecc. 90; Johnson v. Moore's Heirs, 11 Ky. (1 Litt.) 371 (1822); Henry Swinburne, *A Treatise of Testaments and Last Wills*, 7th ed., 2 vols. (Dublin, 1793), pt. 2, sec. 3, pp. 77–79; Yvonne Pitts, *Family, Law, and Inheritance in America: A Social and Legal History of Nineteenth-Century Kentucky* (New York: Cambridge University Press, 2013), 54–61, 64–66. If John Randolph had left all of his property to his family, his niece Elizabeth Bryan later acknowledged, "we should all have thought him in his senses." ETB to NBT, 6 January 1840, TCP.

13. NBT to ETB, 19 September 1833, BCRTP; Conway Robinson, *The Practice in the Courts of Law and Equity in Virginia*, 3 vols. (Richmond, 1832), 3:334–42; Thomas Jarman, *Jarman on Wills*, ed. J. C. Perkins, 2nd Amer. ed., 2 vols. (Boston, 1849), 1:58–64. For madness and testamentary capacity, see chapter 8.

14. Lelia Tucker to HSGT, 11 October 1833, RTFP, misc. reel 4224, frames 251–52; Lelia Tucker to NBT, 8 February 1834, TCP; ETB to NBT, 6 January 1840, ibid.; Anne Royall, *Mrs. Royall's Southern Tour, or Second Series of the Black Book* (Washington, DC, 1830), 121; John Mayfield, "The Marketplace of Values: Honor and Enterprise in the Old South," in *The Field of Honor: Essays on Southern Character and American Identity*, ed. John Mayfield and Todd Hagstette (Columbia: University of South Carolina Press, 2017), 17.

15. ETB to Lelia Tucker, 15 August 1833, BCRTP; [ETB], Statement on will of JR, n.d., ibid., box 3 (in JR MSS–MS 5273, this statement is transcribed as an attachment to ETB to Lelia Tucker, 15 August 1833); ETB to NBT, 18 July 1833, 10 September 1833, TCP; HSGT to NBT, 27 August 1833, ibid.

16. NBT to Thomas A. Smith, 9 July 1834, 2 October 1834, 20 October 1838, TCP; Susan and Ersey to NBT, 24 October 1842, ibid.; B. T. Archer to NBT, 19 February 1845, ibid.; A. T. Burnley to NBT, 9 December 1847, ibid.; NBT to Burnley, 25 January 1848, ibid.; [NBT], "Slavery," *Southern Literary Messenger* 2, no. 5 (April 1836): 338.

17. HSGT to NBT, 29 December 1837 ("nine children"), 19 July 1833 ("banishment"), 27 August 1833, TCP; William Leigh to Peachy R. Gilmer, 18 August 1833, 30 September 1833, WLL; Entry for HSGT, 1840 United States Federal Census, Jefferson County, VA, Ancestry.com.

18. Act of 15 March 1832, Va. Rev. Code Supp. (1833), ch. 187, pp. 246–48; Act of 11 March 1834, Acts of General Assembly 1833–34, ch. 68, secs. 6–7, p. 80; William G. Shade, *Democratizing the Old Dominion: Virginia and the Second Party System, 1824–1861* (Charlottesville: University Press of Virginia, 1996), 195–213.

19. Bruce Dain, *A Hideous Monster of the Mind: American Race Theory in the Early Republic* (Cambridge, MA: Harvard University Press, 2002), 31–36, 165–69; David R. Roediger, *The Wages of Whiteness: Race and the Making of the American Working Class*, rev. ed. (London: Verso, 2007), 71–77.

20. George A. Baxter, *An Essay on the Abolition of Slavery* (Richmond, 1836), 6; Eugene D. Genovese and Elizabeth Fox-Genovese, *Fatal Self-Deception: Slaveholding Paternalism in the Old South* (New York: Cambridge University Press, 2011), 92–102; Christa Dierksheide, *Amelioration and Empire: Progress and Slavery in the Plantation Americas* (Charlottesville: University of Virginia Press, 2014), 75–82. On Ohio laws discouraging free Black settlement, see chapter 11.

21. *Farmers' Register* 4, no. 1 (May 1836): 3–4; V[ictor] Moreau Randolph to Richard

Randolph, 2 October 1858, in L. Minor Blackford, *Mine Eyes Have Seen the Glory: The Story of a Virginia Lady, Mary Berkeley Minor Blackford, 1802–1896* (Cambridge, MA: Harvard University Press, 1954), 109; *Richmond Enquirer*, 25 August 1854, 18 June 1858; Melvin Patrick Ely, *Israel on the Appomattox: A Southern Experiment in Black Freedom from the 1790s through the Civil War* (New York: Alfred A. Knopf, 2004), 388–93. One of the newspaper letter writers became a leader of the Ku Klux Klan. Ross Frederick Bagby, "The Randolph Slave Saga: Communities in Collision" (PhD diss., Ohio State University, 1998), 35n44.

22. Joseph P. Reidy, *Illusions of Emancipation: The Pursuit of Freedom and Equality in the Twilight of Slavery* (Chapel Hill: University of North Carolina Press, 2019), 238–51 (quoted at 240, 245).

23. Russell Kirk, *John Randolph of Roanoke: A Study in American Politics*, 4th ed. (Indianapolis: Liberty Fund, 1997), 155–56; Matthew Mason, *Slavery and Politics in the Early American Republic* (Chapel Hill: University of North Carolina Press, 2006), 30; Padraig Riley, *Slavery and the Democratic Conscience: Political Life in Jeffersonian America* (Philadelphia: University of Pennsylvania Press, 2016), 128.

24. Select Committee on Indiana Territory Petition, 7th Cong., 2nd sess., HR Rep. 76, *American State Papers: Public Lands*, 1:146; Annals of Cong., 8th Cong., 2nd sess., 1016; John Craig Hammond, *Slavery, Freedom, and Expansion in the Early American West* (Charlottesville: University of Virginia Press, 2007), 36–46, 103–13.

25. Robert H. Gudmestad, *A Troublesome Commerce: The Transformation of the Interstate Slave Trade* (Baton Rouge: Louisiana State University Press, 2003), 35–42; William G. Thomas III, *A Question of Freedom: The Families Who Challenged Slavery from the Nation's Founding to the Civil War* (New Haven, CT: Yale University Press, 2020), 195–98, 231.

26. Annals of Cong., 14th Cong., 1st sess., 1115–17; Nicholas Wood, "John Randolph of Roanoke and the Politics of Slavery in the Early Republic," *Virginia Magazine of History and Biography* 120, no. 2 (2012): 118–22. Slave trading in the District remained legal until 1850.

27. [American Colonization Society], *A View of Exertions Lately Made for the Purpose of Colonizing the Free People of Colour, in the United States, in Africa, or Elsewhere* (Washington, DC, 1817), 9–10. Black abolitionist David Walker quoted John Randolph's remarks as proof of the organization's proslavery objective. Walker, *Appeal . . . to the Colored Citizens of the World* (Boston, 1829), 54–55.

28. [ACS], *View of Exertions*, 5; Annals of Cong., 14th Cong., 2nd sess., 481–83; Nicholas Guyatt, *Bind Us Apart: How Enlightened Americans Invented Racial Segregation* (New York: Basic Books, 2016), 267–72, 330.

29. JR to Henry Middleton Rutledge, 24 July 1815, JR MSS ("great error"); JR to James Mercer Garnett, 3 July 1815, ibid.; JR, Inscriptions in Books of Common Prayer given to John Randolph Bryan and John St. George Randolph, 8 August 1818, JR MSS and JR MSS–MS 5273; JR to Harmanus Bleecker, 30 January 1821, JR MSS, box 8; Lauren F. Winner, *A Cheerful and Comfortable Faith: Anglican Religious Practice in the Elite Households of Eighteenth-Century Virginia* (New Haven, CT: Yale University Press, 2010), 100–11, 181–87.

30. JR, Diary, 1 January 1818–1 January 1819, entry for 23–24 August 1818, JRCD; JR to William Meade, 21 December 1818, JRCD (quoting Madame de Staël, *Germany* (London, 1813), 3:315); JR to Brockenbrough, 25 September 1818, Garland, 2:100–01; Francis Scott Key to William Meade, 29 September 1818, Francis Scott Key Papers, 1808–1841, UVA; Diana Hochstedt Butler, *Standing against the Whirlwind: Evan-*

gelical Episcopalians in Nineteenth-Century America (New York: Oxford University Press, 1995), 32–34.

31. JR to Brockenbrough, 25 September 1818, Garland, 2:101–02; JR, Diary, 1 January 1818–1 January 1819, entry for 30 August 1818; Powhatan Bouldin, *Home Reminiscences of John Randolph of Roanoke* (Richmond, 1878), 84–86, 126; Robert W. Prichard, *The Nature of Salvation: Theological Consensus in the Episcopal Church, 1801–73* (Urbana: University of Illinois Press, 1997), 105.

32. JR to James Mercer Garnett, 16 November 1818, JR MSS; JR, Will, May 1819, in *Richmond Enquirer*, 26 July 1836 (partial text in Garland, 2:149–50).

33. Robert Pierce Forbes, *The Missouri Compromise and Its Aftermath: Slavery and the Meaning of America* (Chapel Hill: University of North Carolina Press, 2007), 47–50.

34. *Daily Advertiser* (Boston), 5 February 1820, quoted in Glover Moore, *The Missouri Controversy, 1819–1821* (Lexington: University of Kentucky Press, 1953), 93 ("God has given us"); W[illiam] H[enry] Sparks, *The Memories of Fifty Years* (Philadelphia, 1870), 226–32.

35. Charles Francis Adams, ed., *Memoirs of John Quincy Adams*, 5 vols. (Philadelphia, 1875), 4:532–33; Francis Walker Gilmer to Dabney Carr, 27 April 1820, in Richard Beale Davis, *Francis Walker Gilmer: Life and Learning in Jefferson's Virginia* (Richmond: Dietz Press, 1939), 173. Virginians openly worried about Randolph's sanity during the spring of 1820. William H. Cabell to Joseph C. Cabell, 20 April 1820, Cabell Family Papers, box 14, UVA.

36. William J. Cooper Jr., *Liberty and Slavery: Southern Politics to 1860* (1983; Columbia: University of South Carolina Press, 2000), 136–37; Hammond, *Slavery, Freedom, and Expansion*, 161–66.

37. Annals of Cong., 16th Cong., 1st sess., 1429 (Plumer paraphrasing "all the misfortunes"); ibid., 2nd sess., 1236–40; Shade, *Democratization of the Old Dominion*, 231–32; Forbes, *Missouri Compromise*, 116–17. After the Missouri debates, Randolph's references to the misfortune of having been born a slaveholder became routine; e.g., Annals of Cong., 18th Cong., 1st sess., 1307–08.

38. JR to Brockenbrough, 24 February 1820, Garland, 2:133; JR to Henry Middleton Rutledge, 20 March 1820, Duke University Library, available on microfilm 7513, UVA.

39. JR to Richard Kidder Randolph, 4 May 1820, JRCD.

40. Norman K. Risjord, *The Old Republicans: Southern Conservatism in the Age of Jefferson* (New York: Columbia University Press, 1965), 213, 222, 226–27; Leonard L. Richards, *The Slave Power: The Free North and Southern Domination, 1780–1860* (Baton Rouge: Louisiana State University Press, 2000), 83–96.

41. JR, *Speeches of Mr. Randolph on the Greek Question; on Internal Improvement; and on the Tariff Bill* (Washington, DC, 1824).

42. Annals of Cong., 18th Cong., 1st sess., 1308, 2256; Adam L. Tate, *Conservatism and Southern Intellectuals, 1789–1861* (Columbia: University of Missouri Press, 2005), 34–37; James L. Huston, *The British Gentry, the Southern Planter, and the Northern Family Farmer: Agriculture and Sectional Antagonism in North America* (Baton Rouge: Louisiana State University Press, 2015), 179–83.

43. David Johnson, *John Randolph of Roanoke* (Baton Rouge: Louisiana State University Press, 2012), 202–09.

44. Reg. Deb., 19th Cong., 1st sess., 117, 396, 398, 401; Andrew R. L. Cayton, "The Debate over the Panama Congress and the Origins of the Second American Party System," *The Historian* 47, no. 2 (February 1985): 219–38.

45. Thomas Hart Benton, *Thirty Years' View* . . . , 2 vols. (New York, 1854), 1:77; Andrew Burstein, *America's Jubilee: How in 1826 a Generation Remembered Fifty Years of Independence* (New York: Alfred A. Knopf, 2001), 181–204.

46. *Niles' Weekly Register*, 30:169 (6 May 1826), 186–88 (13 May 1826); JR to Littleton Waller Tazewell, 7 March 1826, University of North Carolina Library, available on microfilm 7513, UVA; Depositions in Coalter's Ex'r v. Bryan of John C. Calhoun, p. 339, and John Taliaferro, pp. 305–06; John C. Fitzpatrick, ed., "The Autobiography of Martin Van Buren," *Annual Report of the American Historical Association for 1918*, 2 vols. (Washington, DC: Government Printing Office, 1920), 2:207.

47. JR to Brockenbrough, 20 February 1826, Garland, 2:266–67; Nicholas Wood, "The Missouri Crisis and the 'Changed Object' of the American Colonization Society," in *New Directions in the Study of African American Recolonization*, ed. Beverly C. Tomek and Matthew J. Hetrick (Gainesville: University Press of Florida, 2017), 160–61.

48. Reg. Deb., 19th Cong., 1st sess., 118–19; JR to J[ohn] S. Skinner, 8 March 1828, in *American Turf Register and Sporting Magazine* 4, no. 11 (July 1833): 576. Critics said the American Colonization Society was more interested in removing free Blacks than freeing slaves, but the pattern shifted about the time Randolph left the society, and 64 percent of the 3,444 persons ultimately colonized from Virginia were newly emancipated. James G. Birney, *Letter on Colonization* (New York, 1834), 10, 20; Eric Burin, *Slavery and the Peculiar Solution: A History of the American Colonization Society* (Gainesville: University Press of Florida, 2005), 35–36, 171–72 (tables 4 and 5).

49. [Jacob Harvey], "A Chapter of Eccentricities," *The New-Mirror* (NY) 2, no. 4 (28 October 1843): 57 (*"Virginia slave"*); JR to Brockenbrough, 30 January 1826, Garland, 2:265 ("good old plan"); Testimony of William Leigh, Bryan v. Meade, in *Richmond Enquirer*, 3 November 1835 ("greater portion"); Marcus Cunliffe, *Chattel Slavery and Wage Slavery: The Anglo-American Context, 1830–1860* (Athens: University of Georgia Press, 1979), 1–31.

50. Harriet Martineau, *Society in America*, 2 vols. (New York, 1837), 2:124; Frances Anne Kemble, *Journal of a Residence on a Georgia Plantation in 1838–39*, ed. John A. Scott (1863; Athens: University of Georgia Press, 1984), 3; Morris Birkbeck, *Notes on a Journey in America from the Coast of Virginia to the Territory of Illinois*, 4th ed. (London, 1818), 21; Huston, *The British Gentry, the Southern Planter, and the Northern Farm Family*, 169–75.

51. JR, Codicil, 31 January 1826, *Coalter's Ex'r*, 42 Va. 22–23.

52. HSGT to NBT, 27 August 1833, 14 November 1833, 20 November 1833, TCP.

53. NBT to ETB, 26 July 1833, BCRTP; Bruce E. Steiner, "A Planter's Troubled Conscience," *Journal of Southern History* 28, no. 3 (August 1962): 343–47.

54. William Leigh to Peachy R. Gilmer, 30 September 1833, 18 August 1833, WLL; Robinson, *Practice in the Courts*, 1:327–28, 3:355–56.

55. Leigh to Gilmer, 18 August 1833, WLL; Deposition of William Leigh, Coalter's Ex'r v. Bryan, p. 520.

56. Leigh to Gilmer, 30 September 1833, 18 August 1833, WLL.

57. NBT to ETB, 19 September 1833, BCRTP ("season of the vision"); HSGT to NBT, 27 August 1833, TCP ("extraordinary wishes"); Leigh to Gilmer, 18 August 1833 ("grossly unnatural"), 21 September 1833, 12 January 1834, WLL.

58. NBT to ETB, 26 July 1833, BCRTP; NBT to Thomas A. Smith, 11 September 1833 (bold script), 2 October 1833, TCP.

59. SGTC to NBT, 26 September 1833, 16 July 1836, TCP; ETB to NBT, 10 September 1833, ibid.; Judith H. Coalter to ETB, 26 April 1836, 18 June 1837, BCTP, group

A, box IV:39; SGTC to Chapman Johnson, 8 April 1837, 19 May 1837, in Coalter's Ex'r v. Bryan, pp. 360–62, 363–68.

60. HSGT to NBT, 19 July 1833, 27 August 1833, 29 September, 1833, TCP; Temple v. Temple, 11 Va. (1 Hen. & M.) 476 (1807) (testamentary capacity presumed). On challenging a will in chancery, see chapter 10.

61. ETB to NBT, 18 July 1833, TCP; NBT to Thomas A. Smith, 11 April 1834, ibid.

62. HSGT to NBT, 19 July 1833, 27 August 1833, ibid.; NBT to Thomas A. Smith, 11 September 1833, 2 October 1833, ibid.; John Coalter to NBT, 14 August 1833, ibid.; HSGT to unknown, 1 July 1834, RTFP, misc. reel 4224, frame 268; NBT to Lucy Tucker, 5 July 1834, TCP.

63. [NBT], *George Balcombe*, 2 vols. (New York, 1836). Although Edgar Allan Poe's review of the book called it *"the best* American novel," no modern critic has ever suggested *George Balcombe* is more than a period piece. Poe, Review of *George Balcombe, Southern Literary Messenger* 3, no. 1 (January 1837): 58.

64. ETB to NBT, 25 March 1836, TCP; SGTC to NBT, 14 January [1837], ibid; John L. Hare, *Will the Circle Be Unbroken? Family and Sectionalism in the Virginia Novels of Kennedy, Caruthers, and Tucker, 1830–1845* (New York: Routledge, 2002), 89–105.

65. HSGT to NBT, 14 November 1833, TCP; William Leigh to Peachy R. Gilmer, 12 January 1834, WLL.

66. HSGT to NBT, 20 November 1833, 28 April 1837, TCP; Separate answer of NBT, Coalter's Ex'r v. Bryan, pp. 83–84; Deposition of Chapman Johnson, ibid., pp. 354–58. On Robert Stanard and Chapman Johnson, see chapter 7.

67. HSGT to NBT, 14 November 1833, TCP.

68. Resort to the General Court for probate was never more than a matter of strategy or convenience. Any Virginia court with jurisdiction could prove a will, and the will once proven would support claims anywhere in the state. Morrison v. Campbell, 23 Va. (2 Rand.) 206, 217–18 (1824); Act of 3 March 1819, ch. 104, sec. 12, Va. Rev. Code (1819), 1:377–78; Act of 16 April 1831, ch. 106, sec. 6, Va. Rev. Code Supp. (1833), 138; Robinson, *Practice in the Courts*, 3:331. William Leigh could have transferred the case to an adjacent district or to the General Court (where he would have recused himself). J[ohn] Marshall to HSGT, 17 November 1833, RTFP, misc. reel 4224, frame 254, LVA; Joseph Tate, *Digest of the Laws of Virginia*, 2nd ed. (Richmond, 1841), 532, 560, 593.

69. NBT to ETB, 10 February 1840, BCRTP; Christopher Michael Curtis, *Jefferson's Freeholders and the Politics of Ownership in the Old Dominion* (New York: Cambridge University Press, 2012), 159–67.

70. Burton v. Scott, 24 Va. (3 Rand.) 399 (1825) (privileging doctors' testimony); Tate, *Digest of the Laws of Virginia*, 888n(a); E. Lee Shepard, "Lawyers Look at Themselves: Professional Consciousness and the Virginia Bar, 1770–1850," *American Journal of Legal History* 25, no. 1 (January 1981): 11–15.

71. *Alexandria Gazette* (DC), 18 November 1833 (from *New York Journal of Commerce*); William Leigh to Peachy R. Gilmer, 12 January 1834, WLL; *Daily National Intelligencer*, 9 December 1833.

Chapter 6: The Slaves' Defenders

1. NBT to Lucy Tucker, 5 July 1834, 8 July 1834, TCP; NBT to Thomas A. Smith, 9 July 1834, ibid.; Act of 16 April 1831, ch. 106, sec. 1, Va. Rev. Code Supp. (1833), 134–35; Act of 9 January 1832, ch. 108, sec. 1, ibid., 136.

2.   *Richmond Whig*, 18 July 1834; Alison Goodyear Freehling, *Drift toward Dissolution: The Virginia Slavery Debate of 1831–1832* (Baton Rouge: Louisiana State University Press, 1982), 59–61; Esther C. M. Steele, "Chapman Johnson," *Virginia Magazine of History and Biography* 35, no. 2 (April 1927): 161–74, and no. 3 (July 1927): 246–57. A few years earlier, Chapman Johnson had handled an important land dispute for Judge Coalter's brother. Coalter v. Hunter, 25 Va. (4 Rand.) 58 (1826).

3.   Francis Scott Key to NBT, 8 February 1834, TCP; John S. Pendleton, "Eulogy on the Late Hon. John Mercer Patton" (November 1858), broadside 1858.P44, UVA; Joseph Packard, "General Walter Jones," *Virginia Law Register* 7, no. 4 (August 1901): 233–38; Mima Queen v. Hepburn, 11 U.S. (7 Cranch) 290 (1813) (Key and Jones opposing counsel); Lessee of Binney v. Chesapeake and Ohio Canal Co., 33 U.S. (8 Pet.) 214 (1834) (Key and Jones co-counsel).

4.   *Richmond Whig*, 18 July 1834; Nicholas v. Burruss, 31 Va. (4 Leigh) 289, 298–99 (1833); Loren Schweninger, *Appealing for Liberty: Freedom Suits in the South* (New York: Oxford University Press, 2018), 51–69.

5.   Although there were questions about whether slaves could use freedom suits to prove or challenge wills, Virginia courts allowed it. Redford's Adm'r v. Peggy, 27 Va. (6 Rand.) 316 (1828); Winn v. Bob, 30 Va. (3 Leigh) 140 (1831); Manns v. Givens, 34 Va. (7 Leigh) 689 (1836); Phoebe v. Boggess, 42 Va. (1 Gratt.) 129 (1844); Mercer v. Kelso's Adm'r, 45 Va. (4 Gratt.) 106 (1847); Everard Hall, *A Digested Index Containing the Points Argued and Determined in the Court of Appeals of Virginia . . .* , 2 vols. (Richmond, 1825–35), 2:385.

6.   Key to NBT, 8 February 1834; William Meade, *Old Churches, Ministers, and Families of Virginia*, 2 vols. (1857; Baltimore: Genealogical Publishing, 1995), 1:33n*.

7.   *Richmond Whig*, 18 July 1834; *New-York Spectator*, 4 August 1834.

8.   *Richmond Whig*, 28 July 1835; John R. Cooke to John G. Mosby, 15 May 1836, TCP.

9.   Deposition of Anna Dudley, Coalter's Ex'r v. Bryan, p. 388; David Lynn Holmes Jr., "William Meade and the Church of Virginia, 1789–1829" (PhD diss., Princeton University, 1971), 29–58; J. E. Booty, ed., "The Autobiography of William Meade," *Historical Magazine of the Protestant Episcopal Church* 31, no. 4 (December 1962): 386.

10.   Ibid., 381; John K. Nelson, *A Blessed Company: Parishes, Parsons, and Parishioners in Anglican Virginia, 1690–1776* (Chapel Hill: University of North Carolina Press, 2001), 289; E. Brooks Holifield, *Theology in America: Christian Thought from the Age of the Puritans to the Civil War* (New Haven: Yale University Press, 2003), 236–37; Deborah A. Lee, " 'Life Is a Solemn Trust': Ann R. Page and the Antislavery Movement in the Upper South" (PhD diss., George Mason University, 2002), 88–91.

11.   Richard Channing Moore to William Meade, 18 July 1817, William Meade Papers, W&M; J[ohn] Johns, *A Memoir of the Life of the Right Rev. William Meade, D.D.* (Baltimore, 1867), 48, 77; Robert Nelson, *Reminiscences of the Right Rev. William Meade* (Shanghai, 1873), 25–26; Janet Moore Lindman, "Acting the Manly Christian: White Evangelical Masculinity in Revolutionary Virginia," *William and Mary Quarterly*, 3rd ser., 57, no. 2 (April 2000): 393–416; Edward L. Bond and Joan R. Gundersen, "The Episcopal Church in Virginia, 1607–2007," *Virginia Magazine of History and Biography* 115, no. 2 (2007): 220–22, 230.

12.   John Frank Waukechon, "The Forgotten Evangelicals: Virginia Episcopalians, 1790–1876" (PhD diss., University of Texas at Austin, 2000), 412–64. Meade's biographers say he freed his slaves when he was young, but he still owned eleven slaves in 1830 and at least one as late as 1843. Emancipation deed, William Meade to Lucy, 29 April 1843, Clarke County Deed Book B:467–68, LVA; Entries for William Meade,

1810, 1820, and 1830 United States Federal Census, Frederick County, VA, Ancestry .com.

13. William Meade to Mary Lee Custis, 9 April 1823, Mary Lee Fitzhugh Custis Papers, 1788–1853, sec. 2, VMHC; Marie Tyler-McGraw, *An African Republic: Black and White Virginians in the Making of Liberia* (Charlottesville: University of Virginia Press, 2007), 30–32, 88–89.

14. William Meade, *Sermon Delivered by the Rev. Wm. Meade at the Opening of the Convention of the Diocese of Virginia . . .* ([Winchester, VA], 1818), 24; Deborah A. Lee and Warren R. Hofstra, "Race, Memory, and the Death of Robert Berkeley: 'A Murder . . . of . . . Horible and Savage Barbarity,'" *Journal of Southern History* 65, no. 1 (February 1999): 41–76.

15. William Meade, Address, 4 July 1825, in *African Repository and Colonial Journal* 1, no. 5 (July 1825): 140, 146–50; ibid., no. 7 (September 1825): 223, and no. 11 (January 1826): 348 (contributions from Meade and Custis families and Frederick County, VA auxiliary).

16. Mary Frances Goodwin, ed., "The Diary of Rev. Frederick D. Goodwin, 1826–27," *Proceedings of the Clarke County Historical Society* 4 (1944): 36; Alexander Clinton Zabriskie, "The Rise and Main Characteristics of the Anglican Evangelical Movement in England and America," *Historical Magazine of the Protestant Episcopal Church* 12, no. 2 (June 1943): 104–05; Holmes, "William Meade and the Church of Virginia," 3. Meade is best remembered today for compiling generations of Virginia history, genealogy, and church lore into a two-volume book he called *Old Churches, Ministers, and Families of Virginia.*

17. William Meade, *Pastoral Letter . . . on the Duty of Affording Religious Instructions to Those in Bondage* (Alexandria, DC, 1834), 4–6, 13–16; Charles F. Irons, *The Origins of Proslavery Christianity: White and Black Evangelicals in Colonial and Antebellum Virginia* (Chapel Hill: University of North Carolina Press, 2008), 161–68, 174–84.

18. T. Felder Dorn, *Challenges on the Emmaus Road: Episcopal Bishops Confront Slavery, Civil War, and Emancipation* (Columbia: University of South Carolina Press, 2013), 44–46.

19. William Meade to Mary Lee Custis, 30 May 1825, Mary Lee Fitzhugh Custis Papers, VMHC; Meade, *Old Churches, Ministers, and Families,* 1:33n*, 90–91n*.

20. JR to HSGT, 6 January 1828, JRCD; JR to HSGT, 3 January 1828, JR MSS–MS 5273; William A. R. Goodwin, ed., *History of the Theological Seminary in Virginia,* 2 vols. (New York: Edwin G. Gorham, 1923), 1:95–96; Gerardo Gurza-Lavalle, "Slave Reform in Virginia, 1816-1865" (PhD diss., University of North Carolina–Chapel Hill, 2008), 80–83.

21. Francis Scott Key to NBT, 8 February 1834, TCP; William Meade to NBT, 4 March 1839, ibid.; William Meade to Mary Meade, 3 June 1834, William Meade Papers, W&M.

22. JR to Joseph H. Nicholson, [3], 10, and 21 December 1806, Joseph Hopper Nicholson Papers, LC; Bruce, 2:620; Marc Leepson, *What So Proudly We Hailed: Francis Scott Key, A Life* (New York: Palgrave Macmillan, 2014), 6–7, 14–16. Randolph was also a close friend of Frank Key's brother-in-law Joseph H. Nicholson, whose decision to leave Congress opened the seat Edward Lloyd took in 1806.

23. Leepson, *What So Proudly We Hailed,* 26, 130–31; Schweninger, *Appealing for Liberty,* 243; "Francis Scott Key," in O Say Can You See: Early Washington, D.C., Law and Family, ed. William G. Thomas III et al., University of Nebraska–Lincoln, https://earlywashingtondc.org/people/per.000001. Key represented enslaved litigants in two significant Supreme Court cases; Mima Queen v. Hepburn, 11 U.S. (7

Cranch) 290 (1813) (hearsay evidence of free ancestry inadmissible), and Fenwick v. Chapman, 34 U.S. (9 Pet.) 461 (1835) (no reenslavement for debt where testator left other sufficient assets).

24. David R. Roediger, *The Wages of Whiteness: Race and the Making of the American Working Class*, rev. ed. (London: Verso, 2007), 44–45; Alan Taylor, *The Internal Enemy: Slavery and War in Virginia, 1772–1832* (New York: W. W. Norton, 2013), 245–83, 298–10. For alternative interpretations of Francis Scott Key's lyrics, see Mark Clague, *O Say Can You Hear? A Cultural Biography of the Star-Spangled Banner* (New York: W. W. Norton, 2022), 189–96.

25. Jonathan M. Bryant, *Dark Places of the Earth: The Voyage of the Slave Ship* Antelope (New York: Liveright, 2015), 65–71, 142–46, 160–72.

26. Henry S. Foote, *Casket of Reminiscences* (Washington, DC, 1874), 13 ("dazzled"); *The Antelope*, 23 U.S. (10 Wheat.) 66, 70–81, 130 (1825).

27. P. J. Staudenraus, *The African Colonization Movement, 1816–1865* (New York: Columbia University Press, 1961), 174, 177–78; Leepson, *What So Proudly We Hailed*, 113–22; Bryant, *Dark Places of the Earth*, 257–60.

28. *Genius of Universal Emancipation*, 3rd ser. (Washington, DC) 3, no. 8 (June 1833): 127; Stanley Harrold, *Border War: Fighting over Slavery before the Civil War* (Chapel Hill: University of North Carolina Press, 2010), 36–39; James Brewer Stewart, "The Emergence of Racial Modernity and the Rise of the White North, 1790–1840," *Journal of the Early Republic* 18, no. 2 (Summer 1998): 194. Key brought criminal libel charges against Benjamin Lundy and his printer, but Lundy skipped town and the printer won acquittal. Jefferson Morley, *Snow-Storm in August: The Struggle for American Freedom and Washington's Race Riot of 1835* (New York: Anchor Books, 2013), 80–82.

29. David Grimsted, *American Mobbing, 1828–1861: Toward Civil War* (New York: Oxford University Press, 1998), 4, 12, 30–31; Morley, *Snow-Storm in August*, 108–09, 128–35, 144–56.

30. *African Repository and Colonial Journal* 12, no. 11 (November 1835): 339–51 (quoted at 345); William G. Thomas III, *A Question of Freedom: The Families Who Challenged Slavery from the Nation's Founding to the Civil War* (New Haven, CT: Yale University Press, 2020), 253–62.

31. *African Repository and Colonial Journal*, 12:348.

32. Key to NBT, 13 August 1840, 22 October 1838, TCP; Leepson, *What So Proudly We Hailed*, 190–91, 196.

33. JR to unknown, 6 May 1826, WCBP, misc. reel 3322; Myron Berman, *Richmond's Jewry: Shabbat in Shockoe, 1769–1976* (Charlottesville: University Press of Virginia, 1979), 70–72.

34. HSGT to NBT, 2 April 1834, TCP.

35. JR, Codicil, 29 August 1831, in Coalter's Ex'r v. Bryan, 42 Va. (1 Gratt.) 18, 28–29 (1844); William Leigh to Peachy R. Gilmer, 16 January 1835, WLL. William Leigh immediately doubted the existence of the London deposits. Leigh to William Meade, 30 July 1834, Episcopal Church, Diocese of Virginia Papers, 1709–1972, sec. 1, VMHC.

36. NBT to Thomas A. Smith, 10 June 1835, TCP; SGTC to NBT, 16 July 1836, ibid.; HSGT to NBT, 28 April 1837, ibid.

37. NBT to Lucy Tucker, 28 April 1843, 8 July 1834, TCP; NBT to ETB, 14 May 1834, 6 June 1834, BCRTP; Thomas G. Peachy to NBT, 7 July 1834, TCP.

38. William Leigh to Peachy R. Gilmer, 12 January 1834, 3 March 1834, WLL.

39. Leigh to Gilmer, 22 November 1834, 16 January 1835, 9 June 1835, ibid.

40. Leigh to Gilmer, 9 June 1835, ibid.; Leigh to Meade, 30 July 1834, Episcopal Church, Diocese of Virginia Papers, VMHC.

CHAPTER 7: A CELEBRITY TRIAL

1.   Laura F. Edwards, *The People and Their Peace: Legal Culture and the Transformation of Inequality in the Post-Revolutionary South* (Chapel Hill: University of North Carolina Press, 2009), 76–77; Lawrence M. Friedman, *The Big Trial: Law as Public Spectacle* (Lawrence: University Press of Kansas, 2015), 2, 4, 17, 86, 96 (claiming only modern media can create celebrity).

2.   Thomas Hamilton, *Men and Manners in America*, 2 vols. (Edinburgh, 1833), 2:99-100.

3.   Cong. Globe, 25th Cong., 2nd sess., app. 71 (Clay). "Dough face" or "doughface" referred to a game in which children covered their faces with dough shaped into grotesque masks to frighten each other, and the epithet belittled Northern politicians who played on fears of disunion to accommodate sectional differences. Joanne B. Freeman, *The Field of Blood: Violence in Congress and the Road to Civil War* (New York: Farrar, Straus and Giroux, 2018), 62–68.

4.   Testimony of John Brockenbrough, Meade v. Hobson, in *Richmond Enquirer*, 12 August 1836.

5.   Cynthia A. Kierner, *Scandal at Bizarre: Rumor and Reputation in Jefferson's Virginia* (Charlottesville: University of Virginia Press, 2004), 103–44.

6.   Testimony of John Brockenbrough, *Richmond Enquirer*, 12 August 1836; Bruce, 2:258–60, 334, 632.

7.   Ann Cary Morris to NBT, 3 July 1835, TCP; HSGT to JRB, 31 January 1834, BCRTP; Frederick Hobson to NBT, 22 April 1835, 19 October 1835, TCP; Kierner, *Scandal at Bizarre*, 13–17, 29–30, 110–11.

8.   Ann Cary Morris to NBT, 11 January 1835, TCP; Kierner, *Scandal at Bizarre*, 103, 107.

9.   Testimony in Meade v. Hobson by Benjamin Watkins Leigh, *Richmond Enquirer*, 5 August 1836, and Thomas Robinson, ibid., 12 August 1836; Deposition of Theodore Dudley, Coalter's Ex'r v. Bryan, p. 274; Hugh Blair Grigsby, Memorandum about JR, n.d., excerpted in Michael O'Brien, *Conjectures of Order: Intellectual Life and the American South, 1810–1860*, 2 vols. (Chapel Hill: University of North Carolina Press, 2004), 2:669.

10.   Michael Grossberg, "Institutionalizing Masculinity: The Law as a Masculine Profession," in *Meanings for Manhood: Constructions of Masculinity in Victorian America*, ed. Mark C. Carnes and Clyde Griffen (Chicago: University of Chicago Press, 1990), 136–37.

11.   HSGT to NBT, 14 November 1833, 20 November 1833, [26 April] 1835, TCP; *Lynchburg Virginian*, 26 November 1832 (Chapman Johnson, Robert Stanard, and Benjamin Watkins Leigh as candidates for next United States senator); *Liberator* (Boston), 25 July 1835; *New-York Daily Tribune*, 18 May 1846 (Robert Stanard obituary); John Randolph Tucker, "Reminiscences of Virginia's Judges and Jurists," *Virginia Law Register* 1, no. 3 supp. (July 1895): 23, 27–28.

12.   *Richmond Dispatch*, 25 February 1853 (Samuel Taylor obituary); *Ex parte* Whitney, 38 U.S. (13 Pet.) 404 (1839) (Daniel Clark estate in New Orleans); Vidal v. Girard's Ex'rs, 43 U.S. (2 How.) 127 (1844); Patterson v. Gaines, 47 U.S. (6 How.) 550 (1848) (Clark estate); Gaines v. New Orleans, 73 U.S. (6 Wall.) 642, 690–91 (1867) (same); W. Hamilton Bryson, ed., *Legal Education in Virginia, 1779–1979: A Biographical Approach* (Charlottesville: University Press of Virginia, 1982), 589, 594. For more on Walter Jones, see chapter 6.

13.   On dialectic and performance in trials involving race and slavery, see Ariela Gross,

"Beyond Black and White: Cultural Approaches to Race and Slavery," *Columbia Law Review* 101, no. 3 (April 2001): 640–90, and for analysis of cases, see Jason A. Gillmer, *Slavery and Freedom in Texas: Stories from the Courtroom, 1821–1871* (Athens: University of Georgia Press, 2017).

14. *Lynchburg Virginian*, 15 September 1835, quoted in Gerardo Gurza-Lavalle, "Slave Reform in Virginia, 1816–1865" (PhD diss., University of North Carolina–Chapel Hill, 2008), 82; Kay Wright Lewis, *A Curse upon the Nation: Race, Freedom, and Extermination in America and the Atlantic World* (Athens: University of Georgia Press, 2017), 103–24.

15. Act of 25 January 1806, ch. 63, sec. 10, Samuel Shepherd, ed., *The Statutes at Large of Virginia*, 3 vols. (Richmond, 1835), 3:252. If the manumitter's unsatisfied debts were less than the value of his slaves, selling part of the slaves would distribute the burden unfairly among them and selling all of them would depart more than necessary from the manumitter's intent. Parks v. Hewlett, 36 Va. (9 Leigh) 511, 523 (1838).

16. Act of 2 March 1819, ch. 111, secs. 61–62, 71–78, Va. Rev. Code (1819), 1:436–37, 440–41; Act of 7 April 1831, ch. 186, secs. 1–3, Va. Rev. Code Supp. (1833), 244–45; Kirt von Daacke, *Freedom Has a Face: Race, Identity, and Community in Jefferson's Virginia* (Charlottesville: University of Virginia Press, 2012), 77–81; Ellen Eslinger, "Free Black Residency in Two Antebellum Virginia Counties: How the Laws Functioned," *Journal of Southern History* 79, no. 2 (May 2013): 261–98.

17. Rex v. Allan (The Slave Grace), [1827] 166 Eng. Rep. 179, 2 Hagg. 94; Commonwealth v. Turner, 26 Va. (5 Rand.) 678, 680–81, 684–86 (Gen. Ct. 1827); Hunter v. Fulcher, 28 Va. (1 Leigh) 172 (1829); Orlando Patterson, *Slavery and Social Death: A Comparative Study* (Cambridge, MA: Harvard University Press, 1982), 209–61; Christopher Tomlins, *Freedom Bound: Law, Labor, and Civic Identity in Colonizing English America, 1580–1865* (New York: Cambridge University Press, 2010), 452–75. Even antislavery judges recognized that African American freedom often depended on positive rather than natural law. Commonwealth v. Aves, 35 Mass. (18 Pick.) 193 (1836).

18. Robert M. Cover, *Justice Accused: Antislavery and the Judicial Process* (New Haven, CT: Yale University Press, 1975), 37–38, 67–73.

19. Sawney v. Carter, 27 Va. (6 Rand.) 173 (1828) (Coalter, J.); Nicholas v. Burruss, 31 Va. (4 Leigh) 289, 295–96 (1833) (Tucker, P.); Loren Schweninger, *Appealing for Liberty: Freedom Suits in the South* (New York: Oxford University Press, 2018), 47.

20. JR to John Randolph Clay, 12 June 1829, JRCD; *Liberator*, 25 August 1837; William Meade, *Old Churches, Ministers, and Families of Virginia*, 2 vols. (1857; Baltimore: Genealogical Publishing, 1995), 1:33n*; James Oakes, *The Ruling Race: A History of American Slaveholders* (1982; New York: W. W. Norton, 1998), 105–22.

21. JR to Josiah Quincy, 18 October 1813, Quincy, 339; Testimony of John Brockenbrough, *Richmond Enquirer*, 12 August 1836; Deposition of William Leigh, Coalter's Ex'r v. Bryan, p. 524; Kenneth S. Greenberg, *Honor and Slavery* (Princeton, NJ: Princeton University Press, 1996), 67, 96. For characterizations of Randolph as a paternalist, see Adam L. Tate, *Conservatism and Southern Intellectuals, 1789–1861* (Columbia: University of Missouri Press, 2005), 117–20; David Johnson, *John Randolph of Roanoke* (Baton Rouge: Louisiana State University Press, 2012), 70–72, and for a summary critique of paternalistic understandings of American slaveholders, see James Oakes, " 'I Own My Slaves, But They Also Own Me': Property and Paternalism in the Slave South," *Reviews in American History* 38, no. 4 (December 2010): 587–94.

22. JR to Josiah Quincy, 20 June 1813, JRCD; JR to Quincy, 22 May 1814, Quincy, 350–53; JR to Harmanus Bleecker, 16 November 1818, JR MSS, box 8; JR to James Mercer Garnett, 16 November 1818, JR MSS.

23. Gordon v. Blackman, 18 S.C. Eq. (1 Rich. Eq.) 61, 66 (1844) ("harsh" to free slaves and send them away because slaves "very much prefer to remain in their present situation"); Elizabeth Fox-Genovese and Eugene D. Genovese, *The Mind of the Master Class: History and Faith in the Southern Slaveholders' Worldview* (New York: Cambridge University Press, 2005), 16–18. After 1830, manumissions in the United States became markedly less common. Peter D. McClelland and Richard J. Zeckhauser, *Demographic Dimensions of the New Republic: American Interregional Migration, Vital Statistics, and Manumissions, 1800–1860* (Cambridge, UK: Cambridge University Press, 1982), 16–17, 80–81.

24. Joseph Packard, *Recollections of a Long Life*, ed. Thomas J. Packard (Washington, DC: Byron S. Adams, 1902), 109–10; William G. Shade, *Democratizing the Old Dominion: Virginia and the Second Party System, 1824–1861* (Charlottesville: University Press of Virginia, 1996), 40, 61, 196, 203, 236. Calling another man a presumptuous "puppy" was an insult meant to provoke a duel, and rebuffing the insult in kind was a demeaning put-down. Joanne B. Freeman, *Affairs of Honor: National Politics in the New Republic* (New Haven, CT: Yale University Press, 2001), xvi.

25. Rivalry between the *Whig* and the *Enquirer* was a set piece in Virginia political life, and John Hampton Pleasants died in a duel with the editor of the *Enquirer* in 1846. Joseph G. Baldwin, *The Flush Times of Alabama and Mississippi: A Series of Sketches* (New York, 1853), 76; David Grimsted, *American Mobbing, 1828–1861: Toward Civil War* (New York: Oxford University Press, 1998), 88–89.

26. Fletcher M. Green, "Duff Green, Militant Journalist of the Old School," *American Historical Review* 52, no. 2 (January 1947): 251; [Edward Vernon Sparhawk], Randolph Court Record, 1835, JR MSS, ms. 4358; *Richmond Whig*, 3 July 1835 (*Whig* hired Sparhawk), 28 July 1835; *Richmond Enquirer*, 3 July 1835 (claiming the parties hired Sparhawk); Wilmer L. Hall, "The Public Records of Virginia: Their Destruction and Preservation," *Virginia Libraries* 4, nos. 1 and 2 (July 1931): 2–22.

27. Act of 3 March 1819, ch. 104, secs. 12–13, Va. Rev. Code (1819), 1:377–78; Bagwell v. Elliott, 23 Va. (2 Rand.) 190 (1824); Boyd v. Cooke, 30 Va. (3 Leigh) 32, 54 (1831).

CHAPTER 8: THE MEANING OF MADNESS

1. F[rederick] W[illiam] Thomas, *John Randolph of Roanoke and Other Sketches of Character* (Philadelphia, 1853), 31; Ann Cary Morris to Joseph C. Cabell, 7 June 1830, quoted in Bruce, 2:298; Deposition of Anna Dudley, Coalter's Ex'r v. Bryan, p. 388.

2. Elijah Mills to Harriet Mills, 10 March 1826, in Henry Cabot Lodge, "Letters of Hon. Elijah H. Mills," *Proceedings of the Massachusetts Historical Society* 19 (September 1881): 49; Depositions in Coalter's Ex'r v. Bryan of Theodore Dudley, p. 275, and Winfield Scott, pp. 594–604.

3. Thomas C. Upham, *Outline of Imperfect and Disordered Mental Action* (New York, 1840), 20–21, 328–32. Modern historians with distinctly different conceptions of madness have emphasized that it must be understood in historical context. Michael Foucault, *History of Madness*, trans. Jonathan Murphy and Jean Khalfa (London: Routledge, 2009), 102–31, 156, 528–30; Andrew Scull, *Madness in Civilization: A Cultural History of Insanity from the Bible to Freud, from the Madhouse to Modern Medi-*

Notes to Pages 135–39 *329*

cine (Princeton, NJ: Princeton University Press, 2015), 10–15. On the words used to name madness in different historical periods, see Lynn Gamwell and Nancy Tomes, *Madness in America: Cultural and Medical Perceptions of Mental Illness before 1914* (Ithaca, NY: Cornell University Press, 1995), 9.

4.   Greenwood v. Greenwood, (1790) 163 Eng. Rep. 930 (K.B.) 943, 3 Curt. (app.) i, xxx; Temple v. Temple, 11 Va. (1 Hen. & M.) 476 (1807); Van Alst v. Hunter, 5 Johns. Ch. 148, 160 (N.Y. 1821); Samuel v. Marshall, 30 Va. (3 Leigh) 567, 573 (1832); William Waller Hening, *New Virginia Justice . . .* , 2nd ed. (Richmond, 1810), 381; Thomas Jarman, *A Treatise on Wills*, ed. J. C. Perkins, 2nd Amer. ed., 2 vols. (Boston, 1849), 1:29–36, 50–53. Married women could make wills only in limited circumstances because marriage gave their husbands control of their property.

5.   Brogdon v. Brown, (1825) 162 Eng. Rep. 356 (Prerog.) 359–60, 2 Add. 441, 448–50; Clark v. Fisher, 1 Paige Ch. 171, 173–74, 176 (N.Y. 1828); Susanna L. Blumenthal, "The Deviance of the Will: Policing the Bounds of Testamentary Freedom in Nineteenth-Century America," *Harvard Law Review* 119, no. 4 (February 2006): 965, 977.

6.   Theodric Romeyn Beck, *Elements of Medical Jurisprudence*, 2 vols. (Albany, NY, 1823); James C. Mohr, "The Paradoxical Advance and Embattled Retreat of the 'Unsound Mind': Evidence of Insanity and the Adjudication of Wills in Nineteenth-Century America," *Historical Reflections* 24, no. 3 (Fall 1998): 417–21.

7.   Frederick A. Rauch, *Psychology; or, A View of the Human Soul*, 2nd ed. (New York, 1841), 152–54; James C. Mohr, *Doctors and the Law: Medical Jurisprudence in Nineteenth-Century America* (Baltimore: Johns Hopkins University Press, 1993), 58–66, 80–81.

8.   Burton v. Scott, 24 Va. (3 Rand.) 399, 403–04 (1825); John Forbes et al., eds., *The Cyclopaedia of Practical Medicine*, Amer. ed., ed. Robley Dunglison, 4 vols. (Philadelphia, 1845), 3:329–32; Susanna L. Blumenthal, *Law and the Modern Mind: Consciousness and Responsibility in American Legal Culture* (Cambridge, MA: Harvard University Press, 2016), 60.

9.   John Haslam, *Medical Jurisprudence As It Relates to Insanity* (London, 1817), 20; Joel Peter Eigen, *Witnessing Insanity: Madness and Mad-Doctors in the English Court* (New Haven, CT: Yale University Press, 1995), 35–39, 49–51.

10.   Vance v. Crawford, 4 Ga. 445, 460 (1848) (dicta); Wheeler v. Alderson, (1831) 162 Eng. Rep. 1268 (Prerog.) 1274, 1278, 3 Hagg. Ecc. 574, 587–88, 598–99; Parramore v. Taylor, 52 Va. (11 Gratt.) 220, 224–28 (1854); Robert Mensel, "Right Feeling and Knowing Right: Insanity in Testators and Criminals in Nineteenth Century American Law," *Oklahoma Law Review* 58, no. 3 (Fall 2005): 424–26.

11.   Early treatises described aversion toward close relatives as a common symptom of insanity. William Cullen, *First Lines of the Practice of Physic*, 3 vols. (Worcester, MA, 1790), 3:193; Beck, *Elements of Medical Jurisprudence*, 1:341.

12.   Dew v. Clark, (1826) 162 Eng. Rep. 410 (Prerog.) 425–28, 3 Add. 79, 122–32; Blumenthal, *Law and the Modern Mind*, 74–75, 117.

13.   Dew v. Clark, 162 Eng. Rep. 415 (quoting John Locke, *An Essay Concerning Human Understanding*, bk. 2, ch. 11, sec. 13); Joseph Chitty, *A Practical Treatise on Medical Jurisprudence*, 2nd Amer. ed. (Philadelphia, 1836), 347; James E. Moran, *Madness on Trial: A Transatlantic History of English Civil Law and Lunacy* (Manchester, UK: Manchester University Press, 2019), 184–88.

14.   Johnson v. Moore's Heirs, 11 Ky. (1 Litt.) 371 (1822); Yvonne Pitts, *Family, Law, and Inheritance in America: A Social and Legal History of Nineteenth-Century Kentucky* (New York: Cambridge University Press, 2013), 71–73.

15. Johnson v. Moore's Heirs, 11 Ky. 373–74.

16. Ibid., 381, 387, 378.

17. Temple v. Temple, 11 Va. 476; Burton v. Scott, 24 Va. 400–07. Loose language in an earlier Virginia opinion incorrectly suggested that the opponents of a will had the burden of proving insanity. Spencer v. Moore, 8 Va. (4 Call) 423, 425 (1798).

18. Redford's Adm'r v. Peggy, 27 Va. (6 Rand.) 316 (1828); Fulleck v. Allinson, (1830) 162 Eng. Rep. 1251 (Prerog.) 1255, 1257–58, 3 Hagg. Ecc. 527, 537–39, 542–47; George Weir's Will, 39 Ky. (9 Dana) 434, 445–47 (1840); Isaac F. Redfield, *The Law of Wills*, 3rd ed., 2 vols. (Boston, 1869), 1:30–51.

19. Clark v. Fisher, 1 Paige Ch. 176; Haslam, *Medical Jurisprudence*, 104–05; Bradley E. S. Fogel, "The Completely Insane Law of Partial Insanity: The Impact of Monomania on Testamentary Capacity," *Real Property, Probate and Trust Journal* 42, no. 1 (Spring 2007): 93, 99.

20. Mercer v. Kelso's Adm'r, 45 Va. (4 Gratt.) 106 (1847); Adrienne D. Davis, "The Private Law of Race and Sex: An Antebellum Perspective," *Stanford Law Review* 51, no. 2 (January 1999): 258. On Virginia's Court of Appeals in manumission cases, see chapter 4.

21. *Richmond Enquirer*, 30 June, 3 July, and 21 July 1835. The legislature had advanced the General Court's summer term from July to the last Monday in June and required at least eleven of the twenty judges to attend. Act of 4 March 1835, ch. 41, secs. 1–2, Acts of the General Assembly of Virginia, 1834–35, p. 32.

22. For the Tucker family's litigation strategy, see chapter 5.

23. *Richmond Whig*, 28 July 1835.

24. *Richmond Enquirer*, 7 July, 10 July, 14 July, 17 July 1835; Funeral Honors to John Marshall, 9 July 1835, Broadsides 1835.F98 Box, Special Collections, LVA; *New-York Spectator*, 20 July 1835 (from *Richmond Compiler*, 14 July 1835).

25. Testimony in Bryan v. Meade by William M. Watkins, Richard Randolph Jr., Henry A. Watkins, and John Marshall, *Richmond Enquirer*, 4 August 1835; William Berkeley and Robert Carrington, ibid., 7 August 1835; William Leigh, ibid., 3 November 1835.

26. William Leigh to Peachy R. Gilmer, 25 June 1833, WLL; Testimony in Bryan v. Meade by John Marshall, *Richmond Enquirer*, 4 August 1835; Wyatt Cardwell, ibid., 23 October 1835; William Leigh, ibid., 30 October and 3 November 1835.

27. Testimony in Bryan v. Meade by William Berkeley, ibid., 7 August 1835; William M. Watkins, John Marshall, Robert Carrington, and John J. Flournoy, ibid., 4 August and 7 August 1835; Wyatt Cardwell, ibid., 23 October 1835; William Leigh, ibid., 30 October and 3 November 1835; JR to John Brockenbrough, 15 November 1831, Garland, 2:347; JR to ETB, 16 November 1831, JR MSS.

28. Testimony of Robert Carrington, Bryan v. Meade, in *Richmond Enquirer*, 7 August 1835.

29. *Richmond Enquirer*, 14 July 1835.

30. Testimony in Bryan v. Meade by William Leigh, ibid., 3 November 1835, and John Marshall, ibid., 4 August 1835 ("kill joy").

31. Testimony of William Leigh, ibid., 3 November 1835.

32. NBT to Thomas A. Smith, 10 July 1835, TCP.

33. Testimony of William Leigh, Bryan v. Meade, in *Richmond Enquirer*, 3 November 1835.

34. Deposition of Nathan Lufborough, Coalter's Ex'r v. Bryan, pp. 326–27; Robert Dawidoff, *The Education of John Randolph* (New York: W. W. Norton, 1979), 87–93; Bertram Wyatt-Brown, *Southern Honor: Ethics and Behavior in the Old*

South, 25th anniv. ed. (New York: Oxford University Press, 2007), 72–73, 121, 179–82.

35. JR to Harmanus Bleecker, 23 September 1814, JR MSS, box 8; John C. Fitzpatrick, ed., "The Autobiography of Martin Van Buren," *Annual Report of the American Historical Association for 1918*, 2 vols. (Washington, DC: Government Printing Office, 1920), 2:431.

36. JR to Josiah Quincy, 1 July 1814, Quincy, 353–54; JR to James Mercer Garnett, 1 November 1823, 1 January 1824, JR MSS; Robert P. Sutton, "Nostalgia, Pessimism, and Malaise: The Doomed Aristocrat in Late-Jeffersonian Virginia," *Virginia Magazine of History and Biography* 76, no. 1 (January 1968): 41–55.

37. William G. Shade, *Democratizing the Old Dominion: Virginia and the Second Party System, 1824–1861* (Charlottesville: University Press of Virginia, 1996), 48–49; Emory G. Evans, *A "Topping People": The Rise and Decline of Virginia's Old Political Elite, 1680–1790* (Charlottesville: University of Virginia Press, 2009), 168, 193–201.

38. JR to Quincy, 1 July 1814, 22 March 1814, Quincy, 354 ("chiefly"), 351; Claire Priest, *Creditor Nation: Property Laws and Institutions in Early America* (Princeton, NJ: Princeton University Press, 2021), 139–45; Holly Brewer, "Entailing Aristocracy in Colonial Virginia: 'Ancient Feudal Restraints' and Revolutionary Reform," *William and Mary Quarterly*, 3rd ser., 54, no. 2 (April 1997): 307–46.

39. JR to Henry Middleton Rutledge, 24 July 1815, JR MSS; JR to unknown, n.d., Garland, 1:19; Stanley N. Katz, "Republicanism and the Law of Inheritance in the American Revolutionary Era," *Michigan Law Review* 76, no. 1 (November 1977): 1–29.

40. SGT, *Blackstone's Commentaries*, 5 vols. (Philadelphia, 1803), 3:119n14; James Kent, *Commentaries on American Law*, 2nd ed., 4 vols. (New York, 1832), 2:329; Charles Augustus Murray, *Travels in North America during the Years 1834, 1835, and 1836*, 2 vols. (New York, 1839), 1:125; T. G., "Primogeniture and Entail," *United States Magazine and Democratic Review* 25, no. 133 (July 1849): 17–27; Jens Beckert, *Inherited Wealth*, trans. Thomas Dunlap (Princeton, NJ: Princeton University Press, 2008), 156–66.

41. Testimony of William Leigh, Bryan v. Meade, in *Richmond Enquirer*, 3 November 1835; William Leigh to JR, 15 April 1820, TCP. For Poe's story and the English will, see Edgar Allan Poe, "The Domain of Arnheim" (1846), in *The Collected Works of Edgar Allan Poe*, 3 vols., ed. Thomas Ollive Mabbott (Cambridge, MA: Harvard University Press, 1969-78), 3:1266–85; Peter Polden, *Peter Thellusson's Will of 1797 and Its Consequences on Chancery Law* (Lewiston, NY: Edwin Mellen, 2002), 127–49.

42. Samuel Taylor to John Robertson, 15 July 1835, Duke University Library, available on microfilm 7513, UVA (Taylor's notes); *Richmond Enquirer*, 17 July 1835.

43. Taylor to Robertson, 15 July 1835; *Richmond Enquirer*, 17 July 1835, 21 July 1835; *New-York Spectator*, 20 July 1835; *Daily National Intelligencer* (DC), 23 July 1835. Samuel Taylor's notes and the posture of the case suggest that the Bryan boy's lawyers relied on *Cartwright v. Cartwright*, (1793) 161 Eng. Rep. 923 (Prerog.), 1 Phill. Ecc. 90, which held that an insane woman's will in favor of her favorite nieces was itself sufficient evidence of a lucid interval. Taylor and Robertson's argument about insane delusion rested on *Dew v. Clark*, and their emphasis on Randolph's settled intentions was an attempt to use *Temple v. Temple*, where a deranged man's will survived because it was consistent with his oft-stated intentions.

44. *Richmond Whig*, 20 July 1835; *Richmond Enquirer*, 21 July 1835.

45. *Daily National Intelligencer*, 23 July 1835 (from *Richmond Enquirer*); *New-York Spectator*, 27 July 1835 (same); *Liberator* (Boston), 25 July 1835, 8 August 1835; *Cleveland Herald*, 5 August 1835.

46. Shade, *Democratizing the Old Dominion*, 238–44; John L. Hare, *Will the Circle Be Unbroken? Family and Sectionalism in the Virginia Novels of Kennedy, Caruthers, and Tucker, 1830–1845* (New York: Routledge, 2002), 117–19.

47. NBT [Edward William Sidney, pseud.], *The Partisan Leader: A Tale of the Future*, ed. C. Hugh Holman (1836; Chapel Hill: University of North Carolina Press, 1971). Critics and historians have speculated that Beverley Tucker meant to continue *The Partisan Leader*'s story line in a second installment, which he abandoned when the novel did not sell well enough. The book was republished in New York (1861) and Richmond (1862) after the Southern states seceded.

48. Beverley D. Tucker, *Nathaniel Beverley Tucker: Prophet of the Confederacy, 1784–1851* (Tokyo: Nan'un-do, 1979), 345–50; William G. Shade, "'The Most Delicate and Exciting Topic': Martin Van Buren, Slavery, and the Election of 1836," *Journal of the Early Republic* 18, no. 3 (Autumn 1998): 468.

49. HSGT to NBT, 26 August 1837, TCP; [Abel P. Upshur], Review of *The Partisan Leader*, *Southern Literary Messenger* 3, no. 1 (January 1837): 73–89; Tucker, *Nathaniel Beverley Tucker*, 375–76.

50. NBT to HSGT, 7 September 1837, TCP; SGTC to JRB, 7 September 1837, BCTP, group A, box IV:39; Chad Vanderford, *The Legacy of St. George Tucker: College Professors in Virginia Confront Slavery and the Rights of States, 1771–1897* (Knoxville: University of Tennessee Press, 2015), 111–25, 129–37. Having once asked Henry Tucker to become professor of law at the new University of Virginia (an offer Tucker declined), Thomas Jefferson later dropped Tucker from his list of suitable candidates for the post because he thought Tucker was too moderate on states' rights. Jefferson to James Madison, 20 January 1826, David B. Mattern et al., eds., *The Papers of James Madison, Retirement Series*, 3 vols. to date (Charlottesville: University of Virginia Press, 2009–), 3:668–70.

51. NBT to Lucy Tucker, 17 September 1837, 15 June 1835, 27 November 1835, 28 April 1843, TCP; NBT to ETB, 24 August 1839, BCTP.

52. Henry Adams, *The Education of Henry Adams* (New York: Modern Library, 1931), 100, 57–59; Henry Adams, *John Randolph* (Boston, 1882), 290–91; Michael O'Brien, *Henry Adams and the Southern Question* (Athens: University of Georgia Press, 2005), 132–39.

53. *Daily National Intelligencer*, 9 May 1836 (from *Richmond Compiler*); Order, 3 May 1836, William Meade v. John C. Bryan, Va. Ct. App. Order Bk. 14, pp. 442–43, misc. microfilm 3970, LVA.

54. HSGT to NBT, 13 May 1836, TCP; NBT to Lucy Tucker, [14 July 1836], ibid.; Conway Robinson, *The Practice in the Courts of Law and Equity in Virginia*, 3 vols. (Richmond, 1832), 3:393.

55. ETB, Statement of views on JR's will, [1836], TCP; SGTC to NBT, 16 July 1836, ibid.; HSGT to NBT, 28 April 1837, ibid.; *Richmond Enquirer*, 26 July 1836, 29 July 1836; *Lynchburg Virginian*, 1 August 1836; Coalter's Ex'r v. Bryan, 42 Va. (1 Gratt.) 18, 32–33 (1844).

56. Testimony of John Brockenbrough, Meade v. Hobson, in *Richmond Enquirer*, 12 August 1836, 26 July 1836.

57. *Richmond Enquirer*, 8 December 1836; William H. Macfarland, *Address on the Character and Public Services of the Late Hon. Benjamin Watkins Leigh* (Richmond, 1851);

Mary Newton Stanard, *Richmond: Its People and Its Story* (Philadelphia: J. B. Lippincott, 1923), 92–95.

58. Testimony of Benjamin Watkins Leigh, Meade v. Hobson, in *Richmond Enquirer*, 2 August 1836 (quoted), 5 August 1836, 9 August 1836.

59. Testimony of Richard Randolph Jr., ibid., 9 August 1836.

60. Testimony of Thomas Robinson, ibid., 12 August 1836; JR to Joseph H. Nicholson, 17 March 1805, Joseph Hopper Nicholson Papers, LC.

61. *Lynchburg Virginian*, 21 July 1836 (from *Richmond Whig*) ("most important"); *Richmond Enquirer*, 15 July 1836, 19 July 1836; *Boston Courier*, 28 July 1836; *Cleveland Herald*, 29 July 1836; *New-Hampshire Statesman and State Journal*, 30 July 1836; Order, 15 July 1836, Meade v. Hobson, transcribed in Tucker v. Randolph's Ex'r, pp. 10–11, and Coalter's Ex'r v. Bryan, pp. 687–90.

62. *Virginia Free Press* (Charlestown), 28 July 1836 ("disinterest conduct"); *Emancipator* (NY), 4 August 1836; *Liberator* (Boston), 13 August 1836. The newspapers mistakenly reprinted Randolph's 1819 will, which had been introduced into evidence but not offered for probate, rather than the 1821 will that the General Court upheld.

63. HSGT to NBT, 1 December 1836, 12 December 1836, 24 April 1837, 13 May 1837, TCP; *Richmond Enquirer*, 15 November 1836, 10 December 1836; Act of 15 March 1832, ch. 95, Va. Rev. Code Supp. (1833), 123–25; Francis T. Brooke, *A Narrative of My Life for My Family* (Richmond, 1849), 56–57; Robert Dennard Tucker, *The Descendants of William Tucker of Throwleigh, Devon* (Spartanburg, SC: Reprint Co., 1991), 295; Note, "The Virginia Special Court of Appeals: Constitutional Relief for an Overburdened Court," *William and Mary Law Review* 8, no. 2 (February 1967): 254.

64. SGTC to NBT, 21 June 1837, TCP; HSGT to NBT, 29 June 1837, 9 November 1836, ibid.; *Richmond Enquirer*, 4 February 1837 (judicial delay).

65. *Lynchburg Virginian*, 6 July 1837 ("By this Will"), 10 July 1837 (from *Richmond Enquirer*, 4 July 1837); *Liberator*, 14 July 1837 ("noble devise"), 25 August 1837 ("high-minded slaveholder"), 29 September 1837 (from *Friend of Man* (Utica, NY), 9 August 1837); *Virginia Free Press*, 13 July 1837 ("We do not suppose"); *Daily Herald and Gazette* (Cleveland, OH), 11 July 1837, 21 July 1837; Minutes and order, 5 June–3 July 1837, Frederick Hobson v. William Meade, Va. Ct. App. Order Bk. 15, pp. 114–25, misc. microfilm 3970, LVA. One judge dissented from the Special Court of Appeals decision.

CHAPTER 9: JOHN WHITE'S ROANOKE

1. Henry Howe, *Historical Collections of Virginia* (Charleston, SC, 1845), 223–24; Powhatan Bouldin, *Home Reminiscences of John Randolph of Roanoke* (Richmond, VA, 1878), 262–64. For enslaved and formerly enslaved persons shaping visitors' perceptions, see Scott E. Casper, *Sarah Johnson's Mount Vernon: The Forgotten History of an American Shrine* (New York: Hill and Wang, 2008).

2. Anne Royall, *Mrs. Royall's Southern Tour, or Second Series of the Black Book* (Washington, DC, 1830), 120–21; Interview of Catherine Slim, 9 June 1937, in Federal Writers' Project, *Slave Narratives: A Folk History of Slavery in the United States from Interviews with Former Slaves*, 17 vols. (Washington, DC: WPA Library of Congress Project, 1941), 12:79; H[enry] C[lay] Bruce, *The New Man: Twenty-Nine Years a Slave, Twenty-Nine Years a Free Man* (York, PA, 1895), 43–49; David H. Burr, Map of Virginia, Maryland and Delaware, in *The American Atlas* (London, 1839).

3. "Grave of John Randolph," *Littell's Living Age* 11, no. 128 (24 October 1846): 195 (from *American Beacon* (Norfolk, VA)); JRB to editor, *Daily Dispatch* (Richmond), 20 May 1878.

4. Testimony of Clem C. Clay, Moton v. Kessens, p. 153; Entry for John White, cert. 285, Charlotte Free Register; David Stefan Doddington, *Contesting Slave Masculinity in the American South* (Cambridge, UK: Cambridge University Press, 2018), 120–23.

5. NBT to ETB, 21 August 1841, BCRTP; JRB to NBT, 2 October 1841, TCP; "Grave of John Randolph," 195.

6. R[obert] L[ewis] Dabney, "Reminiscences of John Randolph," *Union Theological Seminary Magazine* 6, no. 1 (October 1894): 18–19; Henry Bibb, *Narrative of the Life and Adventures of Henry Bibb, An American Slave* (1849), in *Slave Narratives*, ed. William L. Andrews and Henry Louis Gates Jr. (New York: Library of America, 2000), 446; Sylvia R. Frey and Betty Wood, *Come Shouting to Zion: African American Protestantism in the American South and British Caribbean to 1830* (Chapel Hill: University of North Carolina Press, 1998), 173–74, 177–78.

7. Bouldin, *Home Reminiscences*, 35; Arthur Singleton [Henry Cogswell Knight], *Letters from the South and West* (Boston, 1824), 64, 74; Philip A. Bruce, *The Plantation Negro as a Freeman: Observations on His Character, Condition, and Prospects in Virginia* (New York, 1889), 204–06; Barbara Heath, "Space and Place within Plantation Quarters in Virginia, 1700–1825," in *Cabin, Quarter, Plantation: Architecture and Landscapes of North American Slavery*, ed. Clifton Ellis and Rebecca Ginsburg (New Haven, CT: Yale University Press, 2010), 156–76. No surviving physical evidence of slave housing at Roanoke has been reported.

8. JR to John Brockenbrough, 15 November 1831, Garland, 2:344–45; JR to ETB, 16 November 1831, JR MSS.

9. James L. Smith, *Autobiography* (1881), in *Don't Carry Me Back! Narratives by Former Virginia Slaves*, ed. Maurice Duke (Richmond: Dietz Press, 1995), 61; Mechal Sobel, *The World They Made Together: Black and White Values in Eighteenth-Century Virginia* (Princeton, NJ: Princeton University Press, 1987), 100–26.

10. Joseph Martin, *A New and Comprehensive Gazetteer of Virginia and the District of Columbia* (Charlottesville, VA, 1835), 61–62 (temperatures); Peter Randolph, *Sketches of Slave Life* and *From Slave Cabin to the Pulpit*, ed. Katherine Clay Bassard (1855 and 1893; Morgantown: West Virginia University Press, 2016), 50–51; Helen Bradley Foster, *"New Raiments of Self": African American Clothing in the Antebellum South* (Oxford, UK: Berg, 1997), 146–50.

11. JR, Will, 4 May 1819, in *Richmond Enquirer*, 26 July 1836; Interview of Charles Grandy, 18 May 1937, in Charles L. Perdue Jr., Thomas E. Barden, and Robert K. Phillips, *Weevils in the Wheat: Interviews with Virginia Ex-Slaves* (Charlottesville: University Press of Virginia, 1976), 116; Theodore D. Weld, *American Slavery As It Is: Testimony of a Thousand Witnesses* (New York, 1839), 42–43. On the diet of the enslaved, see Richard Sutch, "The Care and Feeding of Slaves," in *Reckoning with Slavery: A Critical Study in the Quantitative History of American Negro Slavery*, ed. Paul A. David et al. (New York: Oxford University Press, 1976), 261–65.

12. Interview of Gabe Hunt, n.d., in *Weevils in the Wheat*, 148; Randolph, *Sketches of Slave Life*, 52; Lynn A. Nelson, *Pharsalia: An Environmental Biography of a Southern Plantation, 1780–1880* (Athens: University of Georgia Press, 2007), 103–08, 133–35.

13. Wyatt Cardwell to NBT, 10 May 1834, TCP. A more critical white observer saw "no look of decent comfort anywhere" in slave country. Charles Dickens, *American Notes for General Circulation* (London, 1850), 93–94.

14. James W. Alexander to John Hall, 16 November 1828, in John Hall, ed., *Forty Years' Familiar Letters of James W. Alexander, D.D.*, 2 vols. (New York, 1860), 1:114; Testimony of Clem C. Clay, Moton v. Kessens, p. 130; Deposition of William Smith, Tucker v. Randolph's Ex'r, pp. 51–52 (Randolph's assault on Juba).

15. B. P. [Benjamin Perley Poore], "Visit to the Estate of the late John Randolph, of Roanoke," *New-York Farmer and American Gardener's Magazine* 8, no. 5 (May 1835): 140; Ben: Perley Poore, "'Roanoke,' the Farm Home of John Randolph," *Southern Planter and Farmer* 39, no. 3 (March 1878): 127–30 (from *American Cultivator*, n.d.); *New York Times*, 29 May 1887 (Ben: Perley Poore obituary).

16. Eliza Lavalette Barksdale, Diary, entry for [1 September] 1836, VMHC; Anya Jabour, *Scarlett's Sisters: Young Women in the Old South* (Chapel Hill: University of North Carolina Press, 2007), 132–33, 139.

17. Brian Connolly and Marisa Fuentes, introduction to "From Archives of Slavery to Liberated Futures?" *History of the Present* 6, no. 2 (Fall 2016): 105; unknown to R. E. Park, 18 November 1908, "Letters Collected by R. E. Park and Booker T. Washington," *Journal of Negro History* 7, no. 2 (April 1922): 209 (White's popularity); Mark Reinhardt, "Who Speaks for Margaret Garner? Slavery, Silence, and the Politics of Ventriloquism," *Critical Inquiry* 29, no. 1 (Autumn 2002): 81–85, 118–19. For John White's exercise of his freedom, see chapter 12.

18. William Leigh to Peachy R. Gilmer, 12 January 1834, 3 March 1834, WLL; Leigh to HSGT, 21 December 1837, TCP; HSGT to NBT, 24 April 1837, 13 May 1837, ibid.

19. Francis Fedric, *Slave Life in Virginia and Kentucky*, ed. C. L. Innes (1859; Baton Rouge: Louisiana State University Press, 2010), 77–79; Mia Bay, *The White Image in the Black Mind: African-American Ideas about White People, 1830–1925* (New York: Oxford University Press, 2000), 174–77; Susan B. Carter et al., eds., *Historical Statistics of the United States: Earliest Times to the Present*, millennial ed., 5 vols. (New York: Cambridge University Press, 2006), 2:2-381–2-382, table Bb212. The plot of the most popular antislavery novel pivots on the death of a slaveholder. Harriet Beecher Stowe, *Uncle Tom's Cabin; or Life among the Lowly* (1852), in *Harriet Beecher Stowe: Three Novels*, ed. Kathryn Kish Sklar (New York: Library of America, 1982), 371.

20. JRB to NBT, 7 October 1833, TCP; John Marshall to HSGT, 17 November 1833, RTFP, misc. reel 4224, frame 254; HSGT to NBT, 13 May 1837, TCP. Randolph Bryan himself was buying land to keep his growing slave population employed. ETB to Mrs. James P. Screven [Hannah Georgia (Bryan) Screven], 30 November 1838, Grinnan Family Papers, UVA, box 3.

21. Entries for Estate of JR, Virginia Auditor of Public Accounts, Personal Property Tax Books, Charlotte County, 1833–44, reel 82, LVA; Joseph Clark Robert, *The Tobacco Kingdom* (1938; Gloucester, MA: Peter Smith, 1965), 143–45. Cardwell placed advertisements for large sales of Randolph's horses in the *Richmond Enquirer*, 22 August through 3 October 1834 and 1 July through 28 October 1836.

22. JRB to [HSGT], 24 January 1843, RTFP, misc. reel 4225, frames 32–33; Deposition of William Leigh, Coalter's Ex'r v. Bryan, p. 523; John J. Zaborney, *Slaves for Hire: Renting Enslaved Laborers in Antebellum Virginia* (Baton Rouge: Louisiana State University Press, 2012), 58–63.

23. Moses Grandy, *Narrative of the Life of Moses Grandy; Late a Slave in the United States of America*, narr. George Thompson (London, 1843), 9–13; Jonathan D. Martin, *Divided Mastery: Slave Hiring in the American South* (Cambridge, MA: Harvard University Press, 2004), 96–102, 139–40, 156–57.

24. State v. Mann, 13 N.C. (2 Dev.) 263, 266 (1829); Commonwealth v. Booth, 4 Va. (2

Va. Cases) 394 (Gen. Ct. 1824); Commonwealth v. Turner, 26 Va. (5 Rand.) 678 (Gen. Ct. 1827); Sally Greene, "*State v. Mann* Exhumed," *North Carolina Law Review* 87, no. 3 (March 2009): 733–34.

25. John Hope Franklin and Loren Schweninger, *Runaway Slaves: Rebels on the Plantation* (New York: Oxford University Press, 1999), 19–23, 33–37, 136–40; Anthony E. Kaye, *Joining Places: Slave Neighborhoods in the Old South* (Chapel Hill: University of North Carolina Press, 2007), 31; Viola Franziska Müller, "Illegal but Tolerated: Slave Refugees in Richmond, Virginia, 1800–1860," in *Fugitive Slaves and Spaces of Freedom in North America*, ed. Damian Alan Pargas (Gainesville: University Press of Florida, 2018), 137–67.

26. On John White's earlier flight from Roanoke, see chapter 2.

27. Ira Berlin, *Generations of Captivity: A History of African-American Slaves* (Cambridge, MA: Harvard University Press, 2003), 230–44; Calvin Schermerhorn, *Money over Mastery, Family over Freedom: Slavery in the Antebellum Upper South* (Baltimore: John Hopkins University Press, 2011), 18–21, 52, 90.

28. HSGT to NBT, 13 May 1837, TCP; Entries for Estate of JR, Virginia Auditor of Public Accounts, Personal Property Tax Books, Charlotte County, 1833–44; Eva Sheppard Wolf, "Manumission and the Two-Race System in Early National Virginia," in *Paths to Freedom: Manumission in the Atlantic World*, ed. Rosemary Brana-Shute and Randy J. Sparks (Columbia: University of South Carolina Press, 2009), 322–24; Sean Condon, "The Slave Owner's Family and Manumission in the Post-Revolutionary Chesapeake Tidewater," ibid., 351–52.

29. Wyatt Cardwell to NBT, 29 January 1835, TCP; [Poore], "Visit to the Estate of the late John Randolph," 141; Fairfax Harrison, *The Roanoke Stud, 1795–1833* (Richmond: Old Dominion Press, 1930), 203.

30. Cardwell to NBT, 24 December 1840, 4 January 1841, TCP; ETB to NBT, 13 August 1840, ibid.; JRB to NBT, 26 November 1840, ibid.; *Friend of Man* (Utica, NY), 29 April 1840; *Liberator* (Boston), 3 July 1840 (from *Friend of Man*).

31. John Randolph once tried to break contact between his slaves and the residents of Israel Hill, but a letter passing greetings to freedpersons at Israel Hill shows that he had failed. Elizabeth Tucker Coalter to JR, 3 March 1829, JR MSS.

32. Melvin Patrick Ely, *Israel on the Appomattox: A Southern Experiment in Black Freedom from the 1790s through the Civil War* (New York: Alfred A. Knopf, 2004), 58–68, 107–74, 204–05, 212–15, 353–57. On disparaging newspaper accounts of Israel Hill, see chapter 5 above.

33. Herbert G. Gutman, *The Black Family in Slavery and Freedom, 1750–1925* (New York: Pantheon, 1976), 335–57; Peter Kolchin, *American Slavery, 1619–1877* (New York: Hill and Wang, 1993), 138–43; Kaye, *Joining Places*, 42–50.

34. Cardwell to NBT, 19 June 1835, 3 June 1838, TCP; HSGT to NBT, 13 May 1837, ibid.; Robert, *Tobacco Kingdom*, 237.

35. Testimony of Robert Carrington, Bryan v. Meade, in *Richmond Enquirer*, 7 August 1835; Deposition of John Marshall, Coalter's Ex'r v. Bryan, pp. 453–54; Robert, *Tobacco Kingdom*, 242–43 (Virginia tobacco crop, 1833–46); Caitlin Rosenthal, *Accounting for Slavery: Masters and Management* (Cambridge, MA: Harvard University Press, 2018), 122–26.

36. Robert, *Tobacco Kingdom*, 18, 249–50; Lorena S. Walsh, *Motives of Honor, Pleasure, and Profit: Plantation Management in the Colonial Chesapeake, 1607–1763* (Chapel Hill: University of North Carolina Press, 2010), 639–57. Measuring productivity by pounds of tobacco per enslaved laborer rather than per acre was a

practice dating to the colonial period that testified to the relative values of labor and land.

37. Cardwell to NBT, 10 May 1834, 29 January 1835, 11 August 1840, 17 September 1845, TCP; Wyatt Cardwell, Accounts as agent for John Randolph's estate, 1834–46, Henry Family Papers, sec. 45, Mss1 H3968a 909-942, VMHC; Harrison, *Roanoke Stud*, 24–25, 42–44.

38. HSGT to NBT, 27 June 1839, TCP; JRB to NBT, 14 December 1839, ibid.; JRB to [HSGT], 24 January 1843, RTFP, misc. reel 4225, frames 32–33; ETB and JRB to NBT, 10 January [1844] (misdated 1843), TCP.

39. William Leigh to HSGT, 21 December 1837, TCP; HSGT to NBT, 28 June 1838, ibid.; Leigh to NBT, 1 January 1839, ibid.; JRB to NBT, 14 December 1839, 30 January 1842, ibid.; JRB to [HSGT], 24 January 1843, RTFP, misc. reel 4225, frames 32–33; Bagwell v. Elliott, 23 Va. (2 Rand.) 190, 200 (1824); Joseph Tate, *Digest of the Laws of Virginia*, 2nd ed. (Richmond, 1841), 405–06 and n(1); HSGT, *Commentaries on the Laws of Virginia*, 3rd ed., 2 vols. (Richmond, 1846), 1:279.

40. Charles Dickens, *American Notes for General Circulation* (London, 1850), 67–68; Alasdair Roberts, *America's First Great Depression: Economic Crisis and Political Disorder after the Panic of 1837* (Ithaca, NY: Cornell University Press, 2012), 14–15; Jessica M. Lepler, *The Many Panics of 1837: People, Politics, and the Creation of a Transatlantic Financial Crisis* (New York: Cambridge University Press, 2013), 124–32, 166–67.

41. JRB to NBT, 26 October 1839, RTFP, misc. reel 4225, frame 40; JRB to HSGT, 9 January 1837, ibid., frame 30; JRB to NBT, 14 December 1839, TCP.

42. HSGT to NBT, 24 January 1840, 13 January 1840, TCP; NBT to Lucy Tucker, 25 August 1839, ibid.; Coalter's Ex'r v. Bryan, 42 Va. (1 Gratt.) 18, 33 (1844).

43. ETB to NBT, 15 January 1842, TCP; JRB to NBT, 30 January 1842, ibid.

44. HSGT to NBT, 16 September 1842, ibid., JRB to [HSGT], 24 January 1843, RTFP, misc. reel 4225, frames 32–33; ETB to Lucy Tucker, 7 September 1843, TCP. John Coalter did mention the slaves' freedom once—to note that Judge Leigh could do nothing about it until he got rid of the 1832 will. John Coalter to HSGT, 24 November 1834, RTFP, misc. reel 4224, frames 286–87.

45. ETB to NBT, 3 August 1842, TCP; Robert Fyson, "The Crisis of 1842: Chartism, the Colliers' Strike, and the Outbreak in the Potteries," in *The Chartist Experience: Studies in Working-Class Radicalism and Culture, 1830–60*, ed. James Epstein and Dorothy Thompson (London: Macmillan, 1982), 194–220; Sam Walter Haynes, *Unfinished Revolution: The Early American Republic in a British World* (Charlottesville: University of Virginia Press, 2010), 183–85. A South Carolina slavery apologist struck a more belligerent tone in an open letter to an English abolitionist about the plight of British workers. "Emancipate them," he urged. "Raise them from the condition of brutes, to the level of human beings—of American slaves at least." James Henry Hammond to Thomas Clarkson, 28 January 1845, in [William Gilmore Simms, ed.], *Selections from the Letters and Speeches of the Hon. James H. Hammond* (New York, 1866), 159.

CHAPTER 10: A DECADE IN CHANCERY

1. Joseph Martin, *A New and Comprehensive Gazetteer of Virginia and the District of Columbia* (Charlottesville, VA, 1835), 198; John O. Peters and Margaret T. Peters,

Virginia's Historic Courthouses (Charlottesville: University Press of Virginia, 1995), 24–25.

2. HSGT to NBT, [November 1837], TCP; Phillip Hamilton, *The Making and Unmaking of a Revolutionary Family: The Tuckers of Virginia, 1752–1830* (Charlottesville: University of Virginia Press, 2003), 79.

3. Henry Howe, *Historical Collections of Virginia* (Charleston, SC, 1845), 321, 324; Caroline Morris, "A History of Madness: Four Venerable Virginia Lunatic Asylums," *Virginia Magazine of History and Biography* 125, no. 2 (2017): 140–44.

4. Chad Vanderford, *The Legacy of St. George Tucker: College Professors in Virginia Confront Slavery and the Rights of the States, 1771–1897* (Knoxville: University of Tennessee Press, 2015), 132–36, 142; Alfred L. Brophy, *University, Court, and Slave: Pro-Slavery Thought in Southern Colleges and Courts and the Coming of Civil War* (New York: Oxford University Press, 2016), 35–40.

5. Robert J. Brugger, *Beverley Tucker: Heart over Head in the Old South* (Baltimore: Johns Hopkins University Press, 1978), 92, 107–13, 135; Bertram Wyatt-Brown, *Hearts of Darkness: Wellsprings of a Southern Literary Tradition* (Baton Rouge: Louisiana State University Press, 2003), 41–42.

6. A. P. Upshur to NBT, 28 July, 12 August, 3 September, and 15 November 1838, 14 January and 28 March 1839, 12 January 1840, TCP; Thomas T. Cropper to NBT, 6 February 1841, ibid.

7. Claude H. Hall, *Abel Parker Upshur: Conservative Virginian, 1790–1844* (Madison: State Historical Society of Wisconsin, 1963), 69–86; Thomas D. Morris, *Southern Slavery and the Law, 1619–1860* (Chapel Hill: University of North Carolina Press, 1996), 372; Ted Maris-Wolf, *Family Bonds: Free Blacks and Re-enslavement Law in Antebellum Virginia* (Chapel Hill: University of North Carolina Press, 2015), 29–31.

8. [Abel P. Upshur], *A Brief Enquiry into the True Nature and Character of Our Federal Government* (Petersburg, VA, 1840); Michael O'Brien, *Conjectures of Order: Intellectual Life and the American South, 1810–1860*, 2 vols. (Chapel Hill: University of North Carolina Press, 2004), 2:833–36, 865–72; Sean Wilentz, *The Rise of American Democracy: Jefferson to Lincoln* (New York: W. W. Norton, 2005), 559–66.

9. NBT to Thomas A. Smith, 10 July 1835, TCP; SGTC to JRB, 7 September 1837, 13 October 1837, BCTP, group A, box IV:39.

10. Ford v. Gardner, 11 Va. (1 Hen. & M.) 72 (1806); Wills v. Spraggins, 44 Va. (3 Gratt.) 555 (1847); Conway Robinson, *The Practice in the Courts of Law and Equity in Virginia*, 3 vols. (Richmond, 1832), 2:75–77. The simple procedure known as probate in common form was the only way to probate a will in Virginia when John Randolph died, but soon after the courts probated Randolph's will, the legislature allowed parties to adopt a more formal procedure that could bind all interested parties except in unusual circumstances. Act of 3 March 1819, ch. 104, sec. 13, Va. Rev. Code (1819), 1:378; Act of 24 March 1838, ch. 92, Acts of the General Assembly of Virginia, 1838–39, pp. 71–72; Coalter's Ex'r v. Bryan, 42 Va. (1 Gratt.) 18, 76–82 (1844).

11. Joseph G. Baldwin, *The Flush Times of Alabama and Mississippi: A Series of Sketches* (New York, 1853), 92; Thomas O. Main, "Traditional Equity and Contemporary Procedure," *Washington Law Review* 78, no. 2 (May 2003): 437–52; Michael Lobban, "Preparing for Fusion: Reforming the Nineteenth-Century Court of Chancery, Part I," *Law and History Review* 22, no. 2 (Summer 2004): 391–98.

12. Act of 3 March 1819, ch. 104, sec. 13, Va. Rev. Code (1819), 1:378; Act of 16 April 1831, ch. 109, secs. 1, 18, 29, Va. Rev. Code Supp. (1833), 136, 142, 145; *Coalter's Ex'r*, 42 Va. 76–80, 85; Dickens v. Bonnewell, 160 Va. 194, 200 (1933); Robinson, *Practice in the*

Courts, 3:393–94; Lewis M. Simes, "The Function of Will Contests," *Michigan Law Review* 44, no. 4 (February 1946): 521.

13. HSGT to NBT, 9 November 1836, 19 November 1837, TCP; SGTC to NBT, 21 June 1837, 28 November 1837, ibid.

14. HSGT to NBT, 29 June 1837, ibid.; Monroe v. James, 18 Va. (4 Munf.) 194, 198–99, 213–14 (1814).

15. Entries for Estate of JR, Virginia Auditor of Public Accounts, Personal Property Tax Books, Charlotte County, 1837 and 1838, reel 82, LVA; Entry for Estate of JR, 1840 United States Federal Census, Charlotte County, VA, Ancestry.com; Susan B. Carter et al., eds., *Historical Statistics of the United States: Earliest Times to the Present*, millennial ed., 5 vols. (New York: Cambridge University Press, 2006), 2:2-381–2-382, table Bb212. Slave prices rose during the course of the chancery litigation, and shortly after final judgment, Judge Leigh was said to have estimated that the slaves manumitted were worth $200,000. E. G. to Brother Benton, July 1845, in *Emancipator and Weekly Chronicle* (Boston), 10 September 1845.

16. Bill of complaint, 11 December 1837, Tucker v. Randolph's Ex'r, pp. 1–4.

17. Answer of William Leigh, 22 February 1838, ibid., pp. 13–22 (quoted at 20); HSGT to NBT, 22 December 1837, TCP; William Leigh to HSGT, 21 December 1837, ibid.

18. JRB to NBT, 4 January 1838, ibid. For Judge Upshur's absence from the probate trials of Randolph's will, see *Daily National Intelligencer* (DC), 23 July 1835; *Richmond Enquirer*, 26 July 1836.

19. NBT to Thomas A. Smith, 11 April 1834, TCP; HSGT to NBT, 28 April 1837, ibid.; NBT to ETB, 10 February 1840, BCRTP; Daniel P. Jordan, *Political Leadership in Jefferson's Virginia* (Charlottesville: University Press of Virginia, 1983), 169. For other large Virginia manumissions, see note 3 in the preface.

20. William Meade to NBT, 4 March 1839, TCP; Corbin Braxton to NBT, 19 October 1839, ibid.; Depositions, November 1838–April 1839, Tucker v. Randolph's Ex'r, pp. 24–94; Answers of William Meade, Francis Scott Key, and Frederick Hobson, ibid., pp. 94–96, 99–100; Orders, 15 November 1839, ibid., pp. 97–99.

21. JRB to NBT, 15 April 1838, 14 December 1839, 30 January 1842, TCP; ETB to NBT, 6 January 1840, ibid.; NBT to ETB, 10 February 1840, BCRTP; NBT to JRB, 17 February 1842, Grinnan Family Papers, box 3, UVA; Bertram Wyatt-Brown, *Southern Honor: Ethics and Behavior in the Old South*, 25th anniv. ed. (New York: Oxford University Press, 2007), 392–93.

22. Opinion of Judge Upshur, 26 November 1839, Tucker v. Randolph's Ex'r, pp. 101–13 (quoted at 111–12, 113).

23. Randolph's Ex'r v. Tucker, 37 Va. (10 Leigh) 655, 662–63 (1840); Muller v. Bayly, 62 Va. (21 Gratt.) 521, 533–34 (1871) (jurisdictional claim in *Randolph's Ex'r* merely colorable). The Court of Appeals had discretion to hear interlocutory appeals on jurisdiction. Act of 16 April 1831, ch. 109, sec. 31, Va. Rev. Code Supp. (1833), 149; Robinson, *Practice in the Courts*, 2:422, 425.

24. Corbin Braxton [SGTC's executor] to NBT, 19 October 1839, 19 March 1840, TCP; Bill of complaint, [1 April 1840], Coalter's Ex'r v. Bryan, pp. 2–4; Act of 16 April 1831, ch. 109, sec. 38, Va. Rev. Code Supp. (1833), 151.

25. Separate answer of William Leigh, 30 October 1840, Coalter's Ex'r v. Bryan, pp. 21–42 (quoted at 24); Separate answer of William Meade, 28 April 1841, ibid., pp. 57–82.

26. Answer of NBT, 11 May 1841, ibid., pp 83–88 (quoted at 83, 88).

27. Stipulation, 14 May 1841, ibid., pp. 627–29; Decree, 14 May 1841, ibid., pp. 8, 630–31.

28. Martin, *New and Comprehensive Gazetteer*, 162–63; J[ames] S[ilk] Buckingham, *The Slave States of America*, 2 vols. (London, 1842), 2:435–36; Suzanne Lebsock, *The Free Women of Petersburg: Status and Culture in a Southern Town, 1784–1860* (New York: W. W. Norton, 1984), 7–10.

29. Department of State, *Compendium of the Enumeration of Inhabitants and Statistics of the United States . . . from the Returns of the Sixth Census* (Washington, DC, 1841), 32–34; L. Diane Barnes, *Artisan Workers in the Upper South: Petersburg, Virginia, 1820–1865* (Baton Rouge: Louisiana State University Press, 2008), 12–36, 131, 215.

30. Lebsock, *Free Women of Petersburg*, 11, 89–94; Barnes, *Artisan Workers*, 132–53;

31. Peters and Peters, *Virginia's Historic Courthouses*, 114–16.

32. Interview of Charles Crawley, 20 February 1937, in *Weevils in the Wheat: Interviews with Virginia Ex-Slaves*, ed. Charles L. Perdue Jr. et al. (Charlottesville: University Press of Virginia, 1976), 79; Interview of Louise Jones, 12 February 1937, ibid., 185.

33. *Daily Richmond Whig*, 19 March 1841; *Staunton Spectator and General Advertiser* (VA), 25 March 1841; *Richmond Enquirer*, 7 July 1848 (Gholson obituary); Christopher Michael Curtis, "'Not a Judicial Act, Yet a Judicious One': Honor, Office, and Democracy," in *The Field of Honor: Essays on Southern Character and American Identity*, ed. John Mayfield and Todd Hagstette (Columbia: University of South Carolina Press, 2017), 108–26.

34. Steven Deyle, *Carry Me Back: The Domestic Slave Trade in American Life* (New York: Oxford University Press, 2005), 40–41; Lacy K. Ford, *Deliver Us from Evil: The Slavery Question in the Old South* (New York: Oxford University Press, 2009), 365–70.

35. *Richmond Whig and Commercial Journal*, 19 January 1832. A frequently quoted rhetorical flourish by Patrick Henry turns Gholson's argument on its head. "Would any one believe that I am Master of Slaves of my own purchase?" Henry wrote to a prominent Quaker planter. "I am drawn along by the general Inconvenience of living without them. I will not, I cannot justify it." Patrick Henry to Robert Pleasants, 18 January 1773, Allinson Family Papers, Haverford College Quaker and Special Collections.

36. *Richmond Whig and Commercial Journal*, 24 January 1832. The General Assembly did make annual appropriations of $18,000 for five years to colonize free Black Virginians in Liberia. Marie Tyler-McGraw, *An African Republic: Black and White Virginians in the Making of Liberia* (Chapel Hill: University of North Carolina Press, 2007), 46–47, 57–59.

37. Morris, *Southern Slavery and the Law*, 404–11. One of the decisions that marked the Virginia court's shift away from leniency in manumission cases involved the emancipatory will of John Coalter's widow. Williamson v. Coalter's Ex'r, 55 Va. (14 Gratt.) 394 (1858). On the Virginia Court of Appeals' earlier decisions in manumission cases, see chapter 4.

38. Loren Schweninger, *Appealing for Liberty: Freedom Suits in the South* (New York: Oxford University Press, 2018), 267–82; Kimberly M. Welch, *Black Litigants in the Antebellum American South* (Chapel Hill: University of North Carolina Press, 2018), 173–76.

39. Orders, 13 June 1850, 4 May 1855, and 11 October 1855, James Young v. Isaac Medley (Cir. Super. Ct., Halifax County, VA, 1855), Halifax County Chancery Order Bk. 2, pp. 262, 575–76, 645–46, LVA; Order, 16 January 1855, James Young v. Isaac Medley (Va. Spec. Ct. App., 1855), ibid., pp. 569–70; Jacob v. Ex'r of Philip Vass (Cir. Super. Ct., Halifax County, 1841), Chancery Records Index

no. 1841-010, Virginia Memory, LVA, https://www.lva.virginia.gov/chancery/case_detail.asp?CFN=083-1841-010; Young v. Ex'r of Philip Vass (Cir. Super. Ct., Halifax County, 1855), Chancery Records Index no. 1855-040, ibid., https://www.lva.virginia.gov/chancery/case_detail.asp?CFN=083-1855-040.

40. Orders, 25 November 1841, June 1842, Coalter's Ex'r v. Bryan, pp. 636–38, 641–44.

41. D[enis] G[eorge] Lubé, *An Analysis of the Principles of Equity Pleading*, ed. J. D. Wheeler, 1st Amer. ed. (New York, 1840), 149–74; Charles E. Clark, "History, Systems and Functions of Pleading," *Virginia Law Review* 11, no. 7 (May 1925): 517–52; Stephen N. Subrin, "David Dudley Field and the Field Code: A Historical Analysis of an Earlier Procedural Vision," *Law and History Review* 6, no. 2 (Autumn 1988): 328–31.

42. Act of 16 April 1831, ch. 108 and ch. 109, secs. 1–16, Va. Rev. Code Supp. (1833), 136–41.

43. Lawrence M. Friedman, *A History of American Law*, 4th ed. (New York: Oxford University Press, 2019), 290–96; E. Lee Shepard, "Lawyers Look at Themselves: Professional Consciousness and the Virginia Bar, 1770–1850," *American Journal of Legal History* 25, no. 1 (January 1981): 1–23.

44. Orders, June 1842, 7 December 1842, Coalter's Ex'r v. Bryan, pp. 639–40, 645–47; *Lynchburg Virginian*, 16 December 1841; *Richmond Enquirer*, 5 July 1842.

45. *Emancipator* (NY), 22 July 1841; *Free Press* (Charlestown, VA), 5 August 1841. One enslaved man said his annual hire in Richmond during this period fluctuated from $75 to $150, so the annual hire value of the 150 or more working adults in the Randolph estate could have been as much as $20,000. Burrell W. Mann to American Colonization Society, 18 September 1847, in Carter G. Woodson, ed., *The Mind of the Negro as Reflected in Letters Written during the Crisis, 1800–1860* (1926; New York: Negro University Press, 1969), 20.

46. *Alexandria Gazette* (VA), 20 November 1841 (from *Petersburg Statesman*, 8 November 1841); James W. Alexander to John Hall, 10 March 1842, in John Hall, ed., *Forty Years' Familiar Letters of James W. Alexander, D.D.*, 2 vols. (New York, 1860), 1:350.

47. HSGT to NBT, 9 November 1836, 30 April 1838, TCP; Argument of Samuel Taylor, *Coalter's Ex'r*, 42 Va. 55.

48. SGTC to NBT, 9 January 1838, TCP; Henry L. Brooke to NBT, 22 July 1842, ibid.; Bill of complaint, [1 April 1840], Coalter's Ex'r v. Bryan, p. 4 (interlineation to name Leigh as a defendant "in his own right"); Answer of William Leigh to amended complaint, February 1842, ibid., p. 99; Robinson, *Practice in the Courts*, 1:331, 3:355–56.

49. Order, 7 December 1842, Coalter's Ex'r v. Bryan, pp. 645–46.

50. The Court of Appeals had discretion to hear the interlocutory appeal. Robinson, *Practice in the Courts*, 2:422, 425.

51. *Coalter's Ex'r*, 42 Va. 86–94.

52. Ibid., 95; Thomas R. R. Cobb, *An Inquiry into the Law of Negro Slavery in the United States of America* (Philadelphia, 1858), 86.

53. Peter Kolchin, *American Slavery: 1619–1877* (New York: Hill and Wang, 1993), 133–38; Kendra Taira Field, *Growing Up with the Country: Family, Race, and Nation after the Civil War* (New Haven, CT: Yale University Press, 2018), 10–12.

54. On Richard Randolph's freedmen, see chapter 2.

55. William L. Andrews, *To Tell a Free Story: The First Century of Afro-American Autobiography, 1760–1865* (Urbana: University of Illinois Press, 1986), 97–166; Calvin Schermerhorn, "Arguing Slavery's Narrative: Southern Regionalists, Ex-Slave

Autobiographers, and the Contested Literary Representations of the Peculiar Institution, 1824–1849," *Journal of American Studies* 46, no. 4 (2012): 1009–33.

56. Peter Randolph, *Sketches of Slave Life* and *From Slave Cabin to the Pulpit*, ed. Katherine Clay Bassard (1855 and 1893; Morgantown: West Virginia University Press, 2016), 17, 59, 84–86, 140–41; Executor of Carter H. Edloe v. Mary Orgain (Cir. Super. Ct., Petersburg, VA, 1855), Chancery Records Index no. 1855-020, Virginia Memory, LVA, https://www.lva.virginia.gov/chancery/case_detail.asp?CFN=730-1855-020. A Richmond paper claimed that Carter Edloe's executor sent the Edloe freedmen to Boston because John Randolph's freedmen had been so poorly received in Ohio. *Richmond Enquirer*, 28 September 1847.

57. Dudley, 203n*; Bruce, 2:471–72, 483–87.

58. Deposition of Theodore Dudley, Coalter's Ex'r v. Bryan, pp. 274, 275–76. For Randolph's boundary disputes, see John Lain and John Randolph v. William Lain, 8 January 1811, Charlotte County Order Bk. 17, p. 179, and John Randolph v. Joseph B. Ingraham, 7 August 1811, Charlotte County Order Bk. 18, p. 48, reels 29 and 30, LVA.

59. Deposition of Thomas Hart Benton, Coalter's Ex'r v. Bryan, pp. 605–11 (quoted at 607).

60. Deposition of Henry A. Watkins, ibid., pp. 429, 426.

61. Deposition of William J. Barksdale, ibid., p. 398.

62. Deposition of John C. Calhoun, ibid., pp. 338, 341. For similar testimony about Randolph's views on slavery, see Depositions of Nathan Lufborough and John Brockenbrough, ibid., pp. 330, 384.

63. Depositions of John Taliaferro and John Marshall, ibid., pp. 306–07 (quoted), 444–45, 453–54, 456.

64. Act of 7 January 1819, ch. 75, sec. 12, Va. Rev. Code (1819), 1:266 (jurors must own $300 of real or tangible personal property); Act of 20 February 1845, ch. 62, Acts of the General Assembly of Virginia, 1844–45, p. 56 (lists jurors in Randolph will case); Entries for listed jurors, 1840 United States Federal Census, 1850 United States Federal Census and Slave Schedules, Ancestry.com; Jonathan Daniel Wells, *The Origins of the Southern Middle Class: 1800–1861* (Chapel Hill: University of North Carolina Press, 2004), 181–92; Barnes, *Artisan Workers*, 45–47, 56–57, 92–96.

65. *Richmond Enquirer*, 20 February 1845, 22 February 1845, 3 August 1849.

66. Judge Leigh would have testified in person rather than through a reading of his deposition. William Leigh to Thomas Leigh, 19 December 1844, WLL; Witness lists, Coalter's Ex'r v. Bryan, p. 719; Robinson, *Practice in the Courts*, 2:351, 355–56.

67. Deposition of William Leigh, Coalter's Ex'r v. Bryan, pp. 490, 520–22, 530–31.

68. Entry of jury verdict, 11 February 1845, Coalter's Ex'r v. Bryan, Petersburg Chancery Order Bk. No. 3, p. 130, LVA; Memorandum entry, 12 February 1845, ibid.

69. Henry L. Brooke to NBT, February 1845, in Frederica H. Trapnell, ed., *Virginia Tucker–Henry L. Brooke Correspondence, 1831–1869* ([Richmond], 1978), 20; ETB to NBT, 11 March 1846, TCP; Motions for new trial and correction of verdict, 13 February 1845, Coalter's Ex'r v. Bryan, Petersburg Chancery Order Bk. No. 3, pp. 130–31; Orders, 13 February 1845, 7 June 1845, 17 December 1845, ibid., pp. 132–33, 168–69, 208–09; Compromise bill of complaint, [13 February 1845], Coalter's Ex'r v. Randolph's Ex'r (Cir. Super. Ct., Petersburg, VA), copy in Tomlin v. Coalter's Heirs (Cir. Super. Ct., Charlotte County, 1855), pp. 54–58, Chancery Records Index no. 037-1855-017, Virginia Memory, LVA, http://www.lva.virginia.gov/chancery/case_detail.asp?CFN=037-1855-017.

70. For the value of Randolph's estate at settlement date, see *Richmond Enquirer*, 18 Feb-

ruary 1845; Bill of complaint, March 1850, Tomlin v. Coalter's Heirs, pp. 166–73; Brief of Henry L. Brooke, Randolph's Adm'r v. Hobson (Va. Ct. App., 1852), p. 138, Special Collections, LVA.

71. Pleasants v. Pleasants, 6 Va. (2 Call) 270, 342, 349 (1799); Medley v. Jones, 19 Va. (5 Munf.) 98, 100 (1816); Henry v. Bollar, 34 Va. (7 Leigh) 19, 21 (1836); Act of 11 February 1831, ch. 190, sec. 1, Va. Rev. Code Supp. (1833), 251; Andrew Fede, *Roadblocks to Freedom: Slavery and Manumission in the United States South* (New Orleans: Quid Pro Books, 2011), 350–59.

72. Peter v. Hargrave, 46 Va. (5 Gratt.) 12, 22 (1848); Paup's Adm'r v. Mingo, 31 Va. (4 Leigh) 163, 186 (1833). The judges' view on damages for wrongful enslavement did not always stop juries from considering them. Melvin Patrick Ely, *Israel on the Appomattox: A Southern Experiment in Black Freedom from the 1790s through the Civil War* (New York: Alfred A. Knopf, 2004), 342. For echoes of the Virginia appeals court's views in the modern debate over reparations for slavery, see Alfred L. Brophy, *Reparations: Pro and Con* (New York: Oxford University Press, 2006), 75–94.

73. Lewis [Garrard] Clarke, *Narrative of the Sufferings of Lewis Clarke* (Boston, 1845), 75. On the cost of slave maintenance, see James L. Huston, *The British Gentry, the Southern Planter, and the Northern Family Farmer: Agriculture and Sectional Antagonism in North America* (Baton Rouge: Louisiana State University Press, 2015), 148; Caitlin Rosenthal, *Accounting for Slavery: Masters and Management* (Cambridge, MA: Harvard University Press, 2018), 79–83.

74. *Coalter's Ex'r*, 42 Va. 90. A Virginia code revision (by two lawyers who appeared in the Randolph will case) enacted four years later gave emancipated slaves the right to recover for labor performed while heirs contested the will that freed them. Va. Code (1849), tit. 30, ch. 107, sec. 8, p. 465; William E. Ross, "History of Virginia Codification," *Virginia Law Register* 11, no. 2 (June 1905): 94–96.

75. HSGT to NBT, 16, 17, 25, and 28 February 1845, TCP; David M. Cobin, *Henry St. George Tucker: Jurist, Teacher, Citizen: 1780–1848* (Stephens City, VA: Commercial Press, 1992), 26; Vanderford, *Legacy of St. George Tucker*, 86–87, 104–05.

76. ETB to NBT, 19 February 1845, TCP.

77. Virginia statutes kept slaves freed by a will in bondage until the executor released them so that unsatisfied creditors could satisfy claims against them and heirs would have a workforce for the next crop season. Act of 17 December 1792, ch. 41, secs. 36–42, Samuel Shepherd, ed., *The Statutes at Large of Virginia*, 3 vols. (Richmond, 1835), 1:127–28; Act of 3 March 1819, ch. 104, secs. 49, 53, Va. Rev. Code (1819), 1:387–88.

78. *Richmond Whig and Public Advertiser*, 18 February 1845; *Richmond Enquirer*, 18 February 1845; *Charleston Mercury* (SC), 20 February 1845; *Daily Cincinnati Gazette*, 21 February 1845, 24 February 1845; *Bangor Daily Whig and Courier* (ME), 28 February 1845; *Mississippi Free Trader and Natchez Gazette*, 8 March 1845; *Troy Times* (OH), 8 March 1845 (two items); *Cadiz Sentinel* (OH), 12 March 1845; *Port-Gibson Herald* (MS), 13 March 1845.

79. *Boston Daily Atlas*, 20 February 1845 (based on *Richmond Enquirer*, 15 February 1845); *Cincinnati Daily Enquirer*, 27 February 1845.

CHAPTER 11: PROMISED LAND

1. Harry N. Scheiber, *Ohio Canal Era: A Case Study of Government and the Economy, 1820–1861* (Athens: Ohio University Press, 1987), 129, 220–23; Nikki M. Taylor,

Frontiers of Freedom: Cincinnati's Black Community, 1802–1868 (Athens: Ohio University Press, 2005), 12–27.

2.   Steven J. Ross, *Workers on the Edge: Work, Leisure, and Politics in Industrializing Cincinnati, 1788–1890* (New York: Columbia University Press, 1985), 26–41, 72–83; Walter Stix Glazer, *Cincinnati in 1840: The Social and Functional Organization of an Urban Community during the Pre-Civil War Period* (Columbus: Ohio State University Press, 1999), 31–34, 49–59, 170n10.

3.   Charles Dickens, *American Notes for General Circulation* (London, 1850), 112; [Frances] Trollope, *Domestic Manners of the Americans*, 4th ed. (London, 1832), 54–55; Moritz Busch, *Travels between the Hudson and the Mississippi, 1851–1852*, trans. and ed. Norman H. Binger (Lexington: University of Kentucky Press, 1971), 139–40.

4.   William Leigh to Rebecca Leigh, 9 July 1845, Leigh Family Correspondence, MS 3339, UVA.

5.   William Leigh to Rebecca Leigh, 7 July 1847, William Leigh Papers, Mss2 L5334 c, VMHC. Judge Leigh wrote this letter on a return trip to Ohio two years later; see the epilogue below.

6.   Alexis de Tocqueville, *Democracy in America*, trans. Arthur Goldhammer (New York: Library of America, 2004), 399; Michael Chevalier, *Society, Manners and Politics in the United States*, trans. T. G. Bradford (Boston, 1839), 210; Bayard Tuckerman, ed., *The Diary of Philip Hone, 1828–1851*, 2 vols. (New York, 1889), 2:276 (16 April 1846).

7.   John Mahard, Meteorological diary, 1834–46, entry for 10 July 1845, Public Library of Cincinnati and Hamilton County; W. H. Beers and Co., *The History of Warren County, Ohio* (Chicago, 1882), 284, 287.

8.   Dickens, *American Notes*, 130–31; Busch, *Travels*, 58.

9.   Donald J. Ratcliffe, *The Politics of Long Division: The Birth of the Second Party System in Ohio, 1818–1828* (Columbus: Ohio State University Press, 2000), 326–28; Andrew R. L. Cayton, *Ohio: The History of a People* (Columbus: Ohio State University Press, 2002), 118–21; Joshua A. Lynn, *Preserving the White Man's Republic: Jacksonian Democracy, Race, and the Transformation of American Conservatism* (Charlottesville: University of Virginia Press, 2019), 28–32, 77–81.

10. *Journal of the Convention of the Territory of the United States North-West of the Ohio* (Chillicothe, OH, 1802), 27–28, 37, 39–40; Matthew Salafia, *Slavery's Borderland: Freedom and Bondage along the Ohio River* (Philadelphia: University of Pennsylvania Press, 2013), 78–84.

11. Act of 5 January 1804, ch. 28, Salmon P. Chase, ed., *The Statutes of Ohio*, 3 vols. (Cincinnati, 1833–35), 1:393–94; Stephen Middleton, *The Black Laws: Race and the Legal Process in Early Ohio* (Athens: Ohio University Press, 2005), 49–50.

12. Salafia, *Slavery's Borderland*, 84–86; Kate Masur, "State Sovereignty and Migration before Reconstruction," *Journal of the Civil War Era* 9, no. 4 (December 2019): 592–93, 598–602.

13. Act of 22 February 1805, ch. 108, secs. 4–5, *Statutes of Ohio* (Chase ed.), 1:513–14; Samantha Seeley, *Race, Removal, and the Right to Remain: Migration and the Making of the United States* (Chapel Hill: University of North Carolina Press, 2021), 232–38; William P. Quigley, "The Quicksands of the Poor Law: Poor Relief Legislation in a Growing Nation, 1790–1820," *Northern Illinois University Law Review* 18, no. 1 (Fall 1997): 19–21.

14. Act of 25 January 1807, ch. 139, *Statutes of Ohio* (Chase ed.), 1:555–56; Paul Finkelman, "The Strange Career of Race Discrimination in Antebellum Ohio," *Case Western Reserve Law Review* 55, no. 2 (Winter 2004): 384–95.

15. *Anti-Slavery Examiner* (New York) 13 (1839): 7–8; Frederick Douglass to *National Anti-Slavery Standard*, 17 September 1847, in Carter Woodson, ed., *The Mind of the Negro as Reflected in Letters Written during the Crisis, 1800–1860* (1926; New York: Negro Universities Press, 1969), 483–84.

16. Ohio's Black population grew from 9,567 in 1830 to 17,400 in 1840 and 25,300 in 1850. Abstract of the Returns of the Fifth Census, HR Doc. 263, 22nd Cong., 1st Sess., p. 31; Department of State, *Compendium of the Enumeration of Inhabitants and Statistics of the United States . . . from the Returns of the Sixth Census* (Washington, DC, 1841), 77; Census Office, *The Seventh Census of the United States: 1850* (Washington, DC, 1853), ix.

17. Ross, *Workers on the Edge*, 142–56, 172–79; Joe William Trotter Jr., *River Jordan: African American Urban Life in the Ohio Valley* (Lexington: University Press of Kentucky, 1998), 27–29, 38–40.

18. Allan Peskin, ed., *North into Freedom: The Autobiography of John Malvin, Free Negro, 1795–1880* (Cleveland: Western Reserve University Press, 1966), 38–39; Interview of Mrs. Colman Freeman, in Benjamin Drew, *A North-Side View of Slavery: The Refugee, or the Narratives of Fugitive Slaves in Canada* (Boston, 1856), 332–33.

19. *African Repository and Colonial Journal* 5, no. 6 (August 1829): 185 (Ohio Supreme Court decision); David Walker, *Appeal . . . to the Colored Citizens of the World* (Boston, 1829), 64, 67; E[dward] S. Abdy, *Journal of a Residence and Tour in the United States . . . from April, 1833, to October, 1834*, 3 vols. (London, 1835), 3:10–11; Taylor, *Frontiers of Freedom*, 63–65, 110–12, 119–21; Sharon A. Roger Hepburn, *Crossing the Border: A Free Black Community in Canada* (Champaign: University of Illinois Press, 2007).

20. S. A. Ferrall [Simon Ansley O'Ferrall], *A Ramble of Six Thousand Miles* (London, 1832), 199–201, 52–53.

21. E. G. to Brother Benton, July 1845, in *Emancipator and Weekly Chronicle* (Boston), 10 September 1845 (from *Watchman of the Valley* (Cincinnati)); *Emancipator* (Boston), 5 August 1846.

22. Eugene H. Berwanger, *The Frontier against Slavery: Western Anti-Negro Prejudice and the Slavery Extension Controversy* (Urbana: University of Illinois Press, 1967), 32–33, 43–45; Trotter, *River Jordan*, 24–25, 30.

23. *Daily Dispatch* (Richmond), 1 August 1880 (William Wickham obituary); Philip J. Schwarz, *Migrants against Slavery: Virginians and the Nation* (Charlottesville: University Press of Virginia, 2001), 124–25, 177–80.

24. Charles Royster, *The Fabulous History of the Dismal Swamp Company: A Story of George Washington's Times* (New York: Alfred A. Knopf, 1999), 84–85, 111–13, 159–77, 241–43, 281–84, 424–28; Michael Trotti, "Freedmen and Enslaved Soil: A Case Study of Manumission, Migration, and Land," *Virginia Magazine of History and Biography* 104, no. 4 (Autumn 1996): 456–67.

25. Act of 26 February 1816, ch. 129, Acts of the General Assembly of Virginia, 1815–16, pp. 240–43 (quoted at 243); Paula Kitty Wright, *Gist's Promised Land: The Little-Known Story of the Largest Relocation of Freed Slaves in U.S. History* (Seaman, OH: Sugar Tree Ridge, 2013), 14–18, 20–21, 34–35.

26. Joan E. Cashin, "Landscape and Memory in Antebellum Virginia," *Virginia Magazine of History and Biography* 102, no. 4 (October 1994): 493–96; Trotti, "Freedmen and Enslaved Soil," 463–65, 469–75.

27. *The Supporter* (Chillicothe, OH), 16 June 1819, in Frank U. Quillin, *The Color Line in Ohio: A History of Race Prejudice in a Typical Northern State* (1913; New York:

Negro Universities Press, 1969), 28–29; *Niles' Weekly Register* 49 (3 October 1835): 76 (from *Cincinnati Gazette*).

28. Abdy, *Journal of a Residence*, 3:25–53, 70–81 (quoted at 39, 38); James Brewer Stewart, "The Emergence of Racial Modernity and the Rise of the White North, 1790–1840," *Journal of the Early Republic* 18, no. 2 (Summer 1998): 181–217.

29. William Leigh to Thomas Leigh, 18 December 1844, William Leigh Papers, Mss2 L5334 c, VMHC.

30. *Emancipator*, 5 August 1846; Stephen E. Maizlish, *The Triumph of Sectionalism: The Transformation of Ohio Politics, 1844–1856* (Kent, OH: Kent State University Press, 1983), 84–90; Norman A. Graebner, "Thomas Corwin and the Election of 1848: A Study in Conservative Politics," *Journal of Southern History* 17, no. 2 (May 1951): 162.

31. W. H. Beers, *History of Warren County*, 372–79; Josiah Morrow, ed., *Life and Speeches of Thomas Corwin* (Cincinnati, 1896), 7–8, 19–20, 92–93, 110.

32. E. G. to Brother Benton, July 1845; *Emancipator*, 5 August 1846; Henry Howe, *Historical Collections of Ohio*, 3 vols. (Columbus, 1890–91), 3:437–39; Van Gosse, *The First Reconstruction: Black Politics in America from the Revolution to the Civil War* (Chapel Hill: University of North Carolina Press, 2021), 506–07, 513.

33. Henry Howe, *Historical Collections of Ohio* (Cincinnati, 1848), 352–54; Frank Wilcox, *The Ohio Canals*, ed. William A. McGill (Kent, OH: Kent State University Press, 1969), 62–63, 71; R. Douglas Hurt, *The Ohio Frontier: Crucible of the Old Northwest, 1720–1830* (Bloomington: Indiana University Press, 1996), 139, 394.

34. Andrew R. L. Cayton and Peter S. Onuf, *The Midwest and the Nation: Rethinking the History of an American Region* (Bloomington: Indiana University Press, 1990), 27; Joyce Alig, ed., *Mercer County, Ohio History, 1978* (Celina, OH: Mercer County Historical Society, 1980), 370, 401–54, 735; Mark Bernstein, *New Bremen* (Wilmington, OH: Orange Frazer Press, 1999), 14; Raymond L. Cohn, *Mass Migration under Sail: European Immigration to the Antebellum United States* (New York: Cambridge University Press, 2009), 113–18.

35. Robert Leslie Jones, *History of Agriculture in Ohio to 1880* (Kent, OH: Kent State University Press, 1983), 27–28; David M. Stothers and Patrick M. Tucker, "The Dunlap Farmstead: A Market-Dependent Farm in the Early History of the Maumee Valley of Ohio," *Archaeology of Eastern North America* 30 (2002): 155–88.

36. Interview of John Spitler, 22 December 1900, in Juda M. Moyer, comp., *Pioneer Recollections: Miami Valley of Ohio, 1797–1850* (Apollo, PA: Closson Press, 2013), 205. John Spitler farmed in Darke County, which adjoins Mercer County to the south.

37. John B. Miller, Diary, 1836–43, Leonard Hill Local History Collection, MS-28, box 1, file 1, Special Collections and Archives, Wright State University; Jon Gjerde, *The Minds of the West: Ethnocultural Evolution in the Rural Middle West, 1830–1917* (Chapel Hill: University of North Carolina Press, 1997), 140–46. John Miller farmed in Miami County, just southeast of Mercer County.

38. Marga Millitzer Hagaman and George Unger, trans., *Transplanted German Farmer: The Life and Times of Christian Iutzi (1788–1857), 1832 Immigrant to Butler County, Ohio, in His Own Words* (Sugarcreek, OH: Carlisle Printing, 2009), 40, 43, 23, 25–32, 34.

39. Nevin O. Winter, *A History of Northwest Ohio*, 3 vols. (Chicago: Lewis Publishing, 1917), 1:377–78; Peter Way, *Common Labour: Workers and the Digging of North American Canals, 1780–1860* (Cambridge, UK: Cambridge University Press, 1993), 153–59.

40. S. S. Scranton, ed., *History of Mercer County, Ohio . . .* (Chicago: Biographical Pub-

lishing, 1907), 66–68; Anna-Lisa Cox, *The Bone and Sinew of the Land: America's Forgotten Black Pioneers and the Struggle for Equality* (New York: Public Affairs, 2018), 3–4.

41. Memorial of Colored People of Mercer County to Governor of Ohio, [June] 1846, Ohio Governors' Papers, reel 10, OHC; J. S. H. to editor, 1 November 1840, *The Friend* (Philadelphia) 14, no. 13 (7 December 1840): 100–01 (from *Ohio Free Press*); Mary Ann Brown, "Vanished Black Rural Communities in Western Ohio," *Perspectives in Vernacular Architecture* 1 (1982): 102–03.

42. Department of State, *Compendium of the Sixth Census*, 77; Census Office, *Seventh Census*, 820, 839; *Minutes of the National Convention of Colored Citizens: Held at Buffalo . . .* (New York, 1843), 32–33. The population estimate for 1846 takes account of 1850 census numbers for German and St. Marys townships in Auglaize County, which (together with parts of less populous townships) remained in Mercer County until 1848.

43. General Land Office, Patents to Augustus Wattles, 15 March 1837, acc. nos. OH0680_.379, OH0680_.427; ibid., 21 August 1837, acc. nos. OH1690_.184, OH1690_.185, OH1690_.186, OH1690_.187, available at https://glorecords.blm.gov/search/default.aspx; Lynne Marie Getz, *Abolitionists, Doctors, Ranchers, and Writers: A Family Journey through American History* (Lawrence: University Press of Kansas, 2017), 18–45. Wattles later bought an additional 103 acres in Mercer County. General Land Office, Patents to Augustus Wattle, 1 June 1845, acc. nos. OH1740_.084, OH1740_.085.

44. Augustus Wattles, "Report on the Condition of the People of Color in the State of Ohio," *Proceedings of the Ohio Anti-Slavery Convention*, 22–24 April 1835, pp. 2–6.

45. Busch, *Travels*, 122–23; *The Friend* 14, no. 13 (7 December 1840): 100; ibid., 48, no. 34 (10 April 1875): 271; *Liberator* (Boston), 1 January 1841 (from *New-York Sun*); *Cleveland Daily Herald*, 26 August 1843.

46. *Minutes of the National Convention of Colored Citizens* (1843), 32–33; Bridget Ford, *Bonds of Union: Religion, Race, and Politics in a Civil War Borderland* (Chapel Hill: University of North Carolina Press, 2016), 116–17; Cox, *Bone and Sinew of the Land*, viii–xii, 5, 146–47, 244n41; Gail Patricia Myers, "Sustainable Communities: Traditions, Knowledge, and Adaptations among Black Farmers in Ohio" (PhD diss., Ohio State University, 2002), 91–109.

47. Darrel E. Bigham, *On Jordan's Banks: Emancipation and Its Aftermath in the Ohio River Valley* (Lexington: University Press of Kentucky, 2006), 40–45.

48. Samuel Ringgold Ward, *Autobiography of a Fugitive Negro* (London, 1855), 22; Ryan P. Jordan, *Slavery and the Meetinghouse: The Quakers and the Abolitionist Dilemma, 1820–1865* (Bloomington: Indiana University Press, 2007), 4–18, 25–30, 42–43; A. Glenn Crothers, *Quakers Living in the Lion's Mouth: The Society of Friends in Northern Virginia, 1730–1865* (Gainesville: University Press of Florida, 2012), 106–35.

49. Richard S. Newman, *The Transformation of American Abolitionism: Fighting Slavery in the Early Republic* (Chapel Hill: University of North Carolina Press, 2002), 8–9, 144–46, 153–54; Thomas D. Hamm, "George F. White and Hicksite Opposition to the Abolitionist Movement," in *Quakers and Abolition*, ed. Brycchan Carey and Geoffrey Plank (Urbana: University of Illinois Press, 2014), 44–46.

50. Jordan, *Slavery and the Meetinghouse*, 47–51, 88–89, 123; Stanley Harrold, *Border War: Fighting over Slavery before the Civil War* (Chapel Hill: University of North Carolina Press, 2010), 96–100; Crothers, *Quakers Living in the Lion's Mouth*, 163–64, 207, 228.

51. *Anti-Slavery Bugle* (Salem, OH), 30 October 1845 (from *Massachusetts Spy*); Manisha Sinha, *The Slave's Cause: A History of Abolition* (New Haven, CT: Yale University Press, 2016), 470–71.

52. Annals of Cong., 6th Cong., 1st sess., 233–34; Crothers, *Quakers Living in the Lion's Mouth*, 139–41, 168, 206–07; Aaron Scott Crawford, "John Randolph of Roanoke and the Politics of Doom: Slavery, Sectionalism, and Self-Deception, 1773–1821" (PhD diss., University of Tennessee, 2012), 113–14, 170–73, 264–65.

53. E. G. to Brother Benton, July 1845; Cong. Globe, 30th Cong., 1st sess., 727 (William Sawyer on Peter Odlin); Robert W. Steele and Mary Davies Steele, *Early Dayton* (Dayton, OH, 1896), 221.

54. *Daily News* (Cincinnati), 29 July 1846; Wilcox, *Ohio Canals*, 16–23, 61–64; Scheiber, *Ohio Canal Era*, 41, 200–05.

55. *Cleveland Herald*, 8 September 1845; *New York Herald*, 11 September 1845; *Cadiz Sentinel* (OH), 17 September 1845; *Democratic Pioneer* (Upper Sandusky, OH), 26 September 1845; *Liberator*, 3 October 1845.

56. *Xenia Torch-Light* (OH), 25 November 1846 (Ohio Board of Equalization land valuations). The register of their manumission indicates that the Roanoke community consisted of about sixty-three families and twenty-four single individuals. Some persons listed as individuals were actually members of families, and newspaper accounts say that Judge Leigh believed he needed to provide for about eighty families. *Daily News*, 20 July 1846.

57. Alig, *Mercer County*, 359; Jones, *History of Agriculture*, 33–48; James L. Huston, *The British Gentry, the Southern Planter, and the Northern Family Farmer: Agriculture and Sectional Antagonism in North America* (Baton Rouge: Louisiana State University Press, 2015), 93–94, 107–08, 164. For the better success of larger farms, see Timothy H. H. Thoresen, *River, Reaper, Rail: Agriculture and Identity in Ohio's Mad River Valley, 1795–1885* (Akron, OH: University of Akron Press, 2018), 18–19, 27–29.

58. *Emancipator*, 10 September 1845 (quoted), 5 August 1846; John Mercer Langston, *From the Virginia Plantation to the National Capitol . . .* (Hartford, CT, 1894), 90–92.

59. *United States Magazine and Democratic Review* 17, no. 85 (July/August 1845): 5; Thomas R. Hietala, *Manifest Design: American Exceptionalism and Empire*, rev. ed. (Ithaca, NY: Cornell University Press, 2003), 167–72.

60. Maizlish, *Triumph of Sectionalism*, 63–66; Michael F. Holt, *The Rise and Fall of the American Whig Party: Jacksonian Politics and the Onset of the Civil War* (New York: Oxford University Press, 1999), 249.

61. Michael Felder, *The Turbulent Era: Riot and Disorder in Jacksonian America* (New York: Oxford University Press, 1980), 45; Jonathan H. Earle, *Jacksonian Antislavery and the Politics of Free Soil, 1824–1854* (Chapel Hill: University of North Carolina Press, 2004), 144–59; Kate Masur, *Until Justice Be Done: America's First Civil Rights Movement from the Revolution to Reconstruction* (New York: W. W. Norton, 2021), 203–06.

62. *Anti-Slavery Bugle*, 9 January 1846; *Cleveland Herald*, 13 January 1846; *Emancipator*, 14 January 1846; *Scioto Gazette* (OH), 15 January 1846; *Liberator*, 16 January 1846; *Cadiz Sentinel*, 21 January 1846; *Cincinnati Weekly Herald*, 28 August 1846; *Troy Times* (OH), 1 October 1836; Maizlish, *Triumph of Sectionalism*, 16–17.

63. *Liberator*, 20 February 1846 (from *Cincinnati Herald*); *Anti-Slavery Bugle*, 6 February 1846; *Journal of the House of Representative of the State of Ohio*, 1845–46, p. 434 (26 January 1846) (Thomas J. Gallagher of Hamilton County); *Journal of the Senate of*

the State of Ohio, 1845–46, p. 355 (26 January 1846) (James H. Ewing of Hamilton County).

64. *Richmond Enquirer*, 22 July–3 October 1845 (advertisements for sale of JR's land); *Weekly Ohio Statesman* (Columbus), 20 August 1845 (notice of same); Deed, William Leigh as executor to John T. Clark, signed 31 January 1846 and recorded 28 March 1846, Charlotte County Deed Book 26:85–87, LVA (sale for $8,000 to benefit manumitted slaves); Thomas Leigh to Sarah Ann Leigh, 30 April 1846, William Leigh Papers, Mss2 L5334 c, VMHC.

65. Thomas Leigh to Sarah Ann Leigh, 30 April 1846.

CHAPTER 12: ANOTHER CANAAN

1. Testimony of Clem C. Clay, Moton v. Kessens, pp. 119–22; Deposition of York Rial, ibid., pp. 849–50, 877–78. Thirteen additional men and women sued for freedom under John Randolph's will a decade later. They were enslaved by the estate of John Randolph's sister-in-law Judith Randolph, but they claimed that they or their ancestors had been allocated to John Randolph's share when he and Judith divided the Randolph family's slaves in 1810. Their case was on appeal for a second time when the Civil War emancipated them. Answer of William W[irt] Henry, Henry L. Brooke v. Judith Randolph's Adm'r (Cir. Super. Ct., Prince Edward County, 1884), Chancery Records Index no. 147-1884-002, Virginia Memory, LVA, p. [20], http://www.lva.virginia.gov/chancery/case_detail.asp?CFN=147-1884-002; Melvin Patrick Ely, *Israel on the Appomattox: A Southern Experiment in Black Freedom from the 1790s through the Civil War* (New York: Alfred A. Knopf, 2004), 382–84.

2. Timothy S. Ailsworth et al., *Charlotte County, Rich Indeed: A History from Prehistoric Times through the Civil War* (Charlotte County, VA: Charlotte County Board of Supervisors, 1979), 74–82; John O. Peters and Margaret T. Peters, *Virginia's Historic Courthouses* (Charlottesville: University Press of Virginia, 1995), 46–51.

3. F[rederick] Johnston, *Memorials of Old Virginia Clerks* (Lynchburg, VA, 1888), 126–29; Ailsworth, *Charlotte County*, 445.

4. Charlotte Free Register, certs. 1, 43–45, 56–57, 94–96, 152, 214; Department of State, *Compendium of the Enumeration of Inhabitants and Statistics of the United States . . . from the Returns of the Sixth Census* (Washington, DC, 1841), 33; P. J. Kernodle, *Lives of Christian Ministers* (Richmond: Central Publishing, 1909), 42–43 (Rev. Edward Almond).

5. Act of 2 March 1819, ch. 111, secs. 67–68, Va. Rev. Code (1819), 1:438–39.

6. Charlotte Free Register, certs. 215–216. Many measurements in Virginia free Black registers were made to one-eighth of an inch. Howard Bodenhorn, *The Color Factor: The Economics of African-American Well-Being in the Nineteenth-Century South* (New York: Oxford University Press, 2015), 215.

7. Charlotte Free Register, certs. 217–223. Phil White later used the surname Cole. Testimony of Fountain Randolph, Moton v. Kessens, pp. 55–57.

8. Order, 4 May 1846, Charlotte County, VA, Order Book 33, pp. 106–07, LVA.

9. Charlotte Free Register, certs. 497–503, 285–292, 361–64, 331–33; Ross Frederick Bagby, "The Randolph Slave Saga: Communities in Collision" (PhD diss., Ohio State University, 1998), 326–52. The estimated mortality figure is (*x*) slaves aged sixteen or older who were taxed to John Randolph in 1833 plus freedmen registered in

1846 who were younger than sixteen in 1833 minus (*y*) total freedmen registered in 1846 who were alive in 1833.

10. Charlotte Free Register, certs. 263, 523–524, 595–596, 251–252; Bagby, "Randolph Slave Saga," 78–79, 321–22.

11. On white readings of marks on enslaved bodies, see Kenneth S. Greenberg, *Honor and Slavery* (Princeton, NJ: Princeton University Press, 1996), 15–16; Ariela J. Gross, *Double Character: Slavery and Mastery in the Antebellum Southern Courtroom* (Athens: University of Georgia Press, 2006), 130–31.

12. Craig Robertson, *The Passport in America: The History of a Document* (New York: Oxford University Press, 2010), 65–79, 131–34; Bodenhorn, *Color Factor*, 23–25, 212. The only term with legal significance was *mulatto*. Virginia law used it mainly to stigmatize freeborn persons with at least one-quarter part of African ancestry and subject them to the laws governing free Blacks. If Winslow Robinson had the same racial perceptions as the white men who took the 1850 federal census, the Roanoke community may have been less racially mixed than the overall African American population in Virginia. The census takers thought that 15 percent of Virginians of color were mulattoes; those Robinson described in that way represented only 7 percent of the people at Roanoke. Bureau of the Census, Negroes in the United States, Bulletin 8 (Washington, DC: Government Printing Office, 1904), 14–17; Thomas D. Morris, *Southern Slavery and the Law, 1619–1860* (Chapel Hill: University of North Carolina Press, 1996), 22–24; Richard H. Steckel, "Miscegenation and the American Slave Schedules," *Journal of Interdisciplinary History* 11, no. 2 (Autumn 1980): 251–263.

13. For a sentimental account by a formerly enslaved man who watched the Roanoke freedmen leave, see Orra Langhorne, "A Virginia Negro as Slave and Freedman," *Southern Workman* 10, no. 2 (February 1881): 14.

14. Joseph Martin, *A New and Comprehensive Gazetteer of Virginia and the District of Columbia* (Charlottesville, VA, 1835), 304–05; David H. Burr, Map of Virginia, Maryland and Delaware, in *The American Atlas* (London, 1839); Joshua D. Rothman, *The Ledger and the Chain: How Domestic Slave Traders Shaped America* (New York: Basic Books, 2021), 229.

15. Testimony of Clem C. Clay, Moton v. Kessens, pp. 122–29; *Boston Daily Atlas*, 3 July 1846; Entries for Thomas Cardwell, 1840 and 1850 United States Federal Census, Charlotte County, VA, Ancestry.com.

16. Albert G. Evans, "Randolph of Roanoke and His People," *New England Magazine*, new ser., 4, no. 4 (December 1891): 445–46; Testimony of Clem C. Clay, Moton v. Kessens, pp. 35, 118, 123, 125–27; Charlotte Free Register, cert. 265 (Clem Clay); Shane White and Graham White, *The Sounds of Slavery: Discovering African American History through Songs, Sermons, and Speech* (Boston: Beacon Press, 2005), 55–66.

17. Martin, *New and Comprehensive Gazetteer*, 373–77; J. T. Peters and H. B. Carden, *History of Fayette County, West Virginia* (Charleston, WV: Jarrett Printing, 1926), 123–27.

18. Emory L. Kemp, *The Great Kanawha Navigation* (Pittsburgh: University of Pittsburgh Press, 2000), 16–18, 24–25.

19. Testimony of Clem C. Clay, Moton v. Kessens, pp. 129, 142; *Xenia Torch-Light* (OH), 9 July 1846 (from *Daily Cincinnati Commercial*); *Hunt's Merchants' Magazine and Commercial Review* 15 (August 1846): 167.

20. *Plain Dealer* (Cleveland), 9 June 1846 ("force and arms"); *Alexandria Gazette* (VA), 22 June 1846; *Times and Compiler* (Richmond), 23 June 1846; *Emancipator* (Boston),

1 July 1846; *Boston Daily Atlas*, 3 July 1846; *Sun* (Baltimore), 3 July 1846. Samuel Jay and Thomas Leigh purchased over 3,000 acres for Judge Leigh between 13 May and 16 June 1846. Mercer County Deed Bks., L:384–440 and 71:529, Recorder's Office, Mercer County Courthouse, Celina, OH.

21. *Cincinnati Daily Enquirer*, 17 June 1846; *Cincinnati Weekly Herald*, 24 June 1846.

22. *Daily Cincinnati Gazette*, 2 July 1846 (quoted); *Daily Times* (Cincinnati), 6 July 1846.

23. *Daily Cincinnati Chronicle*, 1 July 1846; *Cincinnati Daily Enquirer*, 2 July 1846; Edward Henry Knight, "The above procession . . . ," [July 1846], pen and wash on paper, Campbell-Knight Family Papers, 1703-1973, Cincinnati History Library and Archives, MS 895, box 15, vol. 5, p. 10; *Robinson and Jones' Cincinnati Directory for 1846* (Cincinnati, 1846), 11, 536; Jeffrey Weidman et al., eds., *Artists in Ohio, 1787-1900: A Biographical Dictionary* (Kent, OH: Kent State University Press, 2000), 495.

24. *Dayton Journal and Advertiser* (OH). 7 July 1846; Harry N. Scheiber, *Ohio Canal Era: A Case Study of Government and the Economy, 1820–1861* (Athens: Ohio University Press, 1987), 40. The headlines on newspaper stories about the freedmen published throughout the country almost invariably read "John Randolph's Negroes," "John Randolph's Slaves," or "John Randolph's Manumitted Slaves."

25. *Dayton Journal and Advertiser*, 7 July 1846; Saidiya V. Hartman, *Scenes of Subjection: Terror, Slavery, and Self-Making in Nineteenth-Century America* (New York: Oxford University Press, 1997), 50–59; James M. Campbell, *Slavery on Trial: Race, Class, and Criminal Justice in Antebellum Richmond, Virginia* (Gainesville: University Press of Florida, 2007), 148–49.

26. *Daily News* (Cincinnati), 13 July 1846 (from *St. Marys Sentinel* (OH), 8 July 1846); *Daily National Intelligencer* (DC), 15 July 1846; *Boston Daily Atlas*, 16 July 1846; C. A. O. McClellan and C. S. Warner, *Map of Auglaize County, Ohio* (Newton, CT, 1860s), https://www.loc.gov/item/2012592387/ (New Bremen).

27. Joyce Alig, ed., *Mercer County, Ohio History, 1978* (Celina, OH: Mercer County Historical Society, 1980), 735–36; Mark Bernstein, *New Bremen* (Wilmington, OH: Orange Frazer Press, 1999), 14; Joseph P. Ferrie, *Yankeys Now: Immigrants in the Antebellum United States, 1840–1860* (New York: Oxford University Press, 1999), 36, 56, 71–81.

28. Testimony of Clem C. Clay, Moton v. Kessens, pp. 132–35; Deposition of York Rial, ibid., pp. 836–37; Frank Wilcox, *The Ohio Canals*, ed. William A. McGill (Kent, OH: Kent State University Press, 1969), 19–21, 31.

29. *Dayton Journal and Advertiser*, 14 July 1846; *Tri-Weekly Courier* (Zanesville, OH), 14 July 1846; Bernstein, *New Bremen*, 33.

30. *Cincinnati Weekly Herald*, 29 July 1846 (satirically headlined "Men of Property and Standing"); *Dayton Journal and Advertiser*, 15 September 1846; *Anti-Slavery Bugle* (Salem, OH), 6 November 1846; Nevin O. Winter, *A History of Northwest Ohio*, 3 vols. (Chicago: Lewis Publishing, 1917), 1:513.

31. Testimony of Clem C. Clay, Moton v. Kessens, pp. 132–35; Depositions of G. B. Coffey and Samuel P. Miles, ibid., pp. 769–72, 803; *Daily News*, 13 July 1846; *Western Christian Advocate* (Cincinnati), 17 July 1846.

32. *Daily News*, 13 July 1846; *Richmond Enquirer*, 24 July 1846 (from *Columbus Free Press*, 11 July 1846); *New-York Daily Tribune*, 14 and 16 July 1846; *Liberator* (Boston), 7 August 1846.

33. Gustave de Beaumont, *Marie, or Slavery in the United States: A Novel of Jacksonian America*, trans. Barbara Chapman (Baltimore: Johns Hopkins University Press,

1999), 117–31, 243–52; Michael Feldberg, *The Turbulent Era: Riot and Disorder in Jacksonian America* (New York: Oxford University Press, 1980), 37–53; Linda K. Kerber, "Abolitionists and Amalgamators: The New York City Riots of 1834," *New York History* 48, no. 1 (January 1967): 28–39.

34. Brent M. S. Campney, *Hostile Heartland: Racism, Repression, and Resistance in the Midwest* (Urbana: University of Illinois Press, 2019), 14–32.

35. Douglass C. North, *The Economic Growth of the United States, 1790–1860* (New York: Prentice-Hall, 1961), 194–99, 205–06, 233; Paul A. Gilje, *Rioting in America* (Bloomington: Indiana University Press, 1996), 89–91; Joshua A. Lynn, *Preserving the White Man's Republic: Jacksonian Democracy, Race, and the Transformation of American Conservatism* (Charlottesville: University of Virginia Press, 2019), 77–81.

36. Donald J. Ratcliffe, "The Decline of Antislavery Politics, 1815–1840," in *Contesting Slavery: The Politics of Bondage and Freedom in the New American Nation* (Charlottesville: University of Virginia Press, 2011), ed. John Craig Hammond and Matthew Mason, 282–86; Richard B. Kielbowicz, "The Law and Mob Law in Attacks on Antislavery Newspapers, 1833–1860," *Law and History Review* 24, no. 3 (Fall 2006): 559–600.

37. Paul Goodman, *Of One Blood: Abolitionism and the Origins of Racial Equality* (Berkeley: University of California Press, 1998), 139–44, 161–62; David Grimsted, *American Mobbing, 1828–1861: Toward Civil War* (New York: Oxford University Press, 1998), 199–245; David R. Roediger, *The Wages of Whiteness: Race and the Making of the American Working Class*, rev. ed. (London: Verso, 2007), 74–77, 140–44.

38. Cong. Globe, 29th Cong., 1st sess., 301–02; *Ohio Statesman* (Columbus), 6 April 1842.

39. *New-York Daily Tribune*, 27 February 1846; ibid., 6, 10, 13, 16, 18, and 23 March 1846; Cong. Globe, 29th Cong., 1st sess., 457–58.

40. Michael F. Holt, *The Rise and Fall of the American Whig Party: Jacksonian Politics and the Onset of the Civil War* (New York: Oxford University Press, 1999), 83–84, 117–18; Robert P. Swierenga, "The Settlement of the Old Northwest: Ethnic Pluralism in a Featureless Plain," *Journal of the Early Republic* 9, no. 1 (Spring 1989): 83–84.

41. Jon Gjerde, *The Minds of the West: Ethnocultural Evolution in the Rural Middle West, 1830–1917* (Chapel Hill: University of North Carolina Press, 1997), 33–49; Bridget Ford, *Bonds of Union: Religion, Race, and Politics in a Civil War Borderland* (Chapel Hill: University of North Carolina Press, 2016), 16–19.

42. *Dayton Journal and Advertiser*, 25 August 1846, 1 September 1846; *Daily Cincinnati Gazette*, 21 August 1846; *Cleveland Herald*, 25 August 1846; *North American* (Philadelphia), 25 September 1847.

43. Cong. Globe, 29th Cong., 2nd sess., 90–91, and app., 80–84; *African Repository and Colonial Journal* 23, no. 2 (February 1847): 45–46; *Cincinnati Enquirer*, 6 October 1846.

44. *New-York Daily Tribune*, 16 July 1846; *Liberator*, 31 July 1846; Leonard U. Hill, *John Johnston and the Indians in the Land of the Three Miamis* (Piqua, OH: n.p., 1967), 11, 20–21, 45–47, 139–40; John P. Bowes, *Land Too Good for Indians: Northern Indian Removal* (Norman: University of Oklahoma Press, 2016), 144–46. Lockport became Lockington, and the Johnston farm is now a state historical site.

45. *Dayton Journal and Advertiser*, 14 July 1846; Depositions in Moton v. Kessens of William Betz, pp. 891–92 (quoted); York Rial, pp. 837–38, 874, 880; David Mitchell, pp. 907–08; Testimony of Clem C. Clay, ibid., p. 137.

46. A[lfred] M. Lorraine to editor, *Western Christian Advocate*, 21 August 1846.

47. *Daily News*, 20 July 1846 (from *St. Marys Sentinel*, 15 July 1846), 27 July 1846; *Daily*

Cincinnati Chronicle, 15 July and 18 July 1846 (from *Sidney Aurora,* 11 July 1846); *Daily Cincinnati Gazette,* 15 July 1846; *Cleveland Herald,* 21 July 1846; *Daily National Intelligencer,* 24 July 1846; *Boston Daily Atlas,* 28 July 1846; *Mississippi Free Trader and Natchez Gazette,* 30 July 1846; *Liberator,* 7 August 1846.

48. *Dayton Journal and Advertiser,* 21 July and 28 July 1846; *Daily Cincinnati Gazette,* 23 July and 31 July 1846, 1 August 1846; *Daily News,* 23 July and 24 July 1846; *Cincinnati Daily Enquirer,* 24 July 1846; *Cleveland Herald,* 27 July 1846; *Cincinnati Weekly Herald,* 29 July 1846; *Western Christian Advocate,* 31 July 1846, 14 August 1846; Jill E. Rowe, *Invisible in Plain Sight: Self-Determination Strategies of Free Blacks in the Old Northwest* (New York: Peter Lang, 2017), 64–66, 78.

49. *Cincinnati Weekly Herald,* 12 August 1846; *Xenia Torch-Light,* 30 July 1846; *Dayton Journal and Advertiser,* 28 July 1846, 4 August 1846; *Western Christian Advocate,* 31 July 1846, 14 August 1846; *Emancipator,* 5 August 1846; *Anti-Slavery Bugle,* 21 August 1846; *Daily Cincinnati Gazette,* 24 August 1846; Christopher Phillips, *The Rivers Ran Backward: The Civil War and the Remaking of the American Middle Border* (New York: Oxford University Press, 2016), 63; Ellen Eslinger, "The Evolution of Racial Politics in Early Ohio," in *The Center of a Great Empire: The Ohio Country in the Early Republic,* ed. Andrew R. L. Cayton and Stuart D. Hobbs (Athens: Ohio University Press, 2005), 92.

50. *Daily Cincinnati Gazette,* 1 August and 24 August 1846; *Dayton Journal and Advertiser,* 4 August 1846; *Piqua Daily Call* (OH), 14 July 1923 (Fountain Randolph interview); Deposition of York Rial, Moton v. Kessens, p. 871.

51. *Daily Cincinnati Gazette,* 31 July 1846; *New-York Daily Tribune,* 5 August 1846; Testimony of Clem C. Clay, Moton v. Kessens, pp. 136–40; Depositions of York Rial, William Betz, David Mitchell, and Howard Scudder, ibid., pp. 837–38, 874, 880, 893, 907, 1002.

52. John Johnston to Jefferson Patterson, 21 August 1846, Patterson Family Papers, 1780–1970, box 1, file 7, Special Collections and Archives, Wright State University; *Cincinnati Weekly Herald,* 5 August 1846 (mob); *Cleveland Herald,* 10 September 1846 (prosecution).

53. Johnston to Patterson, 21 August 1846.

54. *Dayton Journal and Advertiser,* 15 September 1846; *Cleveland Herald,* 25 August 1846; *Daily Cincinnati Gazette,* 5 September 1846; *Sandusky Clarion,* 8 September 1846; *Xenia Torch-Light,* 10 September 1846.

55. *Dayton Journal and Advertiser,* 15 September 1846; *North American,* 25 September 1846.

56. August Wattles to Mordecai Bartley, 16 August 1846, Ohio Governors' Papers, reel 10, OHC; James A. Shedd to Bartley, 19 August 1846, ibid.; James Watson Riley to Bartley, 21 August 1846, ibid. A letter Wattles wrote a month later admitted to more local opposition. *Dayton Journal and Advertiser,* 15 September 1846 (from *Piqua Register* and *St. Marys Sentinel*).

57. Memorial of Colored People of Mercer County to Governor of Ohio, [after 15 August] 1846, Ohio Governors' Papers, reel 10.

58. *Cincinnati Weekly Herald,* 28 August 1846 ("Contemptible"); *Daily Cincinnati Gazette,* 5 September 1846; *Troy Times* (OH), 1 October 1846; Cong. Globe, 29th Cong., 2nd sess., 91 (William Sawyer); Kate Masur, *Until Justice Be Done: America's First Civil Rights Movement from the Revolution to Reconstruction* (New York: W. W. Norton, 2021), 203–04.

59. Eric Foner, *Free Soil, Free Labor, Free Men: The Ideology of the Republican Party*

before the Civil War (New York: Oxford University Press, 1995), 267; Thomas R. Hietala, *Manifest Design: American Exceptionalism and Empire*, rev. ed. (Ithaca, NY: Cornell University Press, 2003), 122–31; Elizabeth R. Varon, *Disunion! The Coming of the American Civil War, 1789–1859* (Chapel Hill: University of North Carolina Press, 2008), 10–12, 180–97.

60. *Daily Cincinnati Gazette*, 24 August 1846; *Cincinnati Weekly Herald*, 19 August 1846.
61. *New-York Daily Tribune*, 4 August 1846; *Liberator*, 21 August 1846.
62. *African Repository and Colonization Journal* 22, no. 9 (September 1846): 271–72.
63. *Mississippi Free Trader and Natchez Gazette*, 8 September 1846; *Lynchburg Virginian*, 10 September 1846 ("imaginary"); *Alexandria Gazette*, 21 September 1846 (from *Richmond Republican*) ("poor negro"); *New Era* (Portsmouth, VA), 8 August 1846.
64. Testimony of Clem C. Clay, Moton v. Kessens, pp. 134, 141; Deposition of York Rial, ibid., pp. 836–37, 872–73.
65. Testimony of Clem C. Clay, ibid., pp. 151–54; *Daily Cincinnati Gazette*, 1 August 1846 (from *Troy Times*); H[enry] C[lay] Bruce, *The New Man: Twenty-Nine Years a Slave, Twenty-Nine Years a Free Man* (York, PA, 1895), 39.
66. Act of 2 March 1819, ch. 111, secs. 61 and 64, Va. Rev. Code (1819), 1:436–38; Act of 22 March 1837, ch. 70, secs. 1 and 3, Acts of General Assembly of Virginia, 1836–37, pp. 47–48; Act of 7 April 1838, ch. 99, sec. 1, Acts of General Assembly, 1838–39, p. 76; Act of 13 March 1841, ch. 74, sec. 5, Acts of the General Assembly of Virginia, 1840–41, pp. 83–84; Ted Maris-Wolf, *Family Bonds: Free Blacks and Re-enslavement Law in Antebellum Virginia* (Chapel Hill: University of North Carolina Press, 2015), 33–36, 142–53.
67. *Alexandria Gazette*, 11 September 1846 (from *Lynchburg Virginian*); *New-York Daily Tribune*, 15 September 1846; *North American*, 15 September 1846; *Dayton Journal and Advertiser*, 22 September 1846; *Cleveland Herald*, 29 September 1846; *Xenia Torch-Light*, 1 October 1846; *Anti-Slavery Bugle*, 2 October 1846. County courts could allow freedmen to remain, but their authority did not extend to a freedman illegally returning from another state. Act of 22 March 1837, ch. 70, sec. 1, Acts of General Assembly of Virginia, 1836–37, pp. 47–48, as codified in Va. Code (1849), ch. 107, sec. 2, p. 466.
68. Orders, 2 June 1851, 6 October 1851, Charlotte County, VA, Order Book 33, pp. 115, 132, LVA; Kirt von Daacke, *Freedom Has a Face: Race, Identity, and Community in Jefferson's Virginia* (Charlottesville: University of Virginia Press, 2012), 100–12; Loren Schweninger, *Appealing for Liberty: Freedom Suits in the South* (New York: Oxford University Press, 2018), 281. Some Roanoke freedmen thought White had gone to Philadelphia because he could not settle in Virginia, and no record of his petition to remain in Virginia survives. But White and his family resided in Charlotte County at the time of the 1850 federal census. They probably registered as free Blacks in 1851 to regularize their status before Betsy and John White left the state to visit their son in Ohio. Another son had moved to Ohio by 1860. Martin Delany to Frederick Douglass, 18 June 1848, in *North Star* (Rochester, NY), 7 July 1848; *Liberator*, 25 June 1852 (John White's death); Charlotte Free Register, certs. 736–737 (2 June 1851), certs. 790–797 (10 October 1851); Entries for John White, Charlotte County, VA, and Moses White, Staunton Township, Miami County, OH, 1850 United States Federal Census, Ancestry.com; Entries for Aaron White, Troy, Miami County, OH, and Moses White, Spring Creek Township, Miami County, OH, 1860 United States Federal Census, ibid.
69. *African Repository and Colonization Journal* 22, no. 10 (October 1846): 321–22; ibid., 23, no. 3 (March 1847): 70; Lynn, *Preserving the White Man's Republic*, 28–32.

EPILOGUE

1. *New-York Daily Tribune*, 13 February 1865; Joseph P. Reidy, *Illusions of Emancipation: The Pursuit of Freedom and Equality in the Twilight of Slavery* (Chapel Hill: University of North Carolina Press, 2019), 78, 345–50; William A. Darity Jr. and Kirsten Mullen, *From Here to Equality: Reparations for Black Americans in the Twenty-First Century* (Chapel Hill: University of North Carolina Press, 2020), 128–42, 156–59.

2. Steven Hahn, *A Nation under Our Feet: Black Political Struggles in the Rural South from Slavery to the Great Migration* (Cambridge, MA: Harvard University Press, 2003), 195–96 (quoted), 128–36, 146; Lynda J. Morgan, *Emancipation in Virginia's Tobacco Belt, 1850–1870* (Athens: University of Georgia Press, 1992), 136–38.

3. Paul W. Gates, *History of Public Land Law Development* (Washington, DC: Government Printing Office, 1968), 443–47; David W. Blight, *Race and Reunion: The Civil War in American Memory* (Cambridge, MA: Harvard University Press, 2001), 45–55.

4. H[enry] C[lay] Bruce, *The New Man: Twenty-Nine Years a Slave, Twenty-Nine Years a Free Man* (York, PA, 1895), 116–17; Frederick Douglass, *Life and Times of Frederick Douglass Written by Himself*, rev. ed. (Boston, 1892), 613–14. On freedmen's economic disadvantages after the Civil War, see Roger L. Ransom and Richard Sutch, *One Kind of Freedom: The Economic Consequences of Emancipation* (New York: Cambridge University Press, 2001), 14–39.

5. Cong. Globe, 40th Cong., 2nd sess., 972, reprinted in *Daily Ohio Statesman* (Columbus), 12 February 1868 (front page).

6. *Mercer County Standard* (Celina, OH), 9 July 1891 ("The Color Line in Agriculture"); S. S. Scranton, ed., *History of Mercer County, Ohio . . .* (Chicago: Biographical Publishing, 1907), 89–90.

7. Deposition of David Mitchell, Moton v. Kessens, pp. 914–15 (quoted); Testimony of Clem C. Clay, ibid., p. 135; Depositions of W. H. Davis, John Coate, G. B. Coffey, Noah Pearson, York Rial, William Betz, Cyrus Long, George E. Lee, and Howard Scudder, ibid., pp. 545–68, 637, 769–72, 785–98, 839, 883–88, 972–74, 988–89, 997–1003.

8. Power of attorney, William Leigh to Joseph Plunkett, 26 October 1846, recorded 16 December 1846, Mercer County Deed Bks., L:623, Recorder's Office, Mercer County Courthouse, Celina, OH; Deeds from William Leigh to purchasers, ibid., M:58–623, N:29–576, O:152–542, P:127–379, Q:101–255, R:101, 194, V:298, X:459.

9. Lewis Tappan to editor of *[New-York] Tribune*, 11 January 1850, Lewis Tappan Papers, reel 4, LC (draft); Census Office, *The Seventh Census of the United States: 1850* (Washington, DC, 1853), 839; Bertram Wyatt-Brown, *Lewis Tappan and the Evangelical War against Slavery* (Baton Rouge: Louisiana State University Press, 1997), 274–78.

10. Cong. Globe, 29th Cong., 2nd sess., 427 ("It would be"); ibid., 30th Cong., 1st sess., app. 728 ("there should be"); William J. McMurray, *History of Auglaize County, Ohio*, 2 vols. (Indianapolis: Historical Publishing, 1923), 1:159–61. Other Democratic congressmen said much the same thing. Thomas R. Hietala, *Manifest Design: American Exceptionalism and Empire*, rev. ed. (Ithaca, NY: Cornell University Press, 2003), 167–72.

11. William Leigh to Rebecca Leigh, 7 July 1847, William Leigh Papers, Mss2 L5334 c, VMHC.

12. Miami County Deed Bks., 24:506, 559, Recorder's Office, Miami County Safety Building, Troy, OH; Charlotte Free Register, certs. 251 (Sampson Rial), 507 (Gabriel

White), 514 (Shadrach White); Helen Dehlia Gilmore, *The History of the John Randolph Freed Slaves of Roanoke, Virginia Who Settled in Miami and Shelby Counties* ([Piqua, OH]: Rossville Springcreek Historical Society, 1981), 18, 27.

13. Miami County Deed Bks., 23:407–12, 24:71, 106–08, 25:295, 604, 613–14, 27:344; Shelby County Deed Bks., O:474–75, P:184, Recorder's Office, Shelby County Annex, Sidney, OH; Charlotte Free Register, certs. 217 (Phill White), 220 (Ellick Gillard), 244 (Meshack Jones), 269 (Nathan Jones), 289 (Moses White), 352 (Theodorick Randolph), 537 (Michael Cole); David Meyers and Elise Meyers Walker, *Historic Black Settlements of Ohio* (Charleston, SC: History Press, 2020), 124–27, 130.

14. Deed, Benjamin F. Brown to Armstead and Johnston Crowder, 21 July 1847, recorded 4 October 1852, Miami County Deed Bks., 27:344; Charlotte Free Register, certs. 216 (Johnson Crowder), 575 (Armstead Crowder). For deeds evidencing other land purchases by Roanoke freedmen that left no public record until years later, see Mashack Jones to Joseph R. Johns and William McKnight, 27 November 1849, recorded 9 November 1853; Allick and Polly Gillard to Silas Williamson, 10 April 1849, recorded 12 March 1855; Moses and Martha White to Daniel Myers, 30 November 1848, recorded 20 October 1859, Miami County Deed Bks., 28:482, 30:396, 35:108. Ohio law encouraged recordation. J. R. Swan, ed., *Statutes of the State of Ohio* (Columbus, 1841), ch. 37, sec. 8, p. 267; ibid., ch. 48, sec. 21, p. 398; ibid., ch. 96, sec. 5, p. 778.

15. Deed, Elijah Coate and Andrew Stevens to Henry Davis, 22 March 1849, recorded 7 August 1865, Miami County Deed Bks., 42:30; Brown v. Brown, 12 Md. 87, 94–96 (1858); Dunlap v. Harrison's Ex'rs, 55 Va. (14 Gratt.) 251, 258–66 (1858); Shaw v. Ward, 175 N.C. 192, 193, 95 S.E. 164, 165 (1918); Loren Schweninger, *Black Property Owners in the South, 1790–1915* (Urbana: University of Illinois Press, 1990), 69–70, 87–90.

16. *Dayton Journal and Advertiser* (OH), 14 September 1847 (from *Cincinnati Herald*); *Anti-Slavery Bugle* (Salem, OH), 17 September 1847.

17. *Dayton Journal and Advertiser*, 14 September 1847; *Anti-Slavery Bugle*, 17 September 1847; Testimony of Louisa Butler, Moton v. Kessens, pp. 176–77; Deposition of M. H. Davis, ibid., pp. 535–49, 582–83, 593–95; Deed, Elijah Coate and Andrew Stevens to Henry Davis, 22 March 1849; Deeds, Henry Davis to trust beneficiaries, 30 December 1864–17 July 1865, ibid., 41:156, 529, 42:30–37; Henry Tucker v. Henry Davis, No. 1040 (Miami County, OH, C.P., 8 December 1864), in Journal, 20:192, Record Vol., 20:555, and Fee Bk. and Execution Docket, 8:1040, Clerk of Courts' Office, Miami County Courthouse, Troy, OH.

18. Acreages and prices are from the Miami and Shelby County deeds cited above.

19. Henry L. Brooke to NBT, 23 June 1845, 16 December 1846, in Frederica H. Trapnell, ed., *Virginia Tucker–Henry L. Brooke Correspondence, 1831–1869* ([Richmond] 1978), 21, 25–26; Depositions of Samuel P. Miles and David Mitchell, Moton v. Kessens, pp. 808–11, 910–23.

20. William Leigh to NBT, 23 May 1848, 17 June 1848, 27 June 1849, 23 February 1851, TCP; Orders, 17 December 1845, 19 June 1846, 3 December 1846, 3 and 4 December 1847, 28 November and 18 December 1848, Coalter's Ex'r v. Bryan, Petersburg Chancery Order Bk. No. 3, pp. 208–09, 270–71, 311–13, 379, 383–88, 409, 438–39, LVA.

21. Patrick Shirreff, *Tour through North America; Together with a Comprehensive View of the Canadas and United States, as Adapted for Agricultural Emigration* (Edinburgh, 1835), 450; James L. Huston, *The British Gentry, the Southern Planter, and the North-*

ern Family Farmer: Agriculture and Sectional Antagonism in North America (Baton Rouge: Louisiana State University Press, 2015), 93–95, 195.

22. Martin R. Delany to Frederick Douglass, 18 June 1848, in *North Star* (Rochester, NY), 7 July 1848; Robert S. Levine, *Martin Delany, Frederick Douglass, and the Politics of Representative Identity* (Chapel Hill: University of North Carolina Press, 1997), 20–22, 36–38.

23. *Richmond Enquirer*, 26 August 1851 (from *Baltimore Patriot*). The report was widely reprinted at the time and again a year later after it appeared in *African Repository* 28, no. 2 (February 1852): 55.

24. W. E. Burghardt Du Bois, "The Negroes of Farmville, Virginia: A Social Study," Bulletin of the Bureau of Labor No. 14, H.R. Rep. No. 55-206, pt. 1 (January 1898), 32–33; Melvin Patrick Ely, *Israel on the Appomattox: A Southern Experiment in Black Freedom from the 1790s through the Civil War* (New York: Alfred A. Knopf, 2004), 360–63, 425–32; Warren Eugene Milteer Jr., *Beyond Slavery's Shadow: Free People of Color in the South* (Chapel Hill: University of North Carolina Press, 2021), 127–35.

25. Deposition of John Coate, Moton v. Kessens, p. 637; David A. Gerber, *Black Ohio and the Color Line, 1860–1915* (Urbana: University of Illinois Press, 1976), 6, 14–15, 62–64.

26. On dispossession of Black farmers in the antebellum West, see Anna-Lisa Cox, *The Bone and Sinew of the Land: America's Forgotten Black Pioneers and the Struggle for Equality* (New York: Public Affairs, 2018).

27. *Mercer County Standard*, 2 June 1905; Notice to Gerhard Kessens, Moton v. Kessens, p. 467. Newspapers throughout Ohio had reported the filing of the test suit, *Moton v. Dewell. Piqua Daily Call* (OH), 28 January 1904, 8 June 1904; *Cincinnati Enquirer*, 7 June 1904; *Bellefontaine Republican* (OH), 10 June 1904; *Gazette* (Cleveland, OH), 18 June 1904.

28. Testimony of Goodrich Giles and Clem C. Clay, Moton v. Kessens, pp. 32–38, 108; *Piqua Daily Call*, 11 July and 25 July 1902, 20, 24, and 30 July 1903, 27 and 29 July 1904; *Dayton Evening Herald* (OH), 8–26 July 1905, 26 July 1907, 19 June 1908, 2 August 1909; *Cincinnati Enquirer*, 28 July 1906.

29. Testimony of Goodrich Giles, Moton v. Kessens, pp. 42–44, 47–48; *Piqua Daily Call*, 20 January 1916; *Dayton Herald*, 18 June 1927; Garner J. Edwards et al., "Letters Collected by R. E. Park and Booker T. Washington," *Journal of Negro History* 7, no. 2 (April 1922): 207–11; Booker T. Washington, *The Story of the Negro*, vol. 1, *The Rise of the Race from Slavery* (New York: Doubleday, Page, 1909), 235–36.

30. *Dayton Evening Herald*, 1 February 1895; Testimony of Fountain Randolph, Moton v. Kessens, pp. 52–93; *Piqua Daily Call*, 11 July 1902, 5 November 1906, 25 July 1916, 14 July 1923; *Dayton Daily News*, 24 July 1924.

31. Testimony of W. E. Henderson, Goodrich Giles, and William G. Fox, Moton v. Kessens, pp. 26–28, 32–33, 198–214. Henderson elsewhere gave a different account to support the petitioners' claim that they did not know about their rights until John Beam told them. Henry Noble Sherwood, "The Settlement of the John Randolph Slaves in Ohio," *Proceedings of the Mississippi Valley Historical Association* 5 (1912): 56.

32. Stephen Middleton, *The Black Laws: Race and the Legal Process in Early Ohio* (Athens: Ohio University Press, 2005), 254–58; Darrel E. Bigham, *On Jordan's Banks: Emancipation and Its Aftermath in the Ohio River Valley* (Lexington: University Press of Kentucky, 2006), 151, 160–61, 275–76.

33. Gerber, *Black Ohio*, 254; Andrew R. L. Cayton, *Ohio: The History of a People* (Columbus: Ohio State University Press, 2002), 271–72, 281–84; David Meyers and

Elise Meyers Walker, *Lynching and Mob Violence in Ohio, 1772–1938* (Jefferson, NC: McFarland, 2019), 168–69, 207–11.

34. Emma Lou Thornbrough, *Indiana Blacks in the Twentieth Century*, ed. Lana Ruegamer (Bloomington: Indiana University Press, 2001), 12–32; Shawn Leigh Alexander, *An Army of Lions: The Civil Rights Struggle before the NAACP* (Philadelphia: University of Pennsylvania Press, 2012), 135–76; Melissa Milewski, *Litigating across the Color Line: Civil Cases between Black and White Southerners from the End of Slavery to Civil Rights* (New York: Oxford University Press, 2018), 116–27.

35. Susan D. Carle, *Defining the Struggle: National Organizing for Racial Justice, 1880–1915* (New York: Oxford University Press, 2013), 205–06; Jennifer Harris, "Barbara E. Pope (1854–1908)," *Legacy* 32, no. 2 (2015): 282, 290–91.

36. Carle, *Defining the Struggle*, 150–51, 153–73; Ana Lucia Araujo, *Reparations for Slavery and the Slave Trade: A Transnational and Comparative History* (London: Bloomsbury Academic, 2017), 95–108.

37. First amended petition, Moton v. Kessens, No. 7879 (C.P., Mercer County, OH, 1912), in Record, Moton v. Kessens, No. 15398 (Ohio Sup. Ct., 1917), 24–40; Testimony of Fountain Randolph and Clem C. Clay, Moton v. Kessens, pp. 82, 110, 116–17; Charlotte Free Register, cert. 363 (Margaret Moton); Entry for Joseph Moton, 1910 United States Federal Census, Concord Township, Miami County, OH, Ancestry.com; Entry for Joseph Moton, 27th Reg. U.S. Colored Infantry, in National Park Service, Civil War Soldiers and Sailors Database, https://www.nps.gov/civilwar/soldiers-and-sailors-database.htm.

38. Deposition of York Rial, Moton v. Kessens, pp. 843–44, 861–63; *Piqua Daily Call*, 1 August 1903; Charlotte Free Register, cert. 589 (York Rial); Department of the Interior, National Park Service, National Register of Historic Places, Nomination Form for York Rial House, Piqua, OH, 9 June 1986, available at https://catalog.archives.gov/id/71990331.

39. Testimony of Gerhard Kessens, Moton v. Kessens, pp. 197–98; Deed, Eustach and Elizabeth Kunkler to Gerhard Kessens, 23 May 1869, ibid., p. 464; Entry for Gerhard G. Kessens, 1910 United States Federal Census, Granville Township, Mercer County, OH, Ancestry.com; Martin Lutz, *Atlas of Mercer County, Ohio* (Celina, OH: J. E. Hamburger, 1900), 30 (sections 14 and 11).

40. Moton v. Dewell, 13 Ohio C.C. (n.s.) 81, 83, 87–88 (3rd Cir., 1910); Gregory S. Alexander, "The Transformation of Trusts as a Legal Category, 1800–1914," *Law and History Review* 5, no. 2 (Autumn 1987): 342–47.

41. Testimony of Gerhard Kessens, Moton v. Kessens, pp. 193–95.

42. John Norton Pomeroy Jr., *A Treatise on Equity Jurisprudence*, 3rd ed., 4 vols. (San Francisco: Bancroft-Whitney, 1905), 2:980–81, 3:2018–19.

43. Lawrence M. Friedman, *A History of American Law*, 4th ed. (New York: Oxford University Press, 2019), 225–26.

44. Jairus Ware Perry, *A Treatise on the Law of Trusts and Trustees*, ed. Edwin A. Howes, 6th ed., 2 vols. (Boston: Little, Brown, 1911), 1:375–79; Harry W. Vanneman, "The Constructive Trust: A Neglected Remedy in Ohio," *Ohio State University Law Journal* 3, no. 1 (December 1936): 3–12.

45. Perry, *Treatise on Trusts*, 2:1398, 1400–21; Comment, "Application of Statute of Limitations to Trusts Arising by Operation of Law," *Michigan Law Review* 15, no. 3 (January 1917): 276–77; Gregory S. Alexander, "The Complexities of Land Reparations," *Law and Social Inquiry* 39, no. 4 (Fall 2014): 876–85.

46. Perry, *Treatise on Trusts*, 2:1406, 1422–23; J. David Hacker, "Decennial Life Tables

for the White Population of the United States, 1790–1900," *Historical Methods* 43, no. 2 (2010): 54–55.

47. Testimony of Fountain Randolph and Clem C. Clay, Moton v. Kessens, pp. 83–88, 144–45; Bigham, *On Jordan's Banks*, 273–76.

48. Journal entry, 3 August 1909, Moton v. Dewell (C.P., Mercer County, OH), in Moton v. Dewell, No. 306 (Ohio Ct. App., 3rd Cir., 1917), Mercer County Clerk of Court, Legal Division, Mercer County Courthouse, Celina, OH.

49. Moton v. Dewell, 13 Ohio C.C. (n.s.) 85–86.

50. *Celina Democrat* (OH), 6 September 1912; Opinion, Moton v. Kessens (C.P., Mercer County, OH, 1912), in Brief for defendant in error, Moton v. Kessens (Ohio Sup. Ct.), 301–10 (quoted at 310); Depositions of York Rial, L. A. Medley, and W. S. Kessler, Moton v. Kessens, pp. 839–43, 929–37, 615–27.

51. Testimony of Fountain Randolph, Clem C. Clay, Elizabeth Moss, and Louisa Butler, Moton v. Kessens, pp. 83–85, 94–95, 157–58, 165; Brief of plaintiffs in error, Moton v. Kessens (Ohio Sup. Ct.), 48–98.

52. Depositions of George L. Christian and E. M. Rowelle, Moton v. Kessens, pp. 524–27, 528–32; Order, 11 June 1851, Coalter's Ex'r v. Bryan, Petersburg Chancery Order Bk. No. 4, p. 194, LVA; Ernest B. Furgurson, *Ashes of Glory: Richmond at War* (New York: Alfred A. Knopf, 1996), 333–36, 338–39.

53. Opinion, Moton v. Kessens (Ohio Ct. App., 3rd Cir., 1916), in Brief for defendant in error, Moton v. Kessens (Ohio Sup. Ct.), 9–10; Charles W. Chesnutt to William E. Henderson, 24 November 1916, in Jesse S. Crissler et al., eds., *An Exemplary Citizen: Letters of Charles W. Chesnutt, 1906–1932* (Palo Alto: Stanford University Press, 2002), 132.

54. Opinion, Moton v. Kessens (Ct. App.), in Brief for defendant in error, Moton v. Kessens (Ohio Sup. Ct.), 18–28; *Celina Democrat*, 30 June 1916; Perry, *Treatise on Trusts*, 2:1404–05, 1421–23.

55. *Cincinnati Enquirer*, 21 March 1917; *Piqua Daily Press* (OH), 21 March 1917; *Celina Democrat*, 23 March, 13 April, and 11 May 1917; Moton v. Kessens, 96 Ohio St. 609, 118 N.E. 1083 (1917).

56. Entries for Armstrong [Armstead] Crowder, Paul Crowder, John Davis, Harrison Gillard, Armistead Jones, Joseph Morton [Moton], and Philip White, in Eric Eugene Johnson, *Ohio's Black Soldiers Who Served in the Civil War* (Bellville, OH: Ohio Genealogical Society, 2014); Douglas R. Egerton, *Thunder at the Gates: The Black Civil War Regiments That Redeemed America* (New York: Basic Books, 2016), 82, 181; Kelly D. Mezurek, *For Their Own Cause: The 27th United States Colored Troops* (Kent, OH: Kent State University Press, 2016), 28–45.

57. John O. Peters and Margaret T. Peters, *Virginia's Historic Courthouses* (Charlottesville: University Press of Virginia, 1995), 114; Mezurek, *For Their Own Cause*, 118–26, 131; A. Wilson Greene, *A Campaign of Giants: The Battle for Petersburg*, vol. 1, *From the Crossing of the James to the Crater* (Chapel Hill: University of North Carolina Press, 2018), 312. On the larger significance of Black troops at Petersburg, see Kevin M. Levin, *Remembering the Battle of the Crater* (Lexington: University Press of Kentucky, 2012), 11–32.

58. Mezurek, *For Their Own Cause*, 152–61, 170–73.

59. Gerber, *Black Ohio*, 34–42, 226–28; Bigham, *On Jordan's Banks*, 160–61, 167–68.

60. John Greenleaf Whittier, "Randolph of Roanoke" (1847), in *The Writings of John Greenleaf Whittier*, vol. 3, *Anti-Slavery Poems: Songs of Labor and Reform* (Boston, 1888), 131–35 (quoted at 131). Abolitionist Theodore Dwight Weld had ridiculed

John Randolph's parsimonious bequests to his household servants, but by the time Harriet Beecher Stowe wrote her key to *Uncle Tom's Cabin* nearly fifteen years later, she quoted Randolph's will approvingly. Weld, *American Slavery As It Is: Testimony of a Thousand Witnesses* (New York, 1839), 42–43; Stowe, *A Key to Uncle Tom's Cabin* (Cleveland, OH, 1853), 37.

61. Josiah Quincy [IV], *Figures of the Past from the Leaves of Old Journals* (Boston, 1883), 228–29; Robert J. Cook, *Civil War Memories: Contesting the Past in the United States since 1865* (Baltimore: Johns Hopkins University Press, 2017), 93–98, 117–18, 136–39. Beverley Tucker's daughter and John Greenleaf Whittier exchanged letters in the same Lost Cause register when she came upon his elegy to Randolph thirty years after he wrote it. Mary Haldane Coleman, "Whittier on John Randolph of Roanoke," *New England Quarterly* 8, no. 4 (December 1935): 551–54.

62. *New-York Spectator*, 19 June 1833.

63. For reflections on why praise and condemnation have not framed the history of slavery in a constructive way, see C. Richard King and David J. Leonard, "Letting America Off the Hook: *Roots, Django Unchained*, and the Divided White Self," in *Reconsidering Roots: Race, Politics, and Memory*, ed. Erica L. Ball and Kellie Carter Jackson (Athens: University of Georgia Press, 2017), 113–27.

64. W. E. B. Du Bois, "The Souls of White Folk" (1920), in *W. E. B. Du Bois: Writings*, ed. Nathan Huggins (New York: Library of America, 1987), 924; Speech of former New York Congressman Martin Grover at the Free Soil Party's second Utica Convention, 22 June 1848, in O. C. Gardiner, *The Great Issue: or, The Three Presidential Candidates* (New York, 1848), 108 ("The question is not whether black men are to be free, but whether we white men are to remain free."); Alexis de Tocqueville, *Democracy in America*, trans. Arthur Goldhammer (New York: Library of America, 2004), 394–97 ("Slavery is being abolished in the United States not in the interest of the Negro but in that of the white man."); Orlando Patterson, *Slavery and Social Death: A Comparative Study* (Cambridge, MA: Harvard University Press, 1982), 240–61.

ILLUSTRATION CREDITS

Frontispiece: Juba with Vixen, attrib. Joseph Wood, c. 1820, photograph of drawing on paper, John Randolph Papers, 1801–30, Virginia Museum of History and Culture, Mss1 R1554 b

Page xv: First will of John Randolph, 17 November 1800, Tucker-Coleman Papers, Special Collections Research Center, William and Mary Libraries, https://digitalarchive.wm.edu/handle/10288/16293

Page xxiv: *John Randolph of Roanoke*, John Sartain after George Catlin, 1831–32, engraving, Library of Congress, LC-DIG-pga-04112

Page 3: The City Hotel, No. 41 North Third St., Philadelphia, M. E. D. Brown, c. 1832, lithograph, Historical Society of Pennsylvania, acc. no. HSP Bb 32 B 813

Page 18: *Roanoke, the Seat of John Randolph*, woodcut, in Henry Howe, *Historical Collections of Virginia* (Charleston, SC, 1845), Albert and Shirley Small Special Collections Library, University of Virginia

Page 32: John Randolph, Gilbert Stuart, 1804–05, oil on canvas, National Gallery of Art, Washington, DC

Page 49: Henry St. George Tucker, attrib. William James Hubard, c. 1833–37, oil on canvas, The Colonial Williamsburg Foundation, Museum Purchase

Page 63: Nathaniel Beverley Tucker, c. 1840–45, daguerreotype, Faculty-Alumni File, Special Collections Research Center, William and Mary Libraries

Page 68: Elizabeth Tucker Bryan, William James Hubard, 1839, oil on canvas, private collection, photograph by Travis Fullerton

Page 74: Charlotte County Courthouse, early-twentieth-century postcard, CourtHouseHistory.com

Page 102: *Richmond from the Hill above the Waterworks*, William James Bennett after George Cooke, 1834, aquatint, Alan M. Voorhees Collection, Library of Virginia

Page 105: William Meade, artist unknown, c. 1840, steel engraving, John Walter Wayland Collection, Stewart Bell Jr. Archives, Handley Regional Library, Winchester, Virginia

Page 121: Francis Scott Key, Joseph Wood, 1816, oil on canvas, Walters Art Museum, Baltimore

Page 133: William Leigh, artist unknown, c. 1845, oil on canvas, private collection, photograph by Neil Steinberg

Page 160: Tobacco field in southern Virginia, Bryan Pollard, 2022, photograph, Dreamstime.com, file 76714240

Page 177: Petersburg Courthouse, c. 1865, stereographic negative, Library of Congress, LC-DIG-cwpb-02773

Page 204: *Cincinnati from Covington, Kentucky*, Robert S. Duncanson, 1850, oil on canvas, Cincinnati Museum Center, CHS.1959.07

Page 207: Map of Ohio, in Sidney E. Morse and Samuel Breese, *The Cerographic Atlas of the United States* (New York, 1842–45), The Huntington Library, https://hdl.huntington.org/digital/collection/p15150coll4/id/13819

Page 231: Procession of the Roanoke freedmen in Cincinnati, Edward Henry Knight, July 1846, pen and wash on paper, Campbell-Knight Family Papers, 1703–1973, Cincinnati Museum Center

Page 236: Map of Virginia, Maryland, and Delaware, in David H. Burr, *The American Atlas* (London, 1839), Library of Congress, Geography and Map Division, https://www.loc.gov/item/2009582191/

Page 248: Miami Canal lock at Lockport (now Lockington), Ohio, 1933, photograph, Library of Congress, HABS OHIO,75-LOCK,1-

Page 257: Randolph freedmen's reunion, c. 1902–05, photograph, Rossville Museum Archive Collection, National Afro-American Museum and Cultural Center, Wilberforce, Ohio

INDEX

Page numbers in *italics* refer to illustrations.

ABOUT THE AUTHOR

GREGORY MAY IS A HISTORIAN WHO WRITES ABOUT THE early American republic. In *A Madman's Will*, he draws on his earlier experience as a lawyer to tell the story of one of the largest and most controversial private emancipations in United States history.

May is a graduate of the College of William and Mary, where he first discovered this untold story while working on a thesis about John Randolph, and the Harvard Law School, where he was an editor of the *Harvard Law Review*. After serving as a law clerk for Justice Lewis Powell on the United States Supreme Court, he practiced law in Washington, DC, and New York for over thirty years. He is the author of *Jefferson's Treasure: How Albert Gallatin Saved the New Nation from Debt*.